kamichama karin

Volume 4

Created by
Koge-Donbo

HAMBURG // LONDON // LOS ANGELES // TOKYO

Kamichama Karin Vol. 4
created by Koge-Donbo

Translation - Nan Rymer
English Adaptation - Lianne Sentar
Retouch and Lettering - Erika "Skooter" Terriquez
Cover Design - Thea Willis

Editor - Carol Fox
Digital Imaging Manager - Chris Buford
Managing Editor - Lindsey Johnston
Editor in Chief - Rob Tokar
VP of Production - Ron Klamert
Publisher - Mike Kiley
President and C.O.O. - John Parker
C.E.O. and Chief Creative Officer - Stuart Levy

A 🔷 **TOKYOPOP**® Manga

TOKYOPOP Inc.
5900 Wilshire Blvd. Suite 2000
Los Angeles, CA 90036

E-mail: info@TOKYOPOP.com
Come visit us online at www.TOKYOPOP.com

ISBN: 1-59532-850-5

First TOKYOPOP printing: June 2006
10 9 8 7 6 5 4 3 2 1
Printed in the USA

Cast of Characters and Story So Far

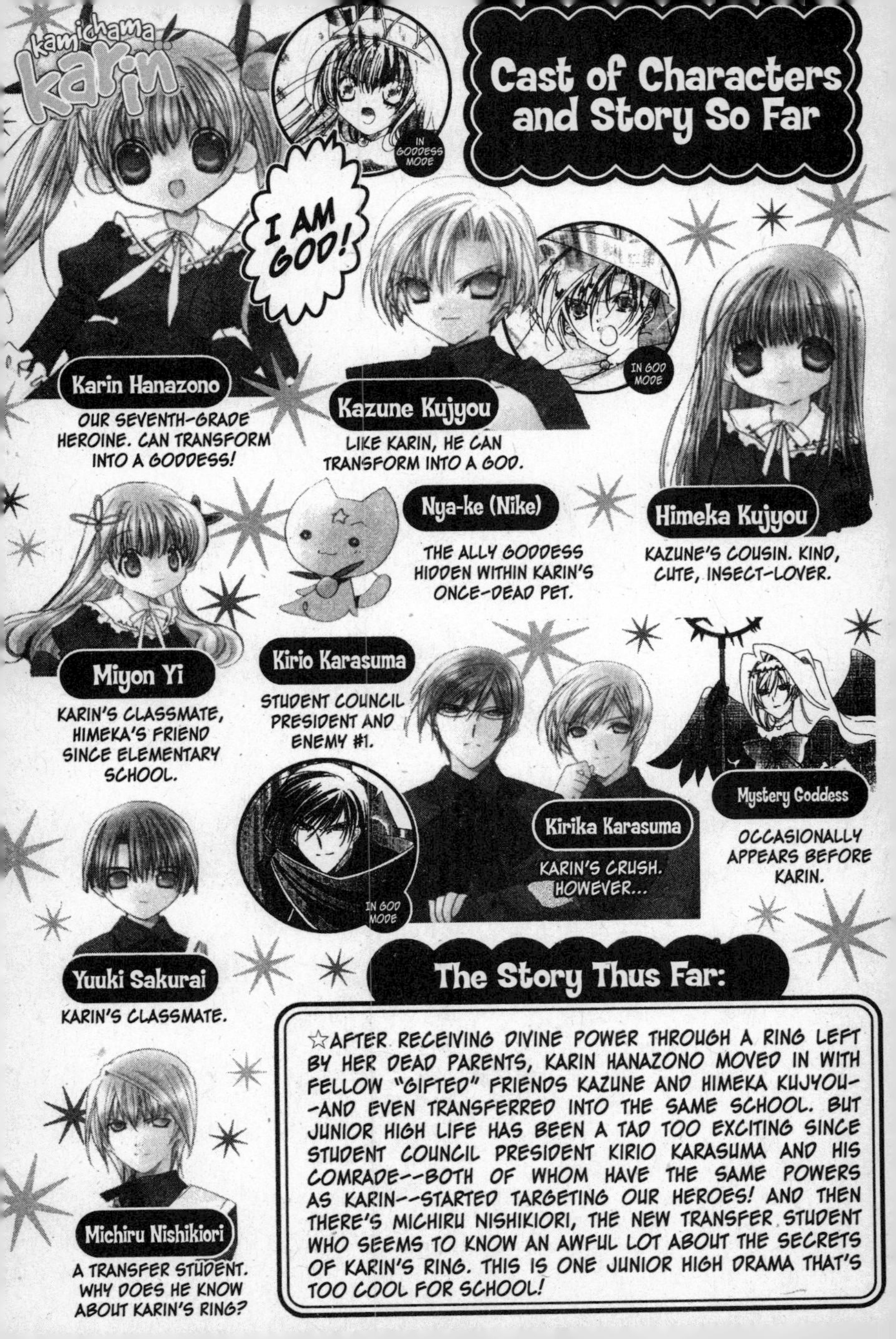

kamichama karin
IN GODDESS MODE
I AM GOD!
IN GOD MODE
IN GOD MODE

Karin Hanazono

OUR SEVENTH-GRADE HEROINE. CAN TRANSFORM INTO A GODDESS!

Kazune Kujyou

LIKE KARIN, HE CAN TRANSFORM INTO A GOD.

Himeka Kujyou

KAZUNE'S COUSIN. KIND, CUTE, INSECT-LOVER.

Nya-ke (Nike)

THE ALLY GODDESS HIDDEN WITHIN KARIN'S ONCE-DEAD PET.

Miyon Yi

KARIN'S CLASSMATE, HIMEKA'S FRIEND SINCE ELEMENTARY SCHOOL.

Kirio Karasuma

STUDENT COUNCIL PRESIDENT AND ENEMY #1.

Kirika Karasuma

KARIN'S CRUSH. HOWEVER...

Mystery Goddess

OCCASIONALLY APPEARS BEFORE KARIN.

Yuuki Sakurai

KARIN'S CLASSMATE.

Michiru Nishikiori

A TRANSFER STUDENT. WHY DOES HE KNOW ABOUT KARIN'S RING?

The Story Thus Far:

☆AFTER RECEIVING DIVINE POWER THROUGH A RING LEFT BY HER DEAD PARENTS, KARIN HANAZONO MOVED IN WITH FELLOW "GIFTED" FRIENDS KAZUNE AND HIMEKA KUJYOU--AND EVEN TRANSFERRED INTO THE SAME SCHOOL. BUT JUNIOR HIGH LIFE HAS BEEN A TAD TOO EXCITING SINCE STUDENT COUNCIL PRESIDENT KIRIO KARASUMA AND HIS COMRADE--BOTH OF WHOM HAVE THE SAME POWERS AS KARIN--STARTED TARGETING OUR HEROES! AND THEN THERE'S MICHIRU NISHIKIORI, THE NEW TRANSFER STUDENT WHO SEEMS TO KNOW AN AWFUL LOT ABOUT THE SECRETS OF KARIN'S RING. THIS IS ONE JUNIOR HIGH DRAMA THAT'S TOO COOL FOR SCHOOL!

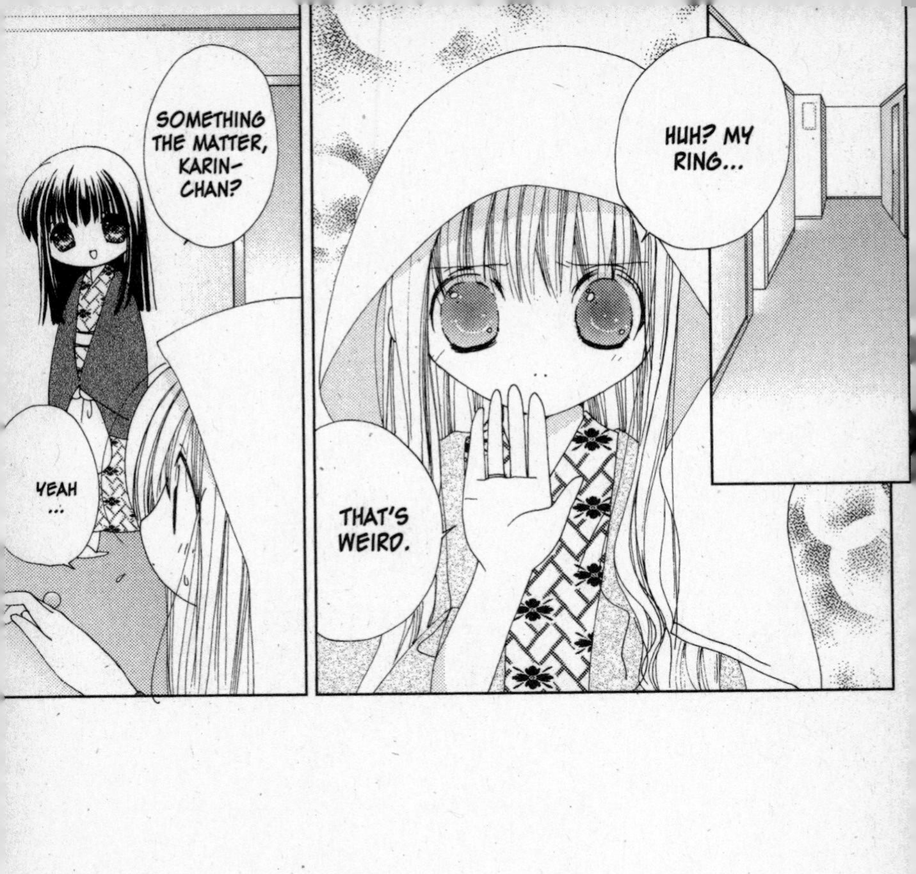
HUH? MY RING...
THAT'S WEIRD.
SOMETHING THE MATTER, KARIN-CHAN?
YEAH ...

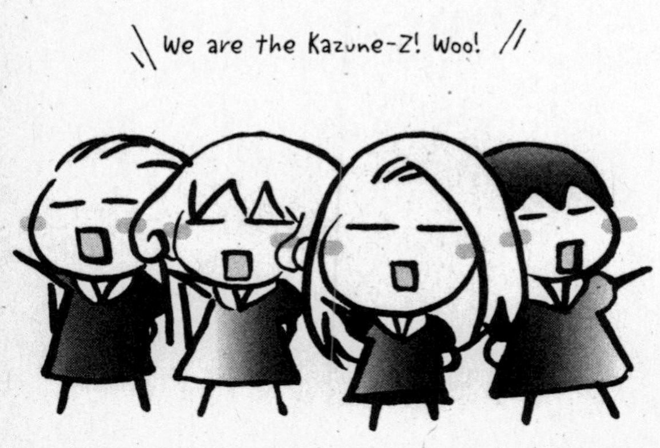
We are the Kazune-Z! Woo!

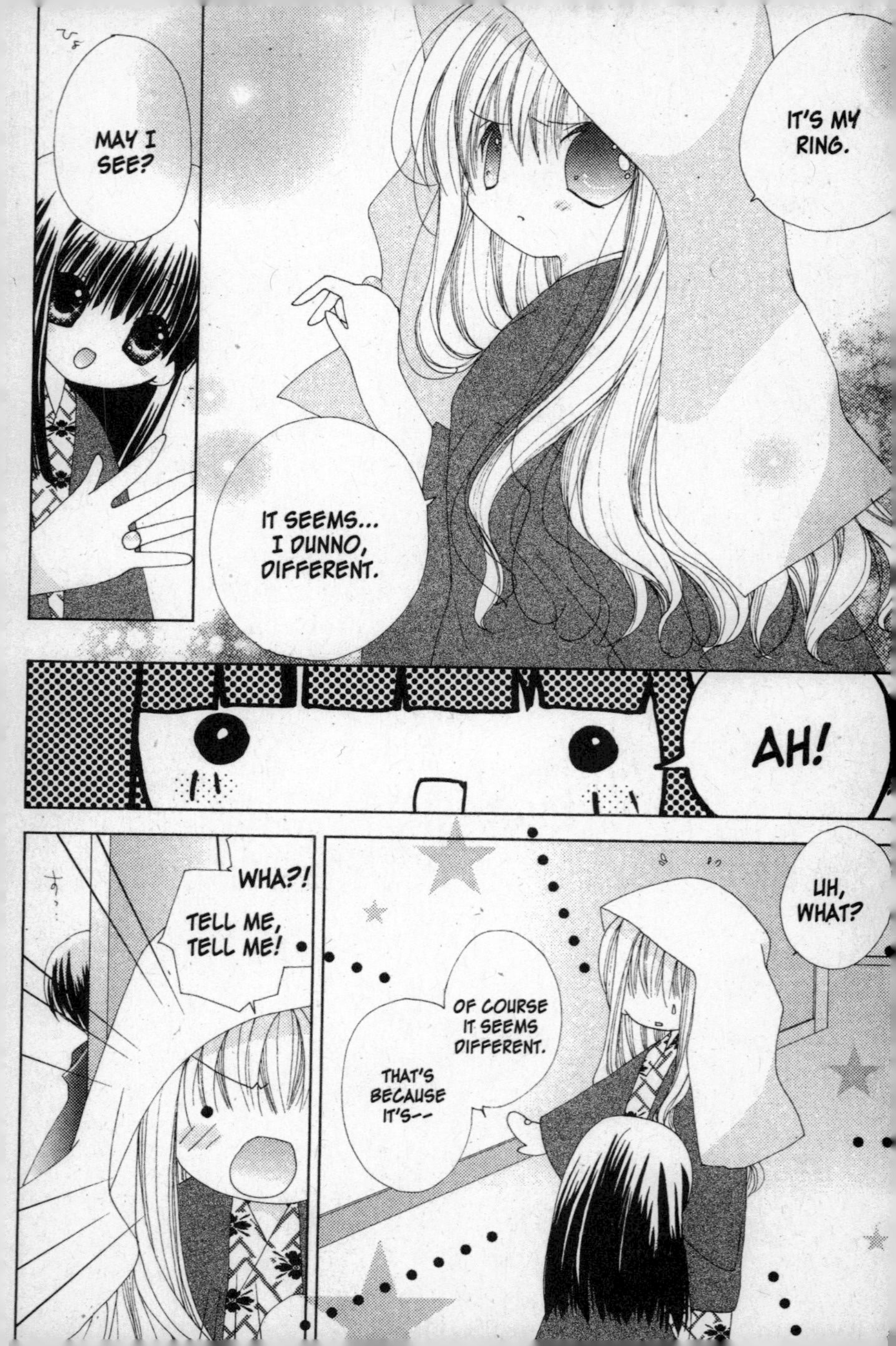
IT'S MY RING.
IT SEEMS... I DUNNO, DIFFERENT.
MAY I SEE?
AH!
UH, WHAT?
OF COURSE IT SEEMS DIFFERENT.
THAT'S BECAUSE IT'S--
WHA?!
TELL ME, TELL ME!

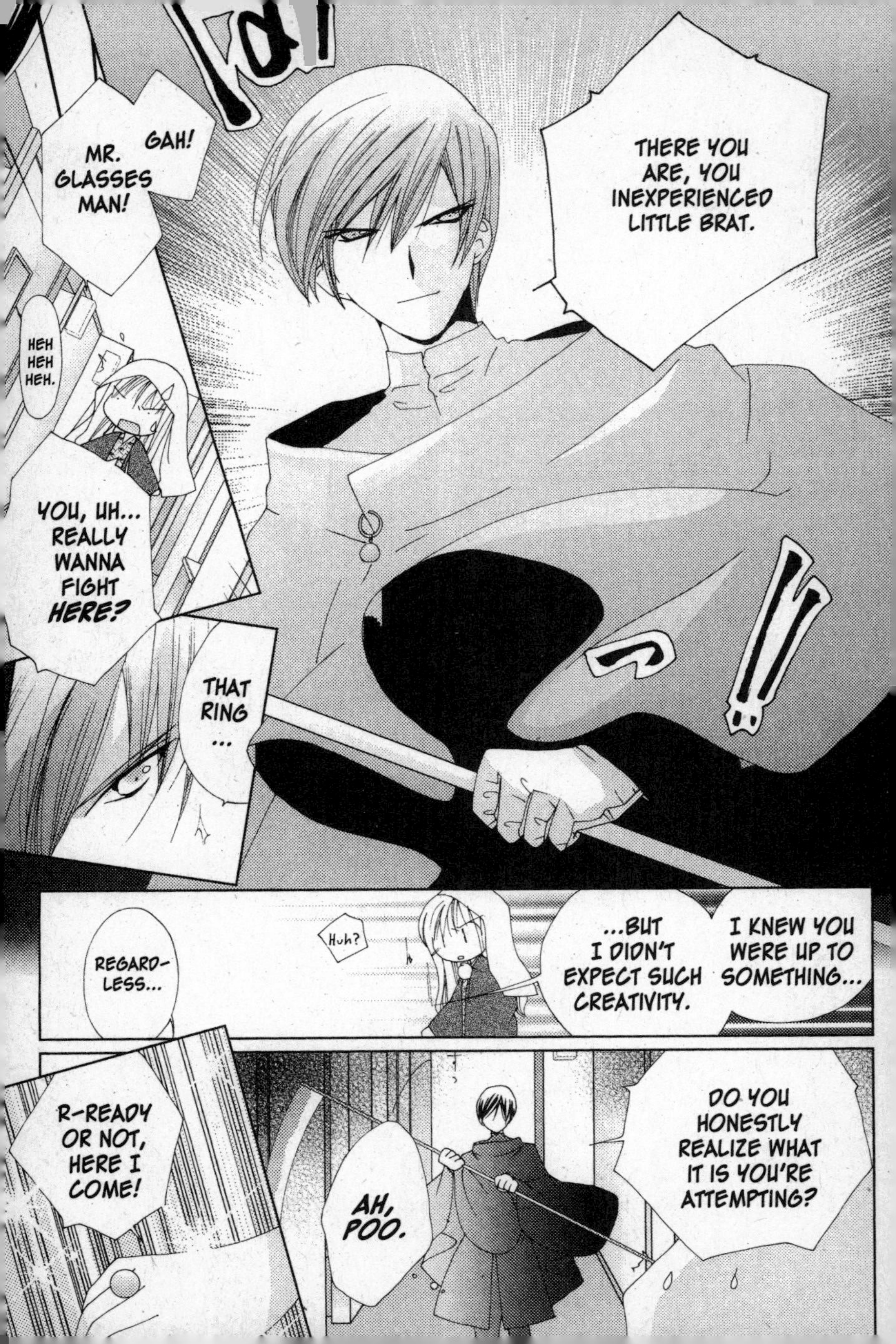
THERE YOU ARE, YOU INEXPERIENCED LITTLE BRAT.
GAH!
MR. GLASSES MAN!
HEH HEH HEH.
YOU, UH... REALLY WANNA FIGHT *HERE?*
THAT RING ...
I KNEW YOU WERE UP TO SOMETHING...
...BUT I DIDN'T EXPECT SUCH CREATIVITY.
Huh?
REGARD-LESS...
DO YOU HONESTLY REALIZE WHAT IT IS YOU'RE ATTEMPTING?
AH, POO.
R-READY OR NOT, HERE I COME!

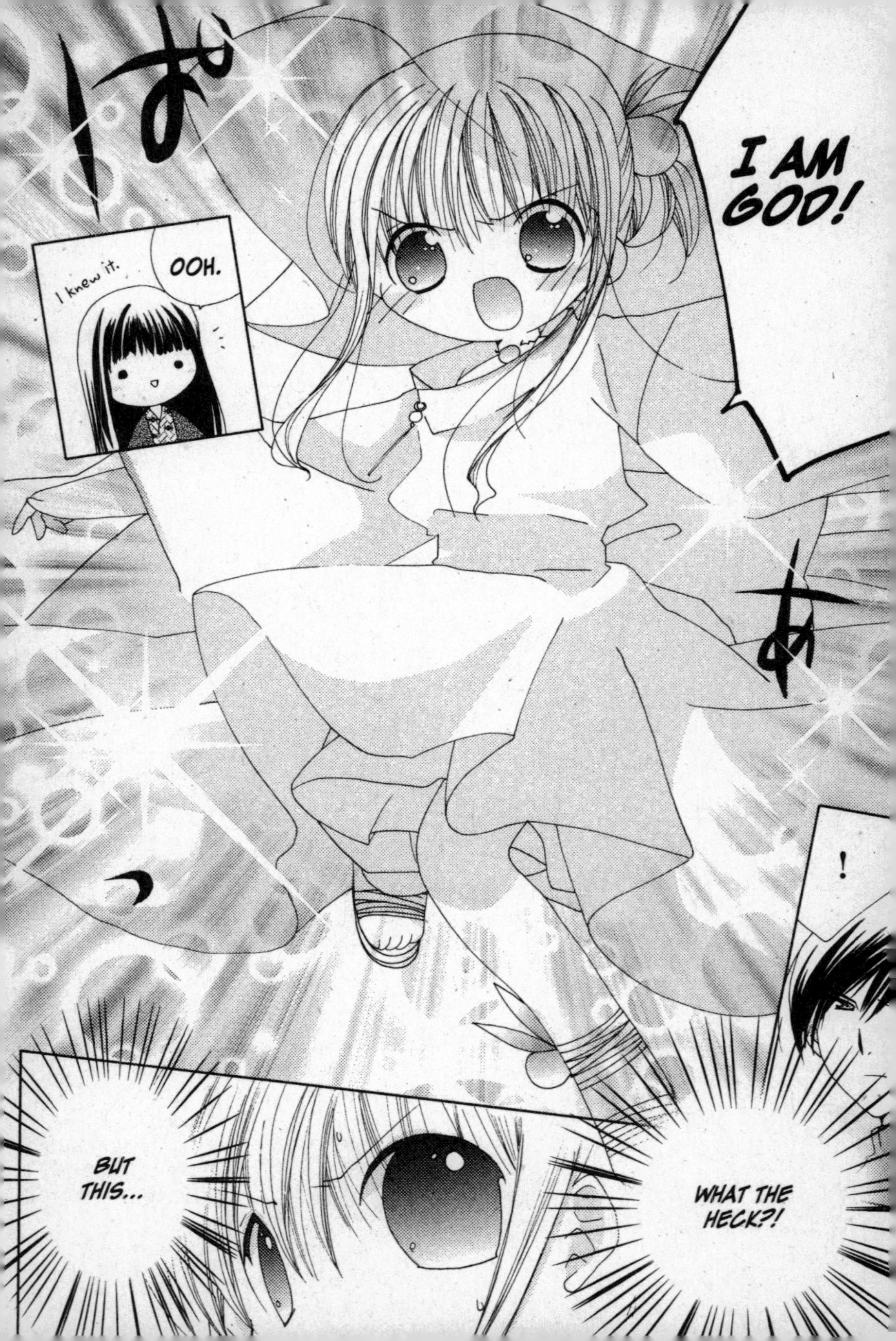
I AM GOD!
OOH.
I knew it.
!
WHAT THE HECK?!
BUT THIS...

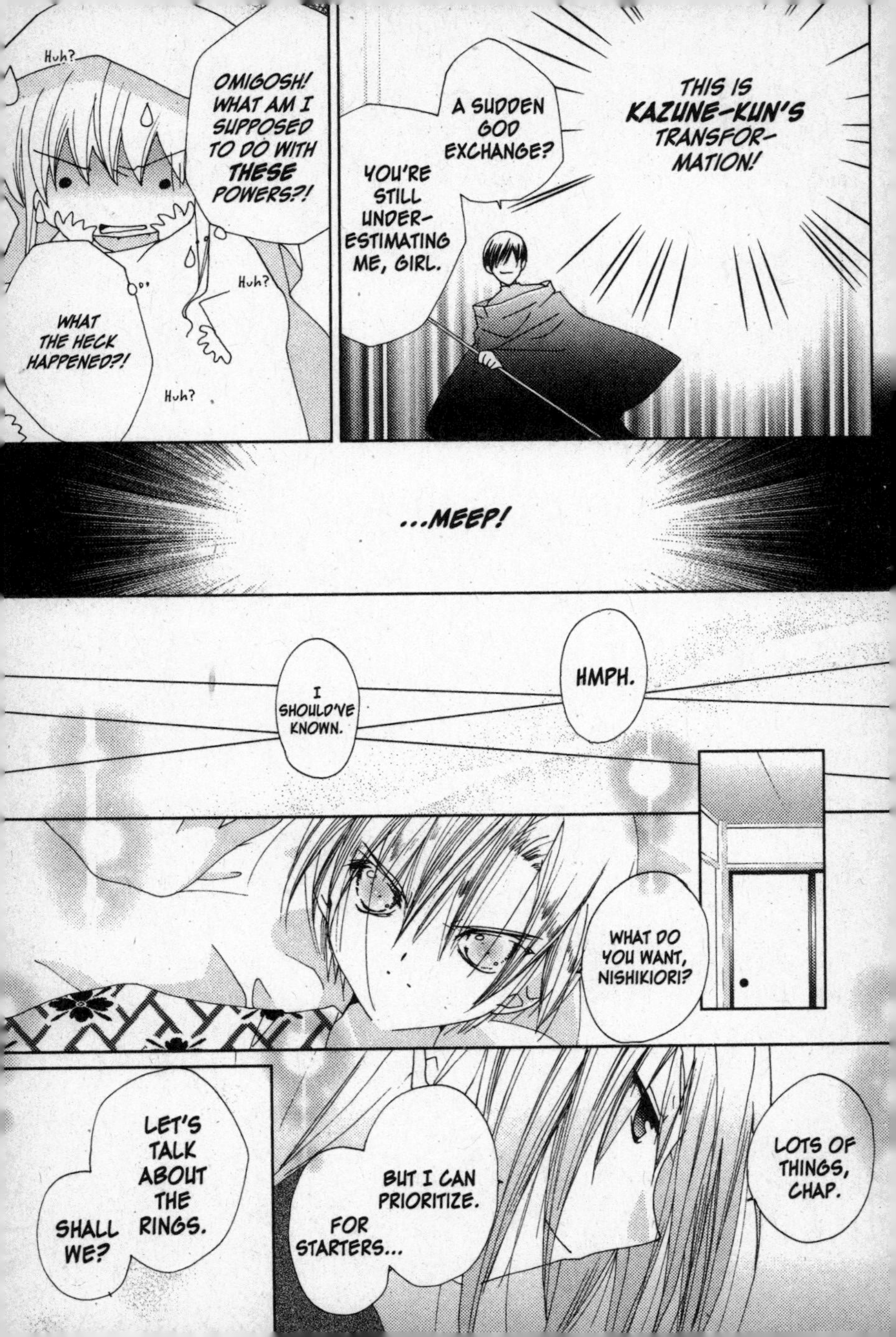
THIS IS KAZUNE-KUN'S TRANSFORMATION!
A SUDDEN GOD EXCHANGE?
YOU'RE STILL UNDER-ESTIMATING ME, GIRL.
OMIGOSH! WHAT AM I SUPPOSED TO DO WITH THESE POWERS?!
Huh?
Huh?
WHAT THE HECK HAPPENED?!
Huh?
...MEEP!
HMPH.
I SHOULD'VE KNOWN.
WHAT DO YOU WANT, NISHIKIORI?
LOTS OF THINGS, CHAP.
BUT I CAN PRIORITIZE.
FOR STARTERS...
LET'S TALK ABOUT THE RINGS.
SHALL WE?

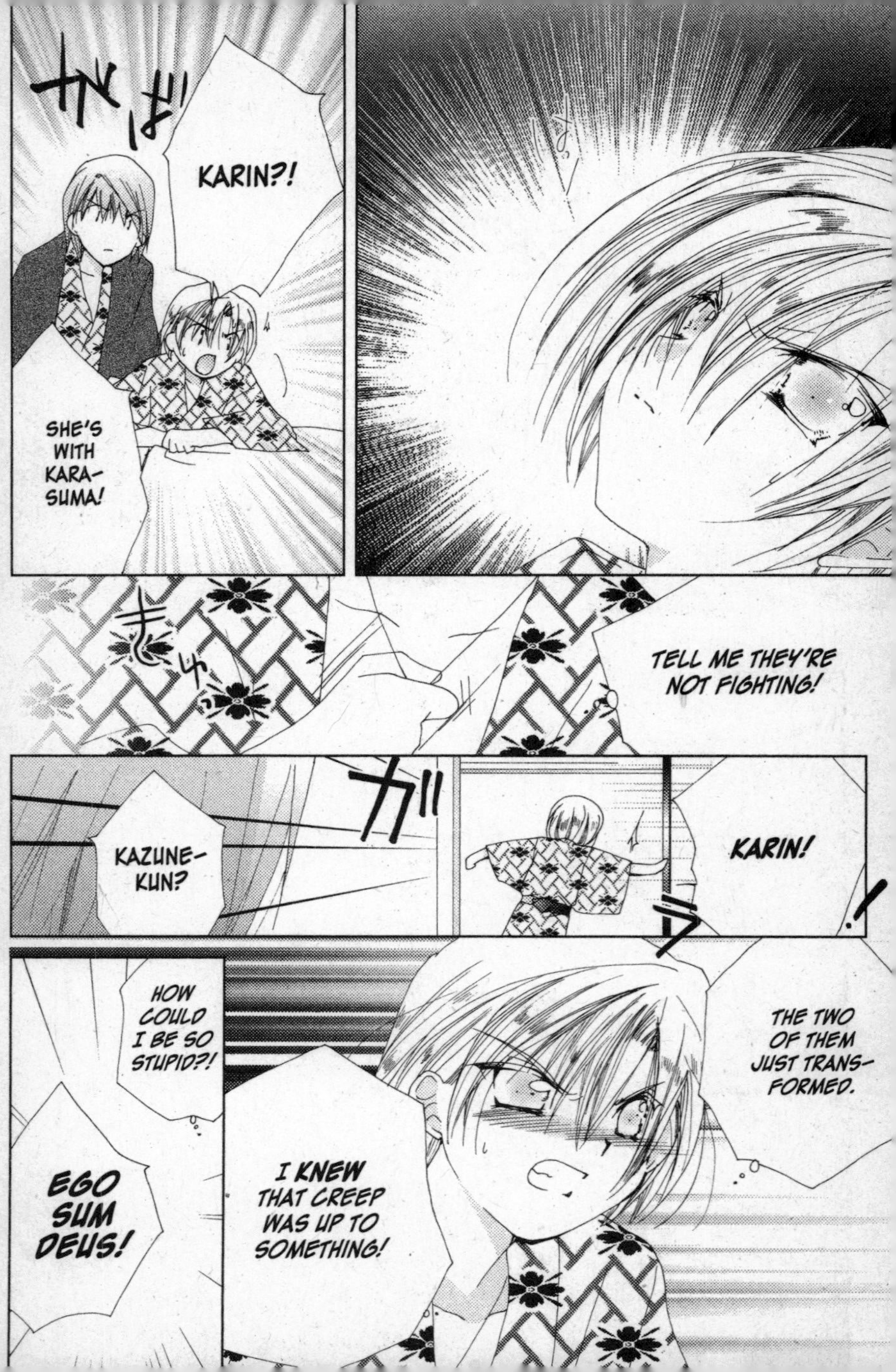
KARIN?!
SHE'S WITH KARA-SUMA!
TELL ME THEY'RE NOT FIGHTING!
KARIN!
KAZUNE-KUN?
THE TWO OF THEM JUST TRANS-FORMED.
I KNEW THAT CREEP WAS UP TO SOMETHING!
HOW COULD I BE SO STUPID?!
EGO SUM DEUS!

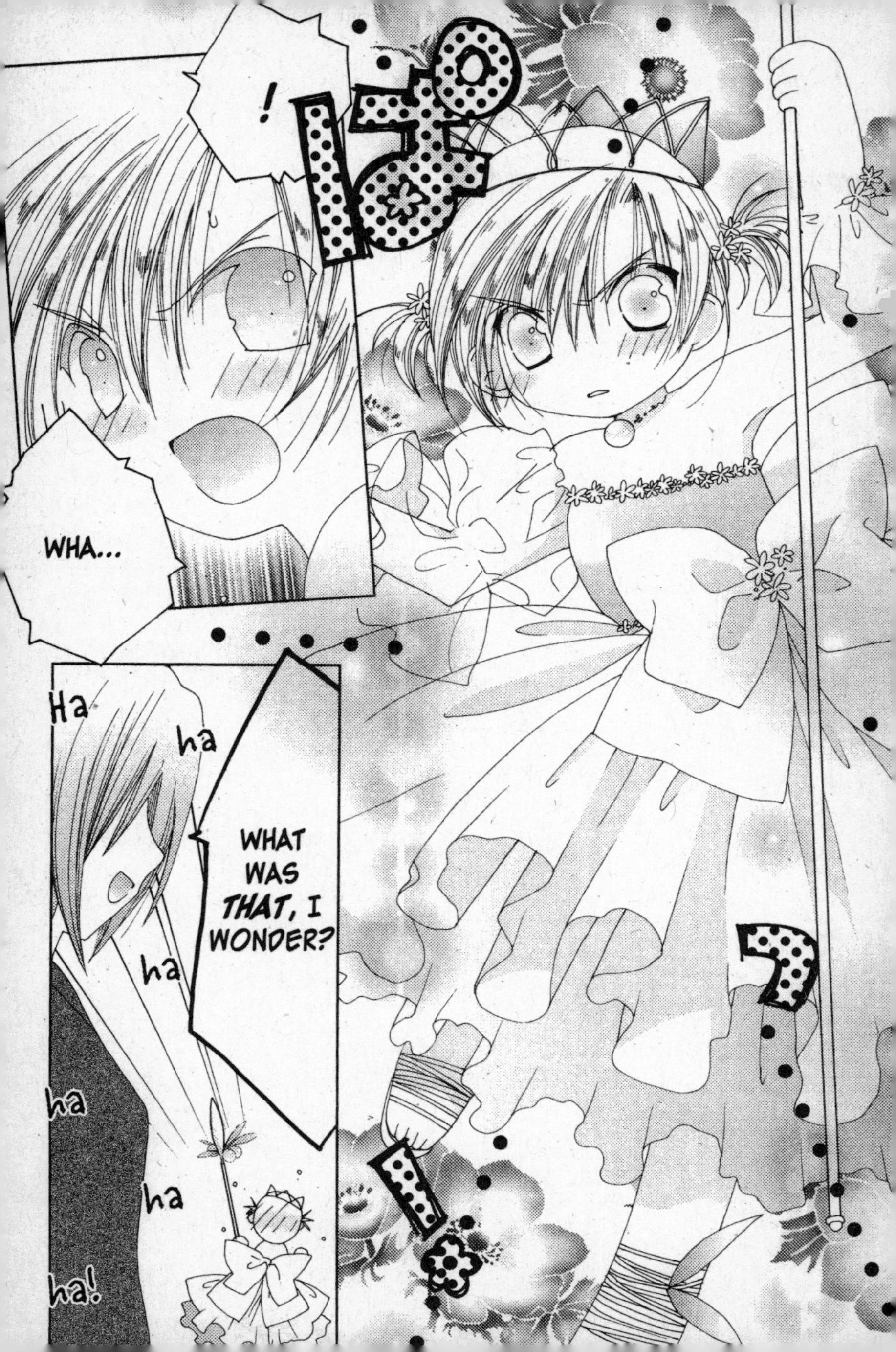
!
WHA...
WHAT WAS THAT, I WONDER?
Ha ha ha ha ha ha!

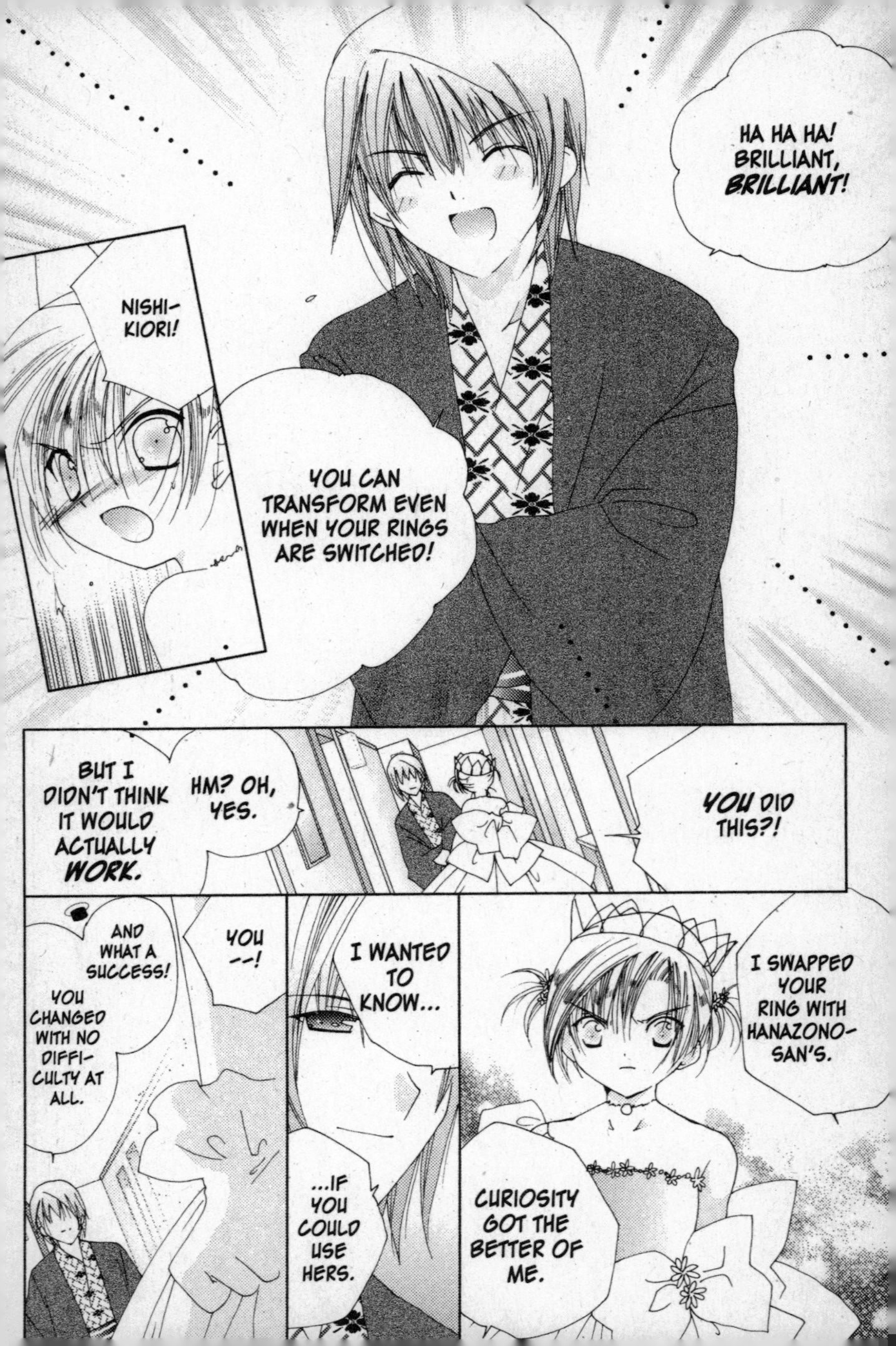
HA HA HA! BRILLIANT, BRILLIANT!
NISHI-KIORI!
YOU CAN TRANSFORM EVEN WHEN YOUR RINGS ARE SWITCHED!
YOU DID THIS?!
HM? OH, YES.
BUT I DIDN'T THINK IT WOULD ACTUALLY WORK.
I SWAPPED YOUR RING WITH HANAZONO-SAN'S.
CURIOSITY GOT THE BETTER OF ME.
I WANTED TO KNOW...
...IF YOU COULD USE HERS.
YOU --!
AND WHAT A SUCCESS!
YOU CHANGED WITH NO DIFFICULTY AT ALL.

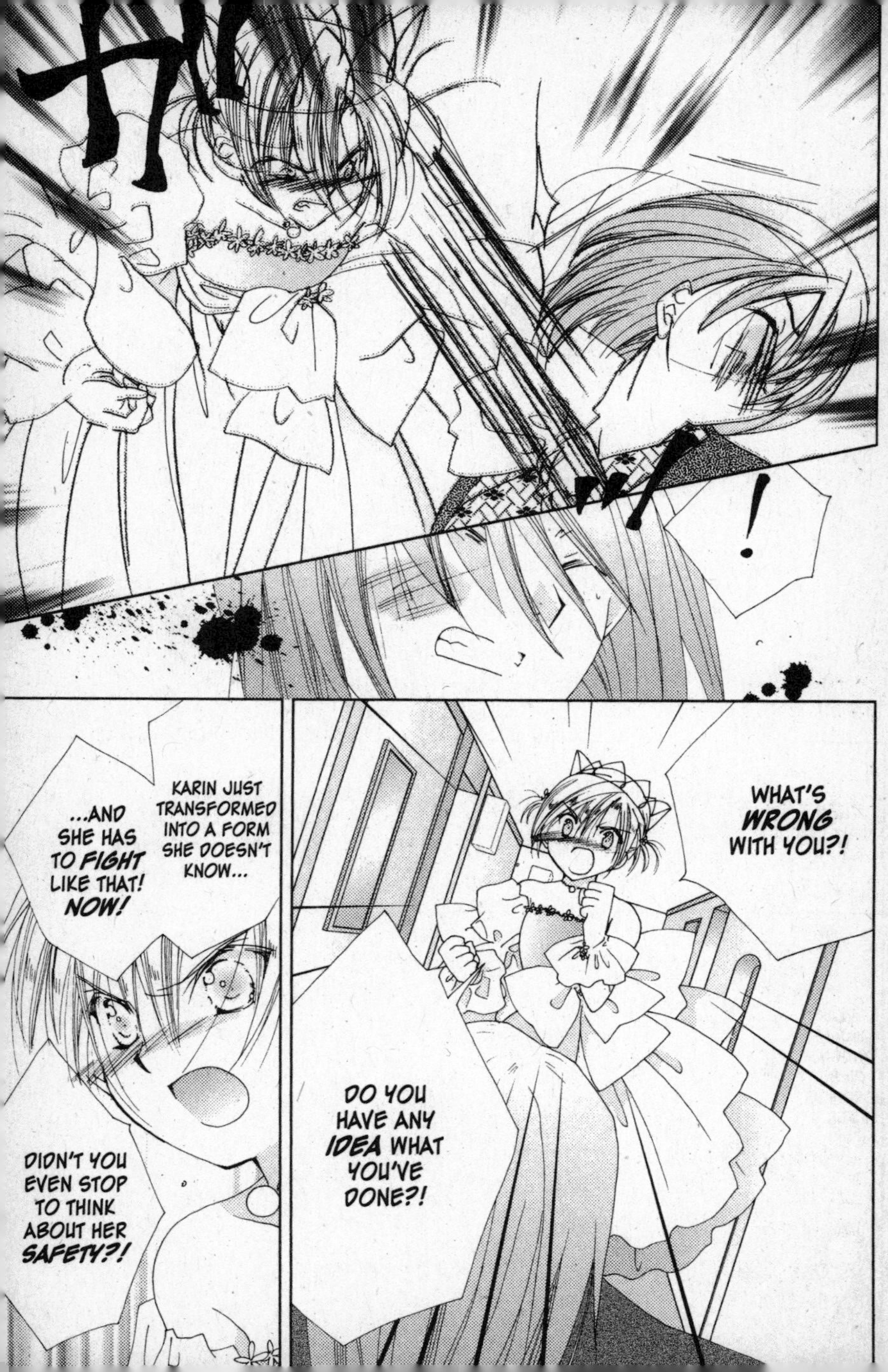
!
WHAT'S WRONG WITH YOU?!
DO YOU HAVE ANY IDEA WHAT YOU'VE DONE?!
KARIN JUST TRANSFORMED INTO A FORM SHE DOESN'T KNOW...
...AND SHE HAS TO FIGHT LIKE THAT! NOW!
DIDN'T YOU EVEN STOP TO THINK ABOUT HER SAFETY?!

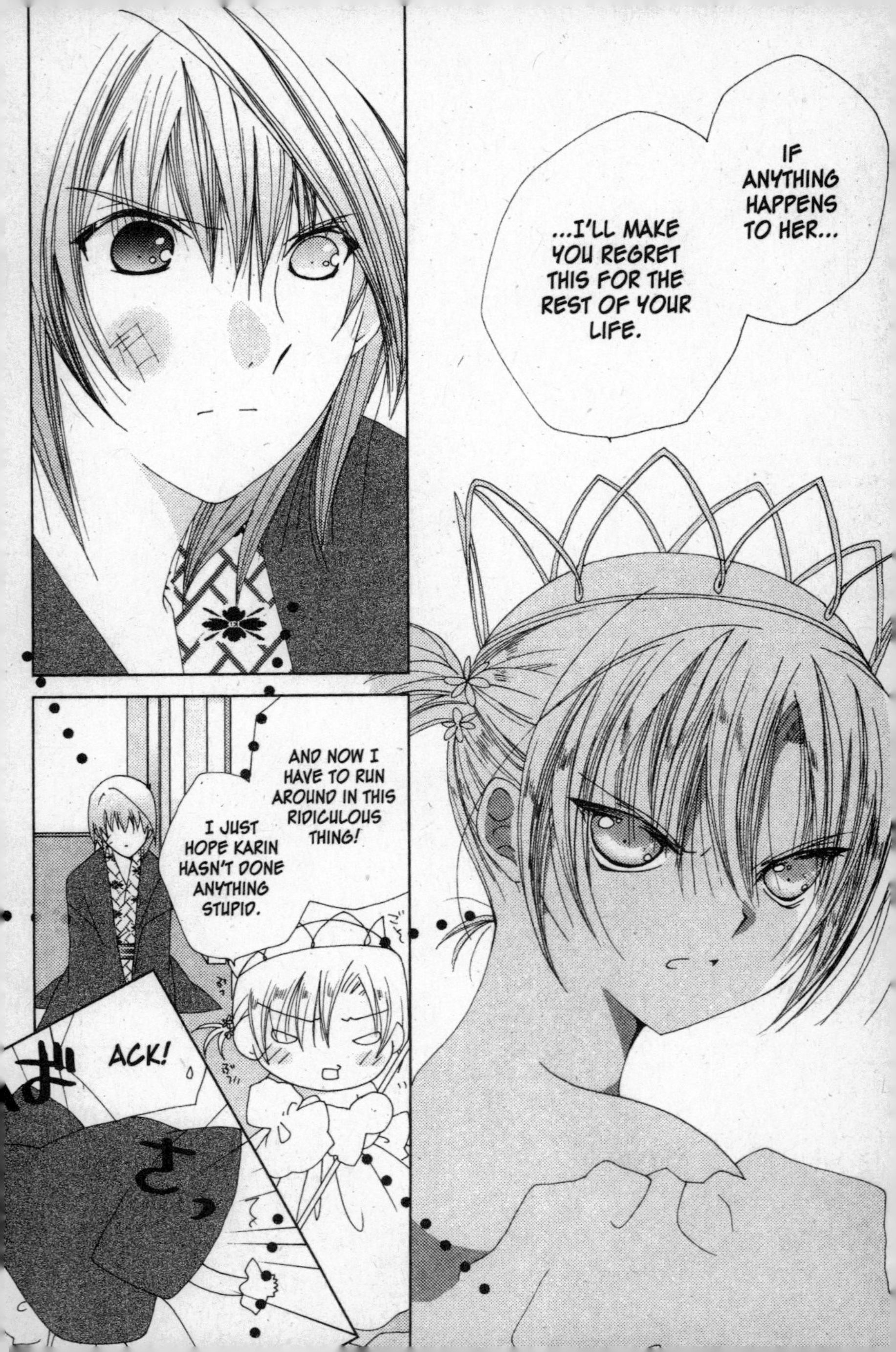

IF ANYTHING HAPPENS TO HER...
...I'LL MAKE YOU REGRET THIS FOR THE REST OF YOUR LIFE.
AND NOW I HAVE TO RUN AROUND IN THIS RIDICULOUS THING!
I JUST HOPE KARIN HASN'T DONE ANYTHING STUPID.
ACK!

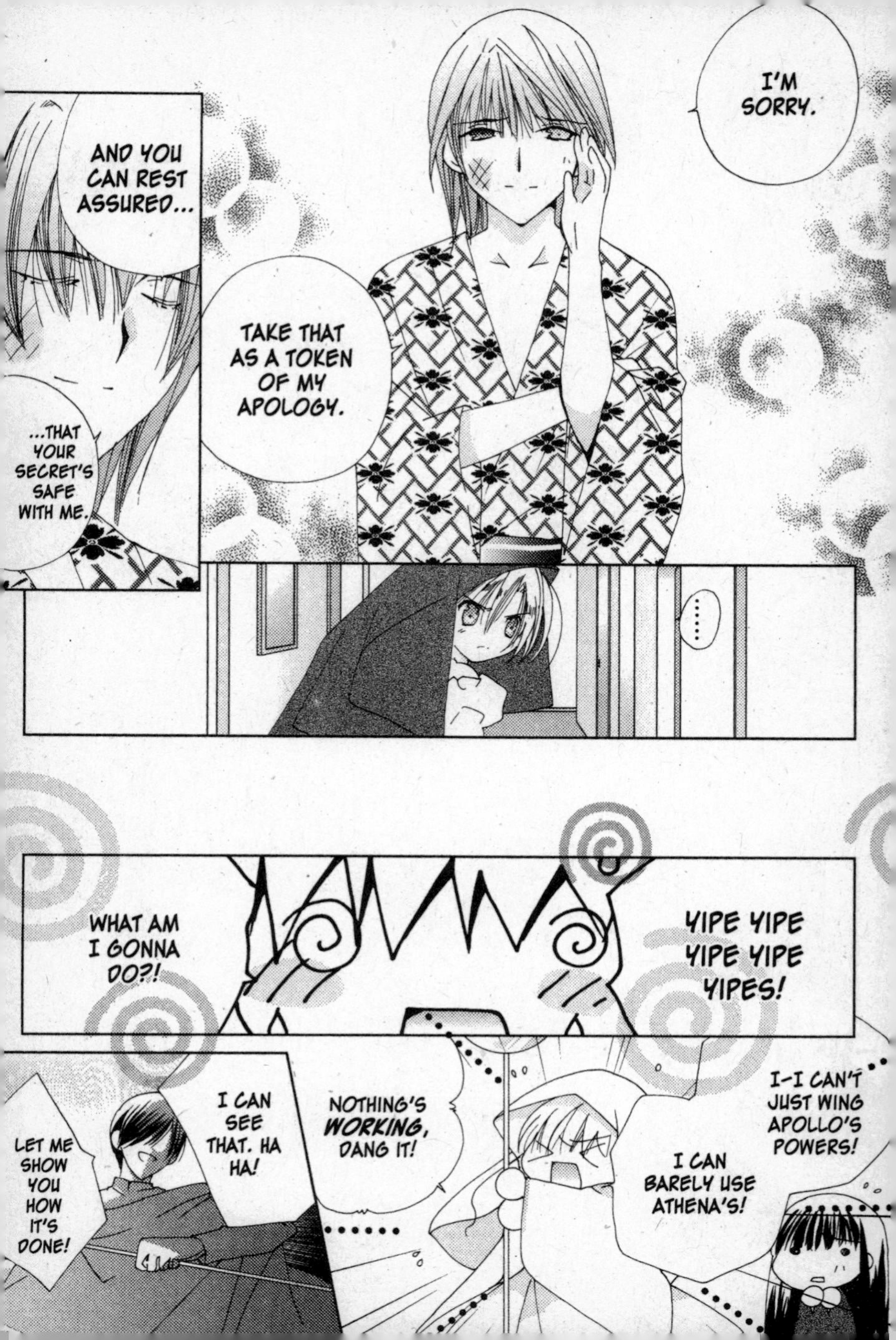
I'M SORRY.
TAKE THAT AS A TOKEN OF MY APOLOGY.
AND YOU CAN REST ASSURED...
...THAT YOUR SECRET'S SAFE WITH ME.
......
YIPE YIPE YIPE YIPE YIPES!
WHAT AM I GONNA DO?!
I-I CAN'T JUST WING APOLLO'S POWERS!
I CAN BARELY USE ATHENA'S!
NOTHING'S *WORKING*, DANG IT!
I CAN SEE THAT. HA HA!
......
LET ME SHOW YOU HOW IT'S DONE!

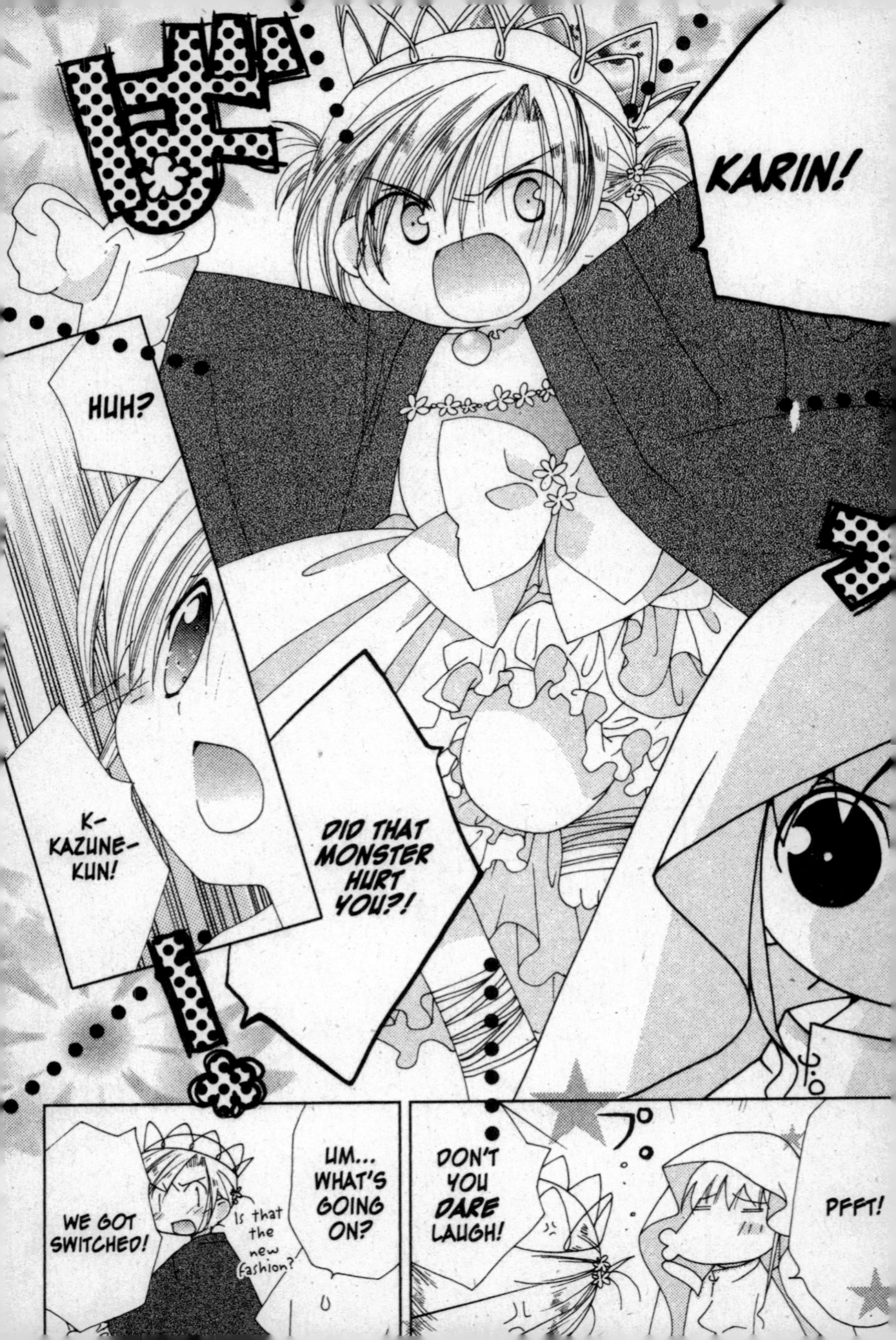
KARIN!
HUH?
DID THAT MONSTER HURT YOU?!
K-KAZUNE-KUN!
PFFT!
DON'T YOU DARE LAUGH!
UM... WHAT'S GOING ON?
Is that the new fashion?
WE GOT SWITCHED!

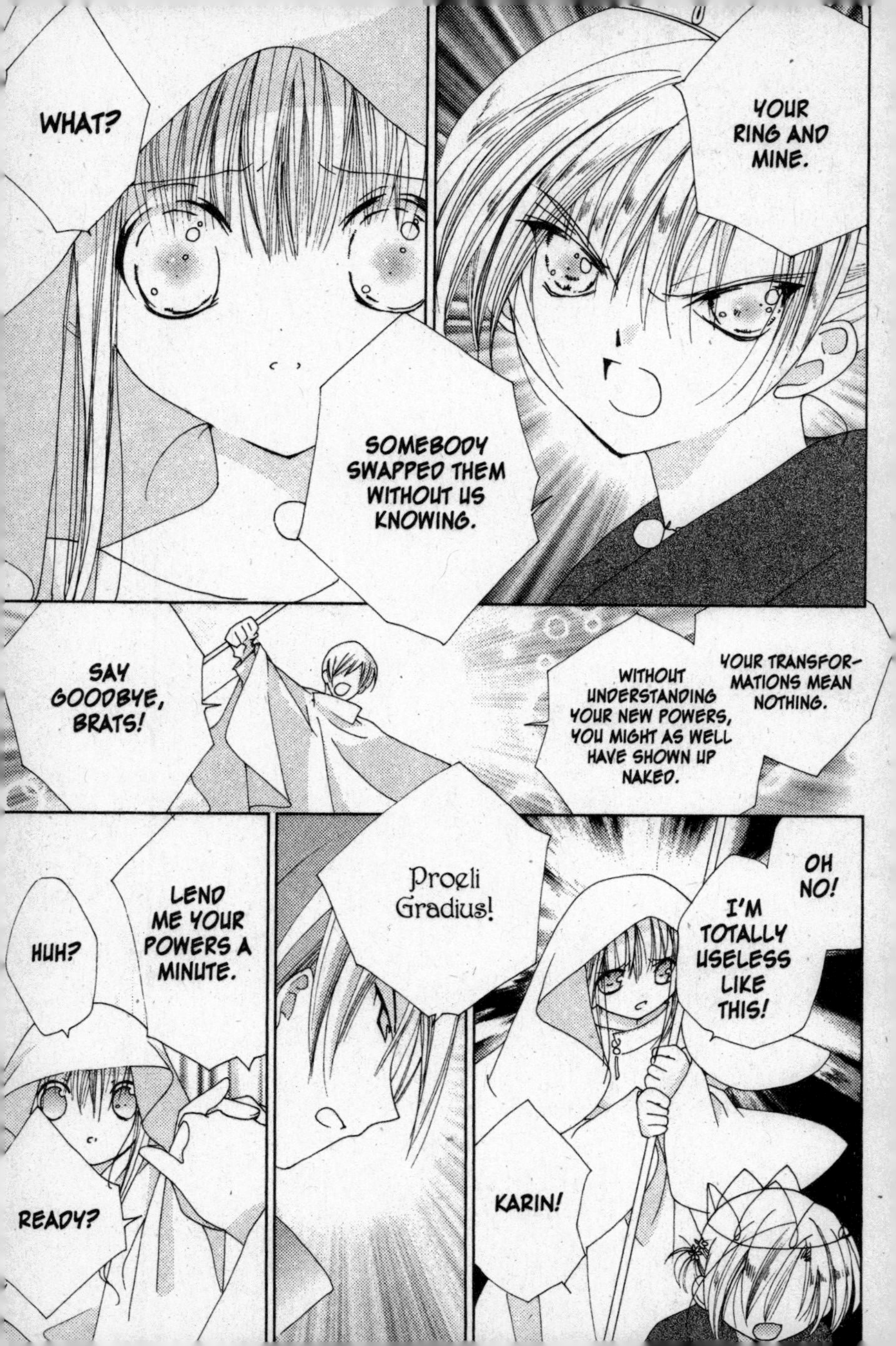
YOUR RING AND MINE.
SOMEBODY SWAPPED THEM WITHOUT US KNOWING.
WHAT?
YOUR TRANSFOR-MATIONS MEAN NOTHING.
WITHOUT UNDERSTANDING YOUR NEW POWERS, YOU MIGHT AS WELL HAVE SHOWN UP NAKED.
SAY GOODBYE, BRATS!
OH NO!
I'M TOTALLY USELESS LIKE THIS!
KARIN!
Proeli Gradius!
LEND ME YOUR POWERS A MINUTE.
HUH?
READY?

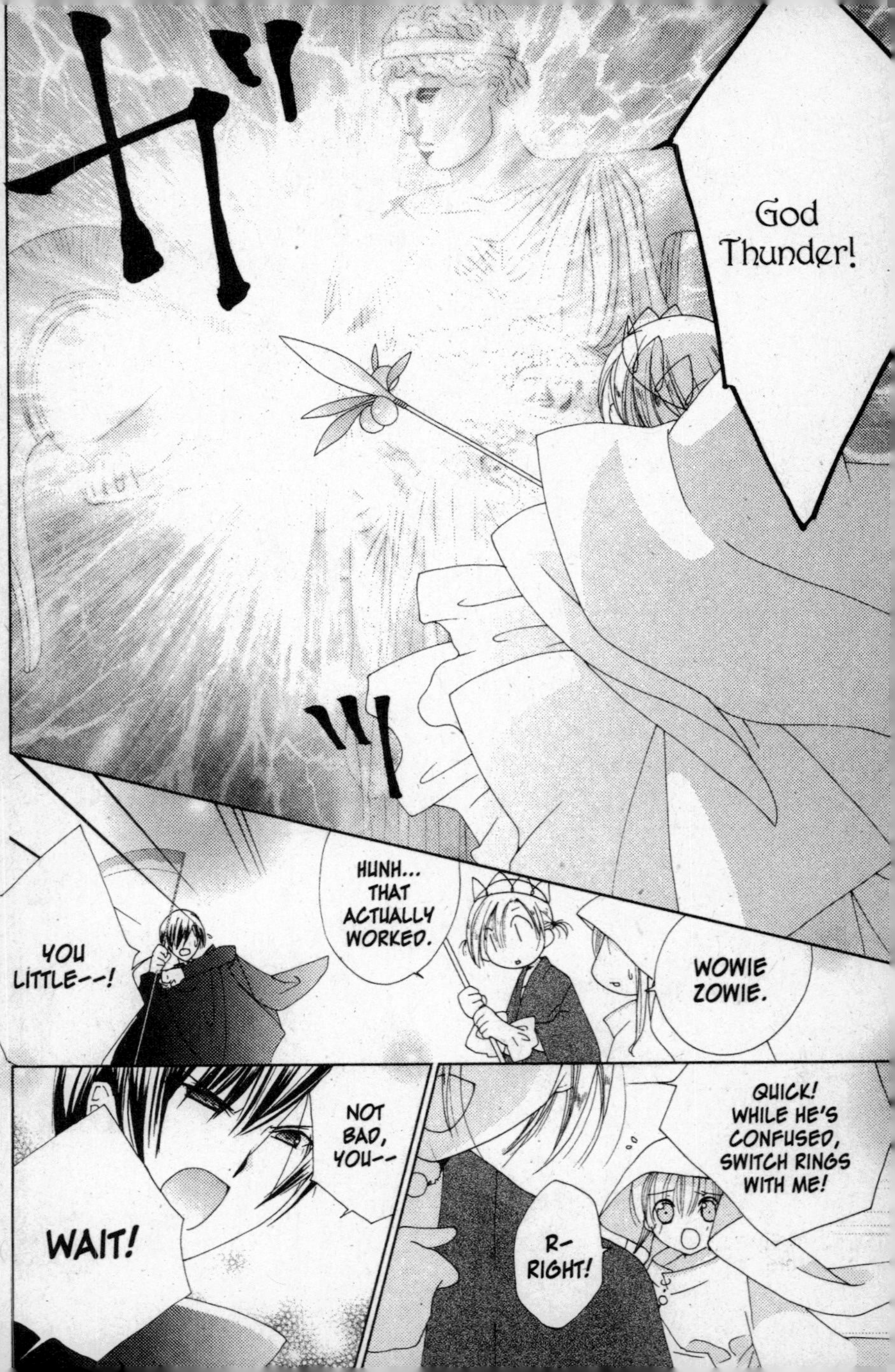
God Thunder!
WOWIE ZOWIE.
HUNH... THAT ACTUALLY WORKED.
YOU LITTLE--!
QUICK! WHILE HE'S CONFUSED, SWITCH RINGS WITH ME!
R- RIGHT!
NOT BAD, YOU--
WAIT!

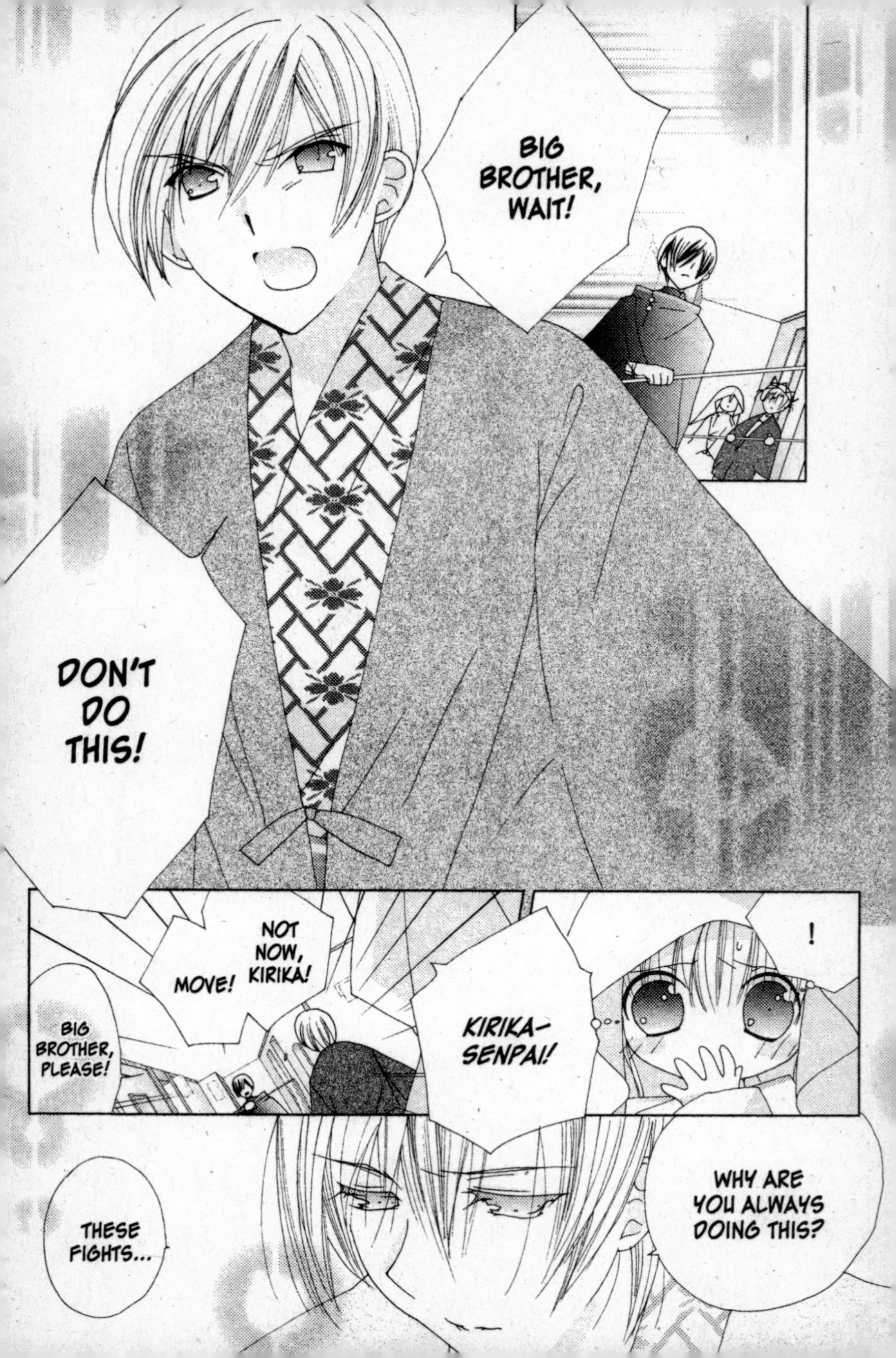
BIG BROTHER, WAIT!
DON'T DO THIS!
!
KIRIKA-SENPAI!
NOT NOW, KIRIKA!
MOVE!
BIG BROTHER, PLEASE!
WHY ARE YOU ALWAYS DOING THIS?
THESE FIGHTS...

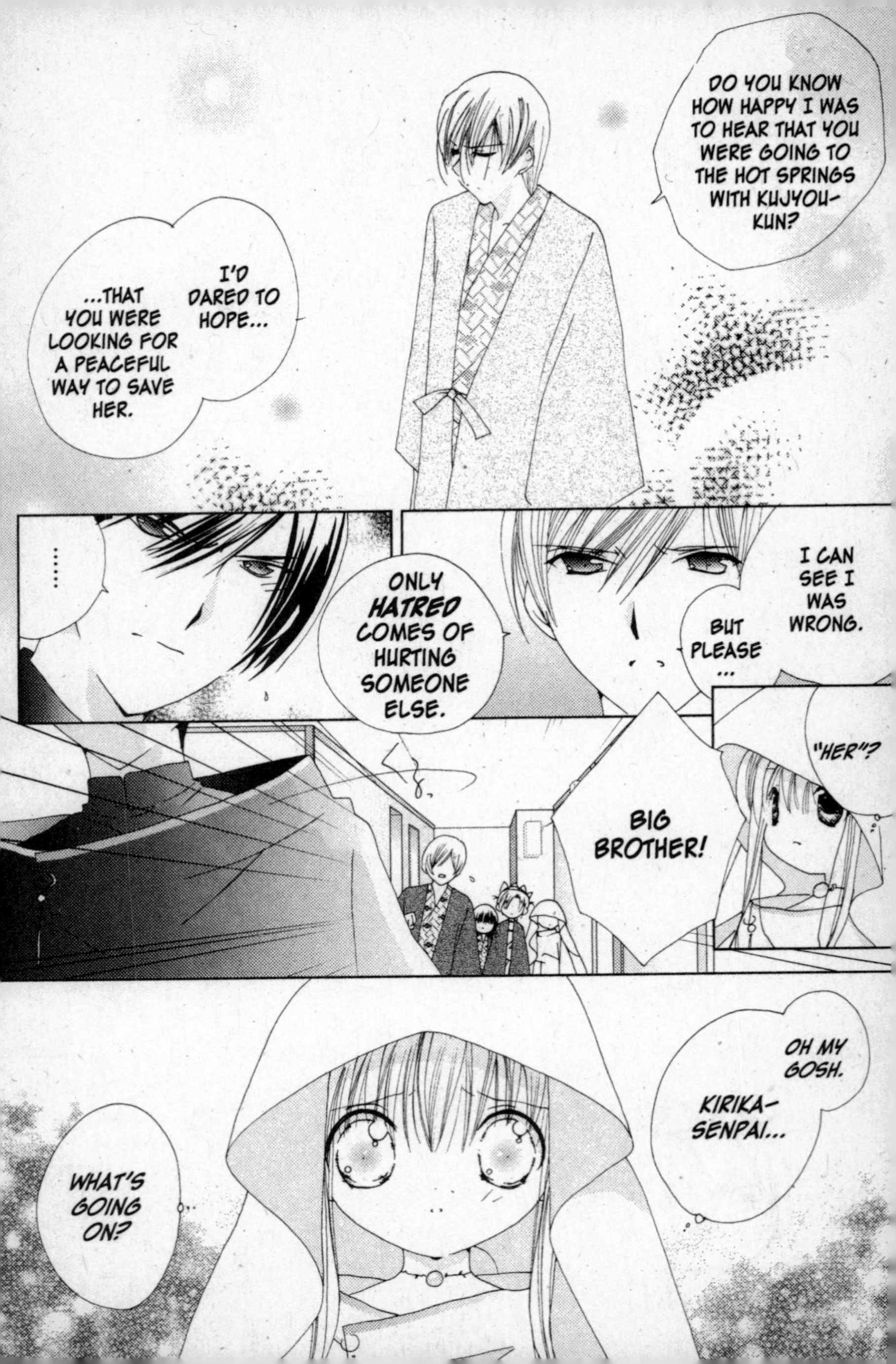
DO YOU KNOW HOW HAPPY I WAS TO HEAR THAT YOU WERE GOING TO THE HOT SPRINGS WITH KUJYOU-KUN?
I'D DARED TO HOPE...
...THAT YOU WERE LOOKING FOR A PEACEFUL WAY TO SAVE HER.
I CAN SEE I WAS WRONG.
BUT PLEASE ...
ONLY HATRED COMES OF HURTING SOMEONE ELSE.
......
"HER"?
BIG BROTHER!
OH MY GOSH.
KIRIKA-SENPAI...
WHAT'S GOING ON?

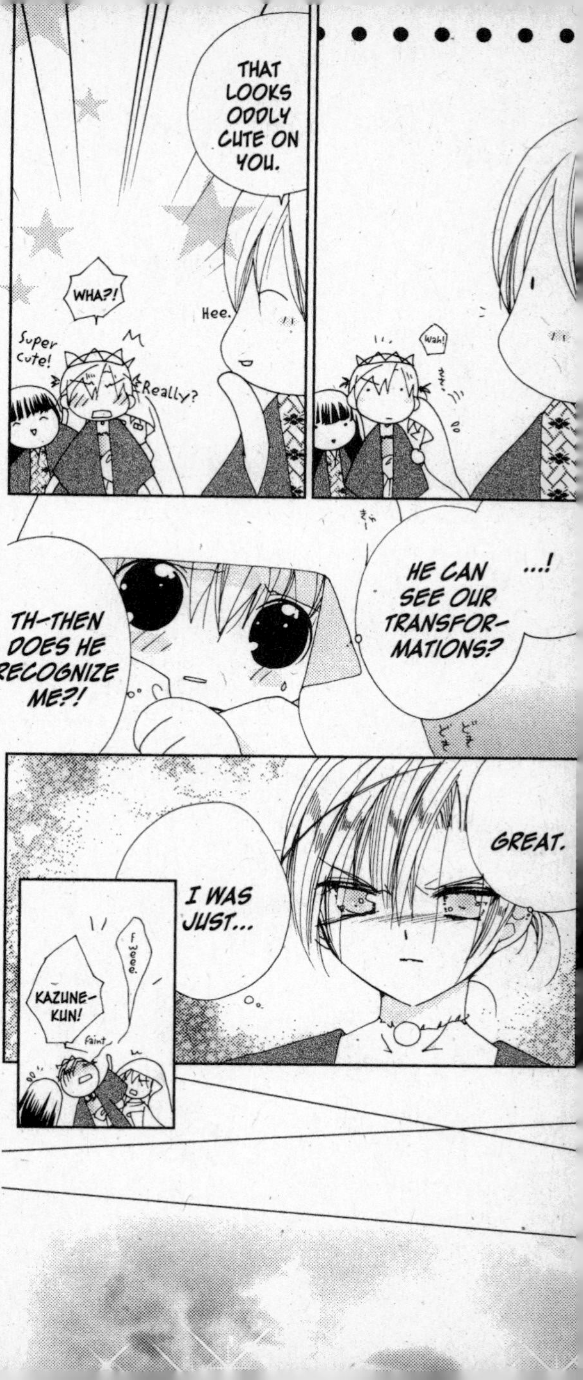
Wah!
THAT LOOKS ODDLY CUTE ON YOU.
Hee.
WHA?!
Really?
Super cute!
...!
HE CAN SEE OUR TRANSFORMATIONS?
TH-THEN DOES HE RECOGNIZE ME?!
GREAT.
I WAS JUST...
Fweee.
KAZUNE-KUN!
Faint

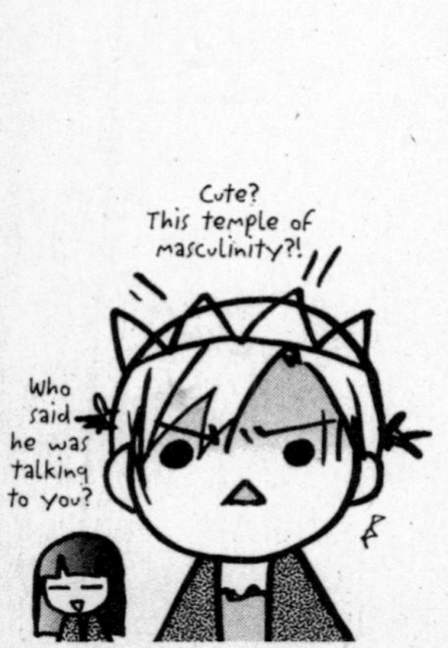
Cute? This temple of masculinity?!
Who said he was talking to you?

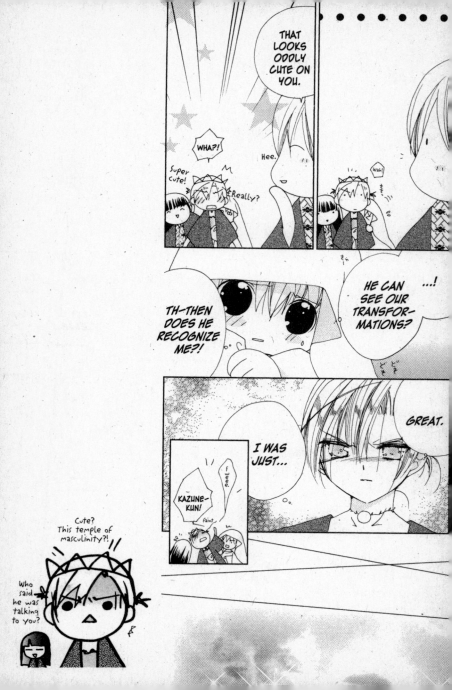

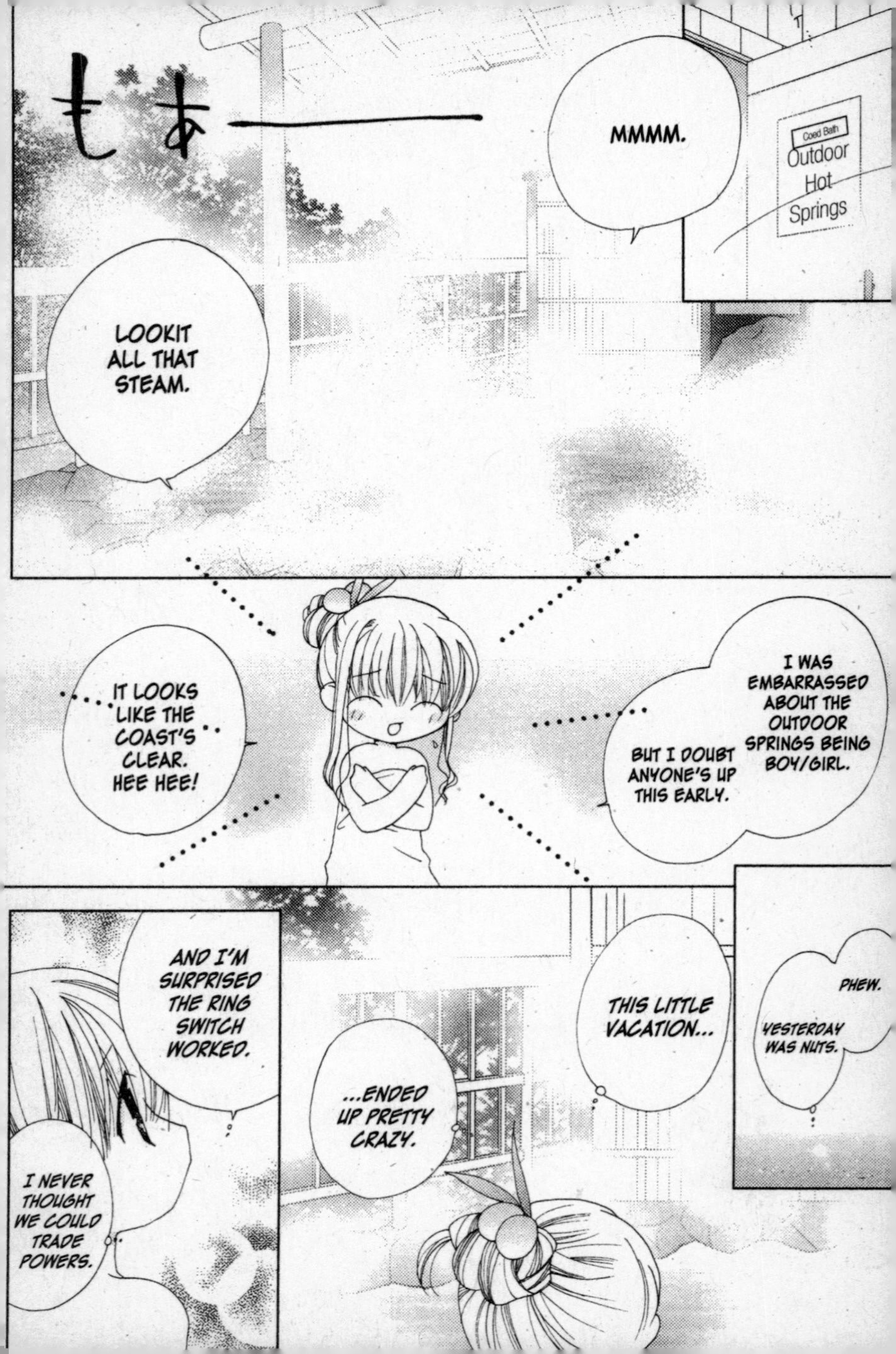
Coed Bath
Outdoor Hot Springs
MMMM.
もあーー
LOOKIT ALL THAT STEAM.
I WAS EMBARRASSED ABOUT THE OUTDOOR SPRINGS BEING BOY/GIRL.
BUT I DOUBT ANYONE'S UP THIS EARLY.
IT LOOKS LIKE THE COAST'S CLEAR. HEE HEE!
PHEW.
YESTERDAY WAS NUTS.
THIS LITTLE VACATION...
...ENDED UP PRETTY CRAZY.
AND I'M SURPRISED THE RING SWITCH WORKED.
I NEVER THOUGHT WE COULD TRADE POWERS.

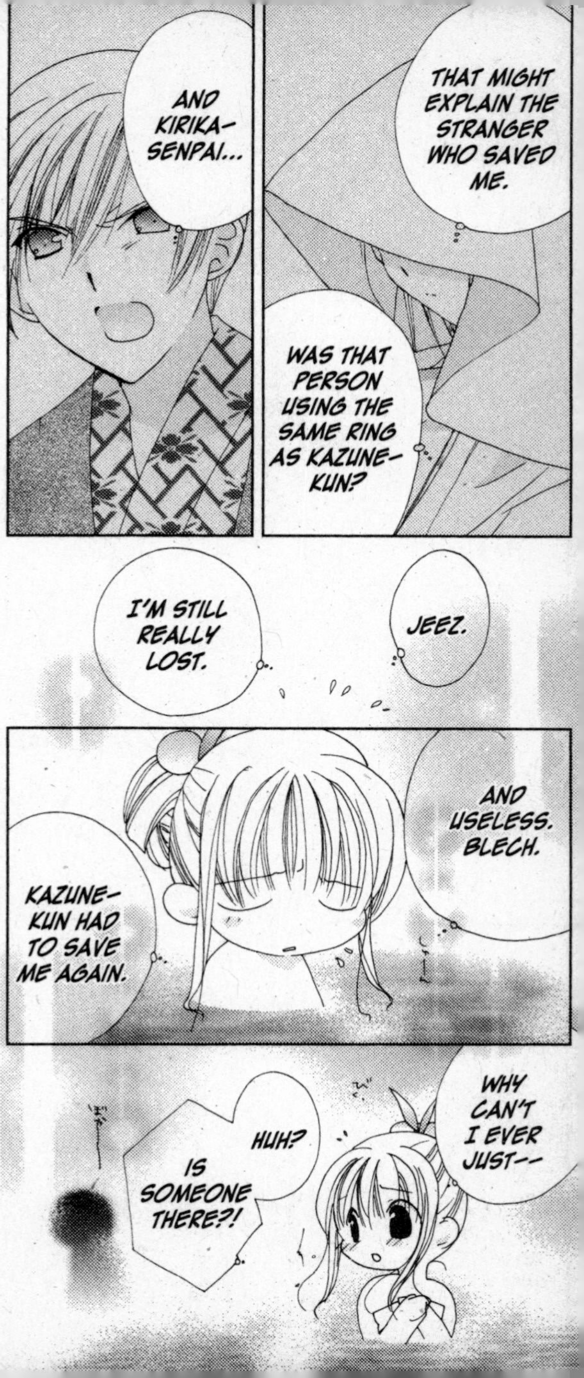
THAT MIGHT EXPLAIN THE STRANGER WHO SAVED ME.
WAS THAT PERSON USING THE SAME RING AS KAZUNE-KUN?
AND KIRIKA-SENPAI...
JEEZ.
I'M STILL REALLY LOST.
AND USELESS. BLECH.
KAZUNE-KUN HAD TO SAVE ME AGAIN.
WHY CAN'T I EVER JUST--
HUH? IS SOMEONE THERE?!

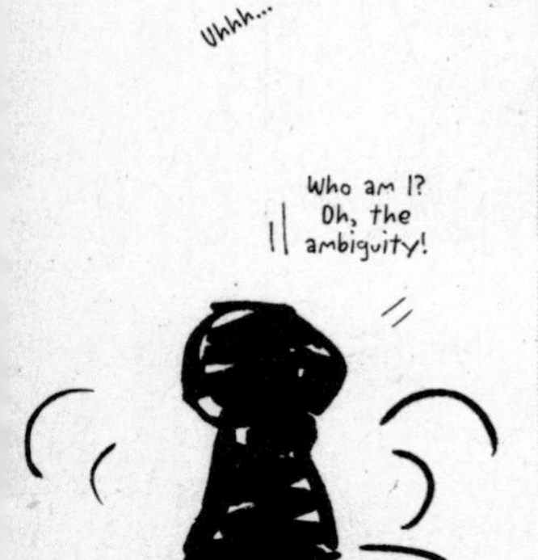
Uhhh...
Who am I? Oh, the ambiguity!

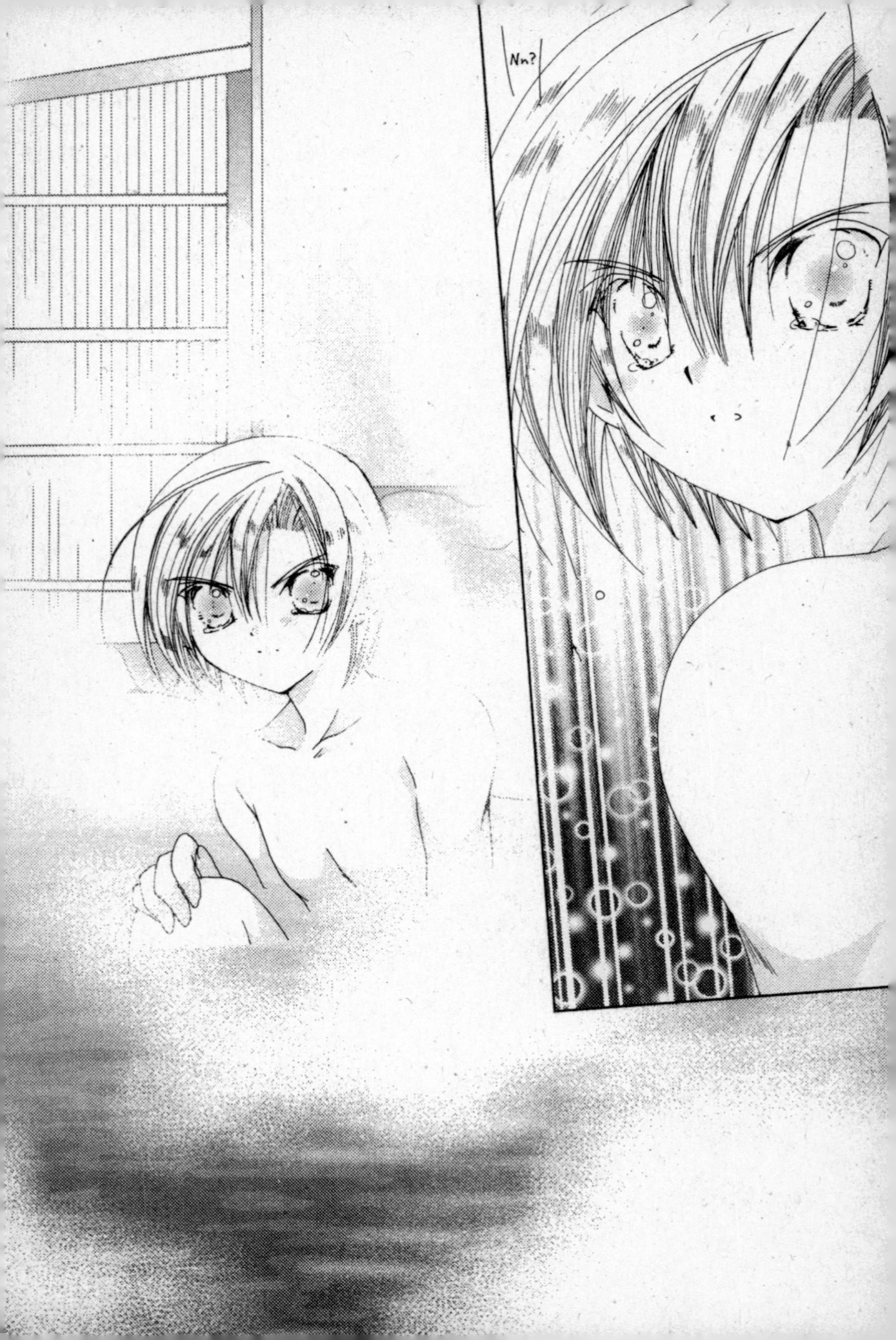
Nn?

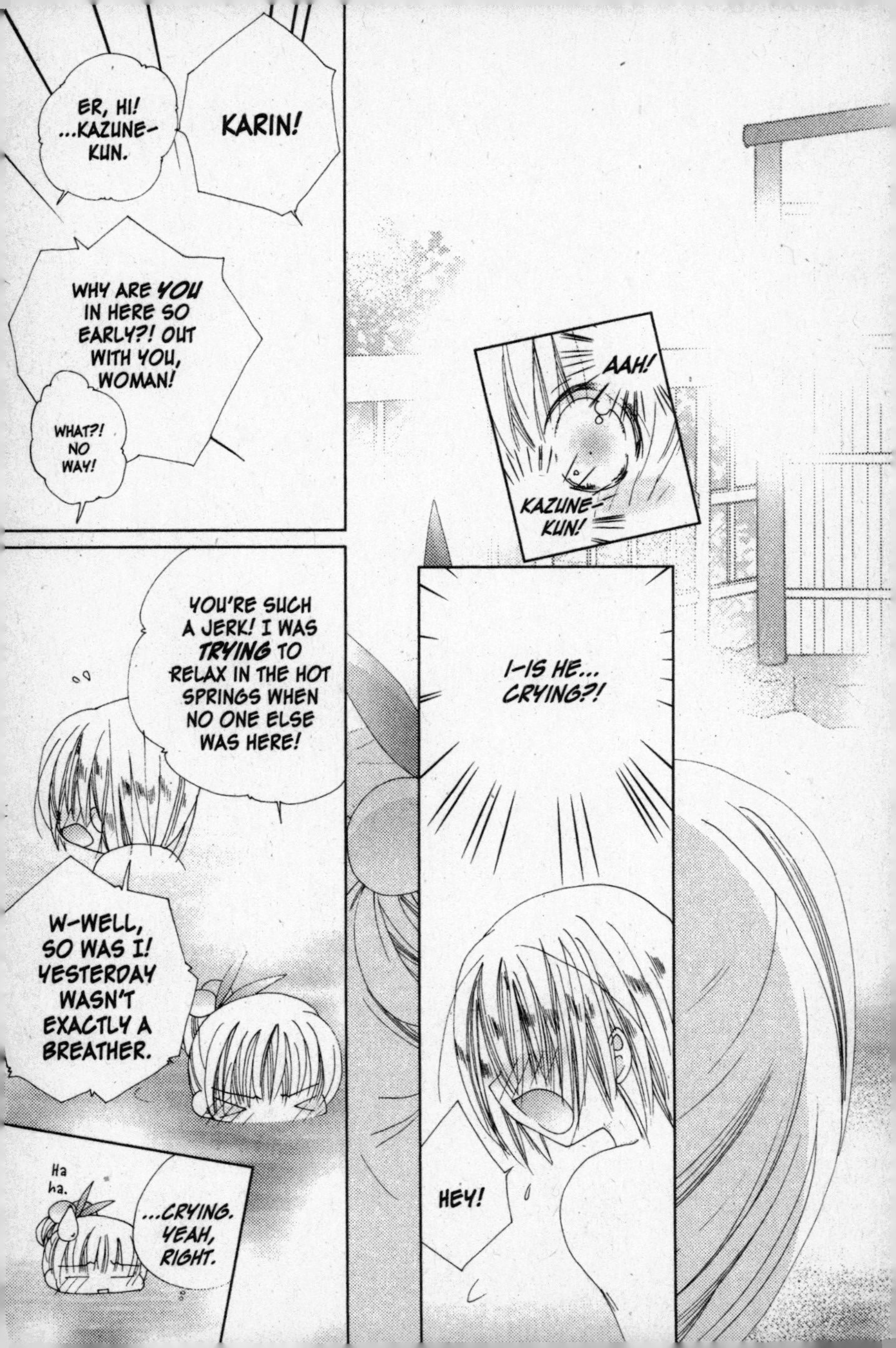

AAH!
KAZUNE-KUN!
I-IS HE... CRYING?!
HEY!
KARIN!
ER, HI! ...KAZUNE-KUN.
WHY ARE YOU IN HERE SO EARLY?! OUT WITH YOU, WOMAN!
WHAT?! NO WAY!
YOU'RE SUCH A JERK! I WAS TRYING TO RELAX IN THE HOT SPRINGS WHEN NO ONE ELSE WAS HERE!
W-WELL, SO WAS I! YESTERDAY WASN'T EXACTLY A BREATHER.
...CRYING. YEAH, RIGHT.
Ha ha.

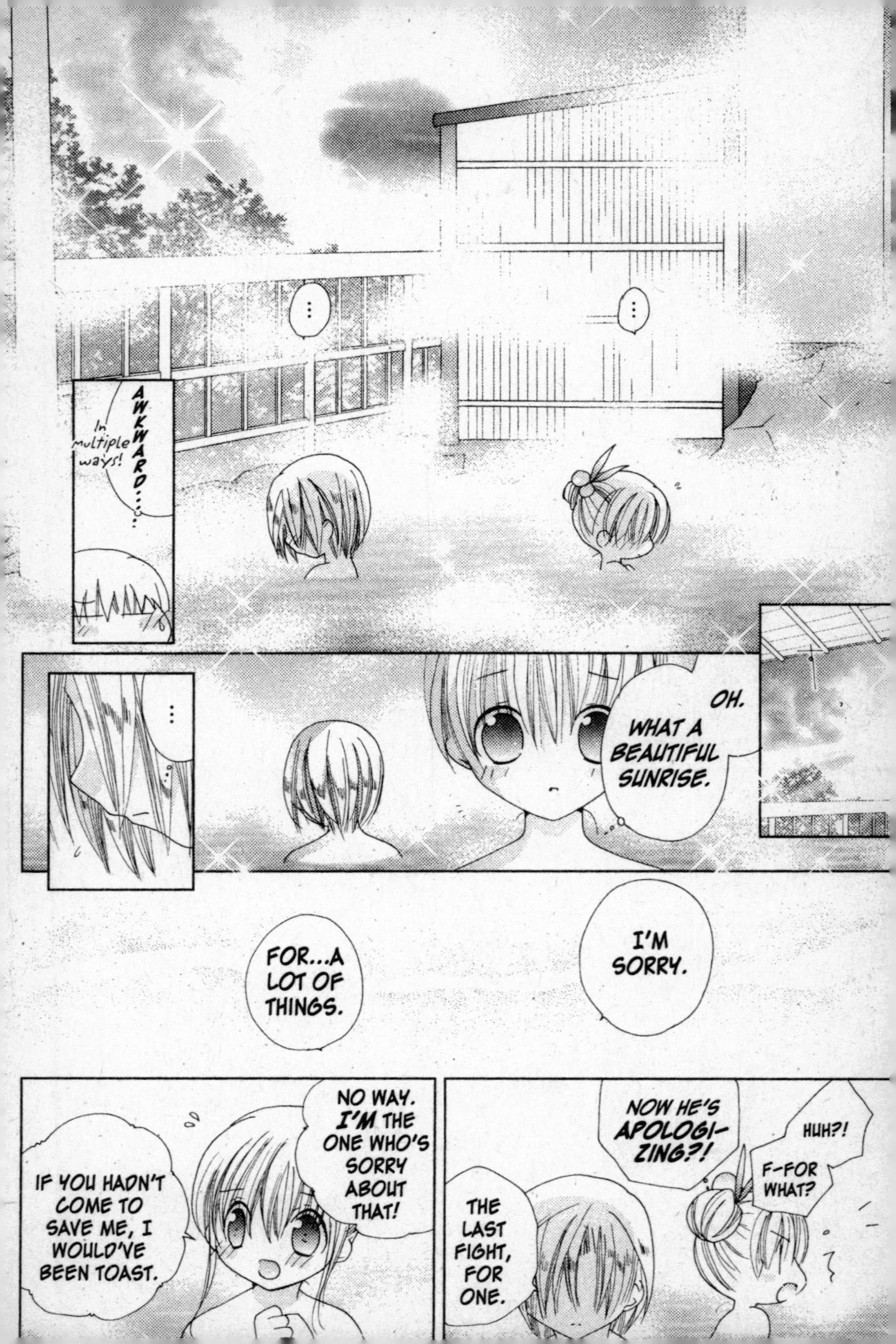
...
...
AWKWARD...
In multiple ways!
OH. WHAT A BEAUTIFUL SUNRISE.
...
...
I'M SORRY.
FOR...A LOT OF THINGS.
HUH?!
F-FOR WHAT?
NOW HE'S APOLOGI-ZING?!
THE LAST FIGHT, FOR ONE.
NO WAY. *I'M* THE ONE WHO'S SORRY ABOUT THAT!
IF YOU HADN'T COME TO SAVE ME, I WOULD'VE BEEN TOAST.

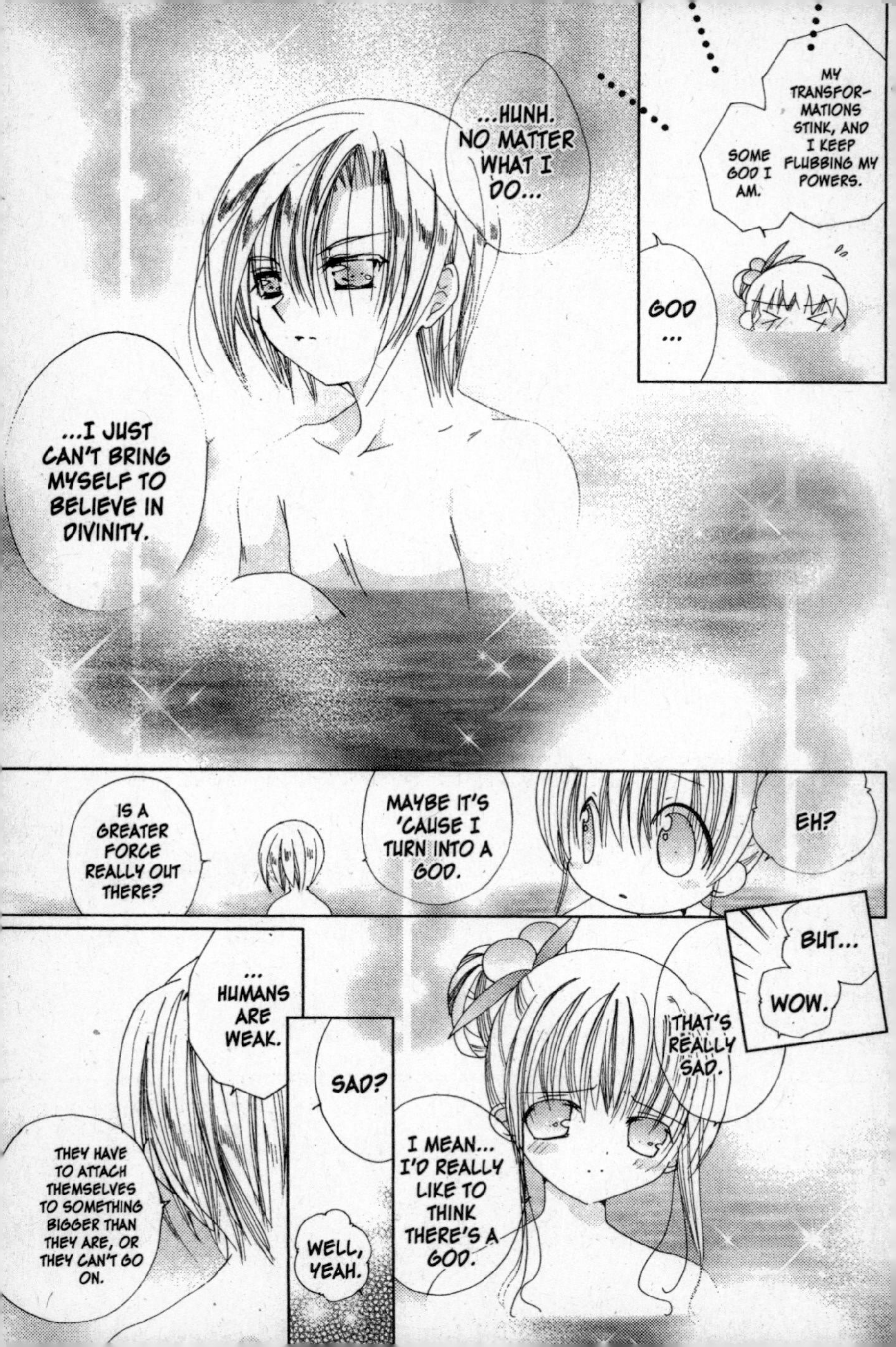
MY TRANSFORMATIONS STINK, AND I KEEP FLUBBING MY POWERS.
SOME GOD I AM.
GOD ...
...HUNH. NO MATTER WHAT I DO...
...I JUST CAN'T BRING MYSELF TO BELIEVE IN DIVINITY.
EH?
MAYBE IT'S 'CAUSE I TURN INTO A GOD.
IS A GREATER FORCE REALLY OUT THERE?
BUT...
WOW.
THAT'S REALLY SAD.
I MEAN... I'D REALLY LIKE TO THINK THERE'S A GOD.
SAD?
WELL, YEAH.
... HUMANS ARE WEAK.
THEY HAVE TO ATTACH THEMSELVES TO SOMETHING BIGGER THAN THEY ARE, OR THEY CAN'T GO ON.

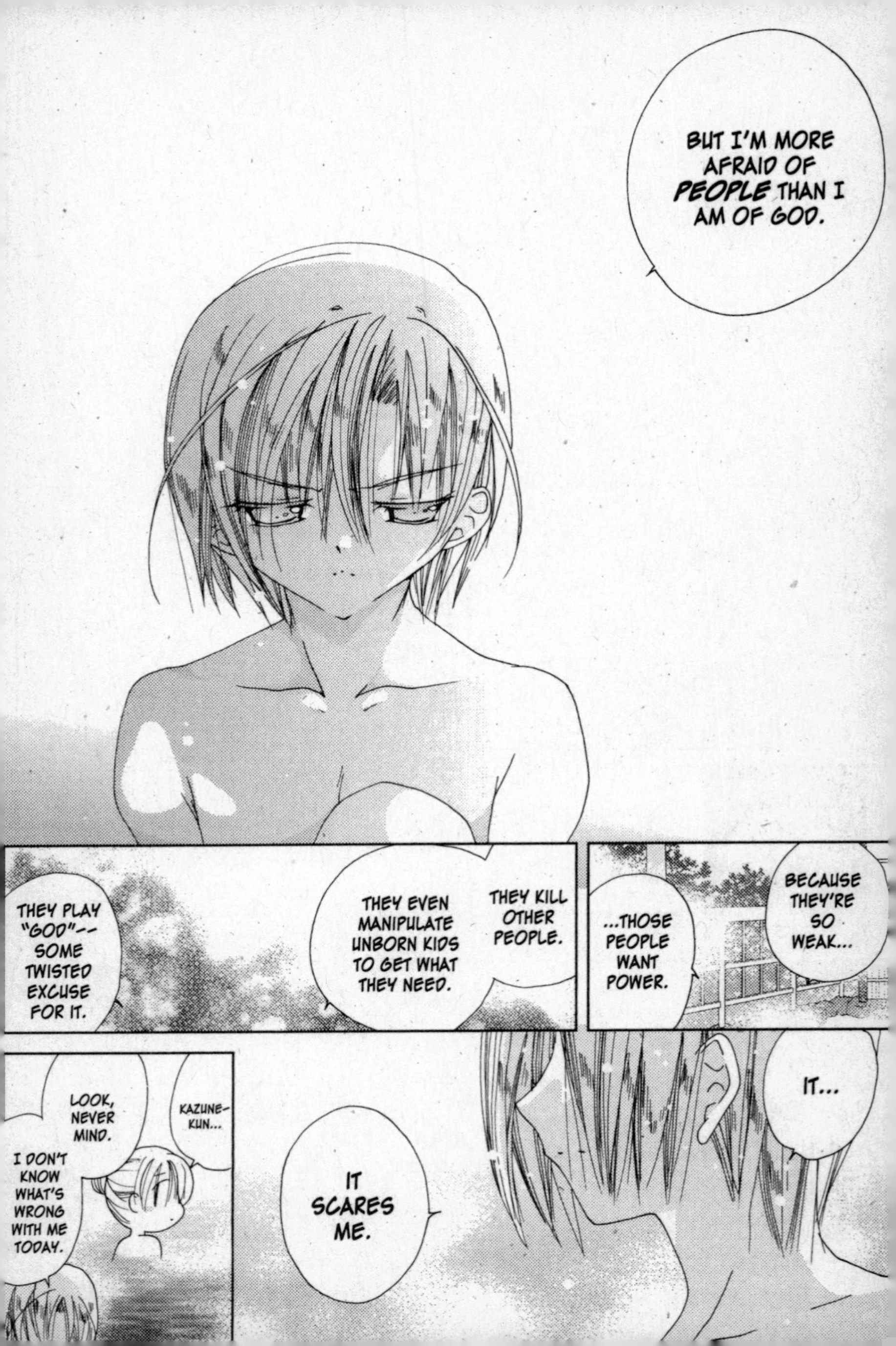
BUT I'M MORE AFRAID OF *PEOPLE* THAN I AM OF GOD.
BECAUSE THEY'RE SO WEAK...
...THOSE PEOPLE WANT POWER.
THEY KILL OTHER PEOPLE.
THEY EVEN MANIPULATE UNBORN KIDS TO GET WHAT THEY NEED.
THEY PLAY "GOD"-- SOME TWISTED EXCUSE FOR IT.
IT...
IT SCARES ME.
KAZUNE-KUN...
LOOK, NEVER MIND.
I DON'T KNOW WHAT'S WRONG WITH ME TODAY.

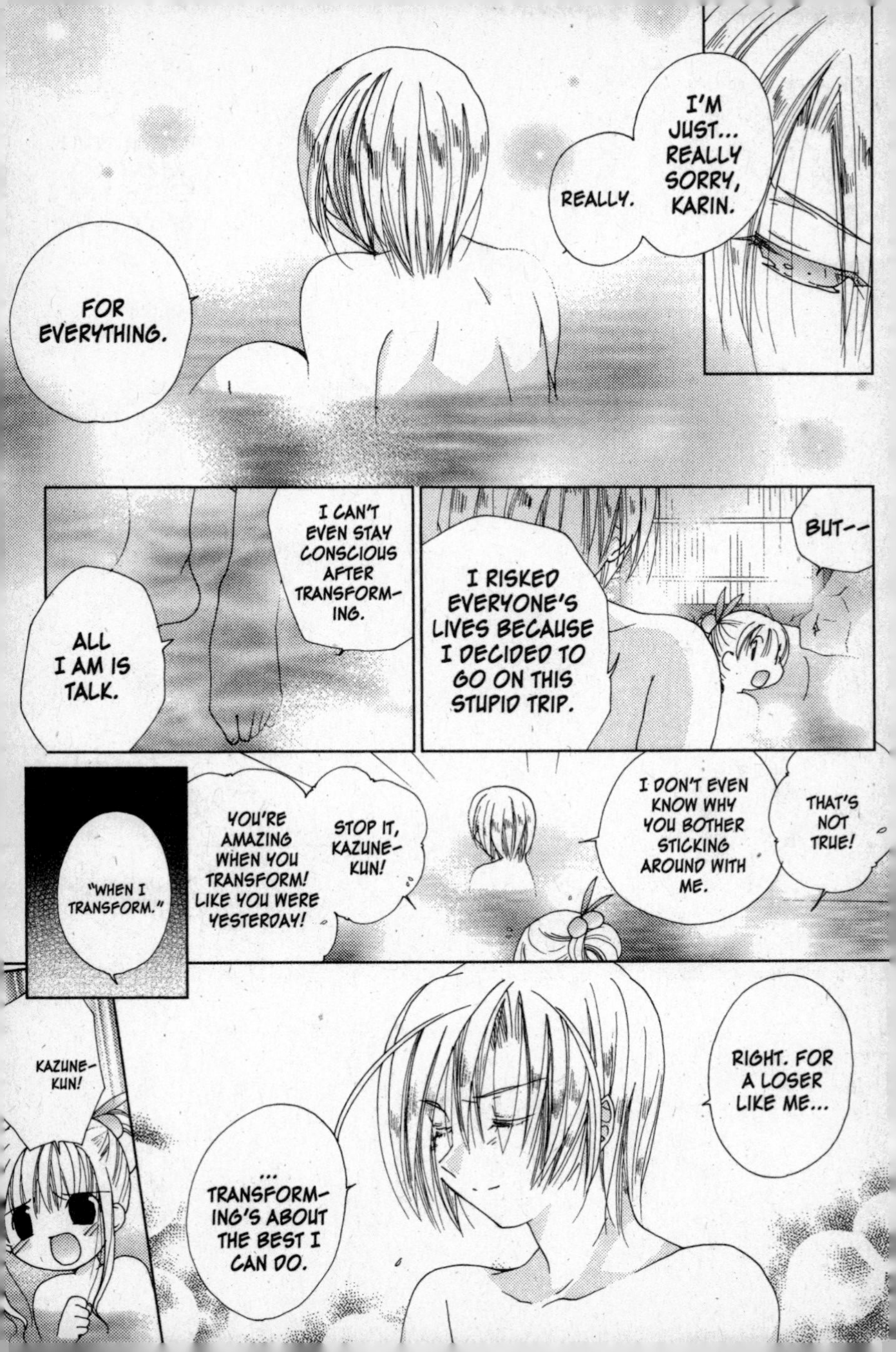

I'M JUST... REALLY SORRY, KARIN.
REALLY.
FOR EVERYTHING.
BUT--
I RISKED EVERYONE'S LIVES BECAUSE I DECIDED TO GO ON THIS STUPID TRIP.
I CAN'T EVEN STAY CONSCIOUS AFTER TRANSFORM-ING.
ALL I AM IS TALK.
THAT'S NOT TRUE!
I DON'T EVEN KNOW WHY YOU BOTHER STICKING AROUND WITH ME.
STOP IT, KAZUNE-KUN!
YOU'RE AMAZING WHEN YOU TRANSFORM! LIKE YOU WERE YESTERDAY!
"WHEN I TRANSFORM."
RIGHT. FOR A LOSER LIKE ME...
... TRANSFORM-ING'S ABOUT THE BEST I CAN DO.
KAZUNE-KUN!

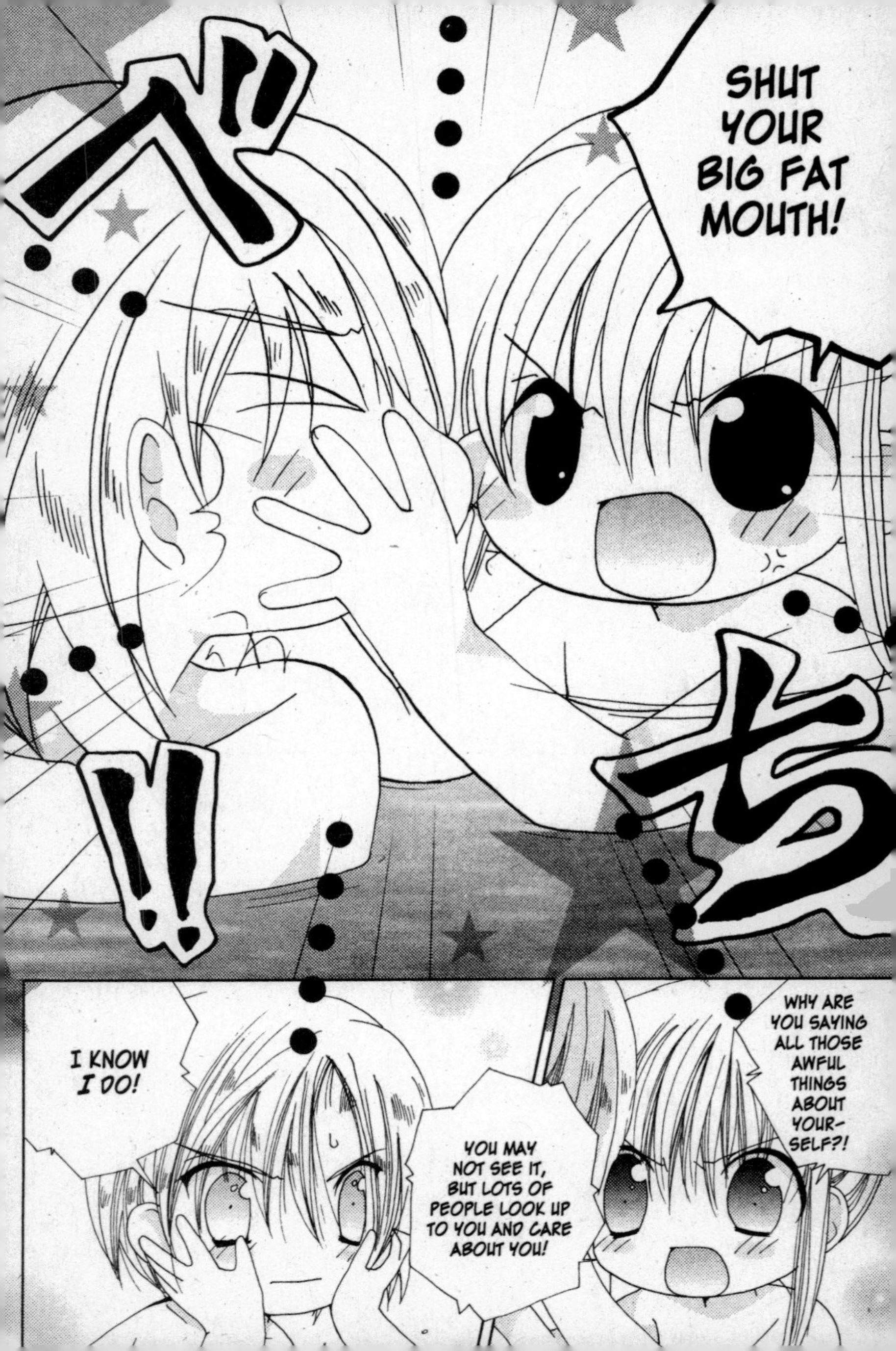
SHUT YOUR BIG FAT MOUTH!
WHY ARE YOU SAYING ALL THOSE AWFUL THINGS ABOUT YOUR-SELF?!
YOU MAY NOT SEE IT, BUT LOTS OF PEOPLE LOOK UP TO YOU AND CARE ABOUT YOU!
I KNOW I DO!

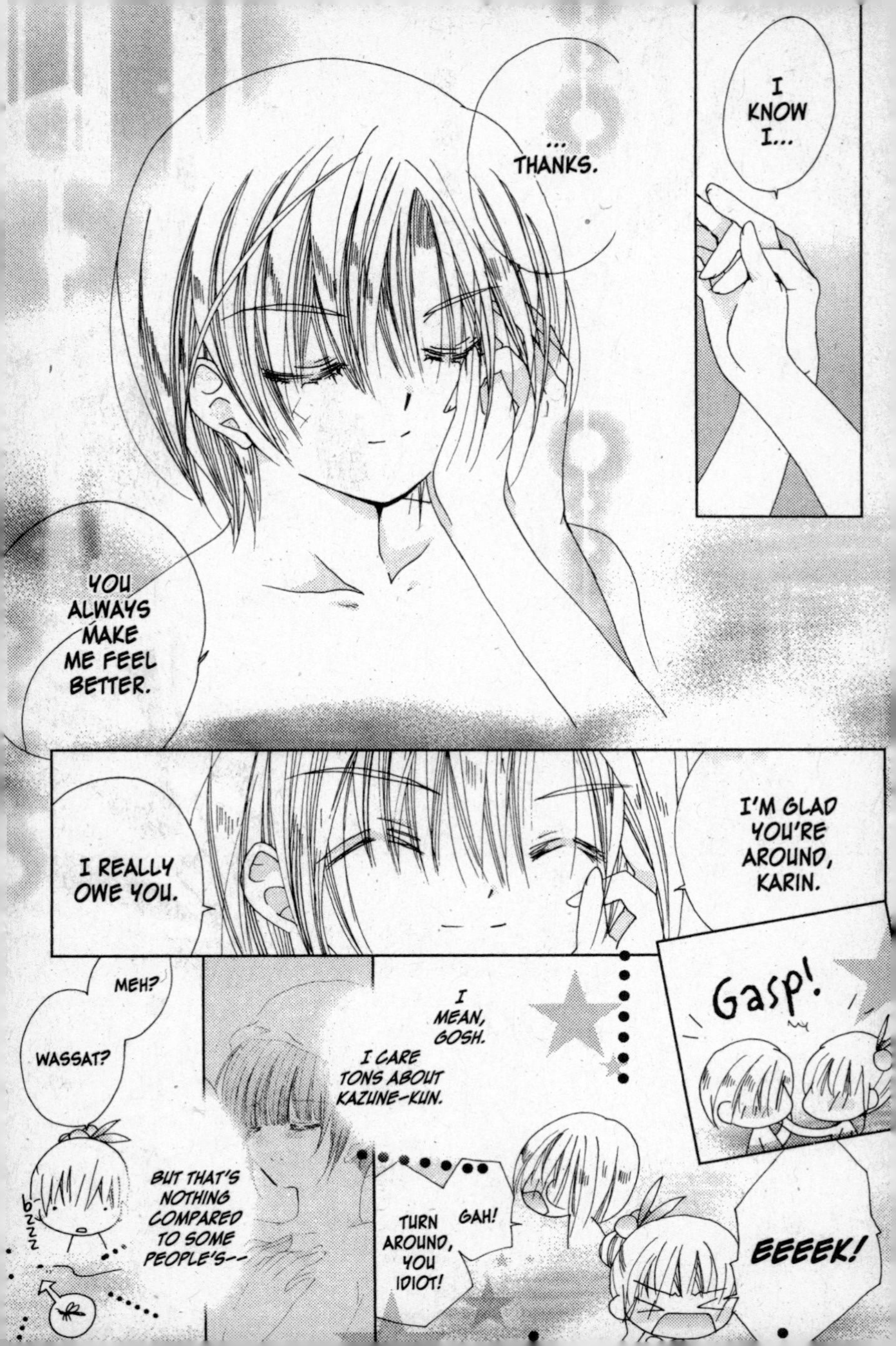
I KNOW I...
...THANKS.
YOU ALWAYS MAKE ME FEEL BETTER.
I'M GLAD YOU'RE AROUND, KARIN.
I REALLY OWE YOU.
Gasp!
EEEEK!
GAH!
TURN AROUND, YOU IDIOT!
I MEAN, GOSH.
I CARE TONS ABOUT KAZUNE-KUN.
BUT THAT'S NOTHING COMPARED TO SOME PEOPLE'S--
MEH?
WASSAT?
bzzz

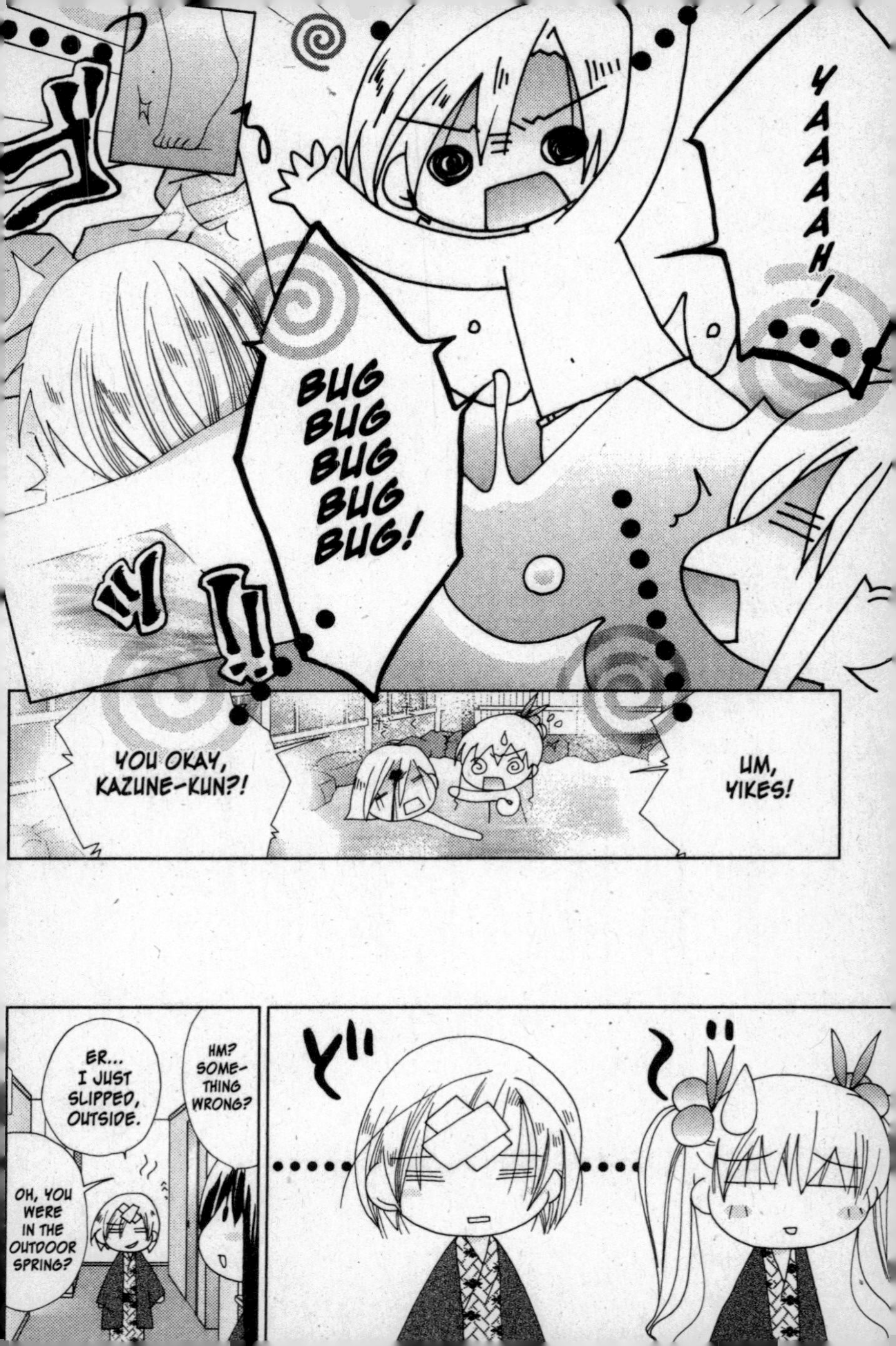
YAAAAAH!
BUG BUG BUG BUG BUG!
UM, YIKES!
YOU OKAY, KAZUNE-KUN?!
HM? SOMETHING WRONG?
ER... I JUST SLIPPED, OUTSIDE.
OH, YOU WERE IN THE OUTDOOR SPRING?

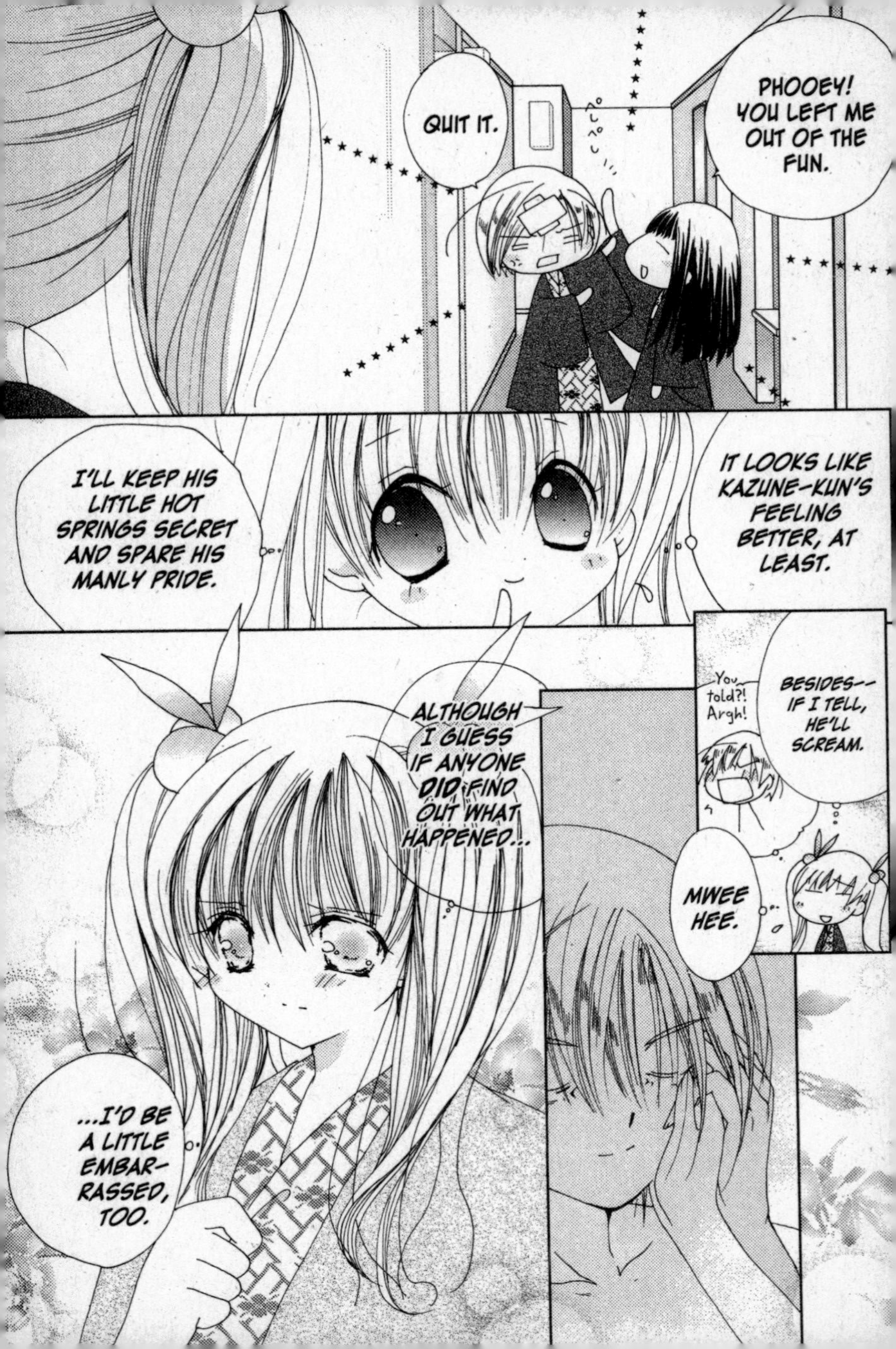
PHOOEY! YOU LEFT ME OUT OF THE FUN.
QUIT IT.
ぺしぺし!!
IT LOOKS LIKE KAZUNE-KUN'S FEELING BETTER, AT LEAST.
I'LL KEEP HIS LITTLE HOT SPRINGS SECRET AND SPARE HIS MANLY PRIDE.
BESIDES-- IF I TELL, HE'LL SCREAM.
You told?! Argh!
MWEE HEE.
ALTHOUGH I GUESS IF ANYONE DID FIND OUT WHAT HAPPENED...
...I'D BE A LITTLE EMBARRASSED, TOO.

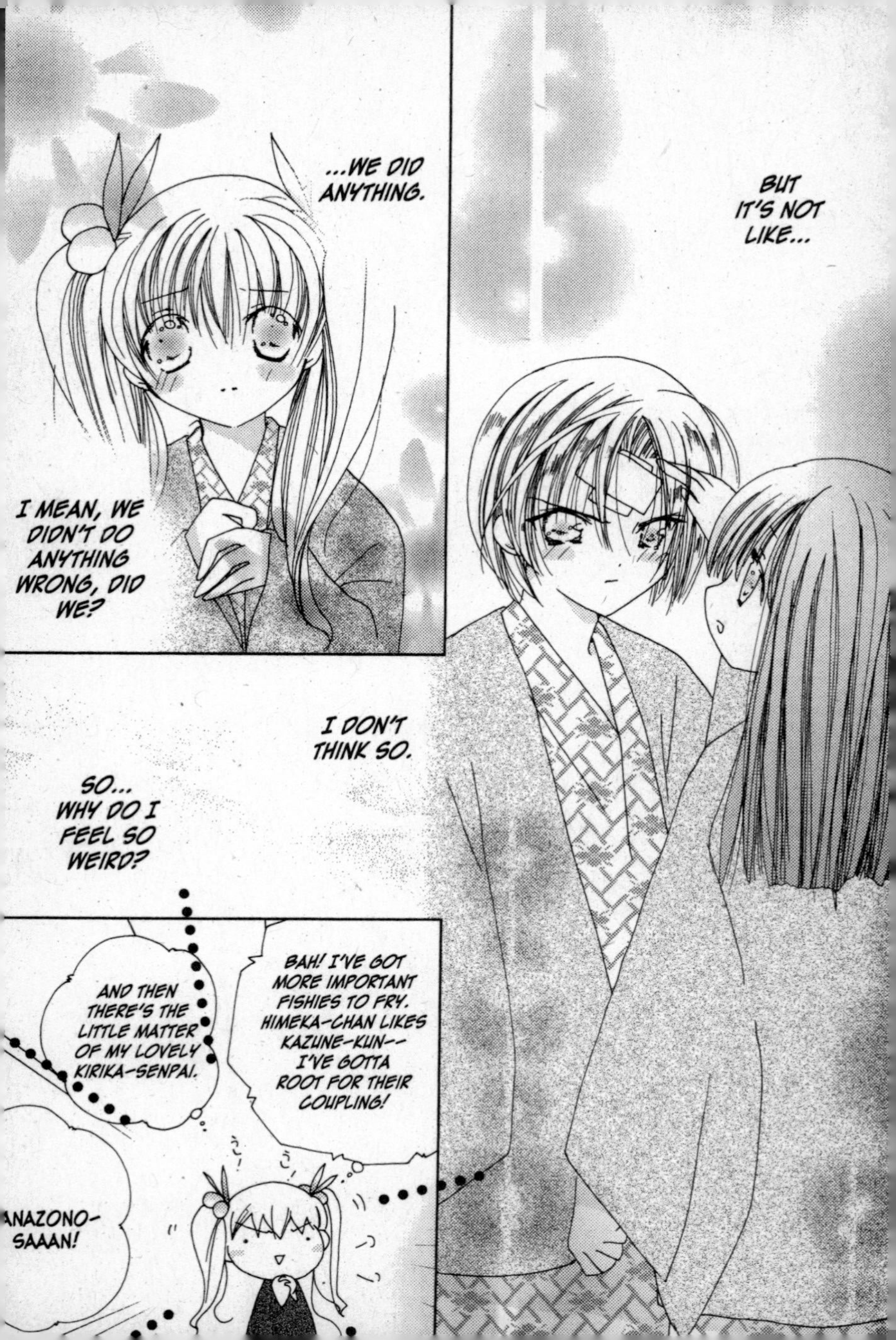
BUT IT'S NOT LIKE...
...WE DID ANYTHING.
I MEAN, WE DIDN'T DO ANYTHING WRONG, DID WE?
I DON'T THINK SO.
SO... WHY DO I FEEL SO WEIRD?
BAH! I'VE GOT MORE IMPORTANT FISHIES TO FRY. HIMEKA-CHAN LIKES KAZUNE-KUN-- I'VE GOTTA ROOT FOR THEIR COUPLING!
AND THEN THERE'S THE LITTLE MATTER OF MY LOVELY KIRIKA-SENPAI.
ANAZONO-SAAAN!

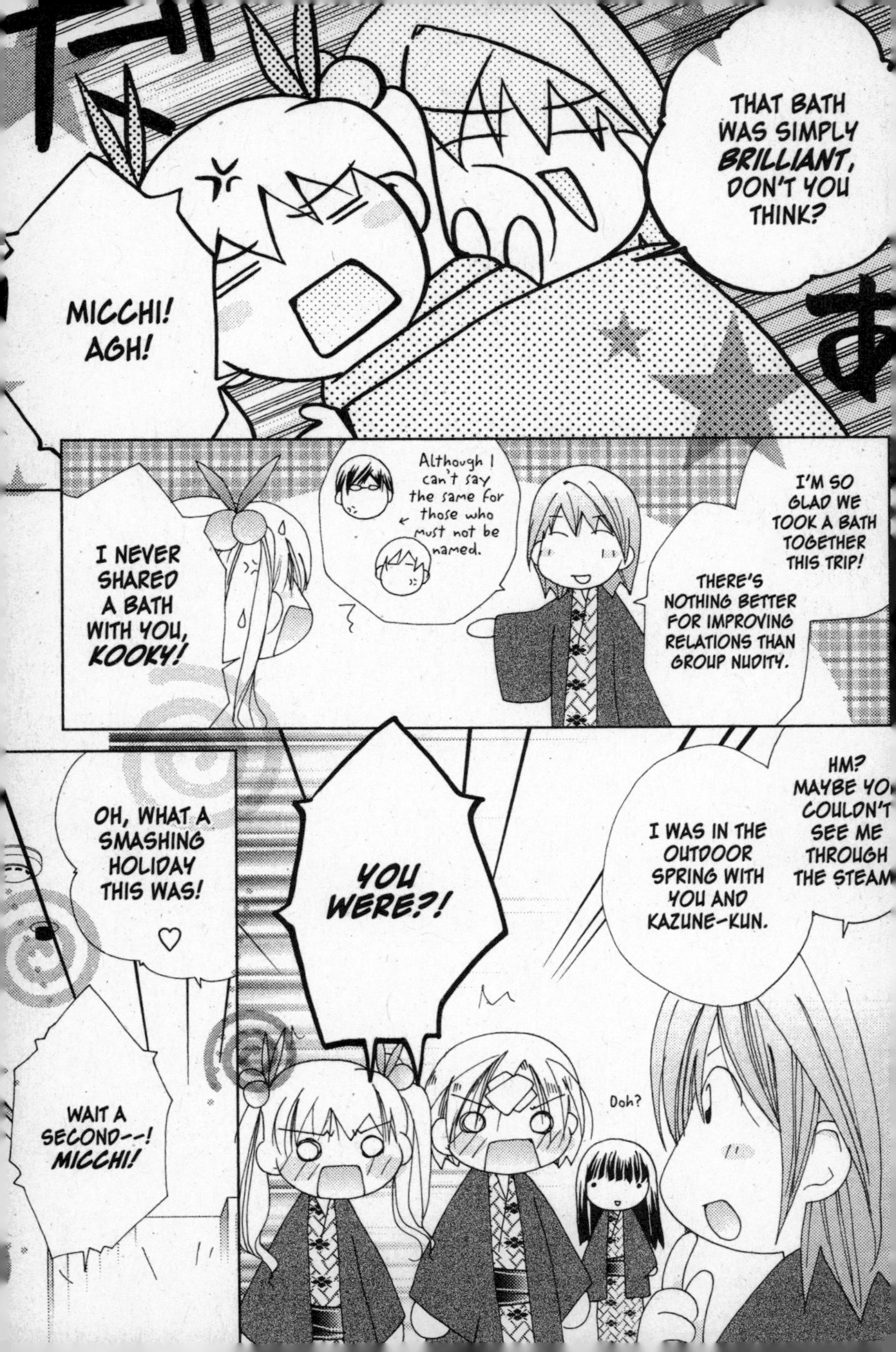
THAT BATH WAS SIMPLY ***BRILLIANT***, DON'T YOU THINK?
MICCHI! AGH!
I'M SO GLAD WE TOOK A BATH TOGETHER THIS TRIP!
THERE'S NOTHING BETTER FOR IMPROVING RELATIONS THAN GROUP NUDITY.
Although I can't say the same for those who must not be named.
I NEVER SHARED A BATH WITH YOU, ***KOOKY!***
HM? MAYBE YO COULDN'T SEE ME THROUGH THE STEAM
I WAS IN THE OUTDOOR SPRING WITH YOU AND KAZUNE-KUN.
Ooh?
YOU WERE?!
OH, WHAT A SMASHING HOLIDAY THIS WAS! ♡
WAIT A SECOND--! ***MICCHI!***

Aaand
they were
wearing
towels.

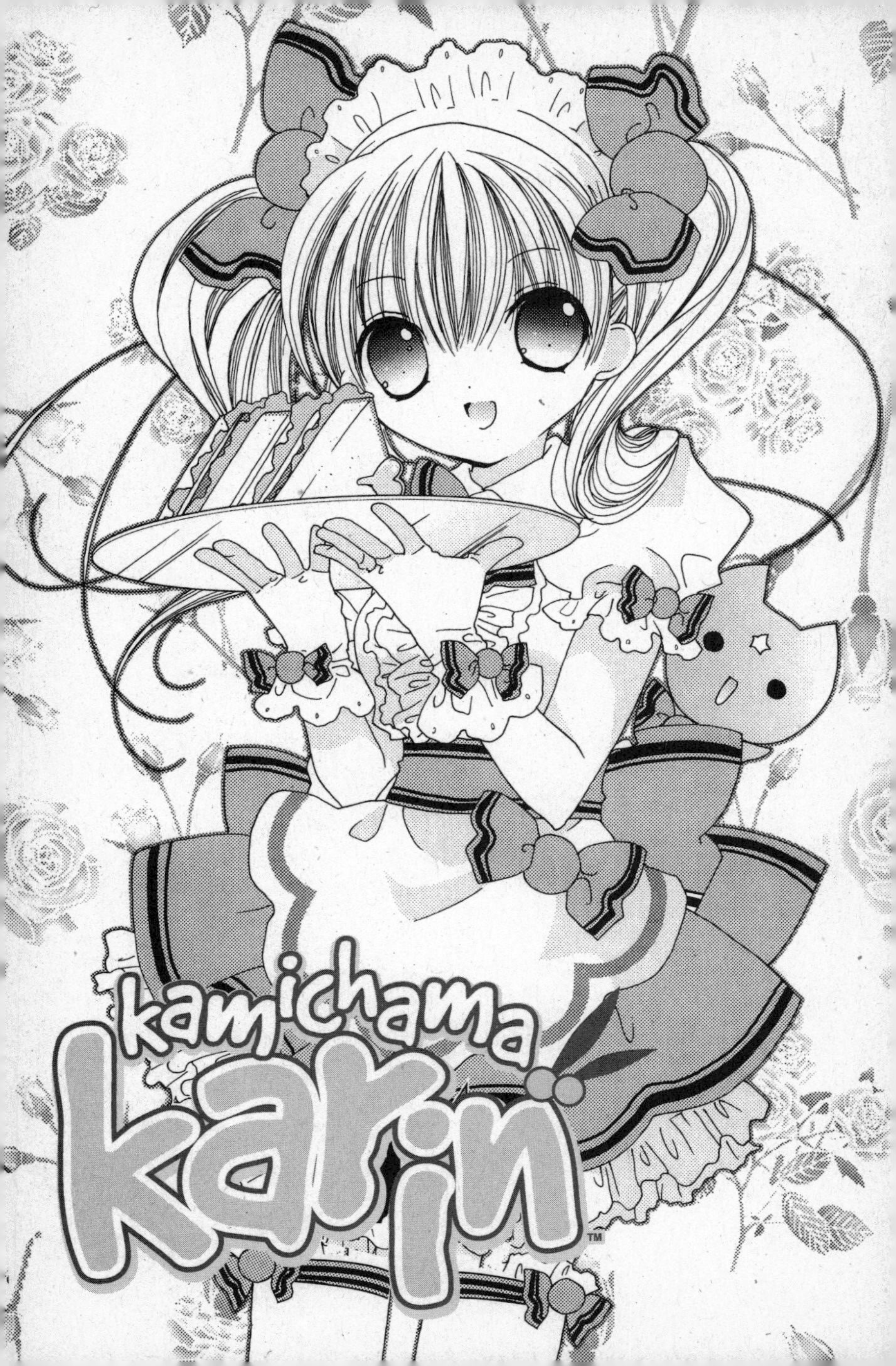
kamichama karin™

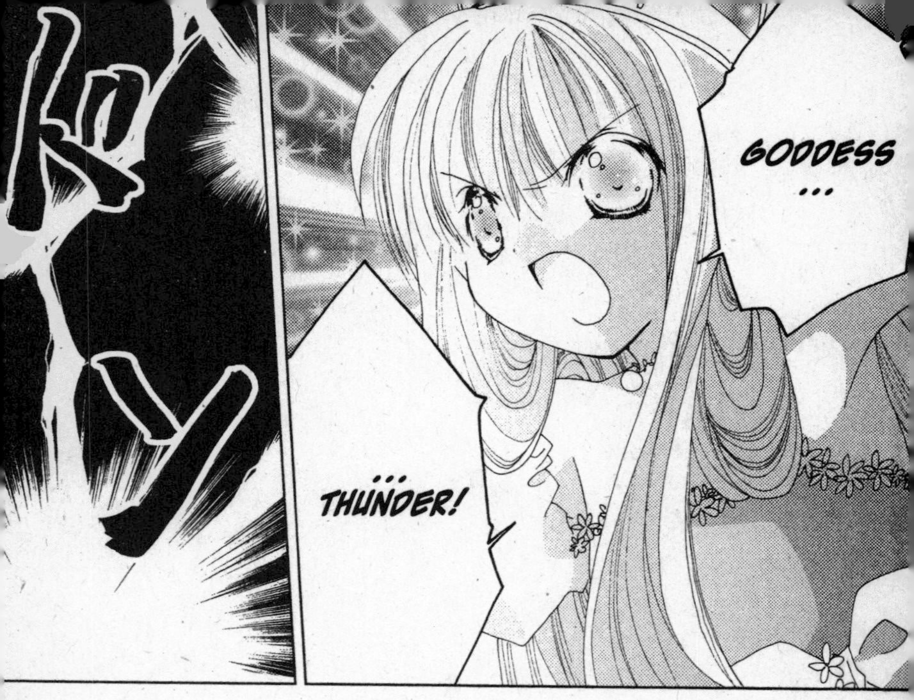
GODDESS ...
...THUNDER!

The original Shi-chan.

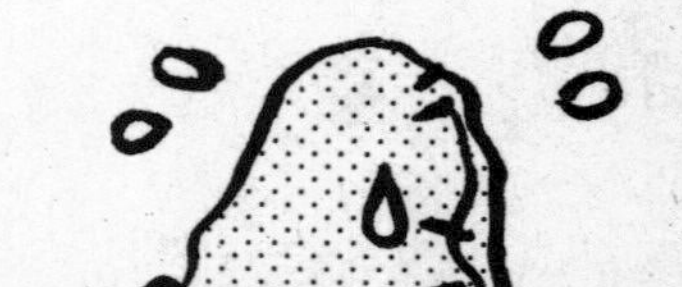

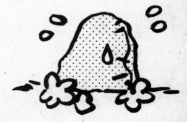

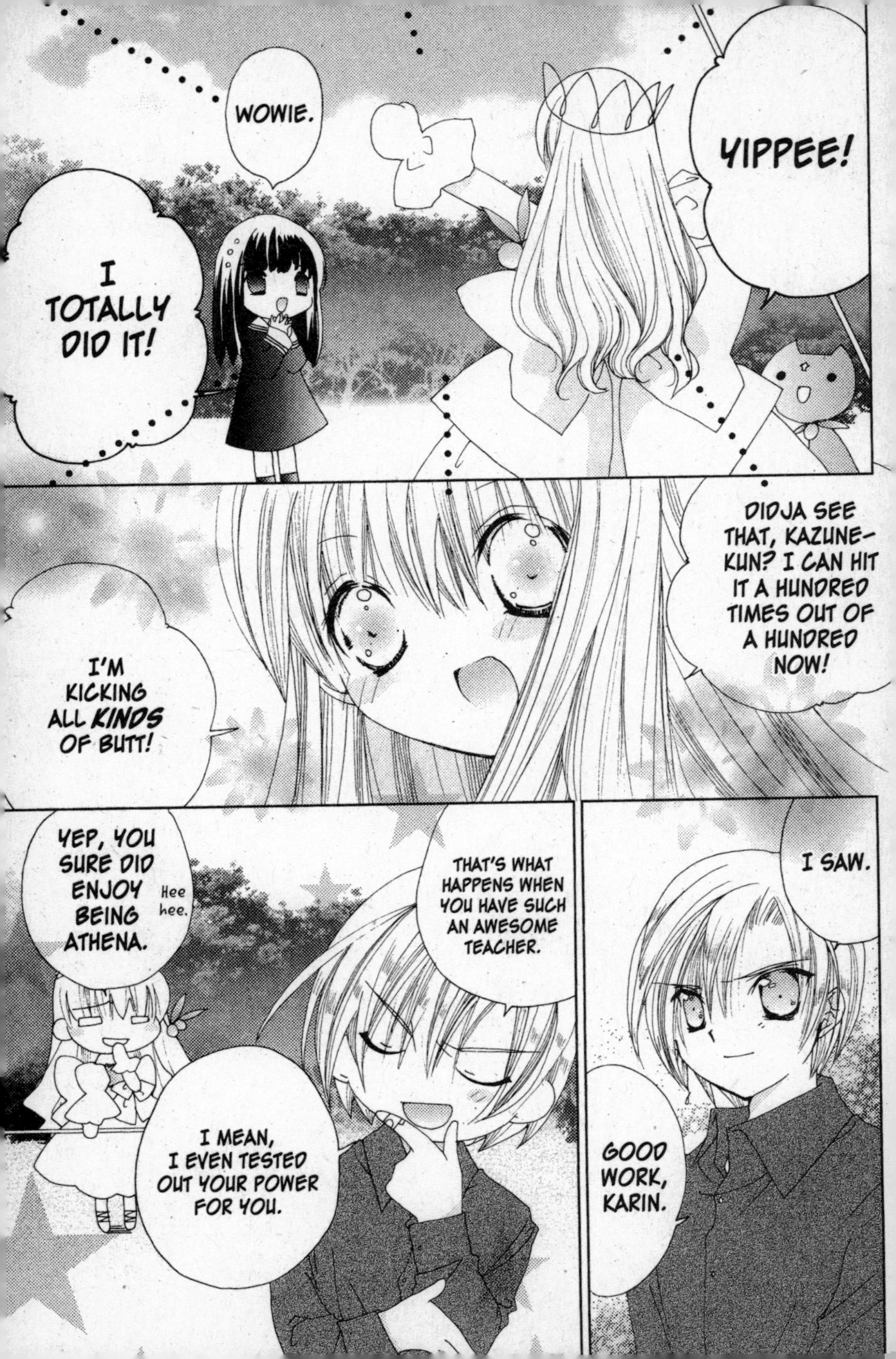
YIPPEE!
WOWIE.
I TOTALLY DID IT!
DIDJA SEE THAT, KAZUNE-KUN? I CAN HIT IT A HUNDRED TIMES OUT OF A HUNDRED NOW!
I'M KICKING ALL *KINDS* OF BUTT!
I SAW.
GOOD WORK, KARIN.
THAT'S WHAT HAPPENS WHEN YOU HAVE SUCH AN AWESOME TEACHER.
YEP, YOU SURE DID ENJOY BEING ATHENA.
Hee hee.
I MEAN, I EVEN TESTED OUT YOUR POWER FOR YOU.

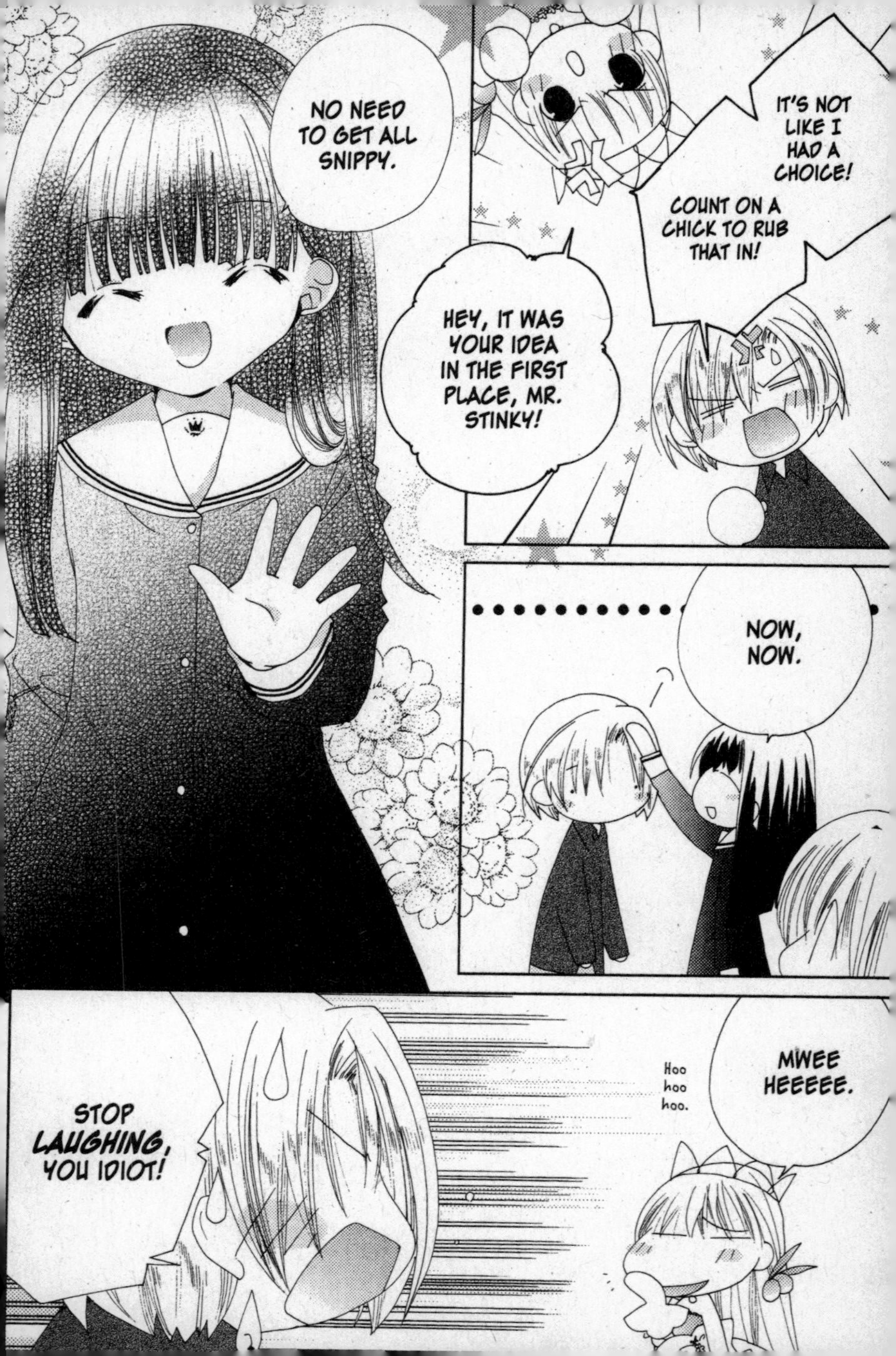
IT'S NOT LIKE I HAD A CHOICE!
COUNT ON A CHICK TO RUB THAT IN!
HEY, IT WAS YOUR IDEA IN THE FIRST PLACE, MR. STINKY!
....
NOW, NOW.
NO NEED TO GET ALL SNIPPY.
MWEE HEEEEE.
Hoo hoo hoo.
STOP LAUGHING, YOU IDIOT!

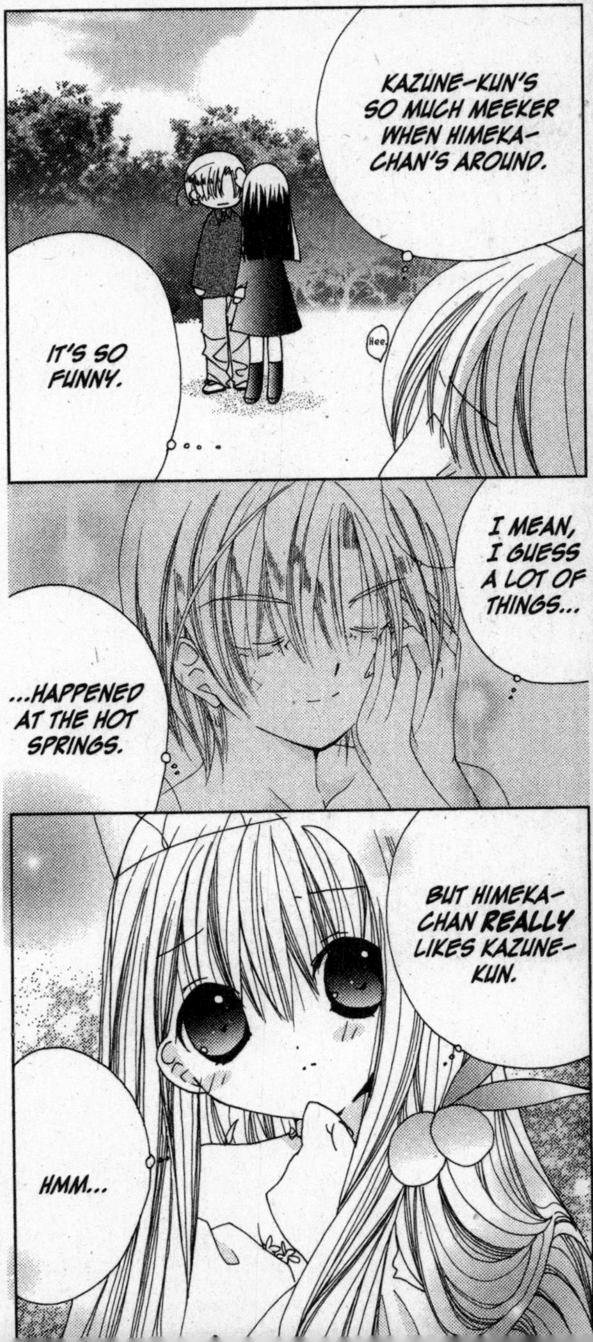
KAZUNE-KUN'S SO MUCH MEEKER WHEN HIMEKA-CHAN'S AROUND.
Hee.
IT'S SO FUNNY.
I MEAN, I GUESS A LOT OF THINGS...
...HAPPENED AT THE HOT SPRINGS.
BUT HIMEKA-CHAN **REALLY** LIKES KAZUNE-KUN.
HMM...
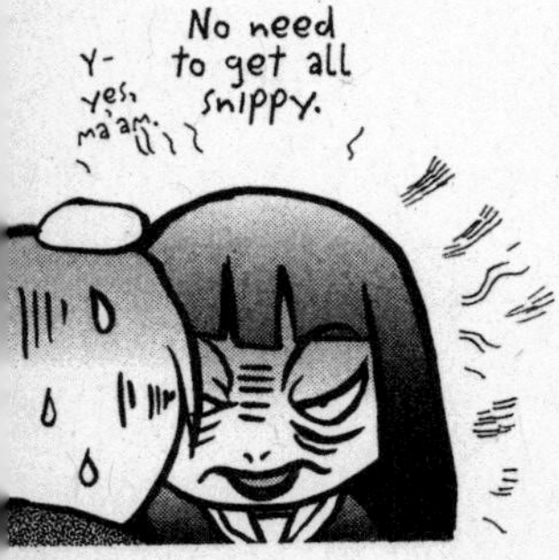
No need to get all snippy.
Y-yes, ma'am.

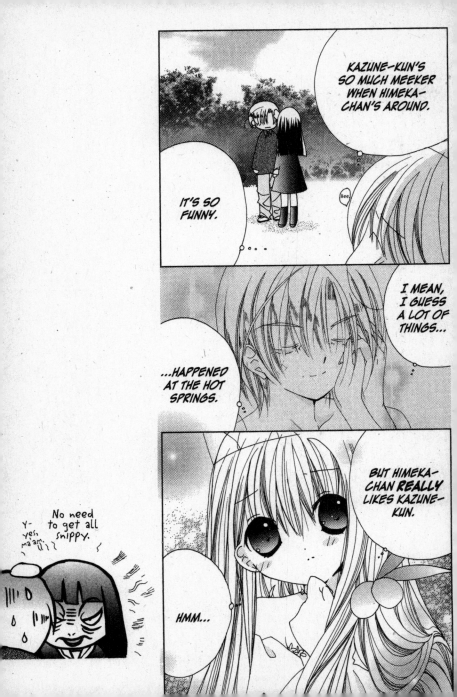

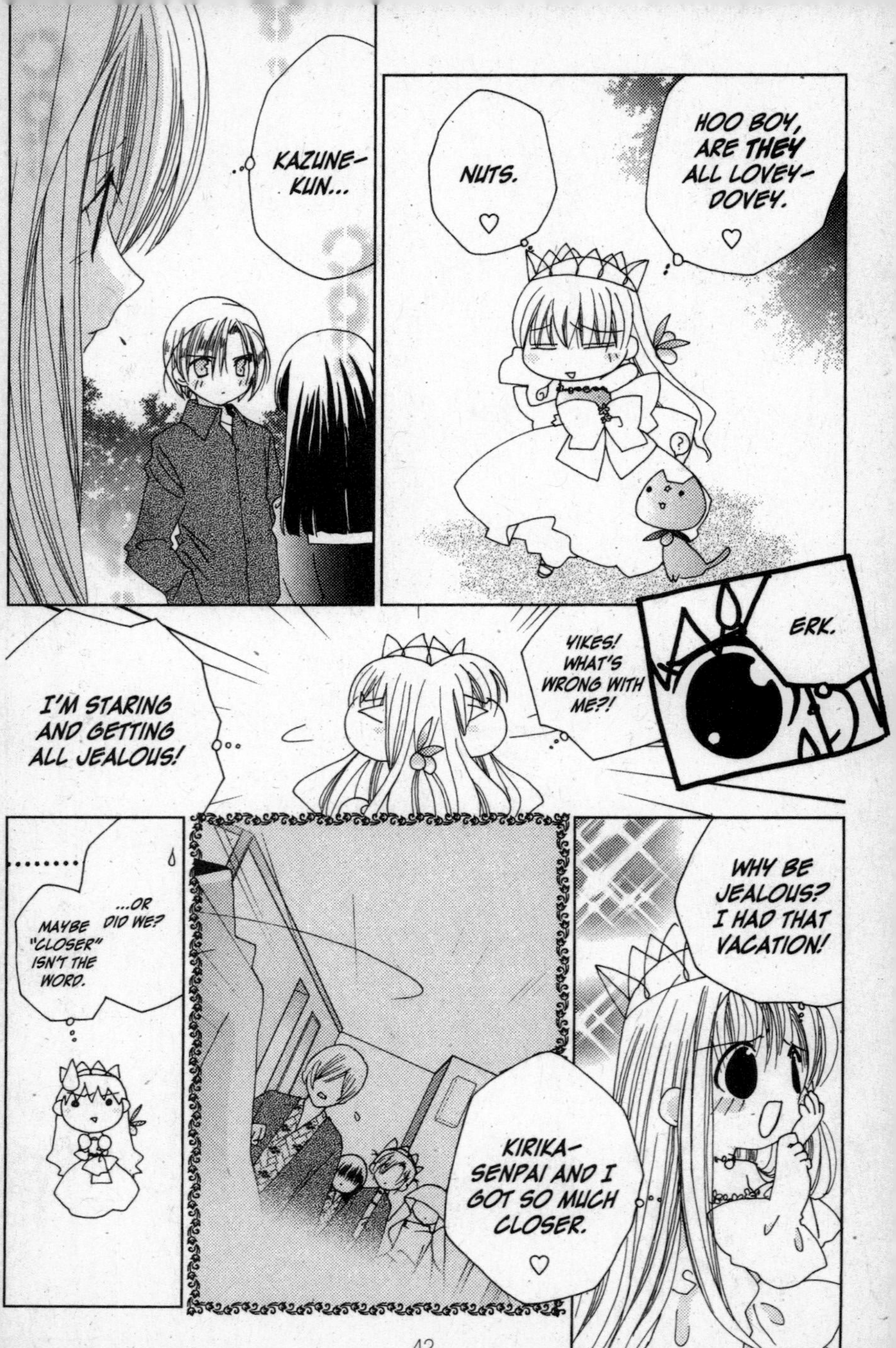
HOO BOY, ARE THEY ALL LOVEY-DOVEY. ♡
NUTS. ♡
...KAZUNE-KUN...
ERK.
YIKES! WHAT'S WRONG WITH ME?!
I'M STARING AND GETTING ALL JEALOUS!
WHY BE JEALOUS? I HAD THAT VACATION!
KIRIKA-SENPAI AND I GOT SO MUCH CLOSER. ♡
......
...OR DID WE?
MAYBE "CLOSER" ISN'T THE WORD.

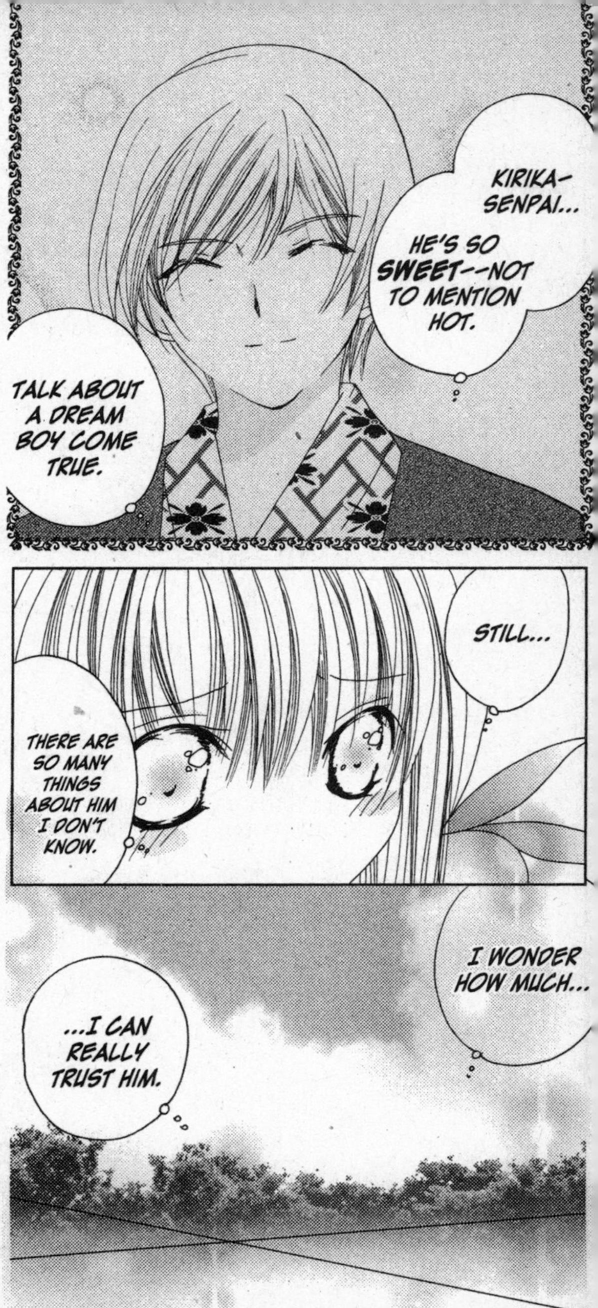
KIRIKA-SENPAI...
HE'S SO SWEET--NOT TO MENTION HOT.
TALK ABOUT A DREAM BOY COME TRUE.
STILL...
THERE ARE SO MANY THINGS ABOUT HIM I DON'T KNOW.
I WONDER HOW MUCH...
...I CAN REALLY TRUST HIM.

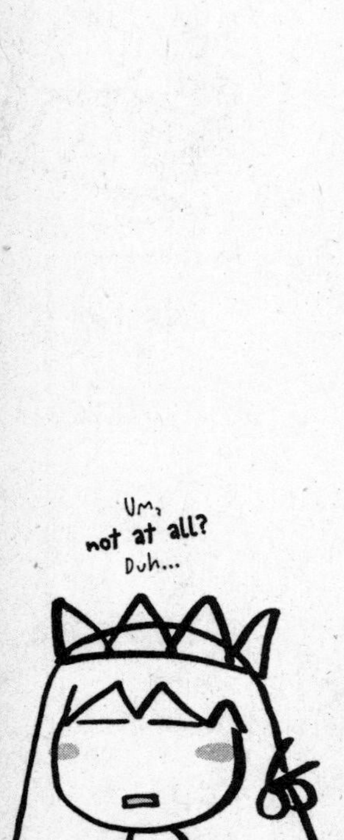
Um, not at all? Duh...

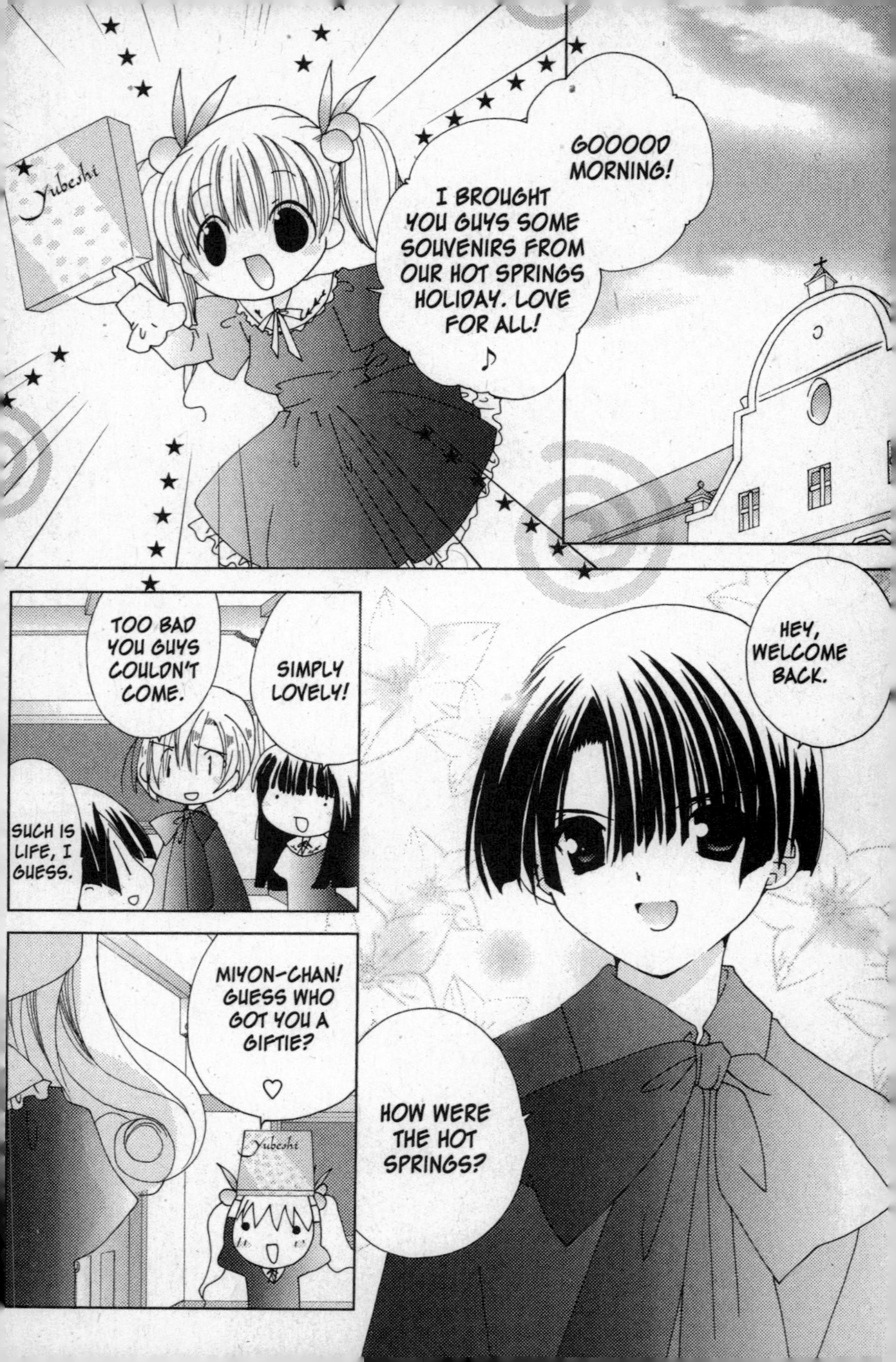
Yubeshi
GOOOOD MORNING!
I BROUGHT YOU GUYS SOME SOUVENIRS FROM OUR HOT SPRINGS HOLIDAY. LOVE FOR ALL! ♪
HEY, WELCOME BACK.
HOW WERE THE HOT SPRINGS?
SIMPLY LOVELY!
TOO BAD YOU GUYS COULDN'T COME.
SUCH IS LIFE, I GUESS.
MIYON-CHAN! GUESS WHO GOT YOU A GIFTIE? ♡
Yubeshi

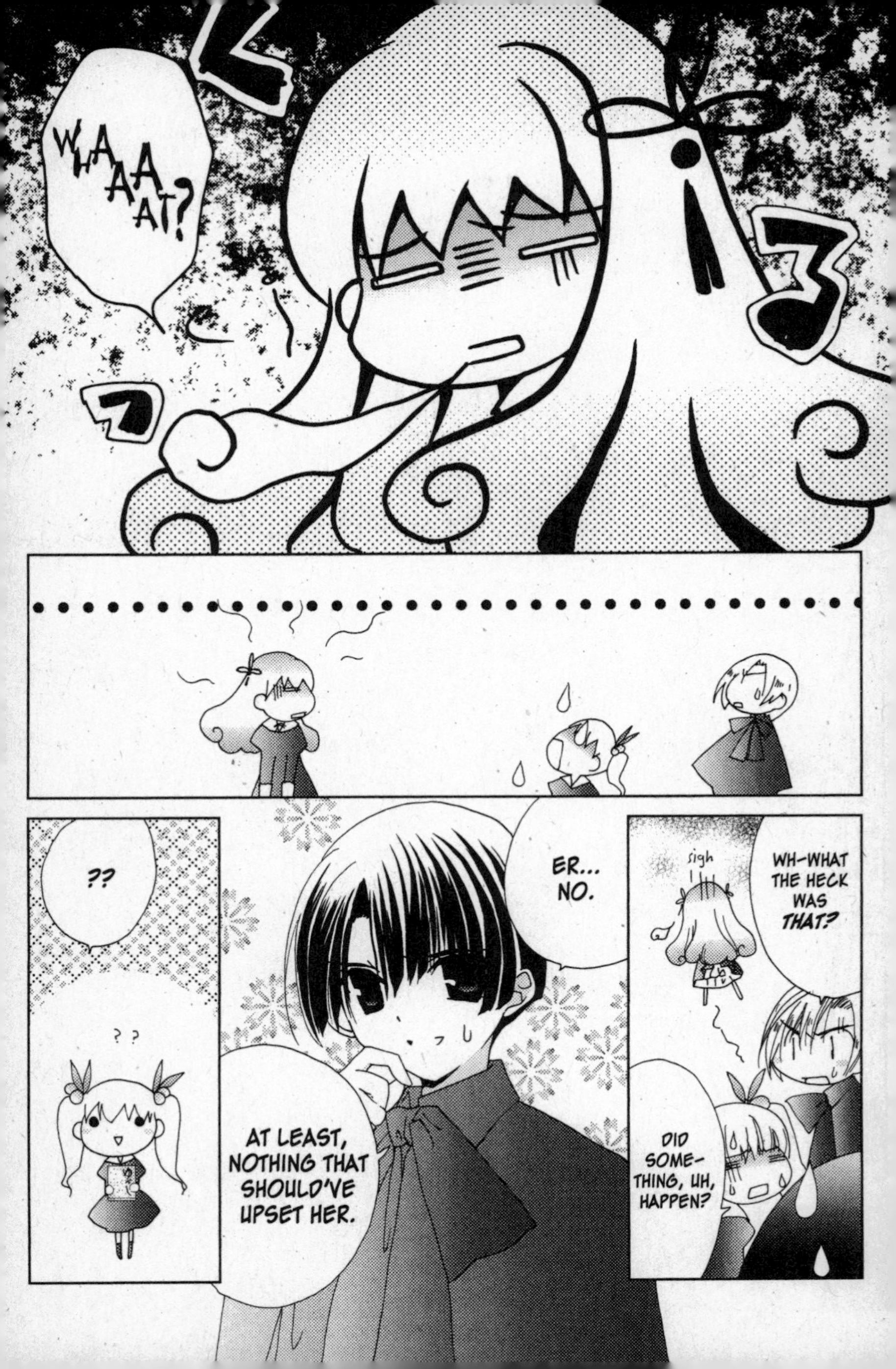
WHAAAAT?
sigh
WH-WHAT THE HECK WAS THAT?
DID SOMETHING, UH, HAPPEN?
ER... NO.
AT LEAST, NOTHING THAT SHOULD'VE UPSET HER.
??
? ?

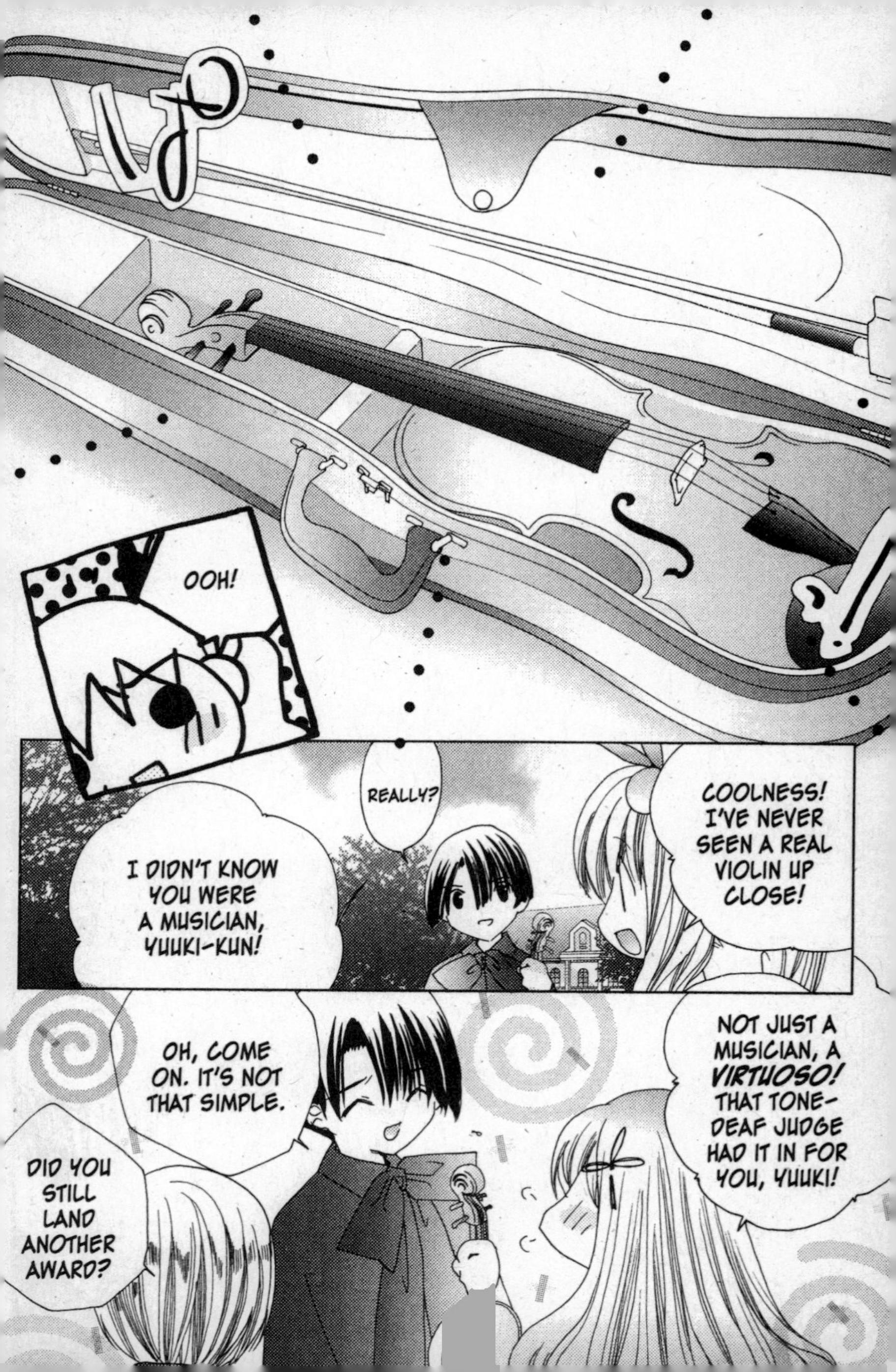
OOH!
COOLNESS! I'VE NEVER SEEN A REAL VIOLIN UP CLOSE!
REALLY?
I DIDN'T KNOW YOU WERE A MUSICIAN, YUUKI-KUN!
NOT JUST A MUSICIAN, A *VIRTUOSO!* THAT TONE-DEAF JUDGE HAD IT IN FOR YOU, YUUKI!
OH, COME ON. IT'S NOT THAT SIMPLE.
DID YOU STILL LAND ANOTHER AWARD?

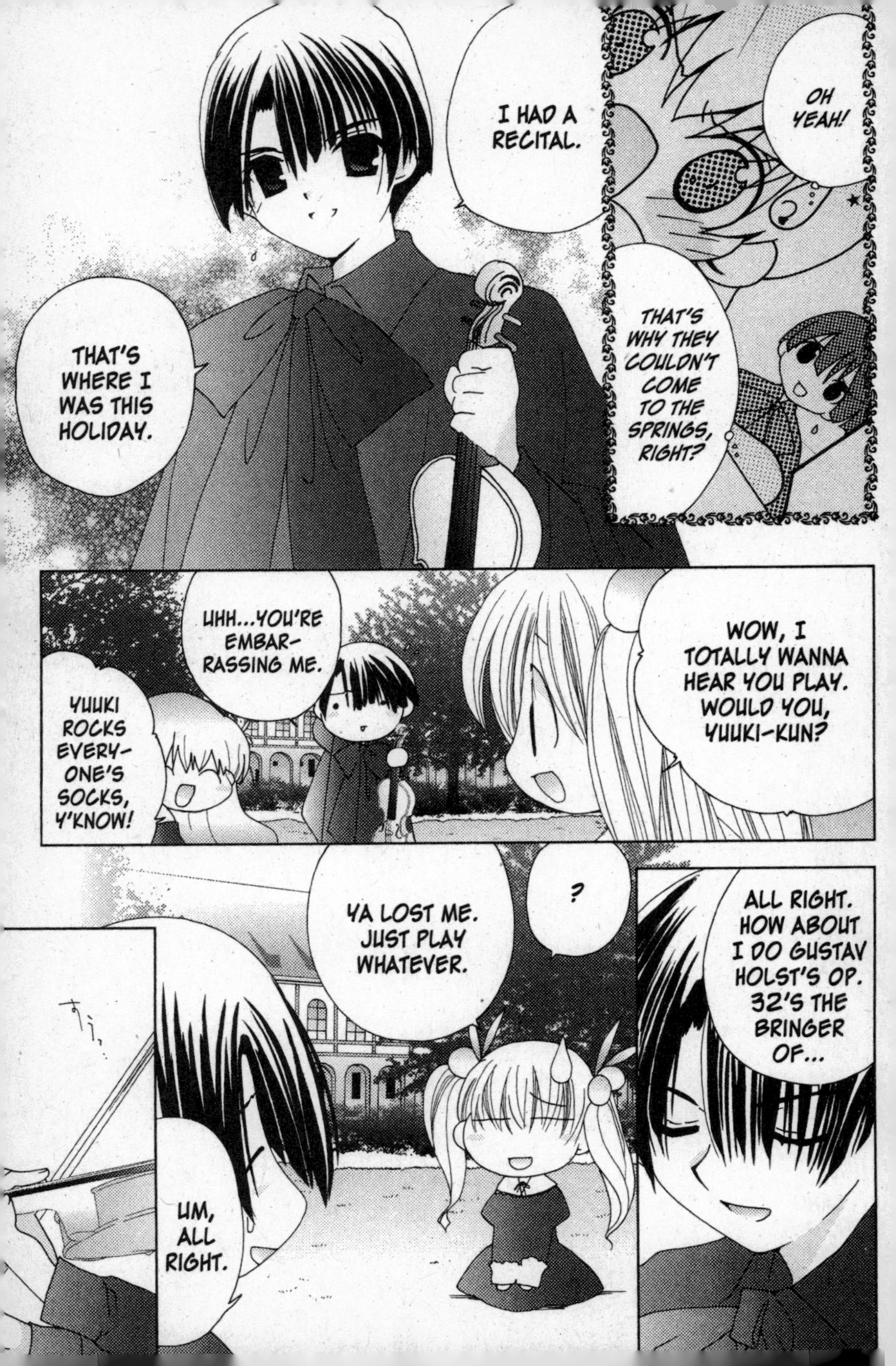
I HAD A RECITAL.
THAT'S WHERE I WAS THIS HOLIDAY.
OH YEAH!
THAT'S WHY THEY COULDN'T COME TO THE SPRINGS, RIGHT?
WOW, I TOTALLY WANNA HEAR YOU PLAY. WOULD YOU, YUUKI-KUN?
UHH...YOU'RE EMBARRASSING ME.
YUUKI ROCKS EVERYONE'S SOCKS, Y'KNOW!
ALL RIGHT. HOW ABOUT I DO GUSTAV HOLST'S OP. 32'S THE BRINGER OF...
?
YA LOST ME. JUST PLAY WHATEVER.
UM, ALL RIGHT.

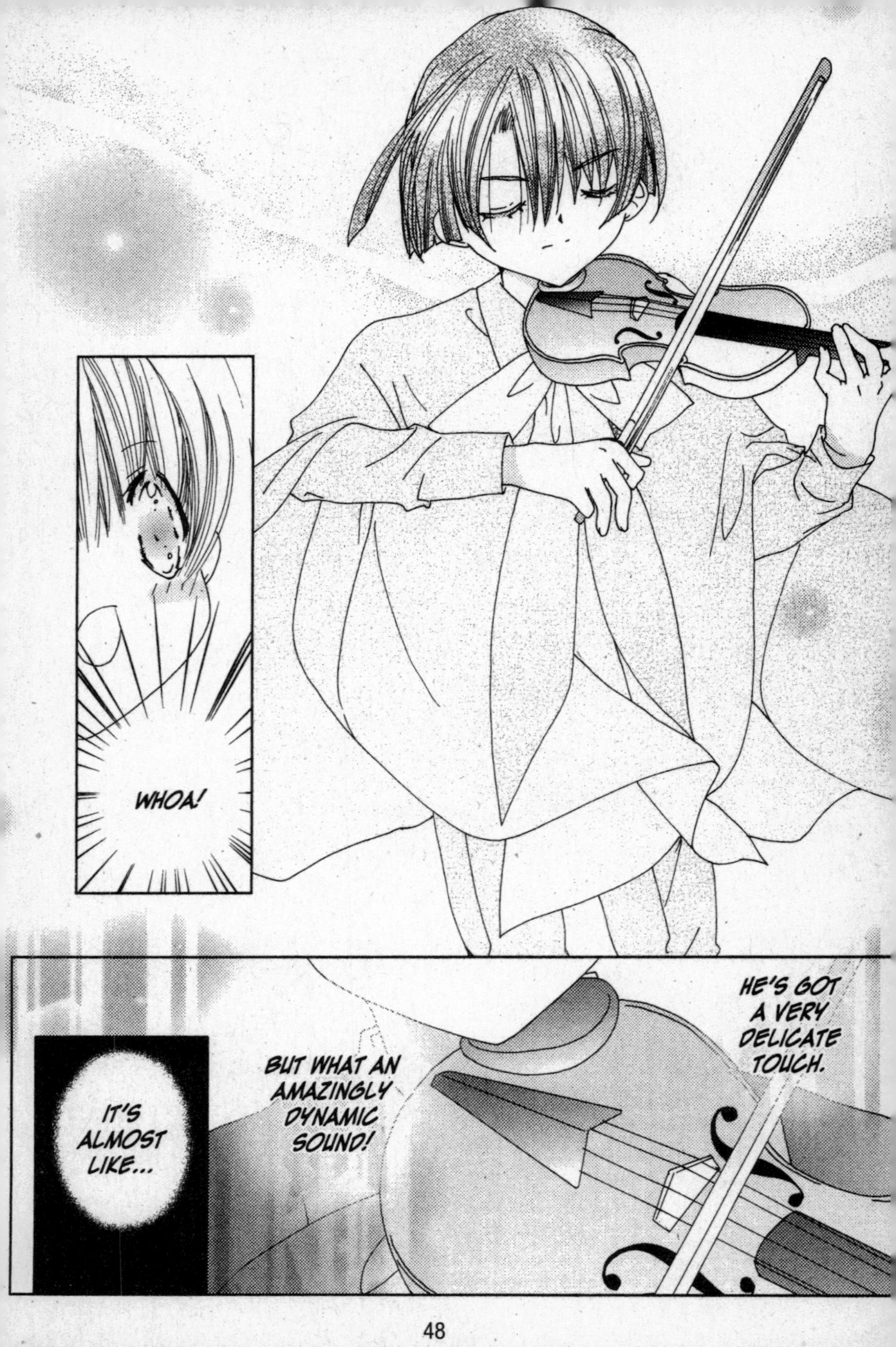
WHOA!
HE'S GOT A VERY DELICATE TOUCH.
BUT WHAT AN AMAZINGLY DYNAMIC SOUND!
IT'S ALMOST LIKE...

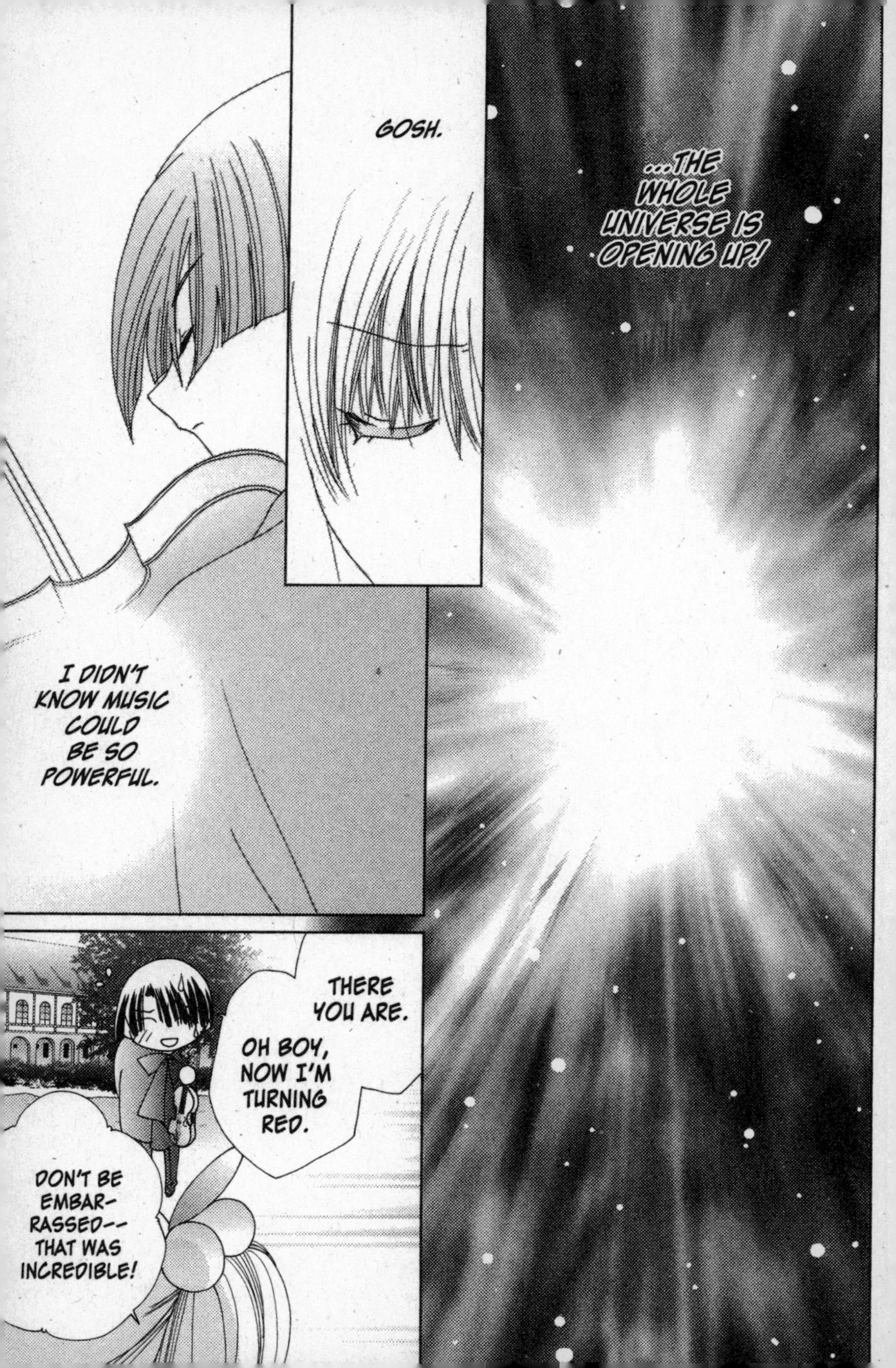
...THE WHOLE UNIVERSE IS OPENING UP!
GOSH.
I DIDN'T KNOW MUSIC COULD BE SO POWERFUL.
THERE YOU ARE.
OH BOY, NOW I'M TURNING RED.
DON'T BE EMBAR-RASSED-- THAT WAS INCREDIBLE!

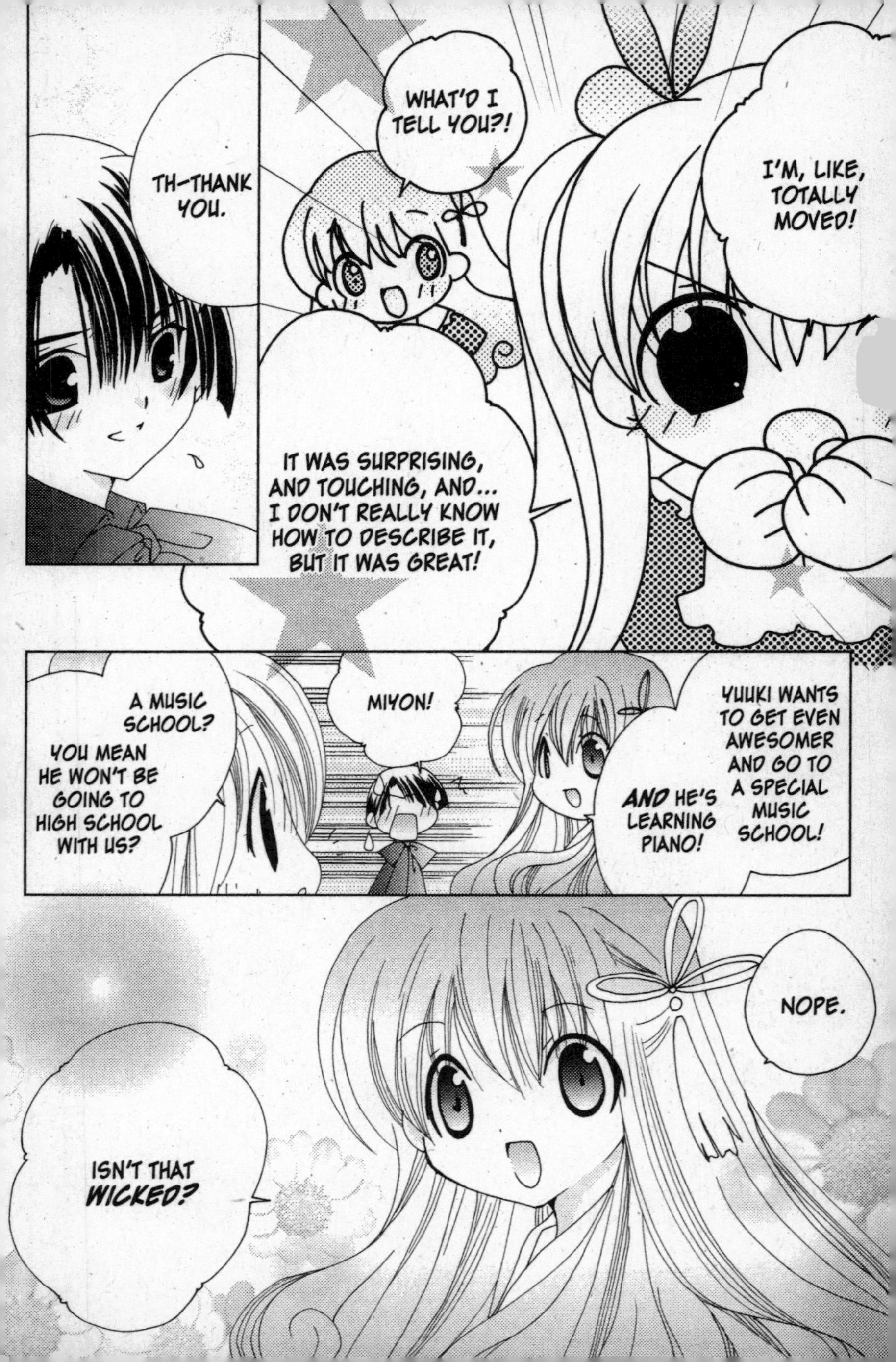
I'M, LIKE, TOTALLY MOVED!
WHAT'D I TELL YOU?!
IT WAS SURPRISING, AND TOUCHING, AND... I DON'T REALLY KNOW HOW TO DESCRIBE IT, BUT IT WAS GREAT!
TH-THANK YOU.
YUUKI WANTS TO GET EVEN AWESOMER AND GO TO A SPECIAL MUSIC SCHOOL!
AND HE'S LEARNING PIANO!
MIYON!
A MUSIC SCHOOL?
YOU MEAN HE WON'T BE GOING TO HIGH SCHOOL WITH US?
NOPE.
ISN'T THAT ***WICKED?***

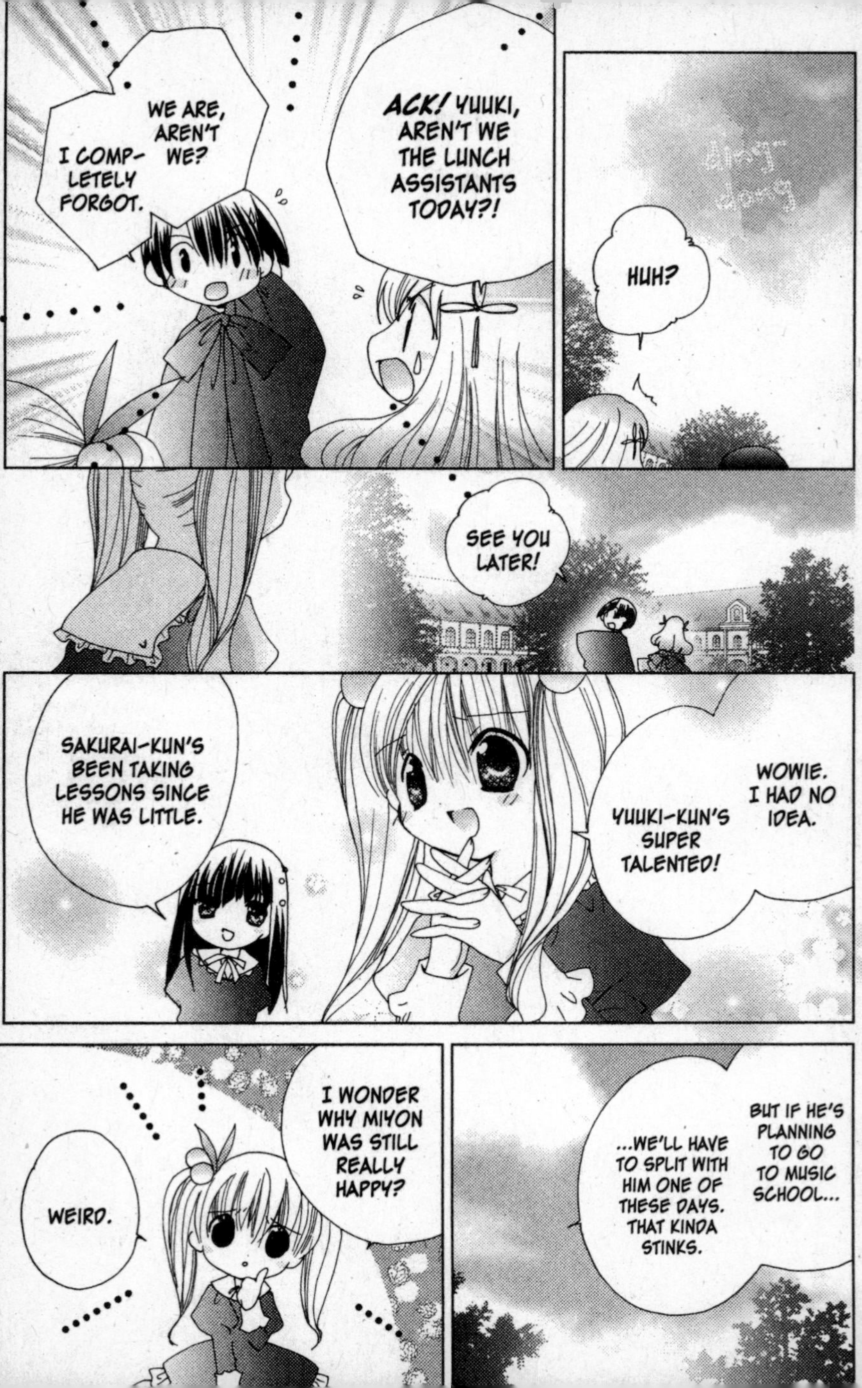
ding-dong
HUH?
ACK! YUUKI, AREN'T WE THE LUNCH ASSISTANTS TODAY?!
WE ARE, AREN'T WE? I COMPLETELY FORGOT.
SEE YOU LATER!
WOWIE. I HAD NO IDEA.
YUUKI-KUN'S SUPER TALENTED!
SAKURAI-KUN'S BEEN TAKING LESSONS SINCE HE WAS LITTLE.
BUT IF HE'S PLANNING TO GO TO MUSIC SCHOOL...
...WE'LL HAVE TO SPLIT WITH HIM ONE OF THESE DAYS. THAT KINDA STINKS.
I WONDER WHY MIYON WAS STILL REALLY HAPPY?
WEIRD.

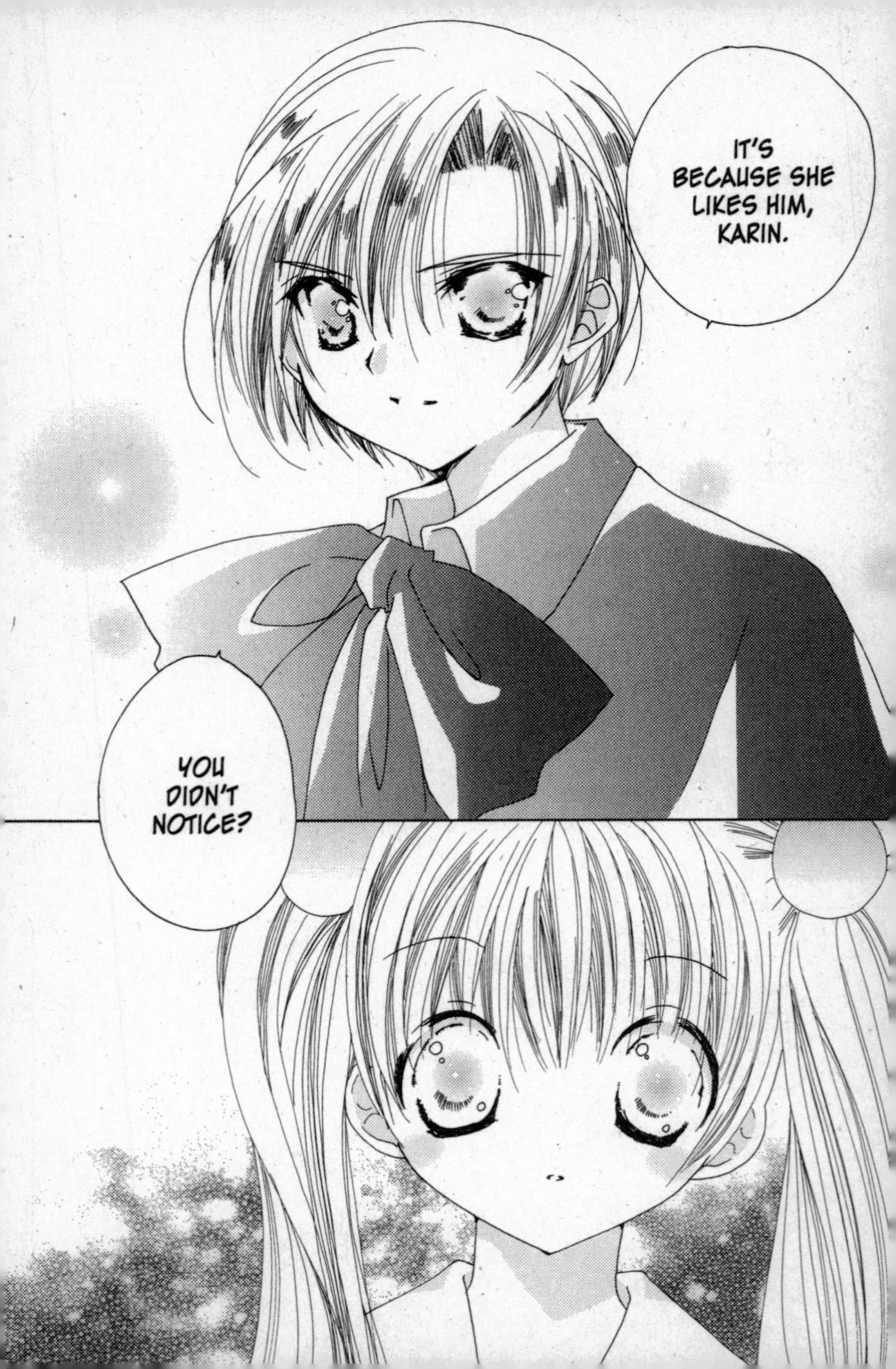
IT'S BECAUSE SHE LIKES HIM, KARIN.
YOU DIDN'T NOTICE?

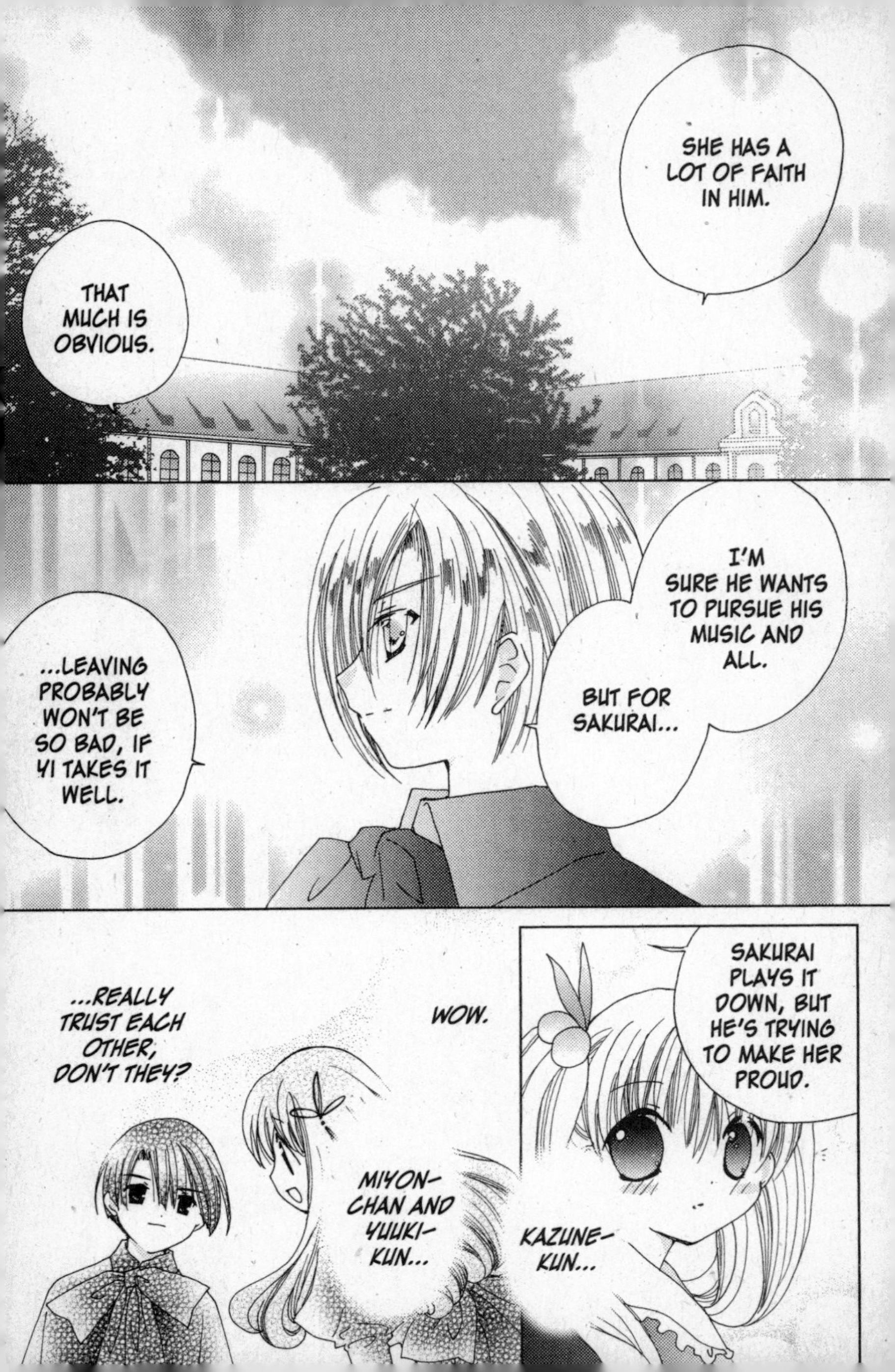
SHE HAS A LOT OF FAITH IN HIM.
THAT MUCH IS OBVIOUS.
I'M SURE HE WANTS TO PURSUE HIS MUSIC AND ALL.
BUT FOR SAKURAI...
...LEAVING PROBABLY WON'T BE SO BAD, IF YI TAKES IT WELL.
SAKURAI PLAYS IT DOWN, BUT HE'S TRYING TO MAKE HER PROUD.
KAZUNE-KUN...
WOW.
MIYON-CHAN AND YUUKI-KUN...
...REALLY TRUST EACH OTHER, DON'T THEY?

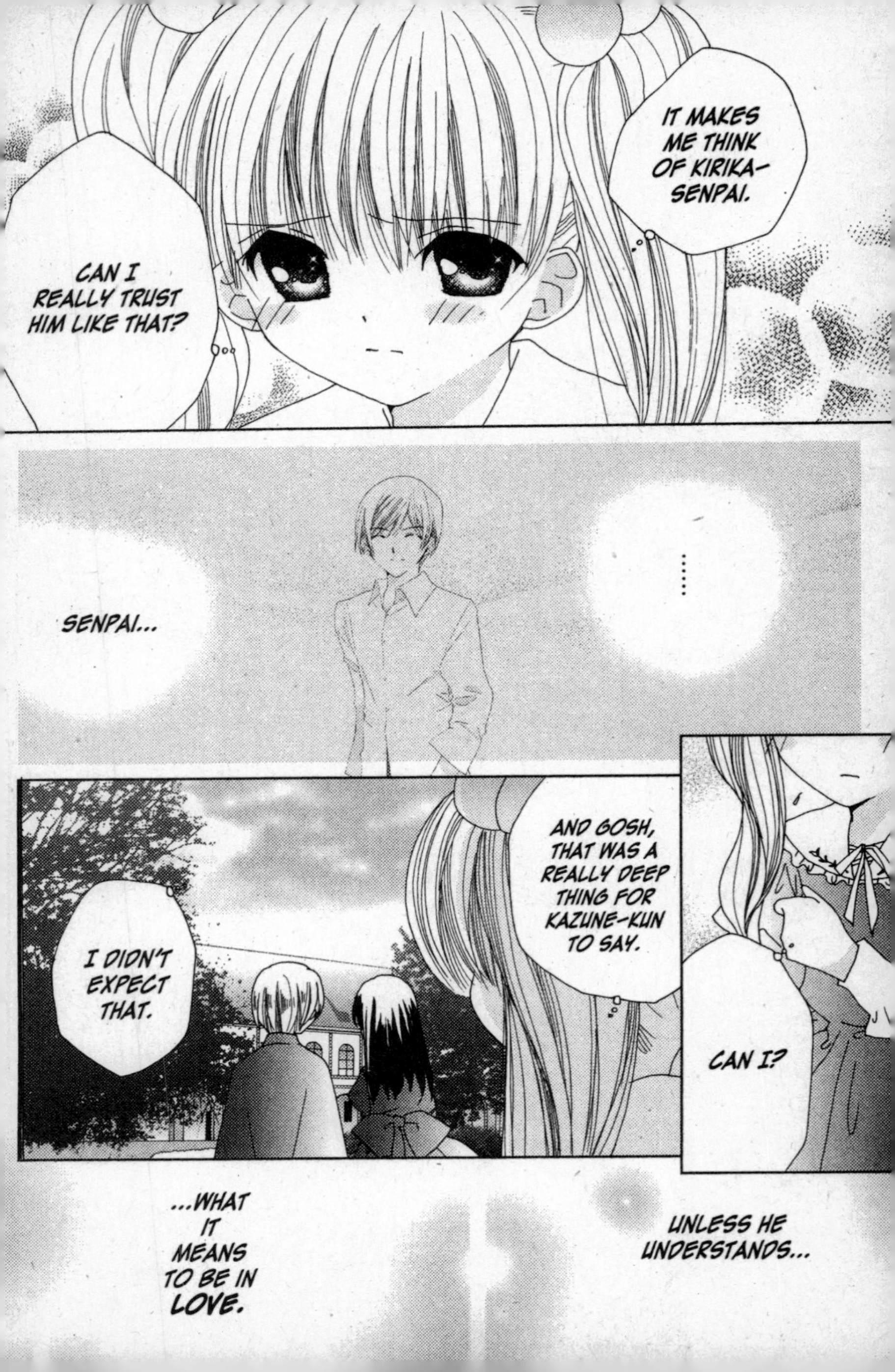
IT MAKES ME THINK OF KIRIKA-SENPAI.
CAN I REALLY TRUST HIM LIKE THAT?
......
SENPAI...
CAN I?
AND GOSH, THAT WAS A REALLY DEEP THING FOR KAZUNE-KUN TO SAY.
I DIDN'T EXPECT THAT.
UNLESS HE UNDERSTANDS...
...WHAT IT MEANS TO BE IN LOVE.

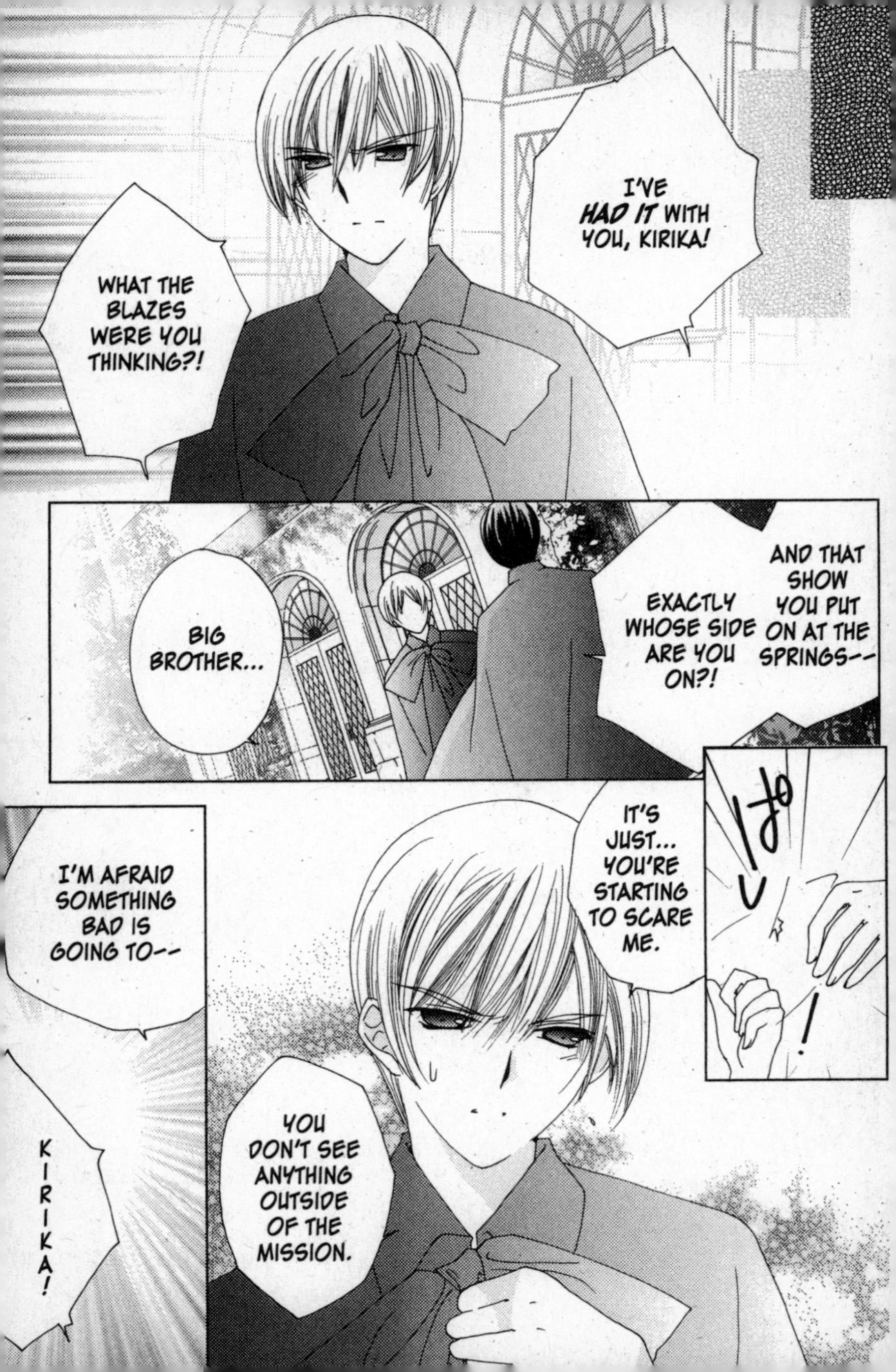
I'VE *HAD IT* WITH YOU, KIRIKA!
WHAT THE BLAZES WERE YOU THINKING?!
AND THAT SHOW YOU PUT ON AT THE SPRINGS--
EXACTLY WHOSE SIDE ARE YOU ON?!
BIG BROTHER...
IT'S JUST... YOU'RE STARTING TO SCARE ME.
YOU DON'T SEE ANYTHING OUTSIDE OF THE MISSION.
I'M AFRAID SOMETHING BAD IS GOING TO--
KIRIKA!

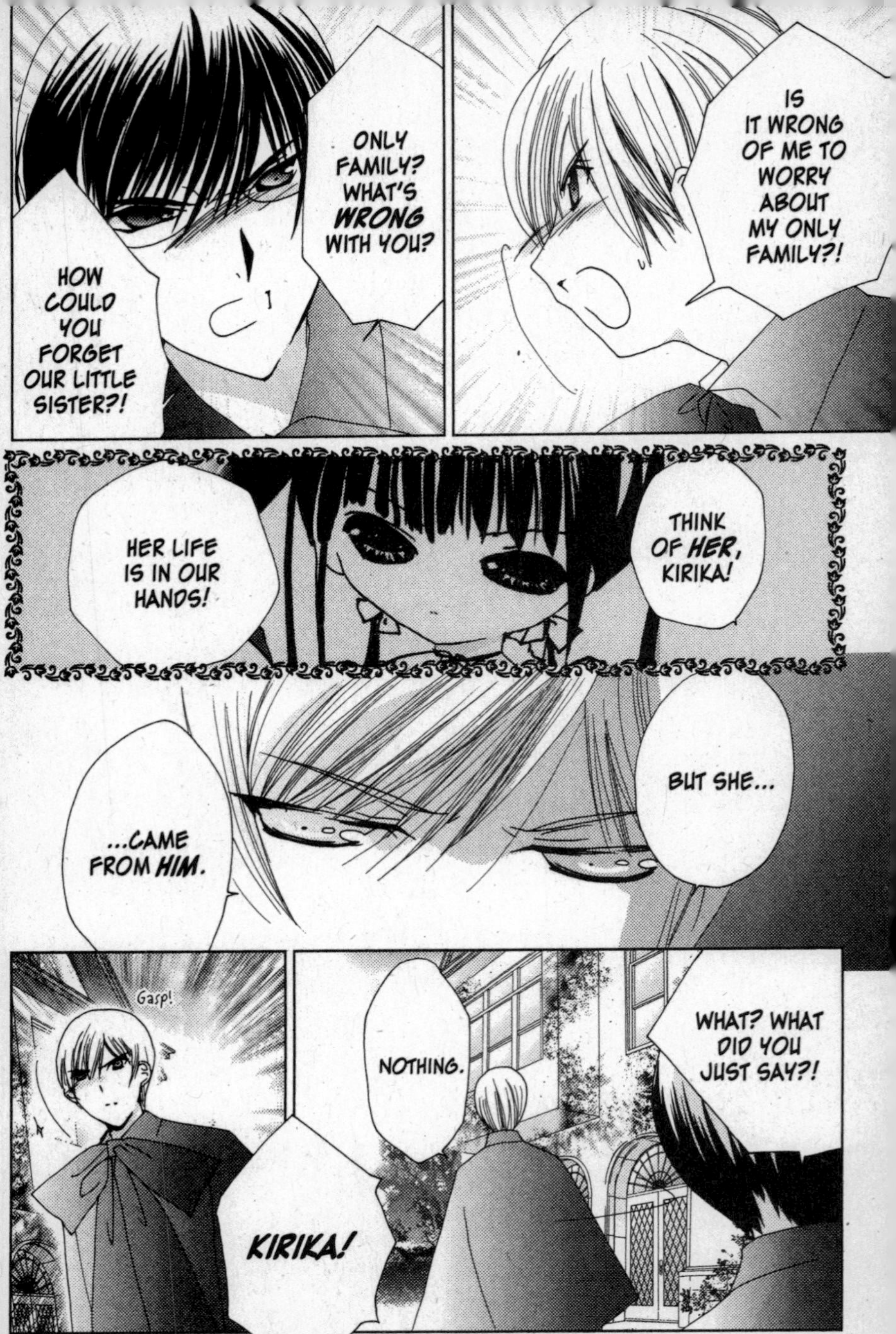
IS IT WRONG OF ME TO WORRY ABOUT MY ONLY FAMILY?!
ONLY FAMILY? WHAT'S *WRONG* WITH YOU?
HOW COULD YOU FORGET OUR LITTLE SISTER?!
THINK OF *HER*, KIRIKA!
HER LIFE IS IN OUR HANDS!
BUT SHE...
...CAME FROM *HIM*.
WHAT? WHAT DID YOU JUST SAY?!
NOTHING.
KIRIKA!
Gasp!

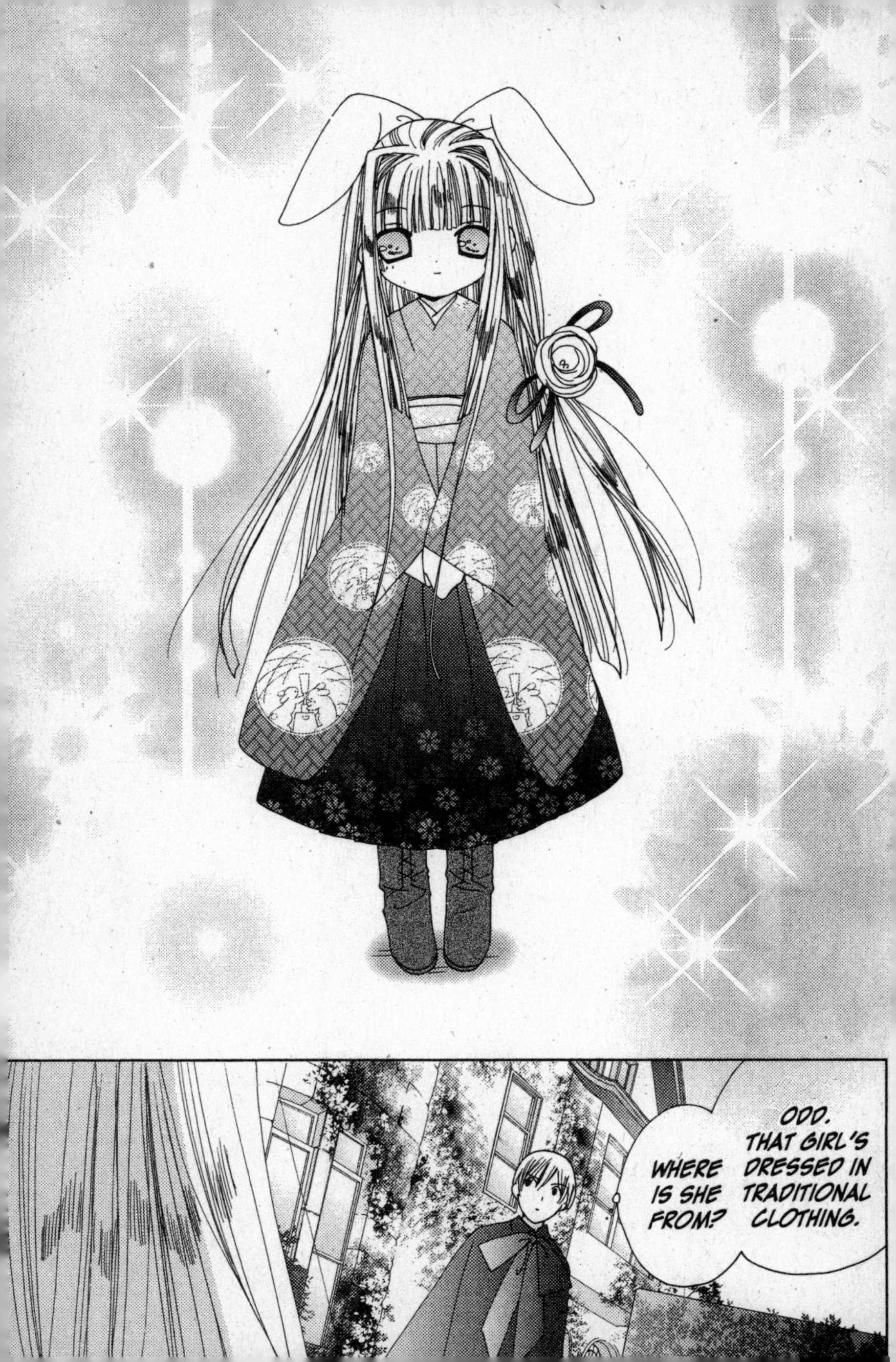
ODD. THAT GIRL'S DRESSED IN TRADITIONAL CLOTHING.
WHERE IS SHE FROM?

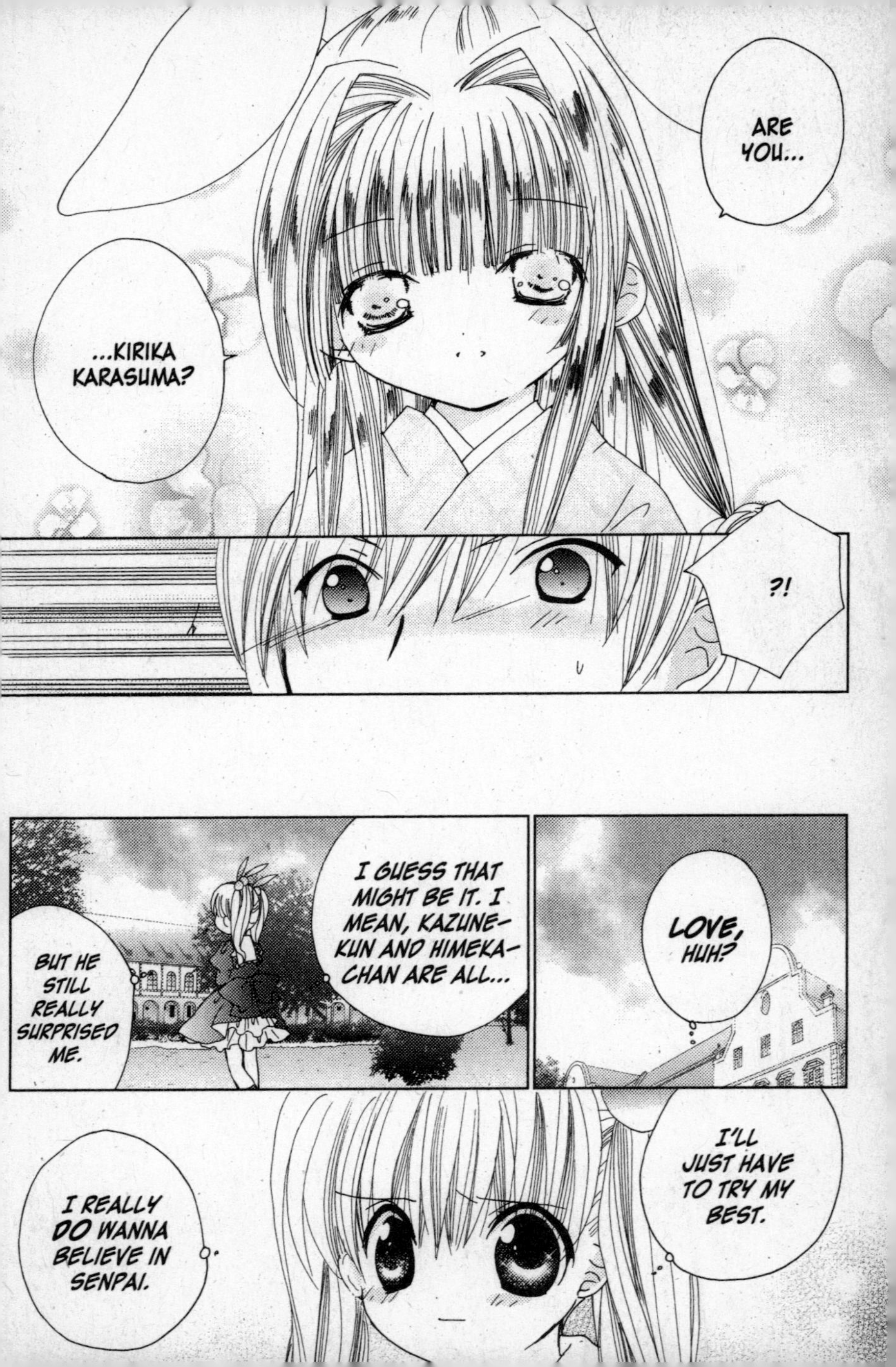
ARE YOU...
...KIRIKA KARASUMA?
?!
LOVE, HUH?
I GUESS THAT MIGHT BE IT. I MEAN, KAZUNE-KUN AND HIMEKA-CHAN ARE ALL...
BUT HE STILL REALLY SURPRISED ME.
I'LL JUST HAVE TO TRY MY BEST.
I REALLY DO WANNA BELIEVE IN SENPAI.

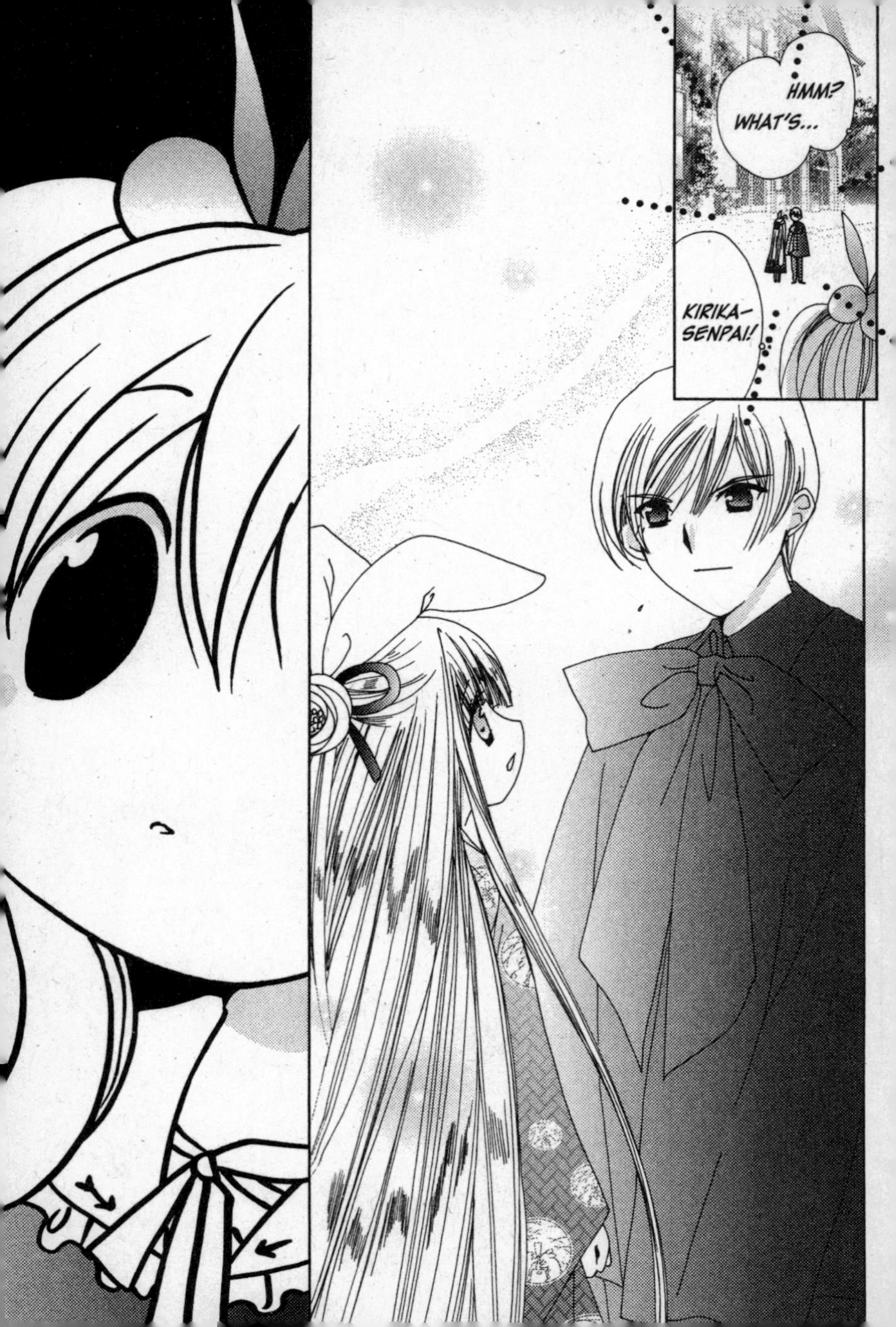
HMM? WHAT'S...
KIRIKA-SENPAI!

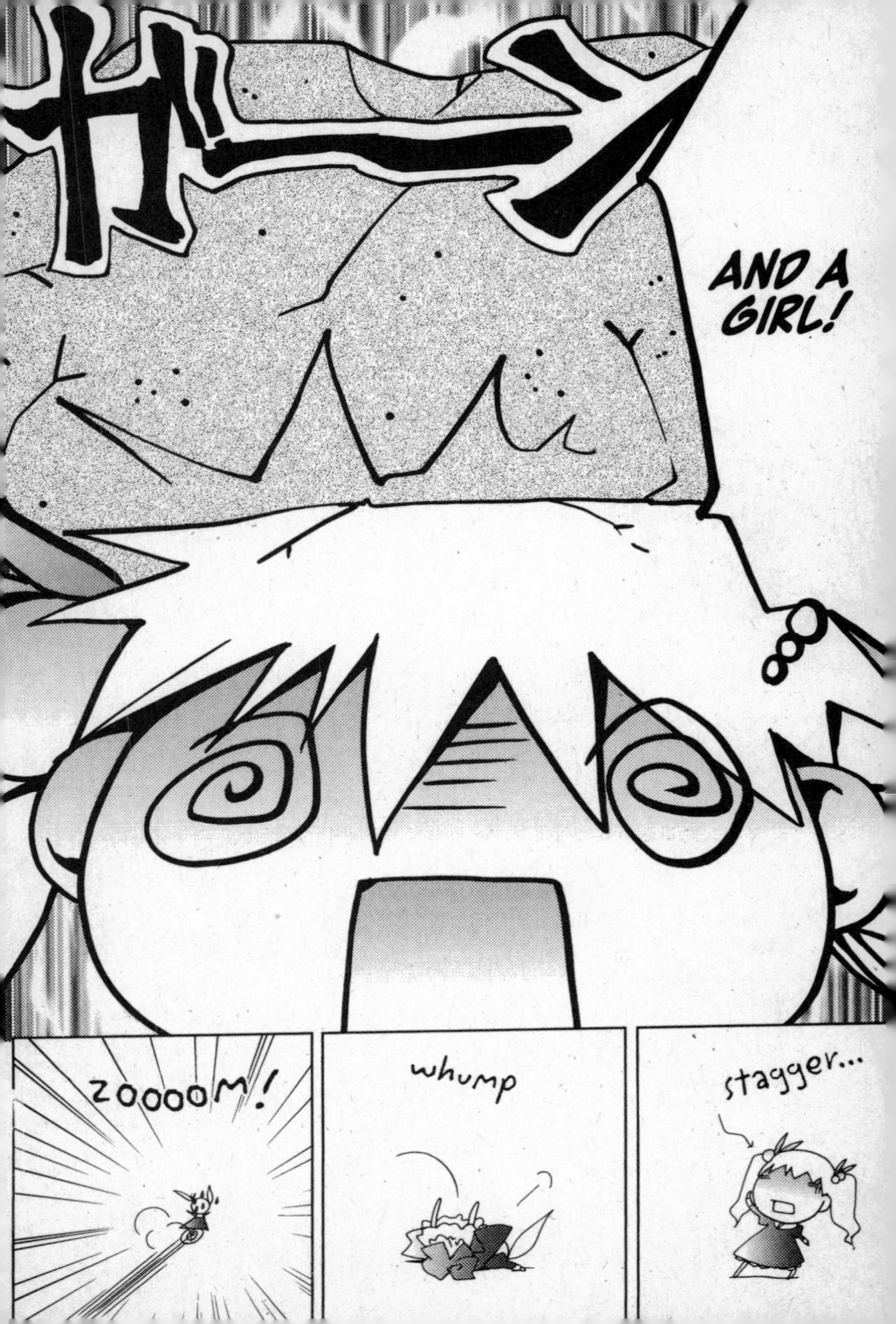
AND A GIRL!
stagger...
whump
ZOOOOOM!

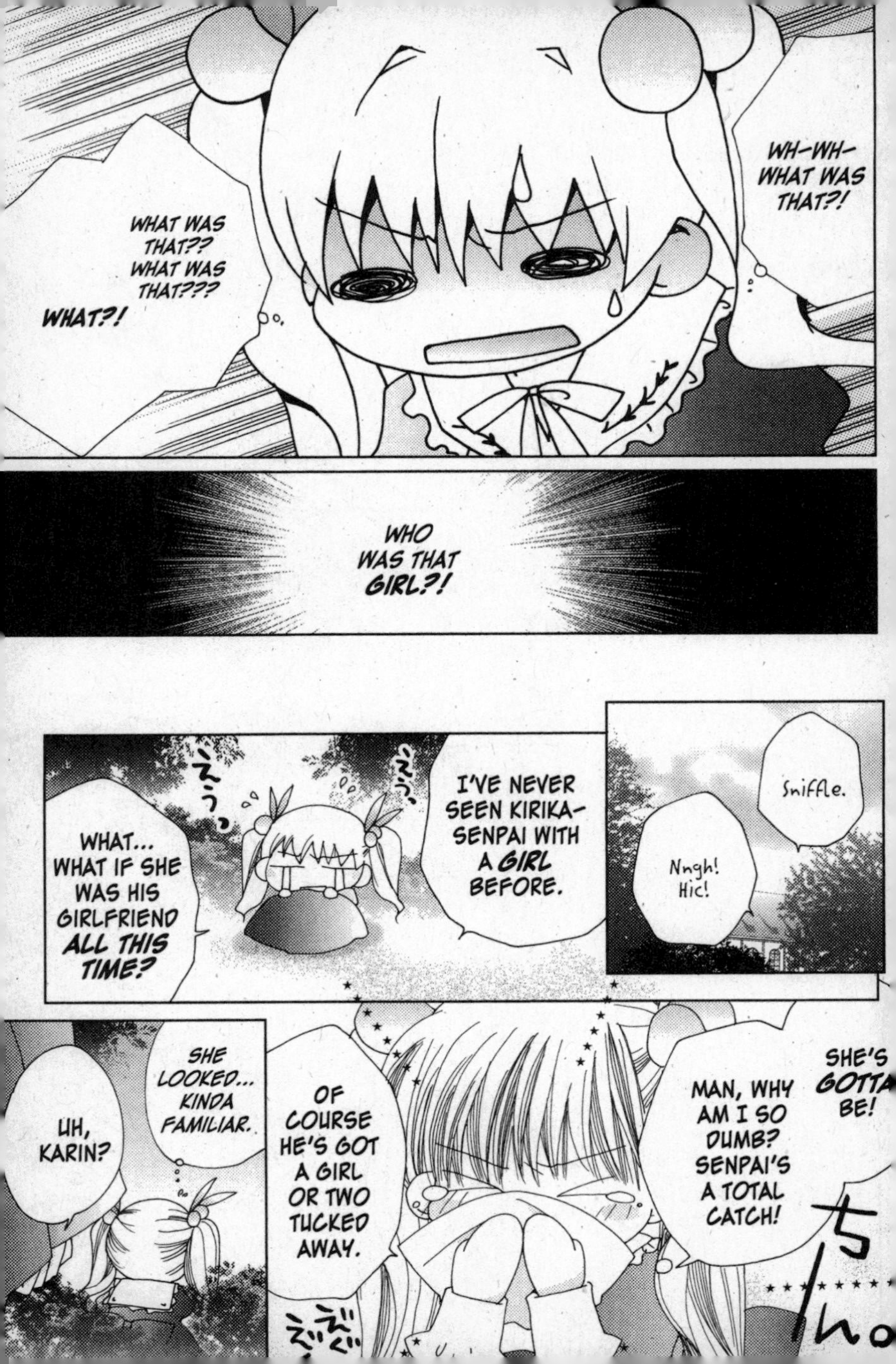
WH-WH-WHAT WAS THAT?!
WHAT WAS THAT?? WHAT WAS THAT??? WHAT?!
WHO WAS THAT GIRL?!
Sniffle.
Nngh! Hic!
I'VE NEVER SEEN KIRIKA-SENPAI WITH A GIRL BEFORE.
WHAT... WHAT IF SHE WAS HIS GIRLFRIEND ALL THIS TIME?
SHE'S GOTTA BE!
MAN, WHY AM I SO DUMB? SENPAI'S A TOTAL CATCH!
OF COURSE HE'S GOT A GIRL OR TWO TUCKED AWAY.
SHE LOOKED... KINDA FAMILIAR.
UH, KARIN?

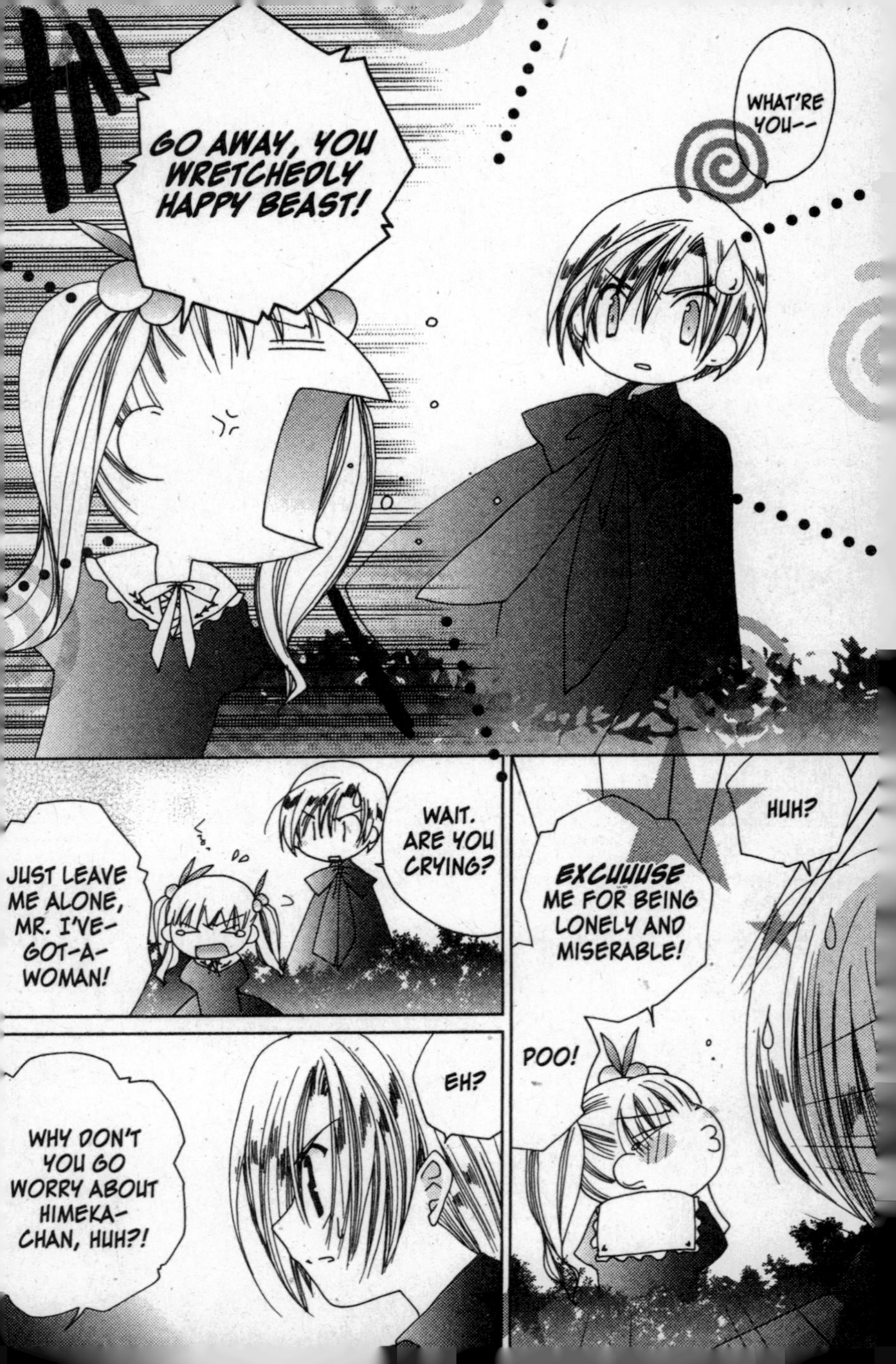
WHAT'RE YOU--
GO AWAY, YOU WRETCHEDLY HAPPY BEAST!
HUH?
EXCUUUUSE ME FOR BEING LONELY AND MISERABLE!
POO!
WAIT. ARE YOU CRYING?
JUST LEAVE ME ALONE, MR. I'VE-GOT-A-WOMAN!
EH?
WHY DON'T YOU GO WORRY ABOUT HIMEKA-CHAN, HUH?!

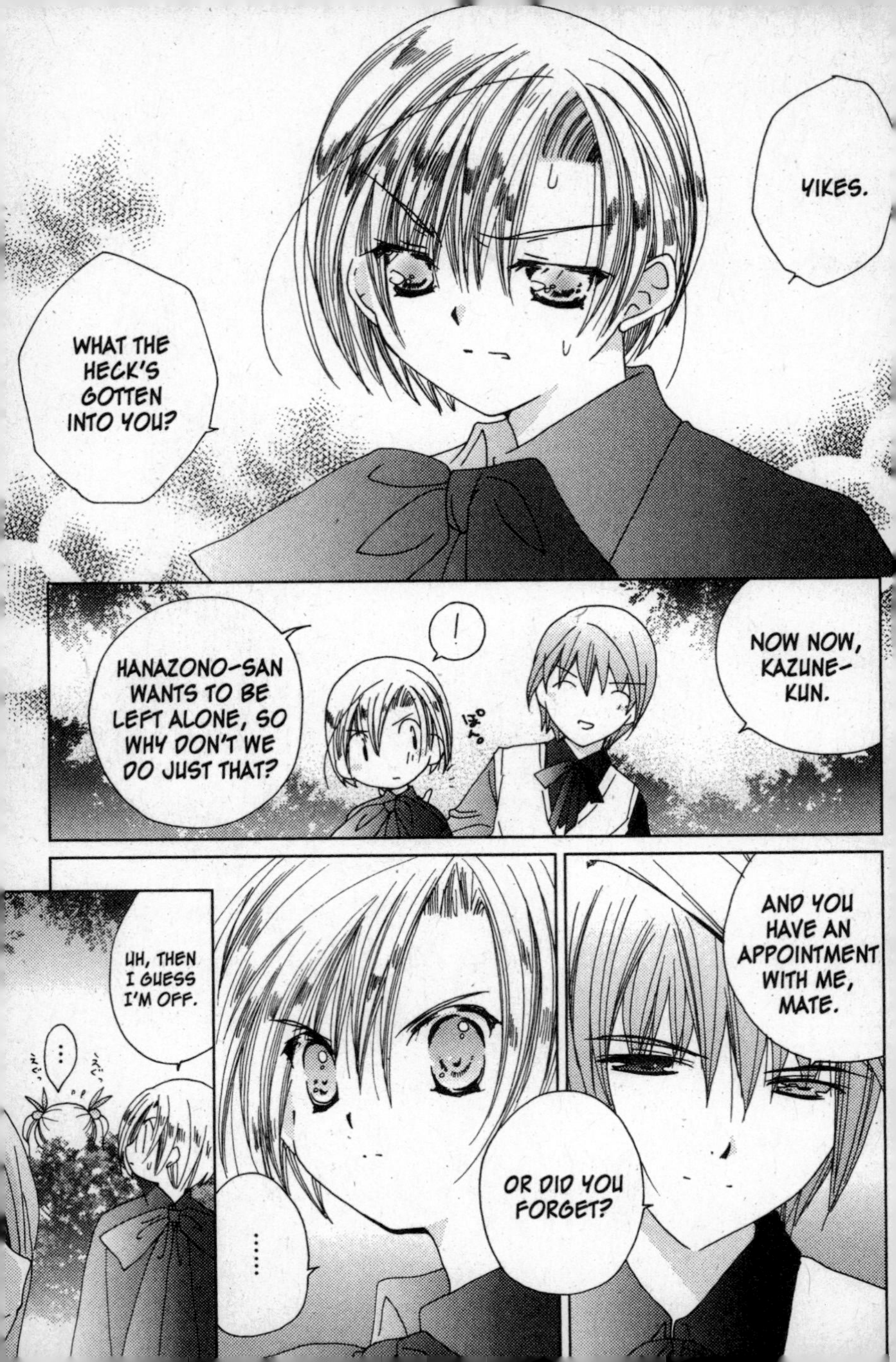
YIKES.
WHAT THE HECK'S GOTTEN INTO YOU?
NOW NOW, KAZUNE-KUN.
!
ぽん。
HANAZONO-SAN WANTS TO BE LEFT ALONE, SO WHY DON'T WE DO JUST THAT?
AND YOU HAVE AN APPOINTMENT WITH ME, MATE.
OR DID YOU FORGET?
......
UH, THEN I GUESS I'M OFF.
...

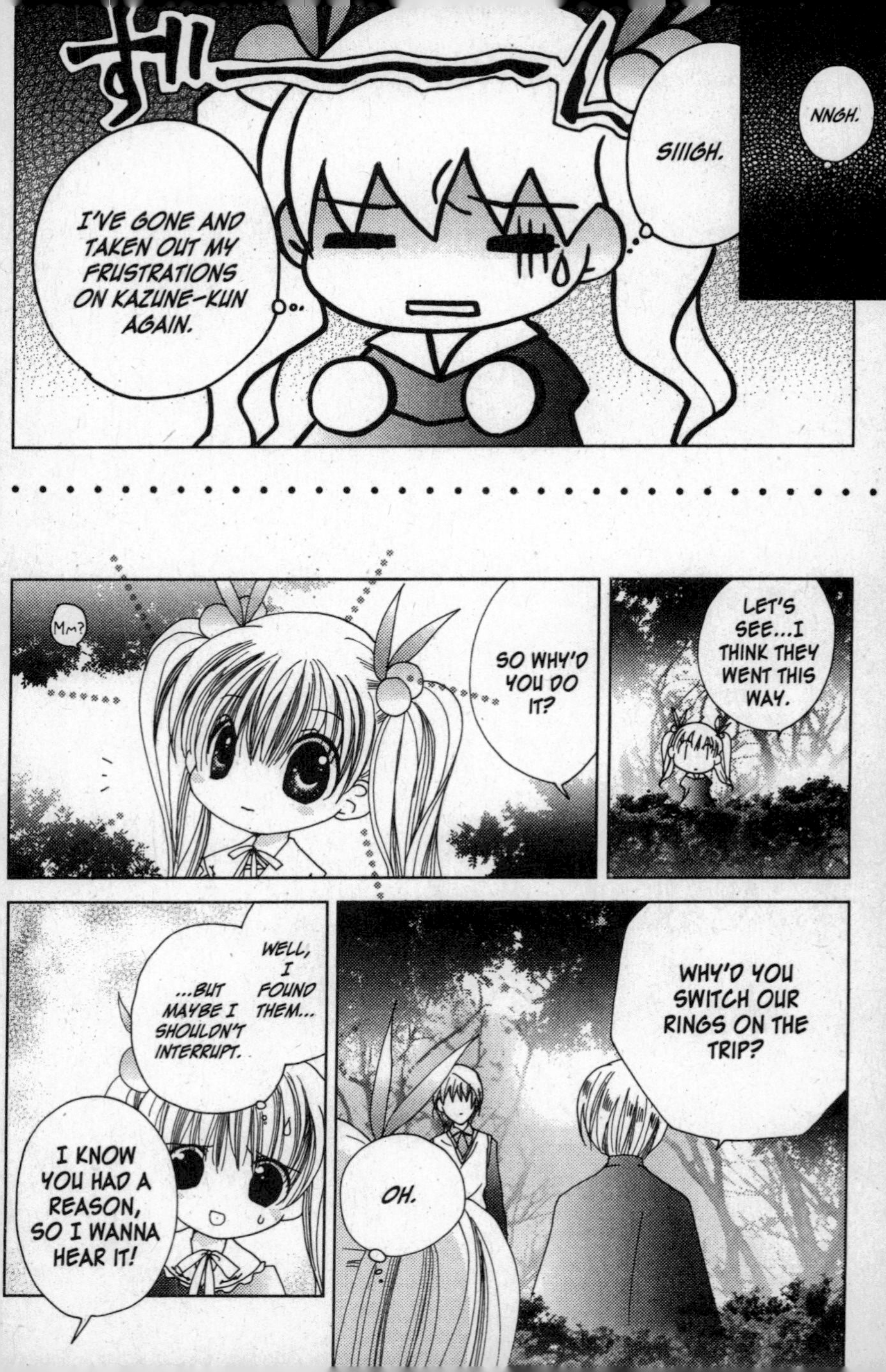

NNGH.
SIIIGH.
I'VE GONE AND TAKEN OUT MY FRUSTRATIONS ON KAZUNE-KUN AGAIN.
LET'S SEE...I THINK THEY WENT THIS WAY.
SO WHY'D YOU DO IT?
Mm?
WHY'D YOU SWITCH OUR RINGS ON THE TRIP?
OH.
WELL, I FOUND THEM...
...BUT MAYBE I SHOULDN'T INTERRUPT.
I KNOW YOU HAD A REASON, SO I WANNA HEAR IT!

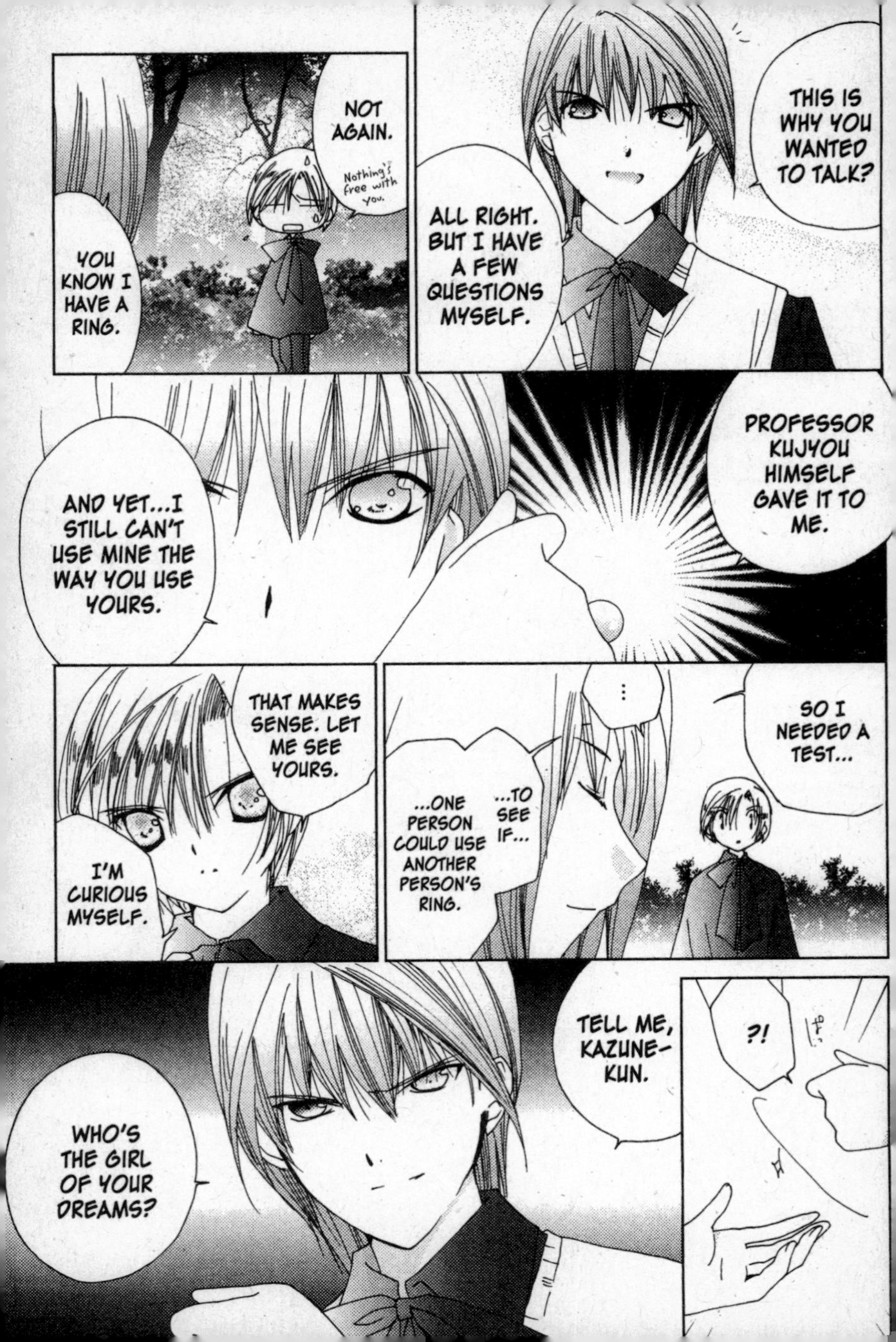
THIS IS WHY YOU WANTED TO TALK?
ALL RIGHT. BUT I HAVE A FEW QUESTIONS MYSELF.
NOT AGAIN.
Nothing's free with you.
YOU KNOW I HAVE A RING.
PROFESSOR KUJYOU HIMSELF GAVE IT TO ME.
AND YET...I STILL CAN'T USE MINE THE WAY YOU USE YOURS.
SO I NEEDED A TEST...
...
...TO SEE IF...
...ONE PERSON COULD USE ANOTHER PERSON'S RING.
THAT MAKES SENSE. LET ME SEE YOURS.
I'M CURIOUS MYSELF.
?!
TELL ME, KAZUNE-KUN.
WHO'S THE GIRL OF YOUR DREAMS?

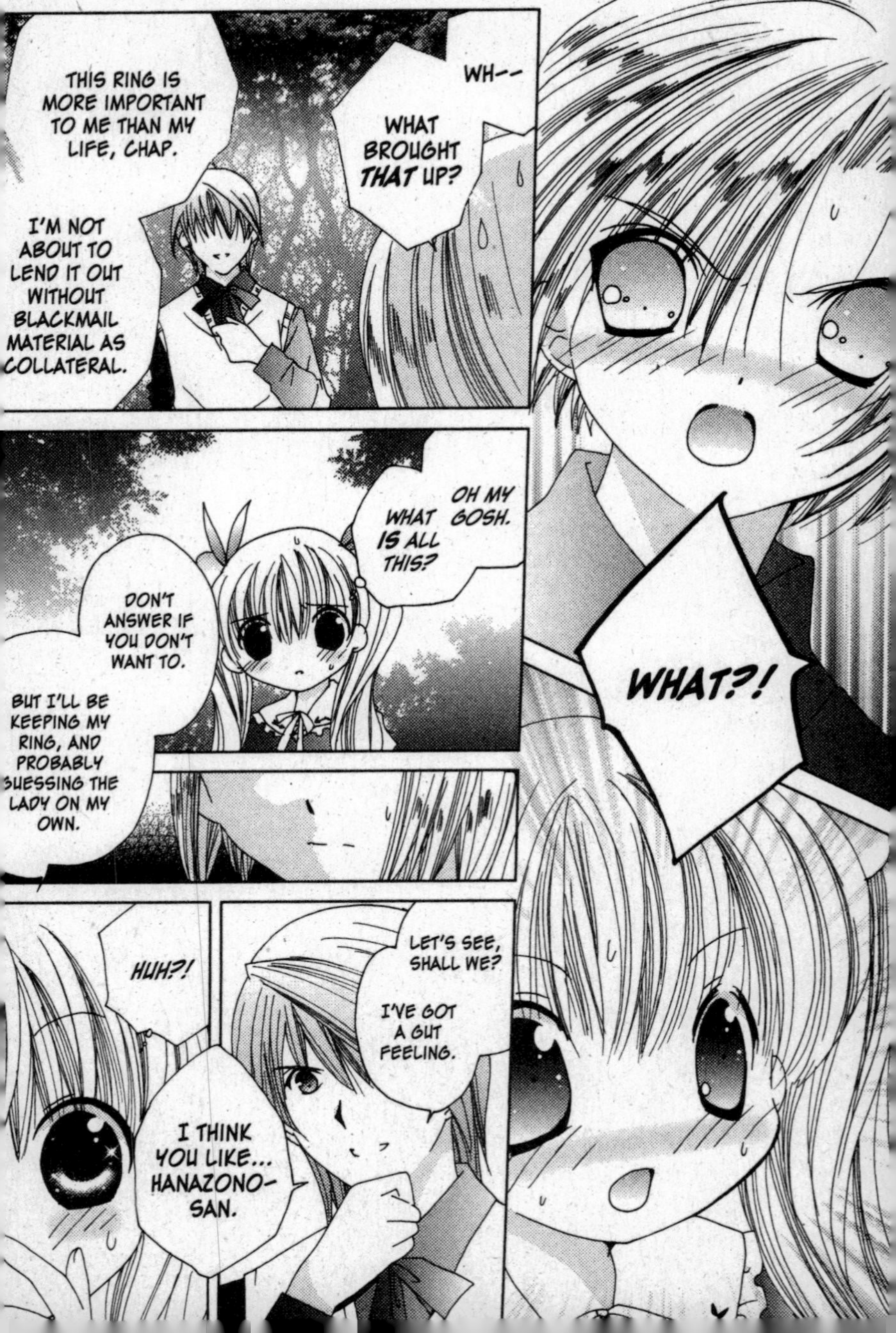
WHAT?!
WH--
WHAT BROUGHT THAT UP?
THIS RING IS MORE IMPORTANT TO ME THAN MY LIFE, CHAP.
I'M NOT ABOUT TO LEND IT OUT WITHOUT BLACKMAIL MATERIAL AS COLLATERAL.
OH MY GOSH.
WHAT IS ALL THIS?
DON'T ANSWER IF YOU DON'T WANT TO.
BUT I'LL BE KEEPING MY RING, AND PROBABLY GUESSING THE LADY ON MY OWN.
LET'S SEE, SHALL WE?
I'VE GOT A GUT FEELING.
I THINK YOU LIKE... HANAZONO-SAN.
HUH?!

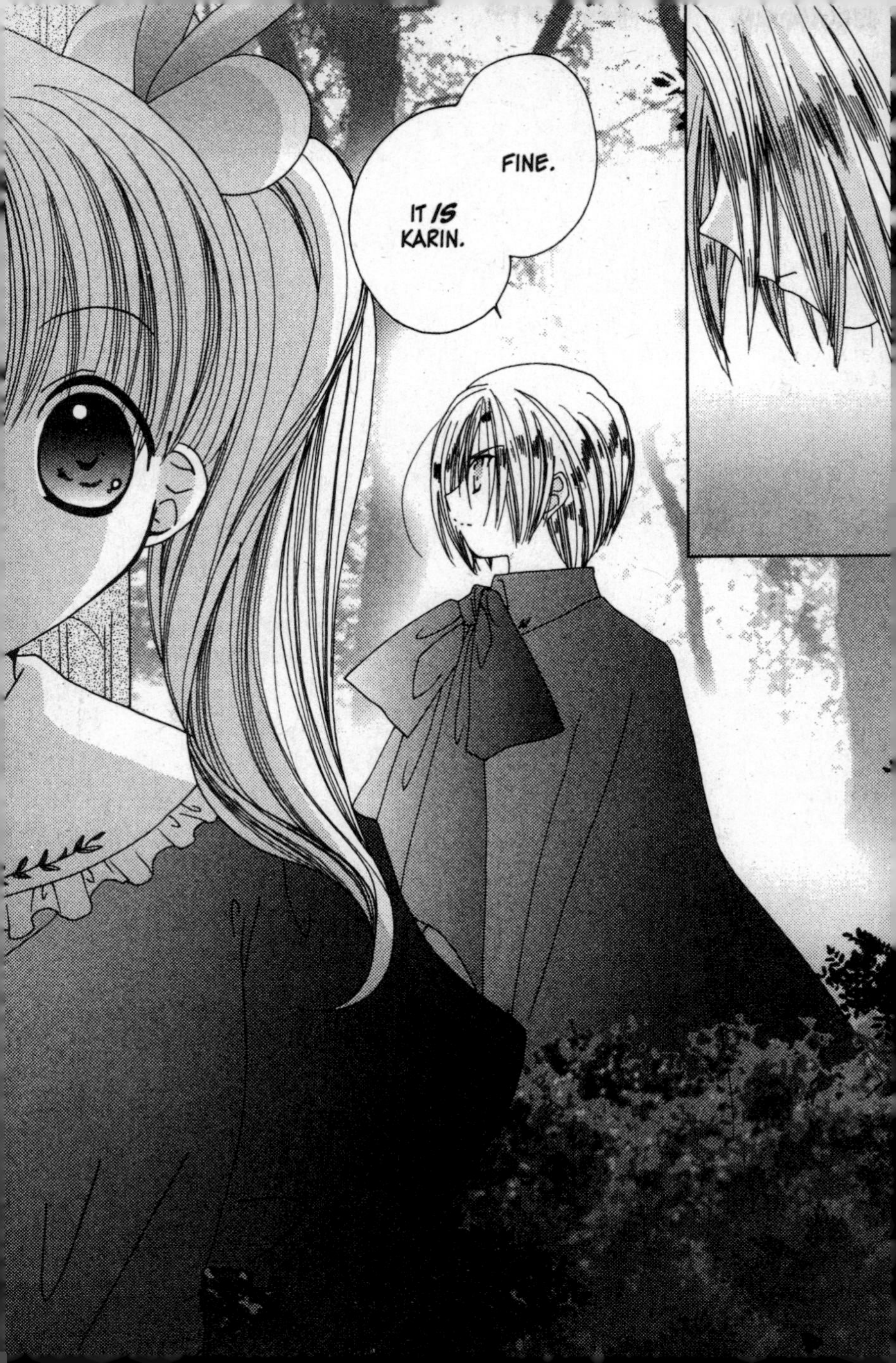
FINE.
IT IS KARIN.

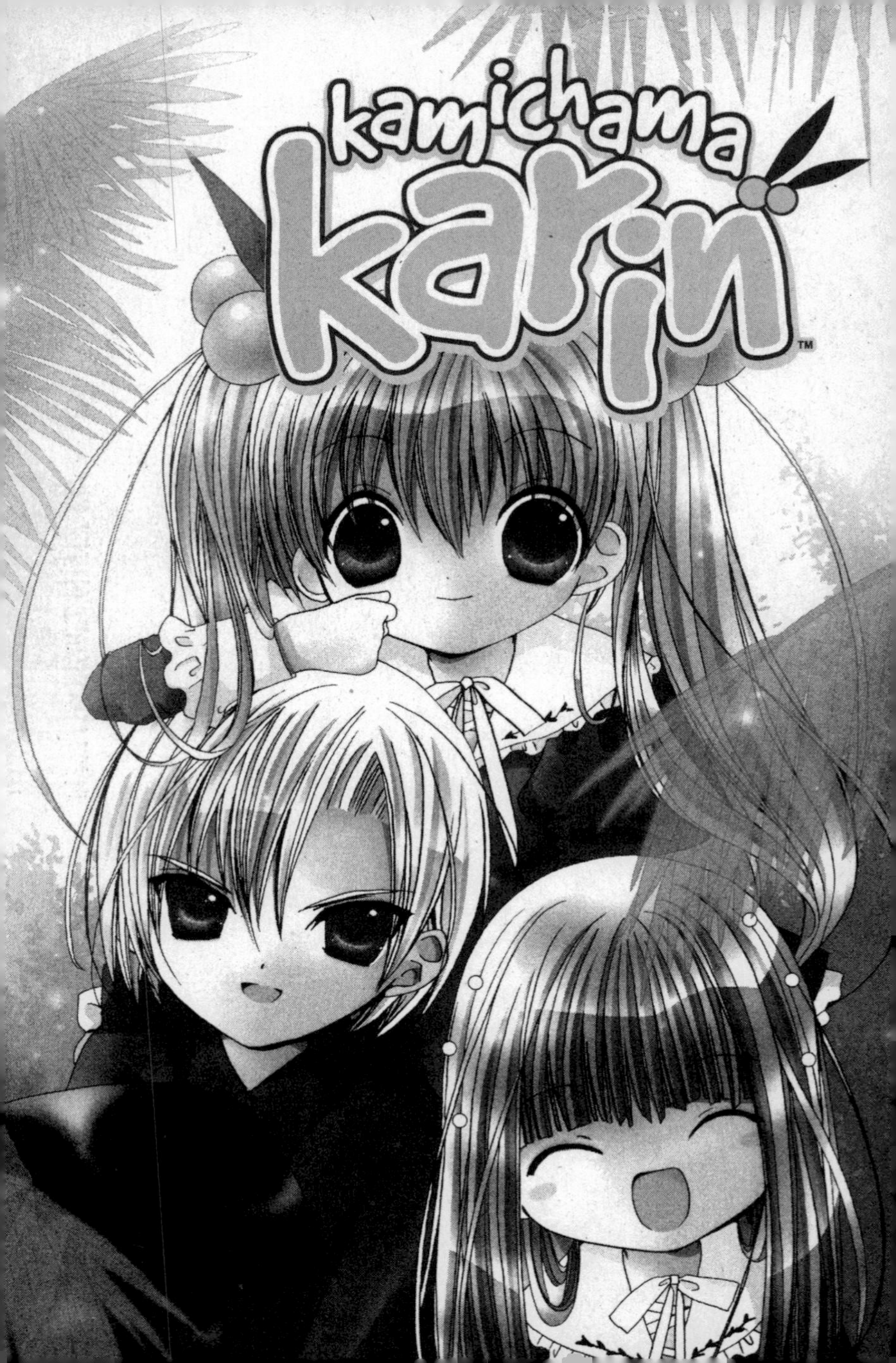
kamichama karin™

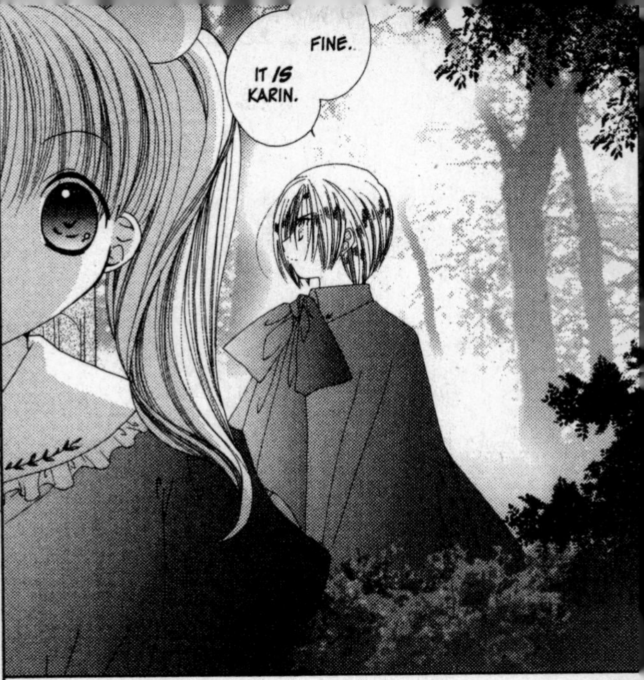
FINE.
IT IS KARIN.
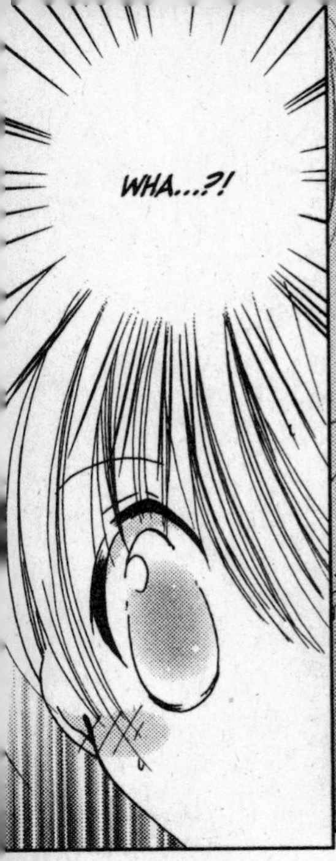
WHA...?!
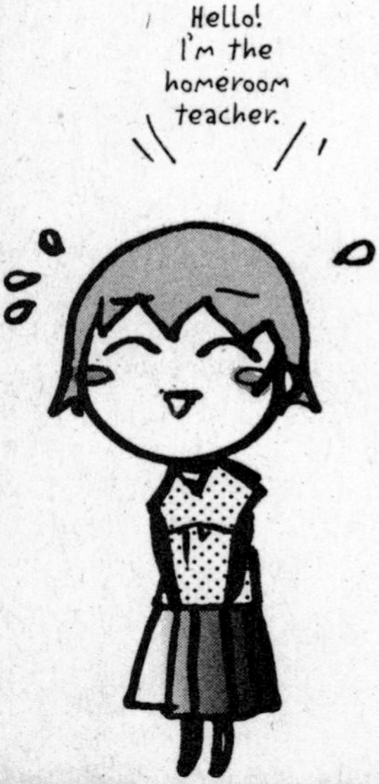
Hello! I'm the homeroom teacher.

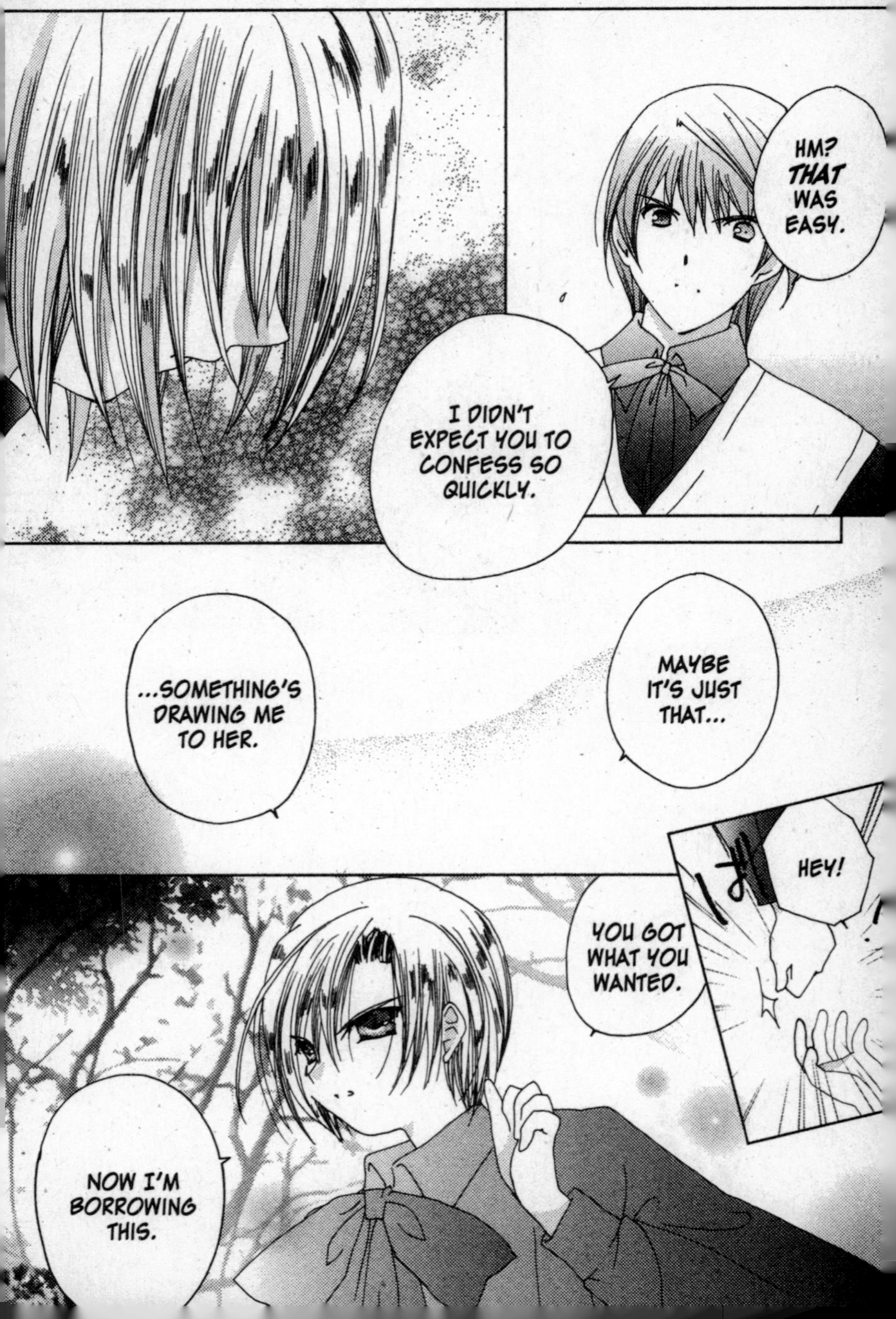
HM? THAT WAS EASY.
I DIDN'T EXPECT YOU TO CONFESS SO QUICKLY.
MAYBE IT'S JUST THAT...
...SOMETHING'S DRAWING ME TO HER.
HEY!
YOU GOT WHAT YOU WANTED.
NOW I'M BORROWING THIS.

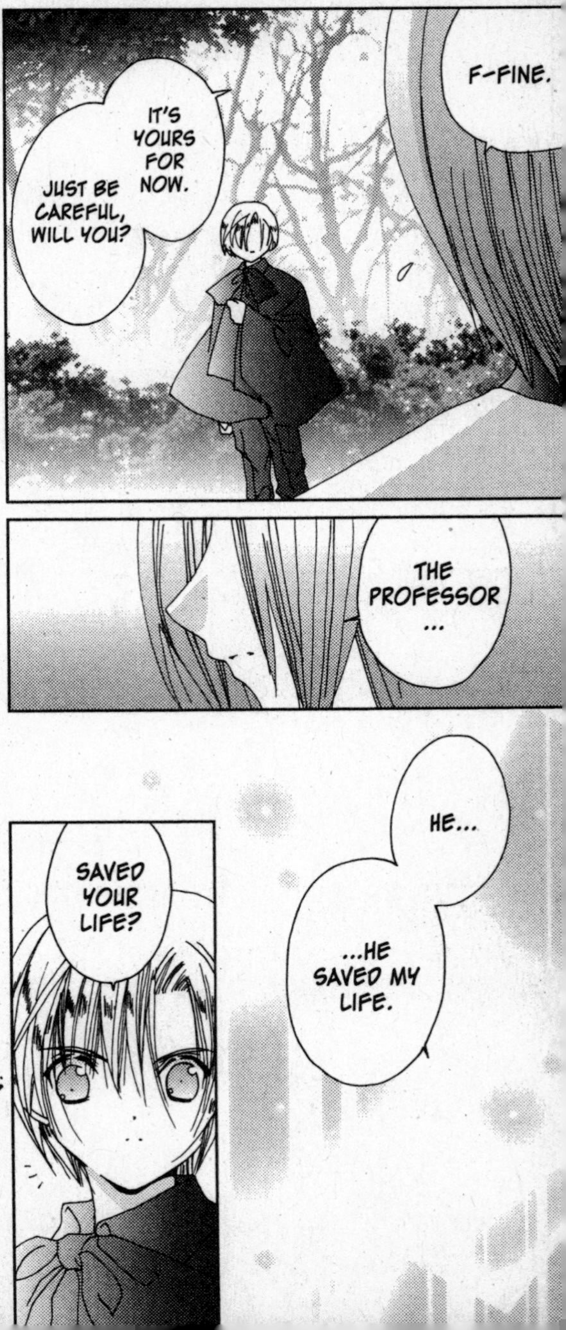
F-FINE.
IT'S YOURS FOR NOW.
JUST BE CAREFUL, WILL YOU?
THE PROFESSOR ...
HE...
...HE SAVED MY LIFE.
SAVED YOUR LIFE?

drag
drag
Something's drawing me to her.

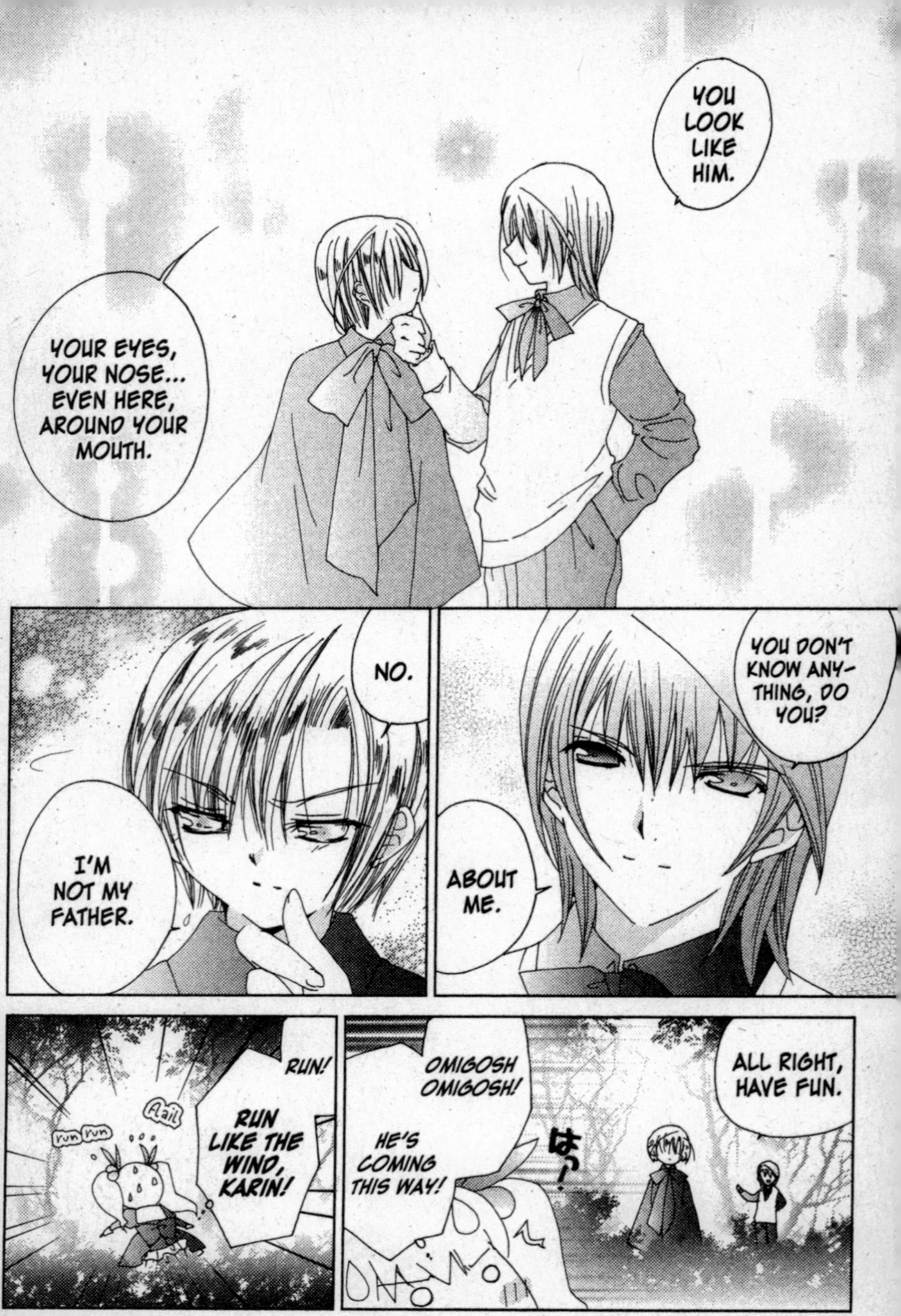
YOU LOOK LIKE HIM.
YOUR EYES, YOUR NOSE... EVEN HERE, AROUND YOUR MOUTH.
YOU DON'T KNOW ANY-THING, DO YOU?
ABOUT ME.
NO.
I'M NOT MY FATHER.
ALL RIGHT, HAVE FUN.
OMIGOSH OMIGOSH!
HE'S COMING THIS WAY!
はっ!
RUN!
RUN LIKE THE WIND, KARIN!
flail
run run

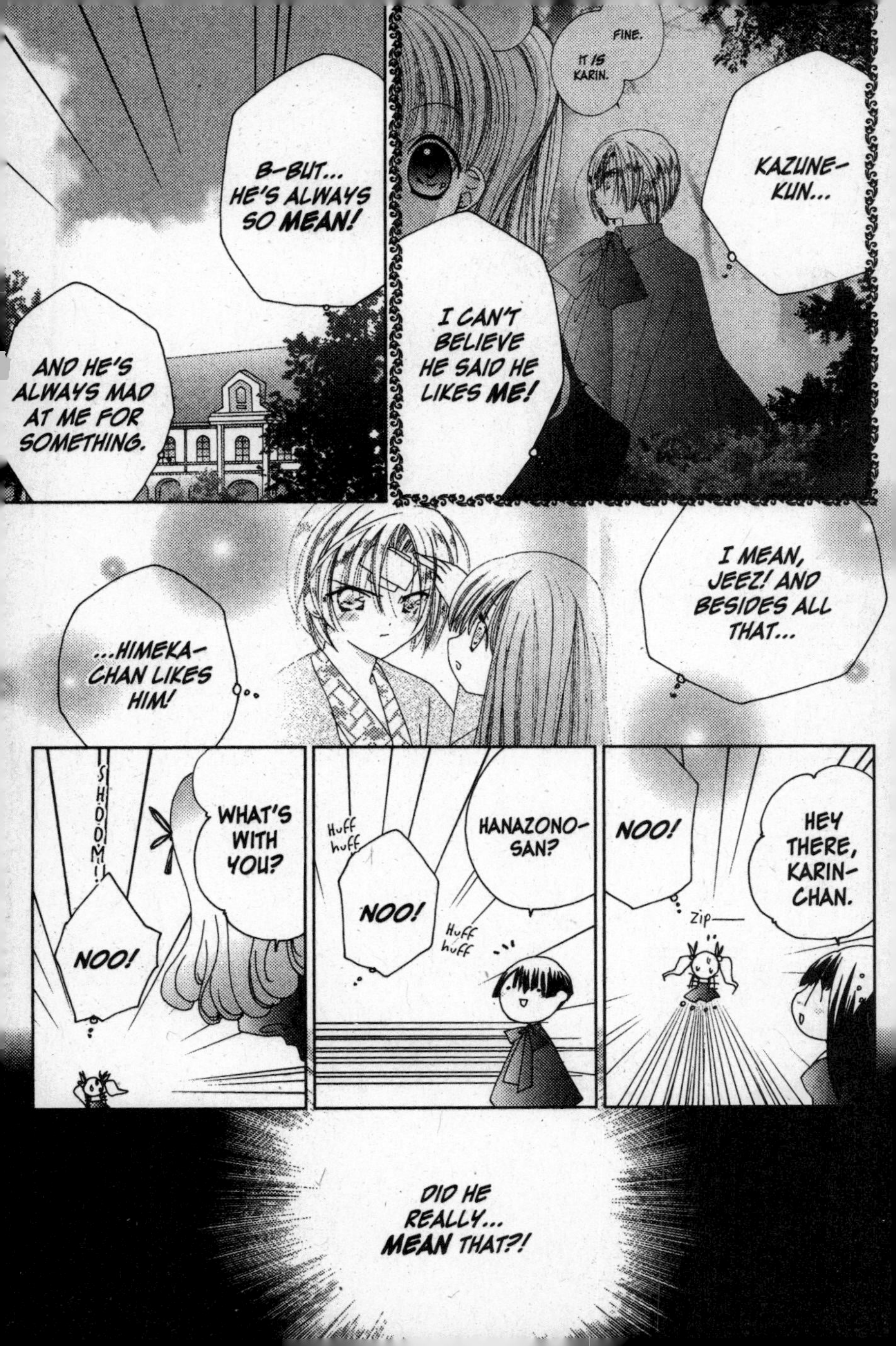
FINE. IT IS KARIN.
KAZUNE-KUN...
I CAN'T BELIEVE HE SAID HE LIKES ME!
B-BUT... HE'S ALWAYS SO MEAN!
AND HE'S ALWAYS MAD AT ME FOR SOMETHING.
I MEAN, JEEZ! AND BESIDES ALL THAT...
...HIMEKA-CHAN LIKES HIM!
HEY THERE, KARIN-CHAN.
NOO!
ZIP—
HANAZONO-SAN?
NOO!
Huff huff
Huff huff
WHAT'S WITH YOU?
SHDOM!
NOO!
DID HE REALLY... MEAN THAT?!

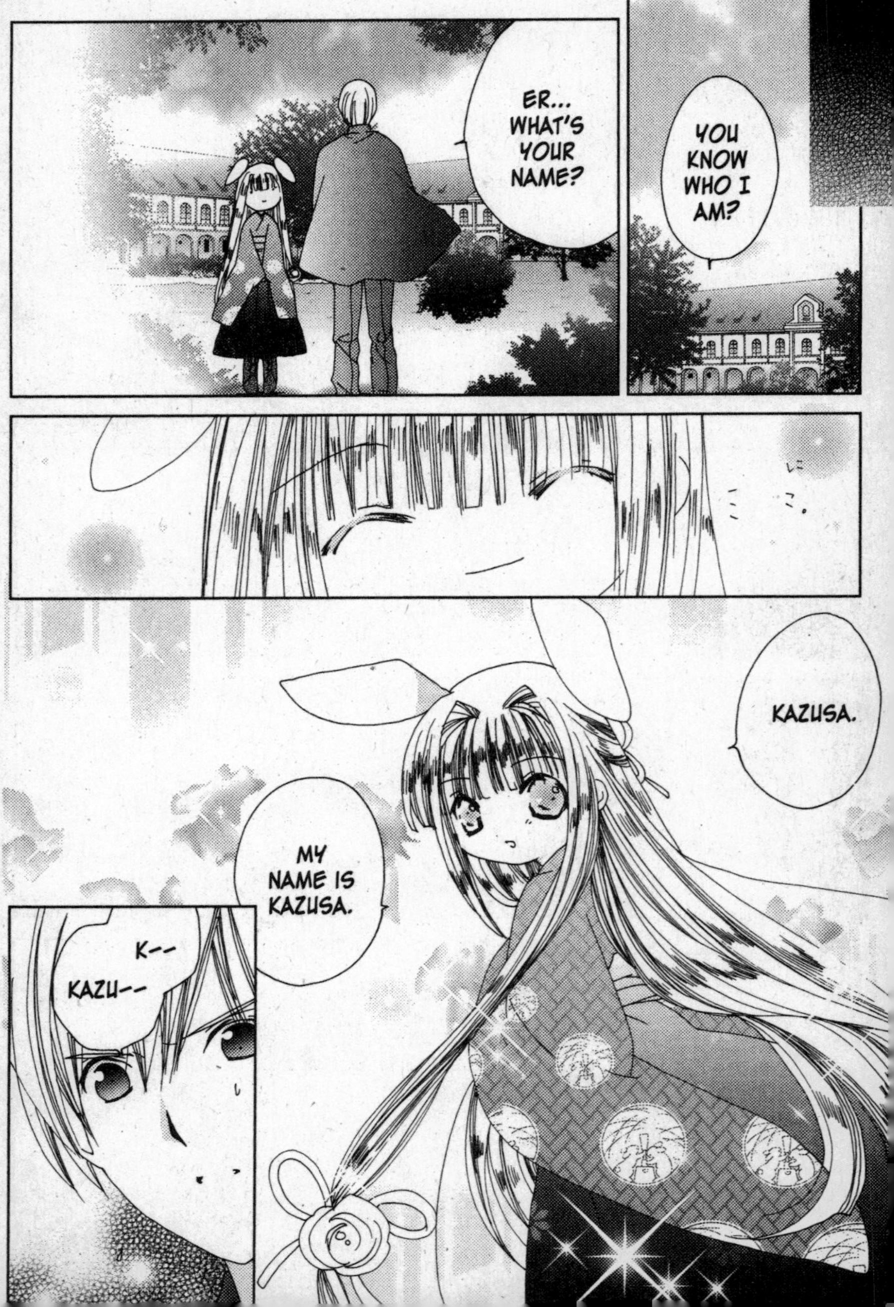
YOU KNOW WHO I AM?
ER... WHAT'S YOUR NAME?
KAZUSA.
MY NAME IS KAZUSA.
K-- KAZU--

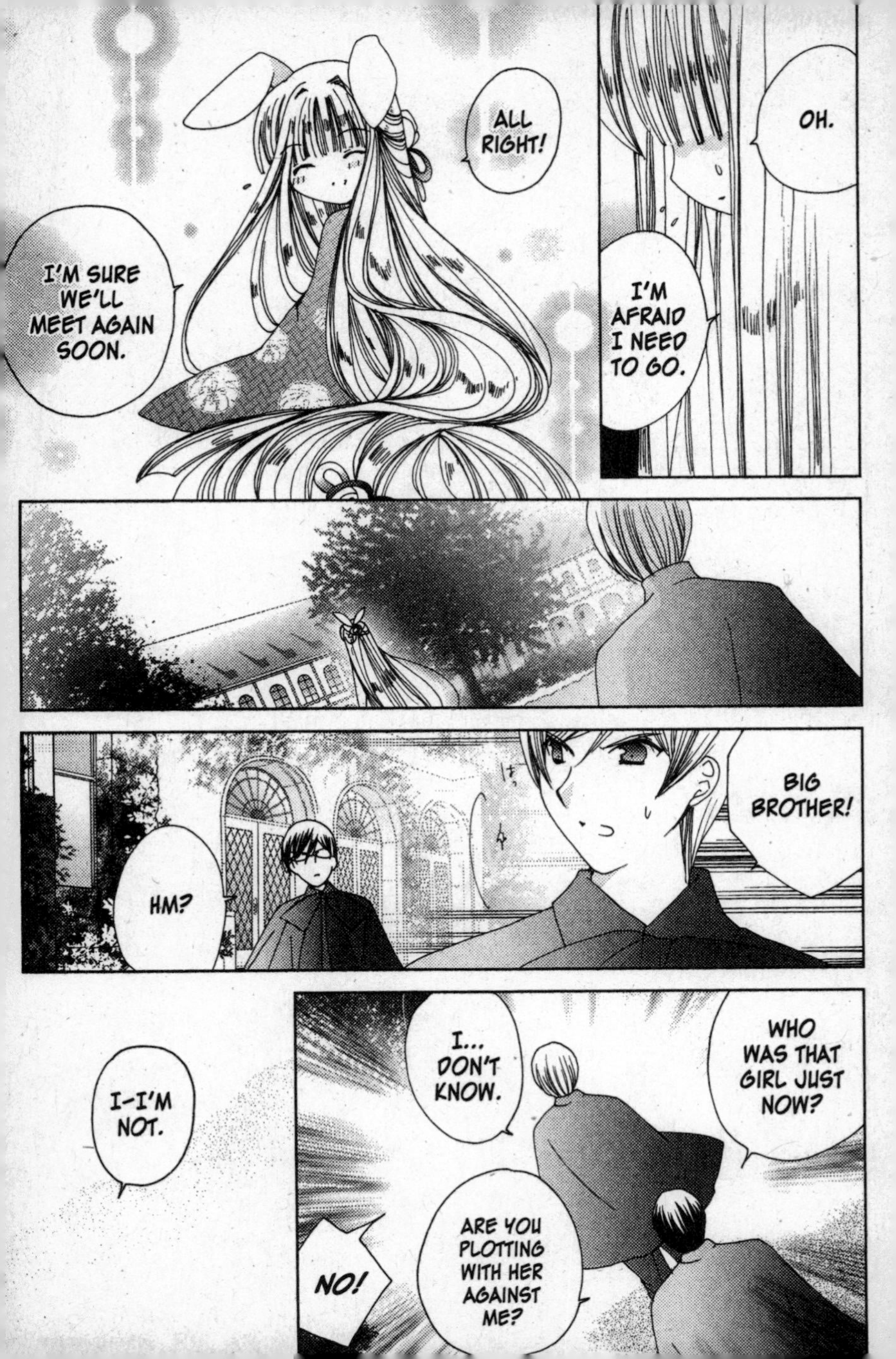
OH.
I'M AFRAID I NEED TO GO.
ALL RIGHT!
I'M SURE WE'LL MEET AGAIN SOON.
BIG BROTHER!
HM?
WHO WAS THAT GIRL JUST NOW?
I... DON'T KNOW.
ARE YOU PLOTTING WITH HER AGAINST ME?
NO!
I-I'M NOT.

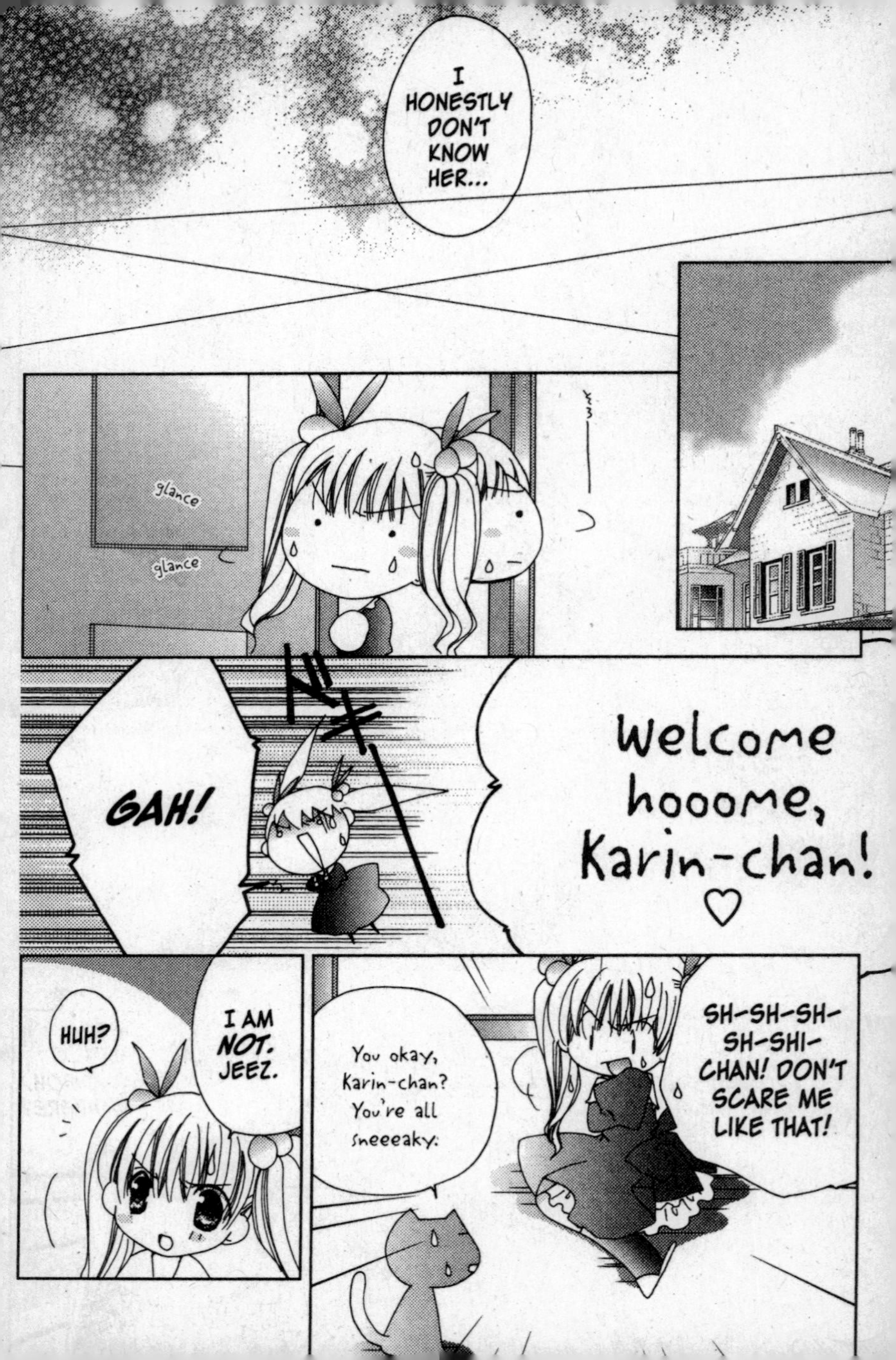
I HONESTLY DON'T KNOW HER...
glance
glance
Welcome hooome, Karin-chan! ♡
GAH!
SH-SH-SH-SH-SHI-CHAN! DON'T SCARE ME LIKE THAT!
You okay, Karin-chan? You're all sneeeaky.
I AM NOT. JEEZ.
HUH?

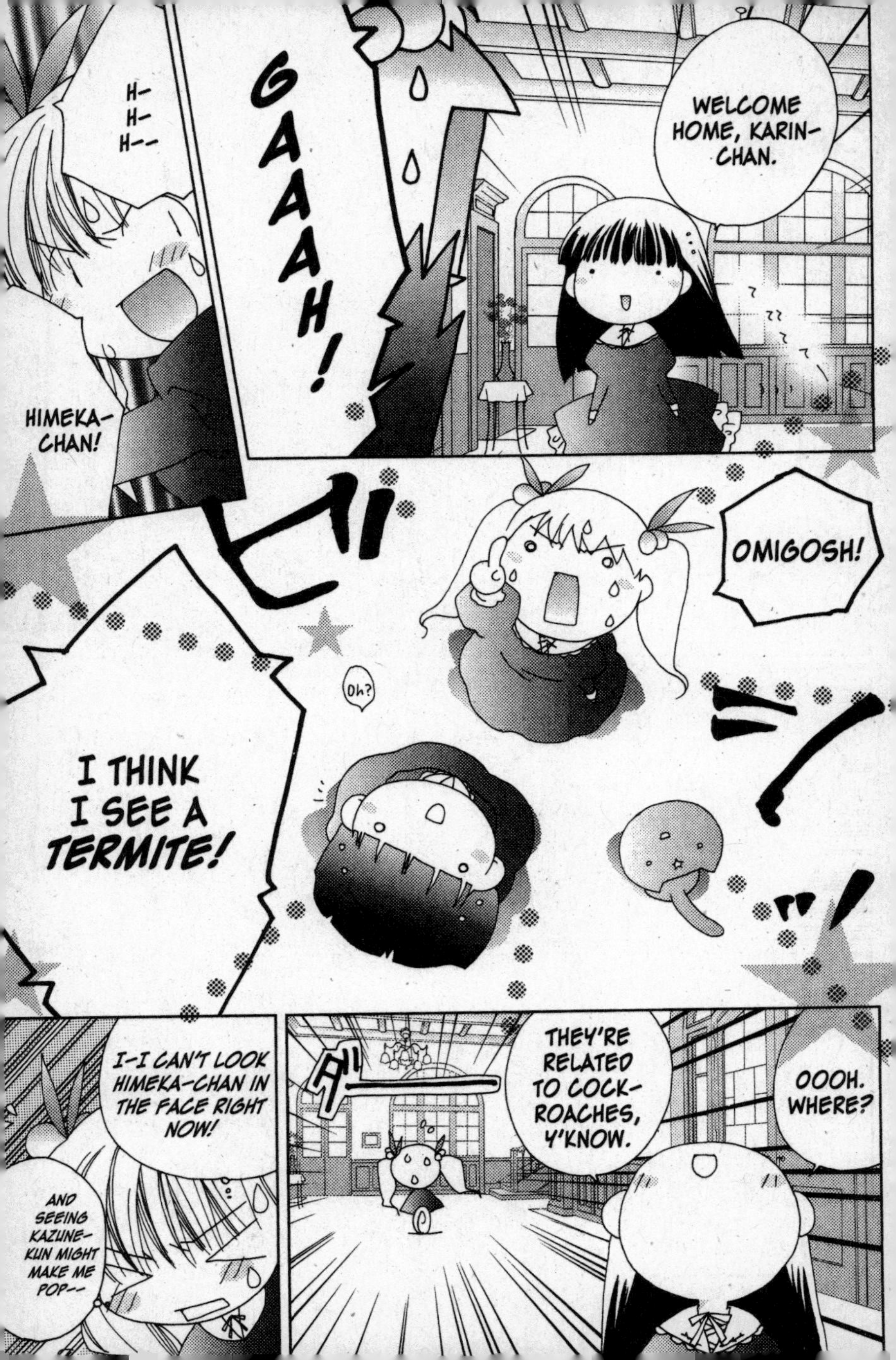
WELCOME HOME, KARIN-CHAN.
GAAAH!
H- H- H--
HIMEKA-CHAN!
OMIGOSH!
Oh?
I THINK I SEE A *TERMITE!*
OOOH. WHERE?
THEY'RE RELATED TO COCK-ROACHES, Y'KNOW.
I-I CAN'T LOOK HIMEKA-CHAN IN THE FACE RIGHT NOW!
AND SEEING KAZUNE-KUN MIGHT MAKE ME POP--

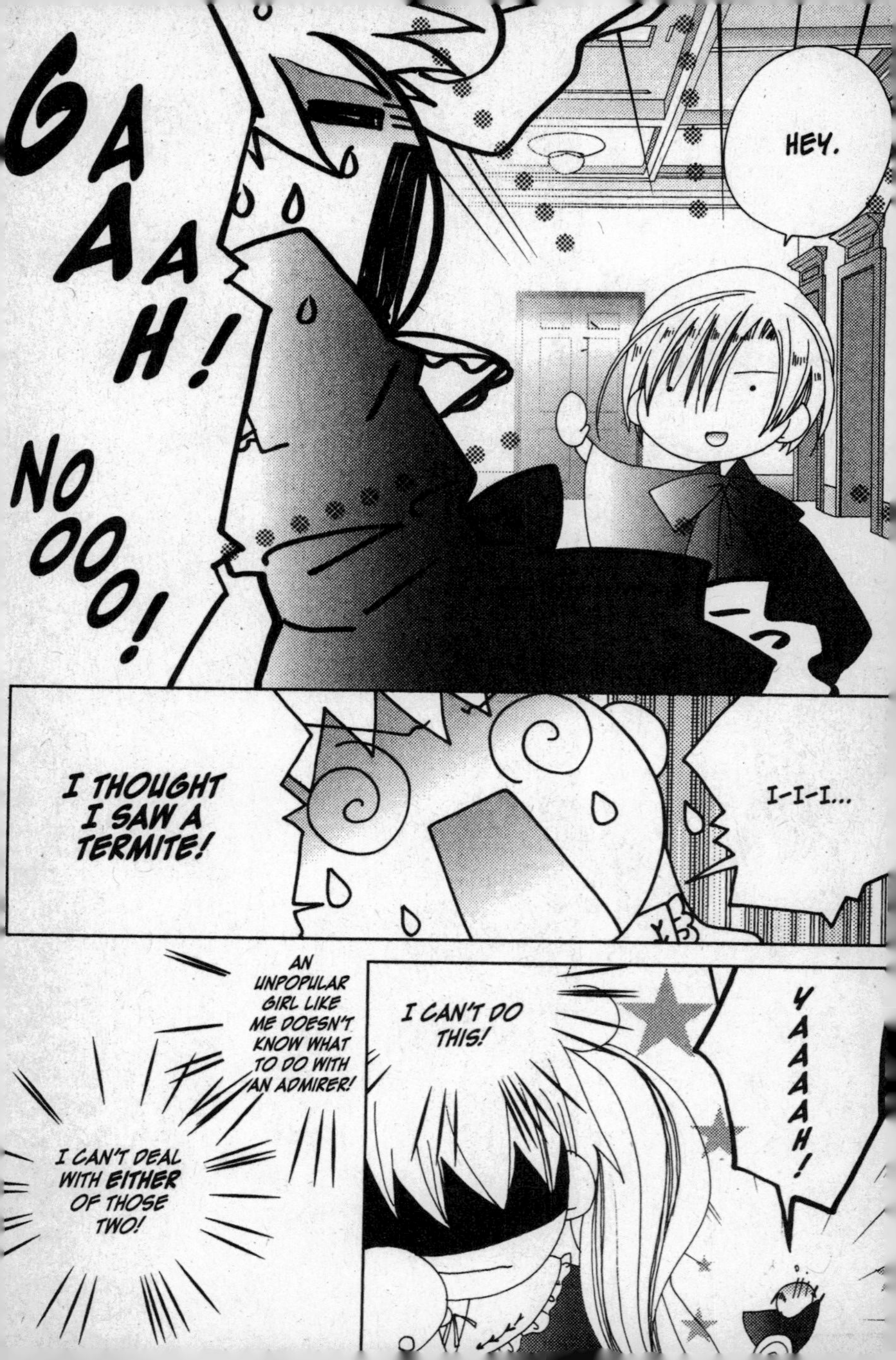
HEY.
GAAAH!
NOOOOO!
I-I-I...
I THOUGHT I SAW A TERMITE!
YAAAAAH!
I CAN'T DO THIS!
AN UNPOPULAR GIRL LIKE ME DOESN'T KNOW WHAT TO DO WITH AN ADMIRER!
I CAN'T DEAL WITH EITHER OF THOSE TWO!

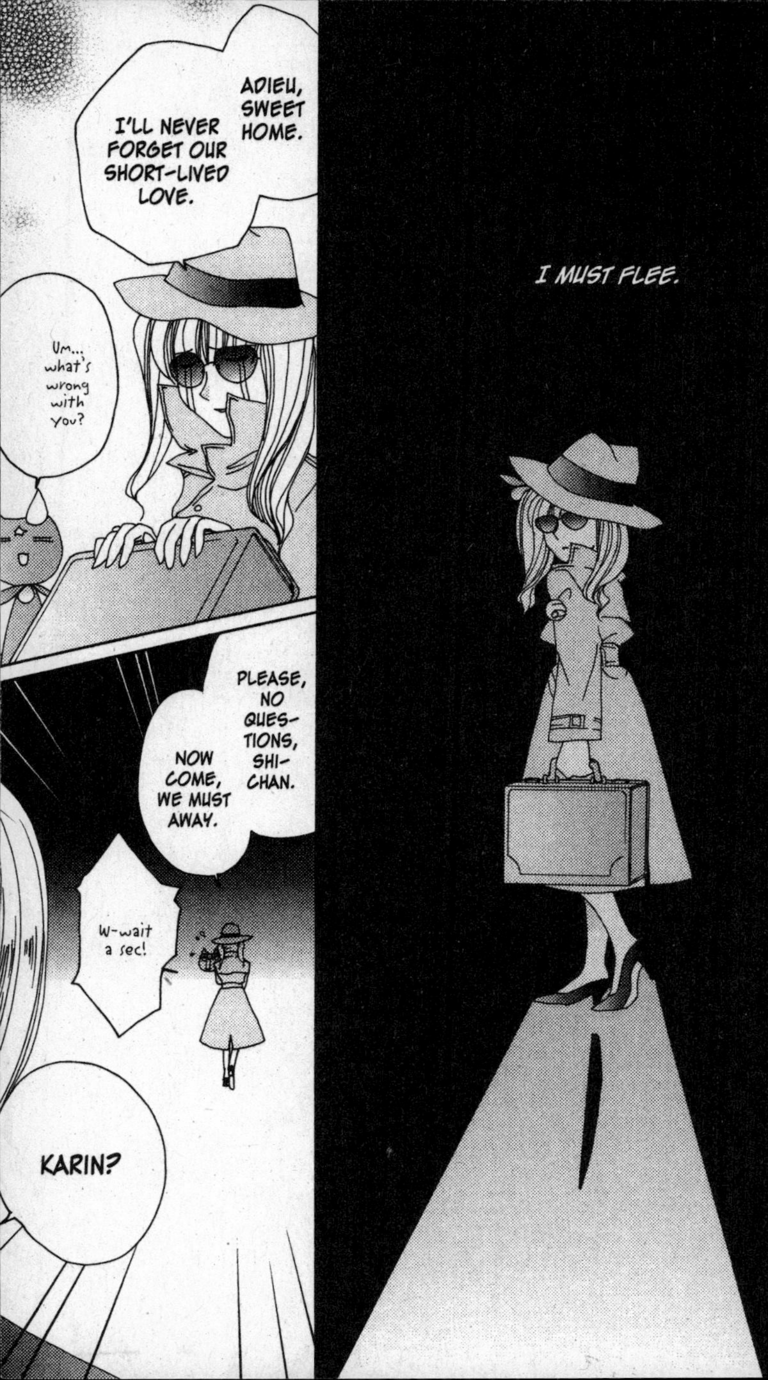
I MUST FLEE.
ADIEU, SWEET HOME.
I'LL NEVER FORGET OUR SHORT-LIVED LOVE.
Um... what's wrong with you?
PLEASE, NO QUESTIONS, SHI-CHAN.
NOW COME, WE MUST AWAY.
W-wait a sec!
KARIN?

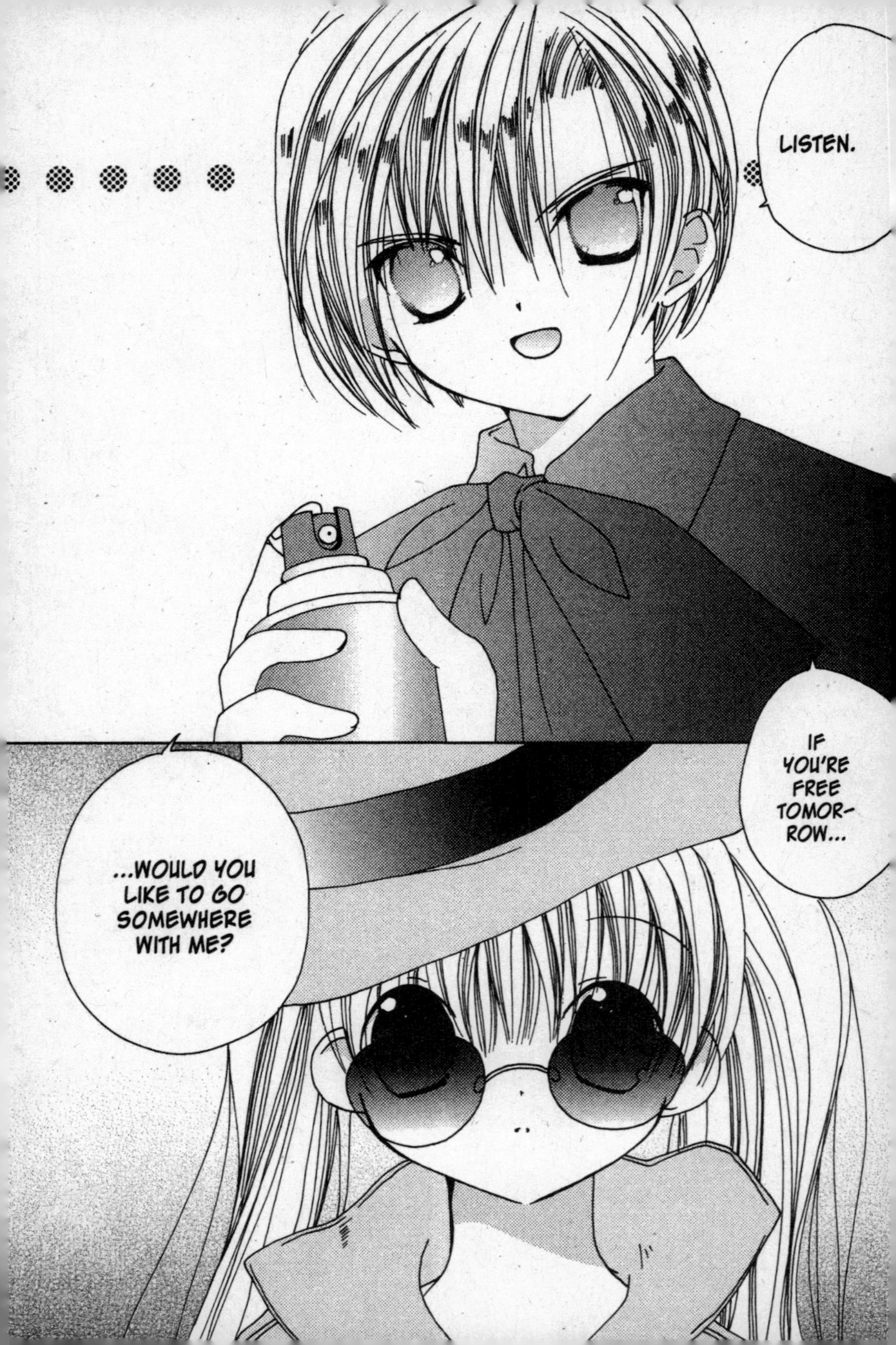
LISTEN.
IF YOU'RE FREE TOMOR-ROW...
...WOULD YOU LIKE TO GO SOMEWHERE WITH ME?

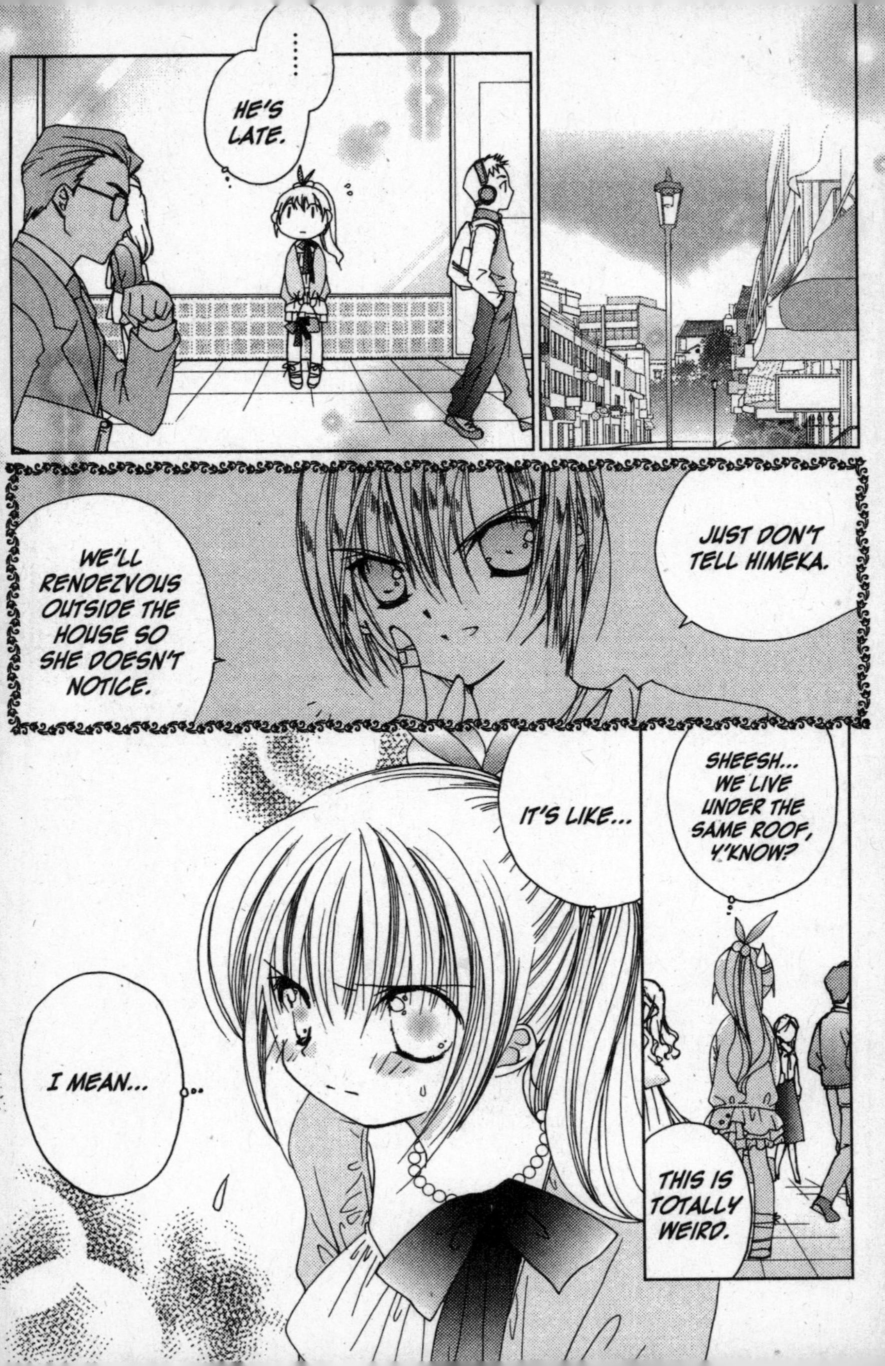
……
HE'S LATE.
JUST DON'T TELL HIMEKA.
WE'LL RENDEZVOUS OUTSIDE THE HOUSE SO SHE DOESN'T NOTICE.
SHEESH... WE LIVE UNDER THE SAME ROOF, Y'KNOW?
THIS IS TOTALLY WEIRD.
IT'S LIKE...
I MEAN...

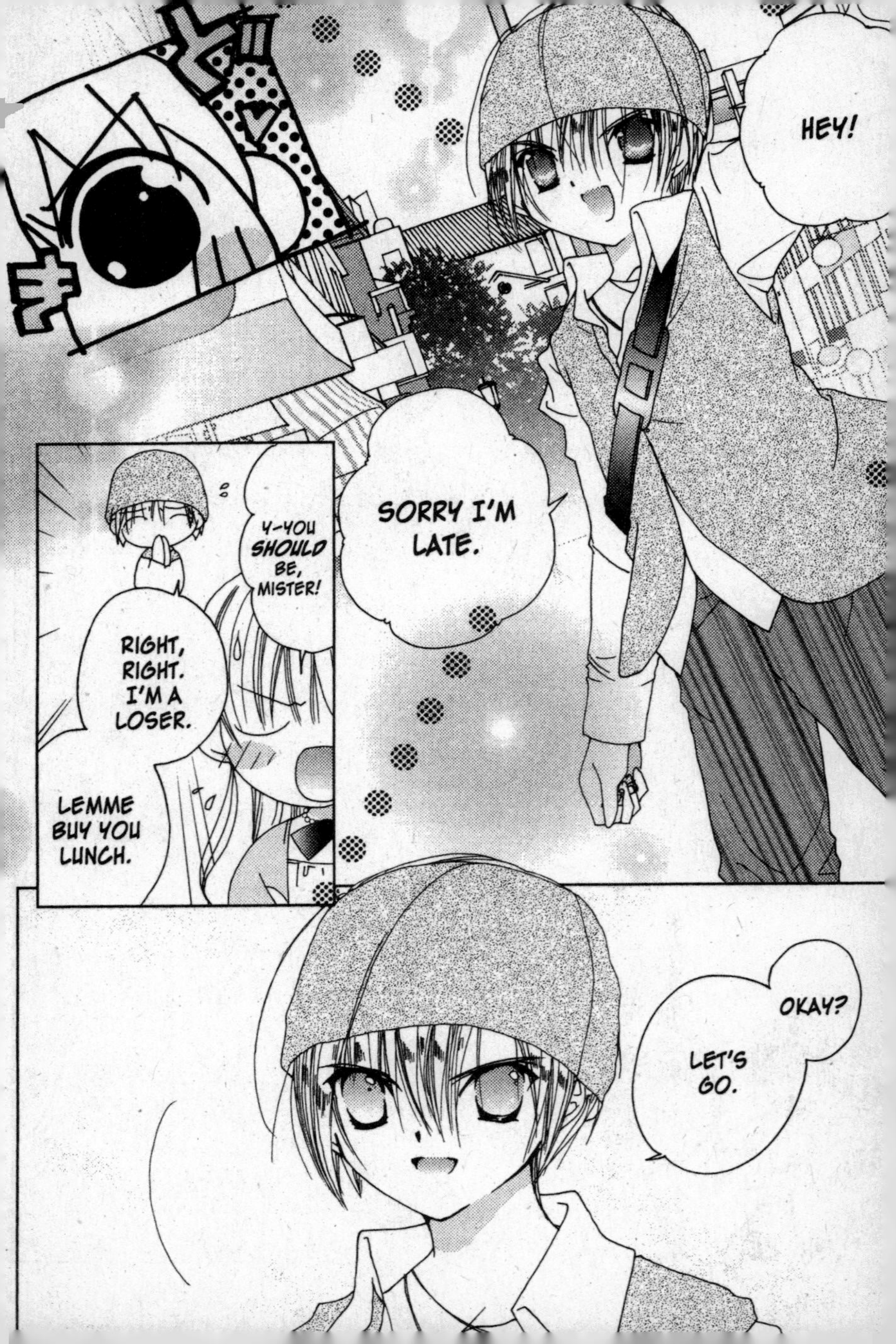
HEY!
SORRY I'M LATE.
Y-YOU SHOULD BE, MISTER!
RIGHT, RIGHT. I'M A LOSER.
LEMME BUY YOU LUNCH.
LET'S GO. OKAY?

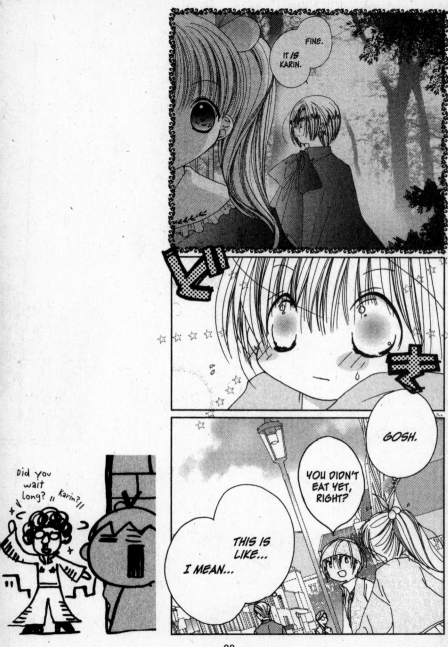

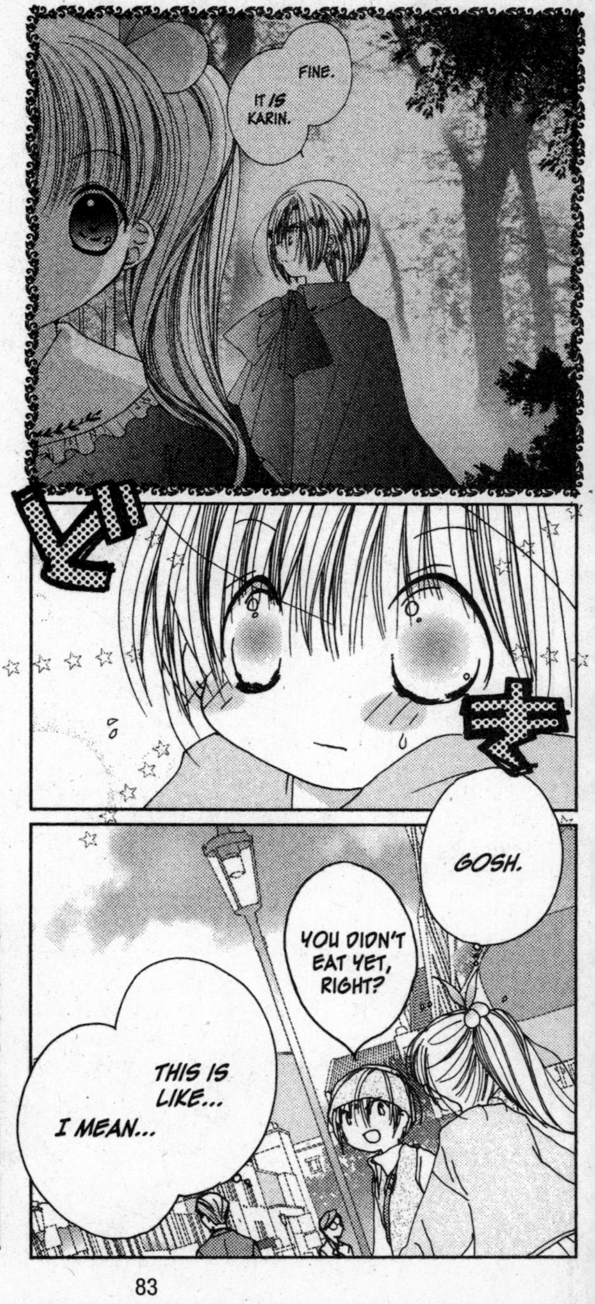
FINE.
IT IS KARIN.
GOSH.
YOU DIDN'T EAT YET, RIGHT?
THIS IS LIKE...
I MEAN...

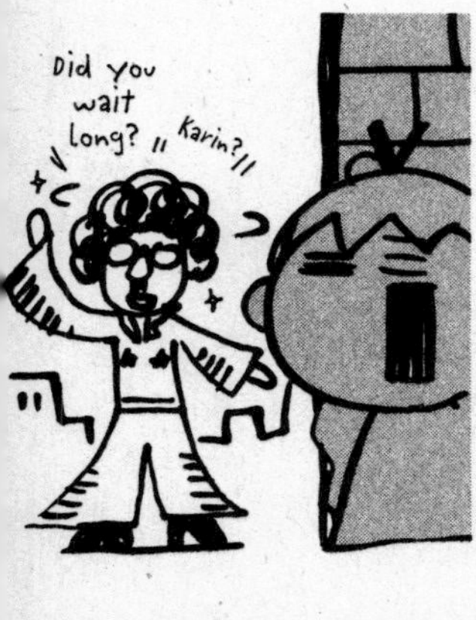
Did you wait long?
Karin?

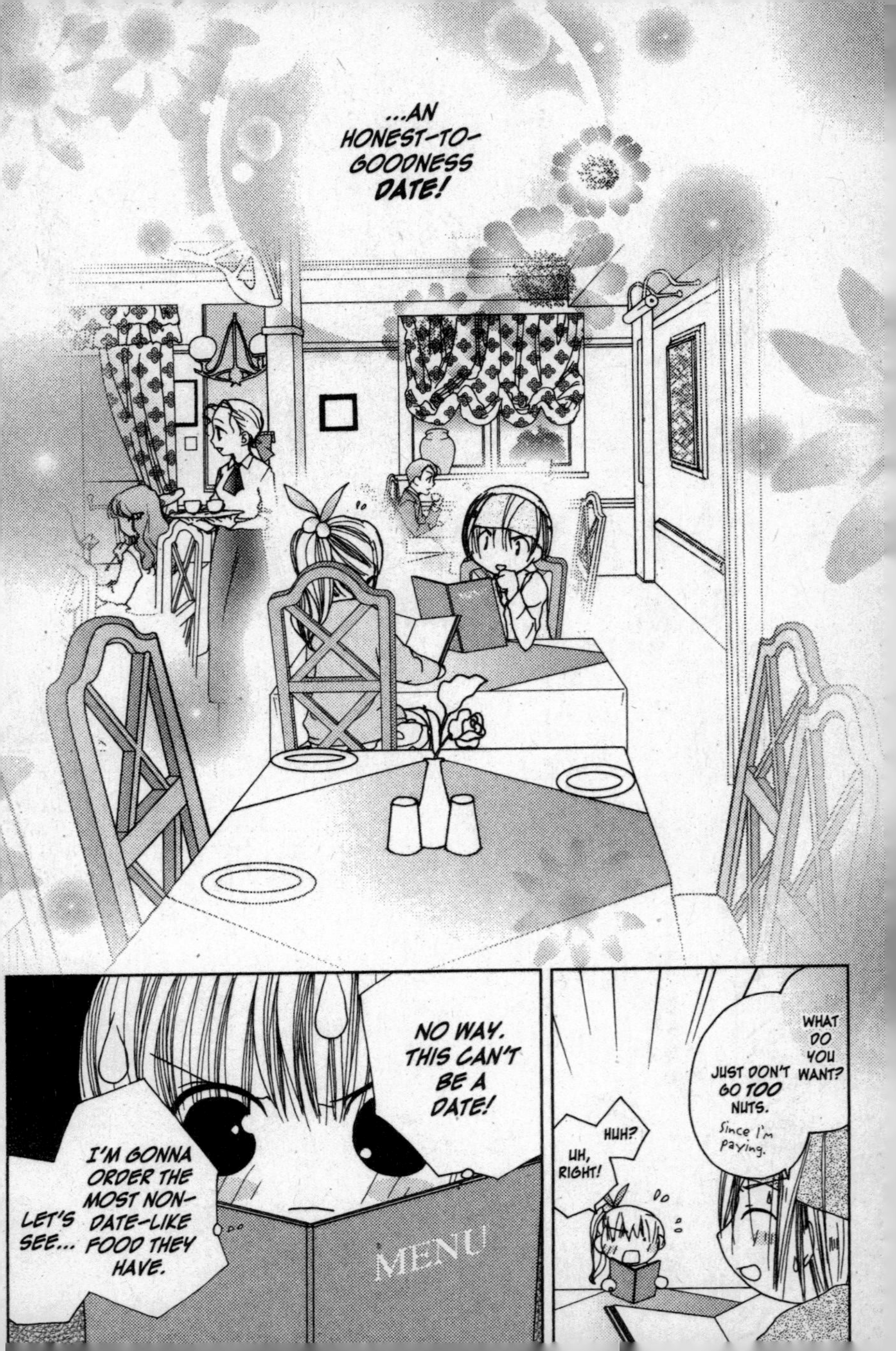
...AN HONEST-TO-GOODNESS DATE!
WHAT DO YOU WANT?
JUST DON'T GO TOO NUTS.
Since I'm paying.
HUH?
UH, RIGHT!
NO WAY. THIS CAN'T BE A DATE!
I'M GONNA ORDER THE MOST NON-DATE-LIKE FOOD THEY HAVE.
LET'S SEE...
MENU

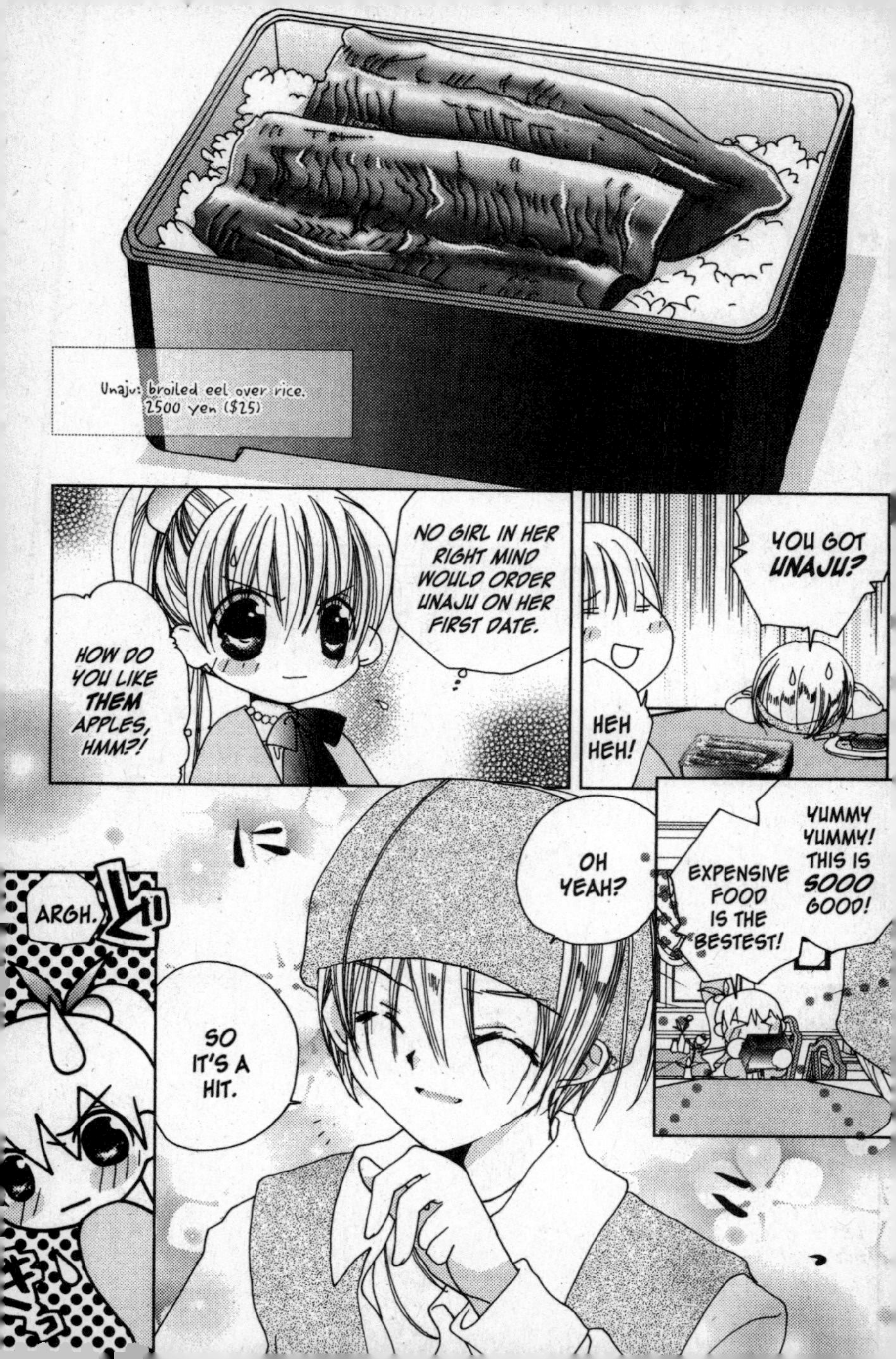
Unaju: broiled eel over rice.
2500 yen ($25)
YOU GOT UNAJU?
HEH HEH!
NO GIRL IN HER RIGHT MIND WOULD ORDER UNAJU ON HER FIRST DATE.
HOW DO YOU LIKE THEM APPLES, HMM?!
YUMMY YUMMY! THIS IS SOOO GOOD!
EXPENSIVE FOOD IS THE BESTEST!
OH YEAH?
SO IT'S A HIT.
ARGH.

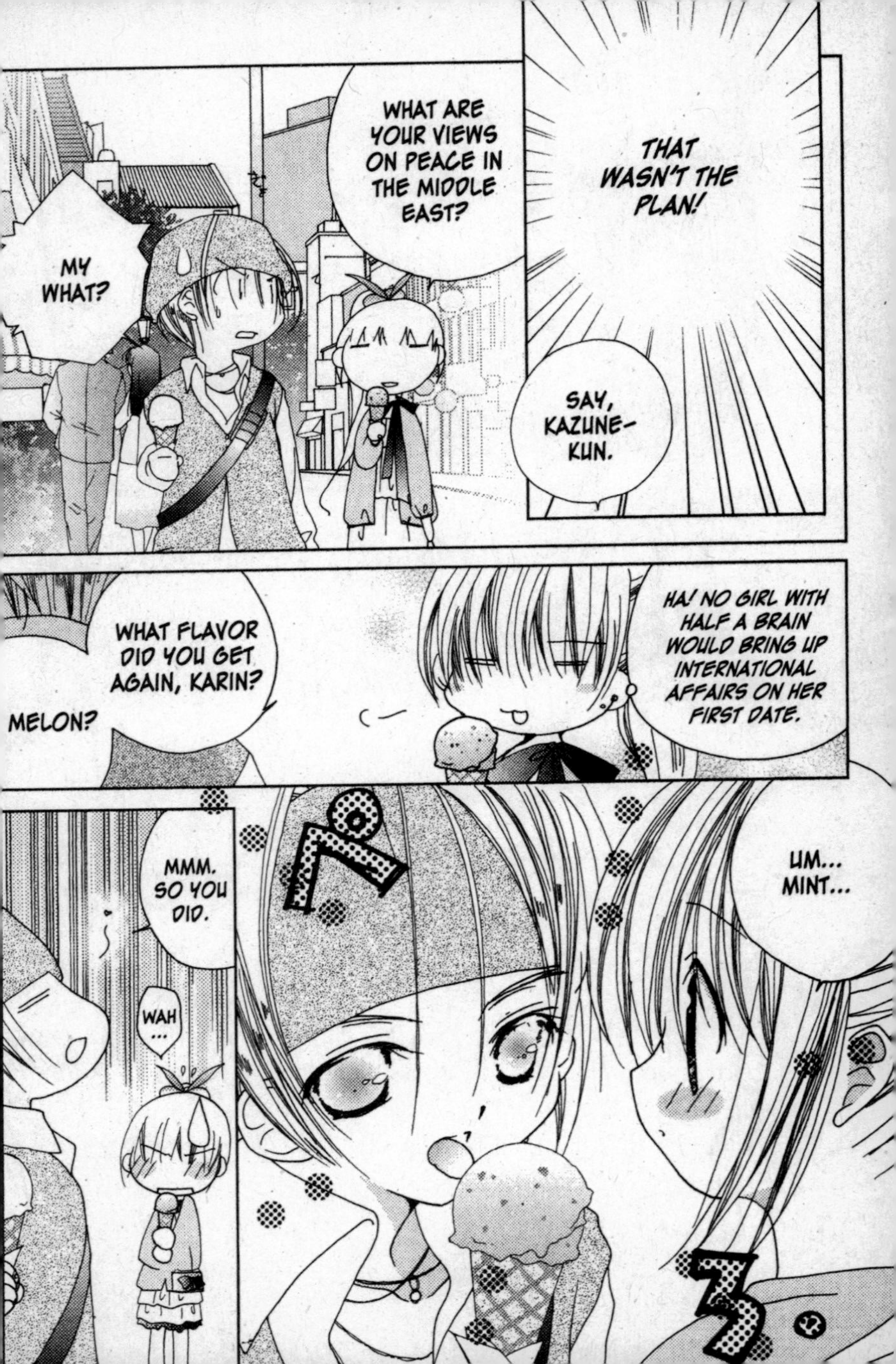
THAT WASN'T THE PLAN!
SAY, KAZUNE-KUN.
WHAT ARE YOUR VIEWS ON PEACE IN THE MIDDLE EAST?
MY WHAT?
HA! NO GIRL WITH HALF A BRAIN WOULD BRING UP INTERNATIONAL AFFAIRS ON HER FIRST DATE.
WHAT FLAVOR DID YOU GET AGAIN, KARIN?
MELON?
UM... MINT...
MMM. SO YOU DID.
WAH...

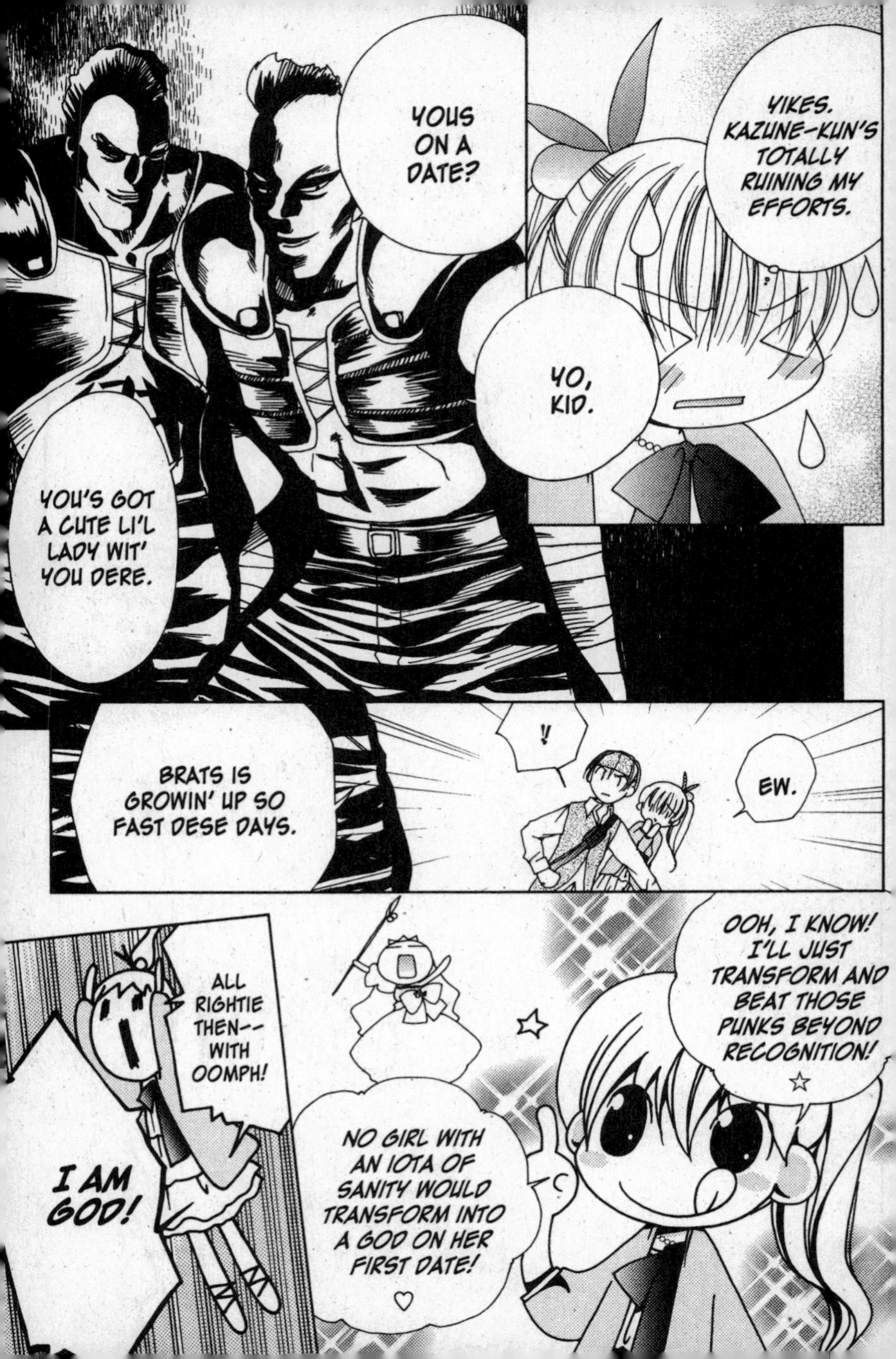
YIKES. KAZUNE-KUN'S TOTALLY RUINING MY EFFORTS.
YO, KID.
YOUS ON A DATE?
YOU'S GOT A CUTE LI'L LADY WIT' YOU DERE.
EW.
!
BRATS IS GROWIN' UP SO FAST DESE DAYS.
OOH, I KNOW! I'LL JUST TRANSFORM AND BEAT THOSE PUNKS BEYOND RECOGNITION!
NO GIRL WITH AN IOTA OF SANITY WOULD TRANSFORM INTO A GOD ON HER FIRST DATE!
ALL RIGHTIE THEN--WITH OOMPH!
I AM GOD!

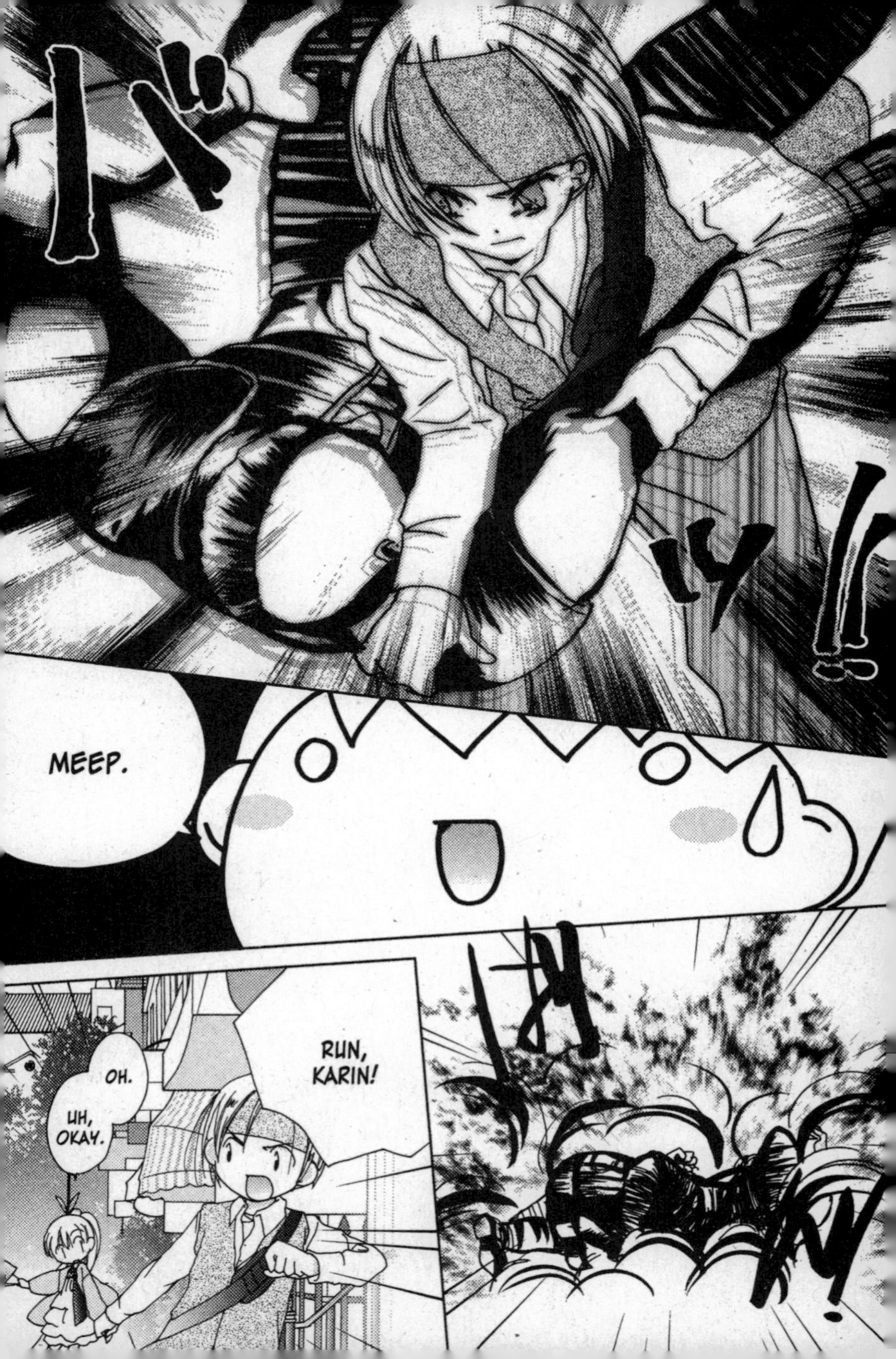
MEEP.
RUN, KARIN!
OH.
UH, OKAY.

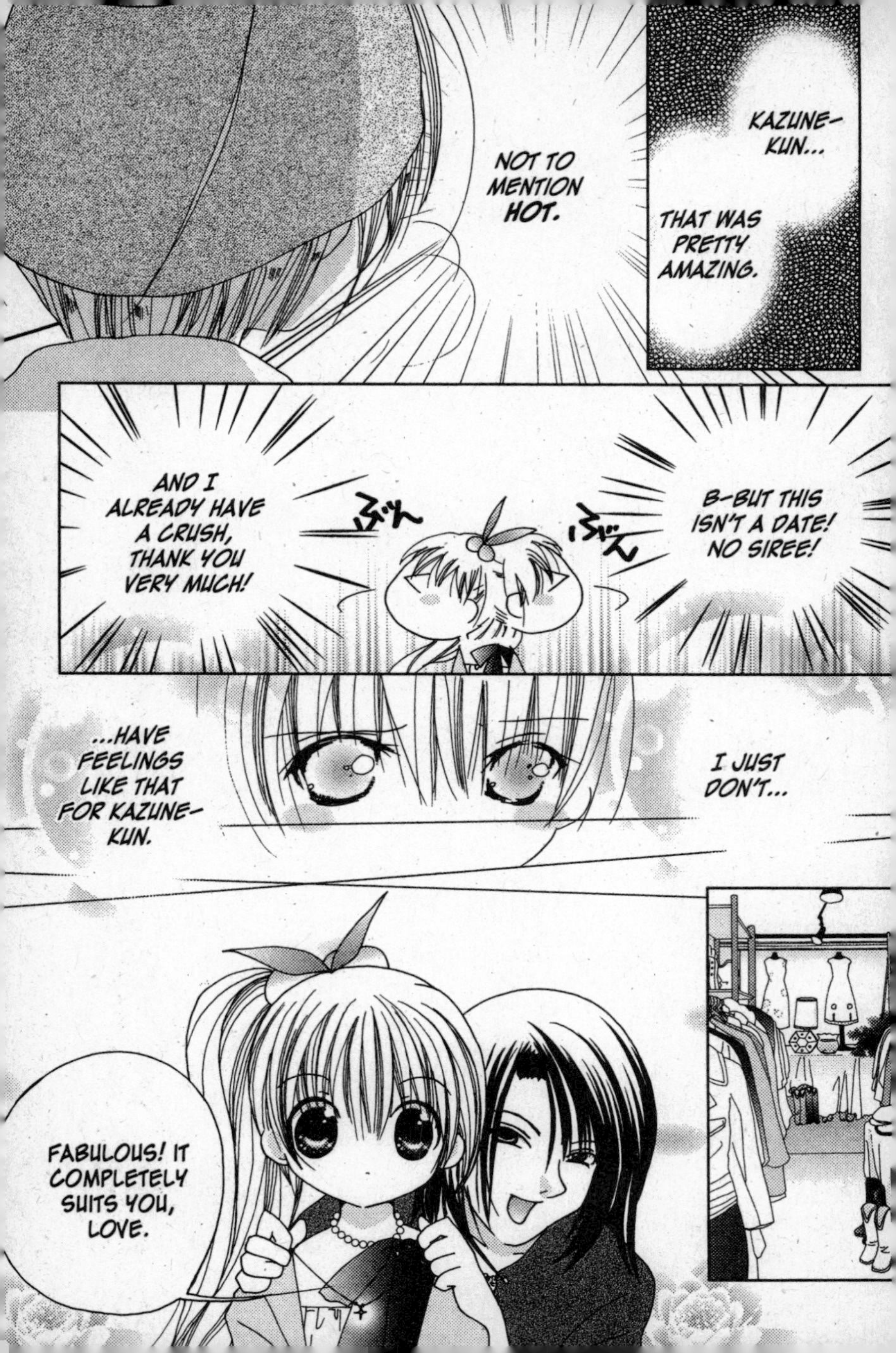
KAZUNE-KUN...
THAT WAS PRETTY AMAZING.
NOT TO MENTION HOT.
B-BUT THIS ISN'T A DATE! NO SIREE!
ぶん
ぶん
AND I ALREADY HAVE A CRUSH, THANK YOU VERY MUCH!
I JUST DON'T...
...HAVE FEELINGS LIKE THAT FOR KAZUNE-KUN.
FABULOUS! IT COMPLETELY SUITS YOU, LOVE.

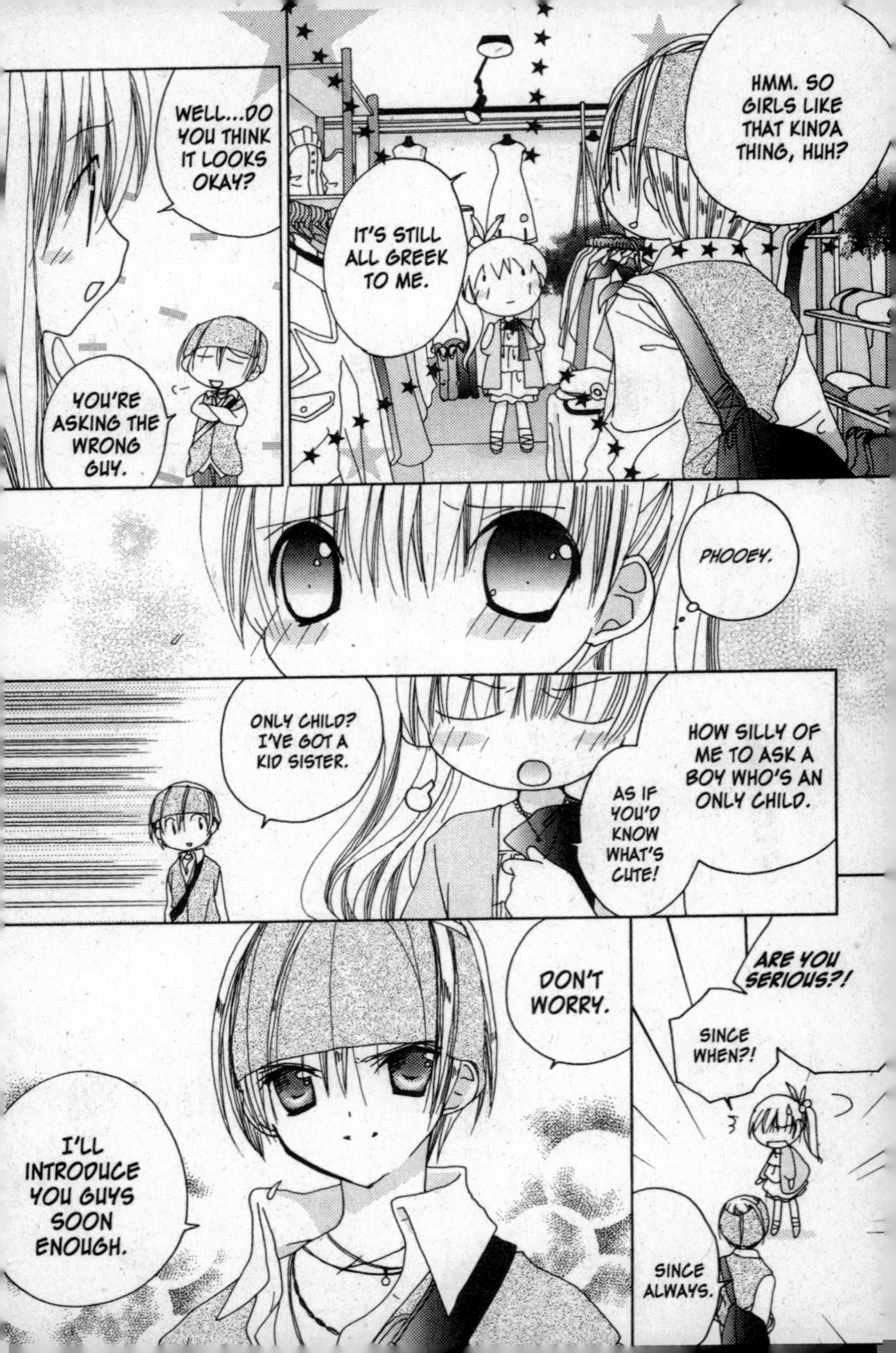
HMM. SO GIRLS LIKE THAT KINDA THING, HUH?
IT'S STILL ALL GREEK TO ME.
WELL...DO YOU THINK IT LOOKS OKAY?
YOU'RE ASKING THE WRONG GUY.
PHOOEY.
HOW SILLY OF ME TO ASK A BOY WHO'S AN ONLY CHILD.
AS IF YOU'D KNOW WHAT'S CUTE!
ONLY CHILD? I'VE GOT A KID SISTER.
ARE YOU SERIOUS?!
SINCE WHEN?!
SINCE ALWAYS.
DON'T WORRY.
I'LL INTRODUCE YOU GUYS SOON ENOUGH.

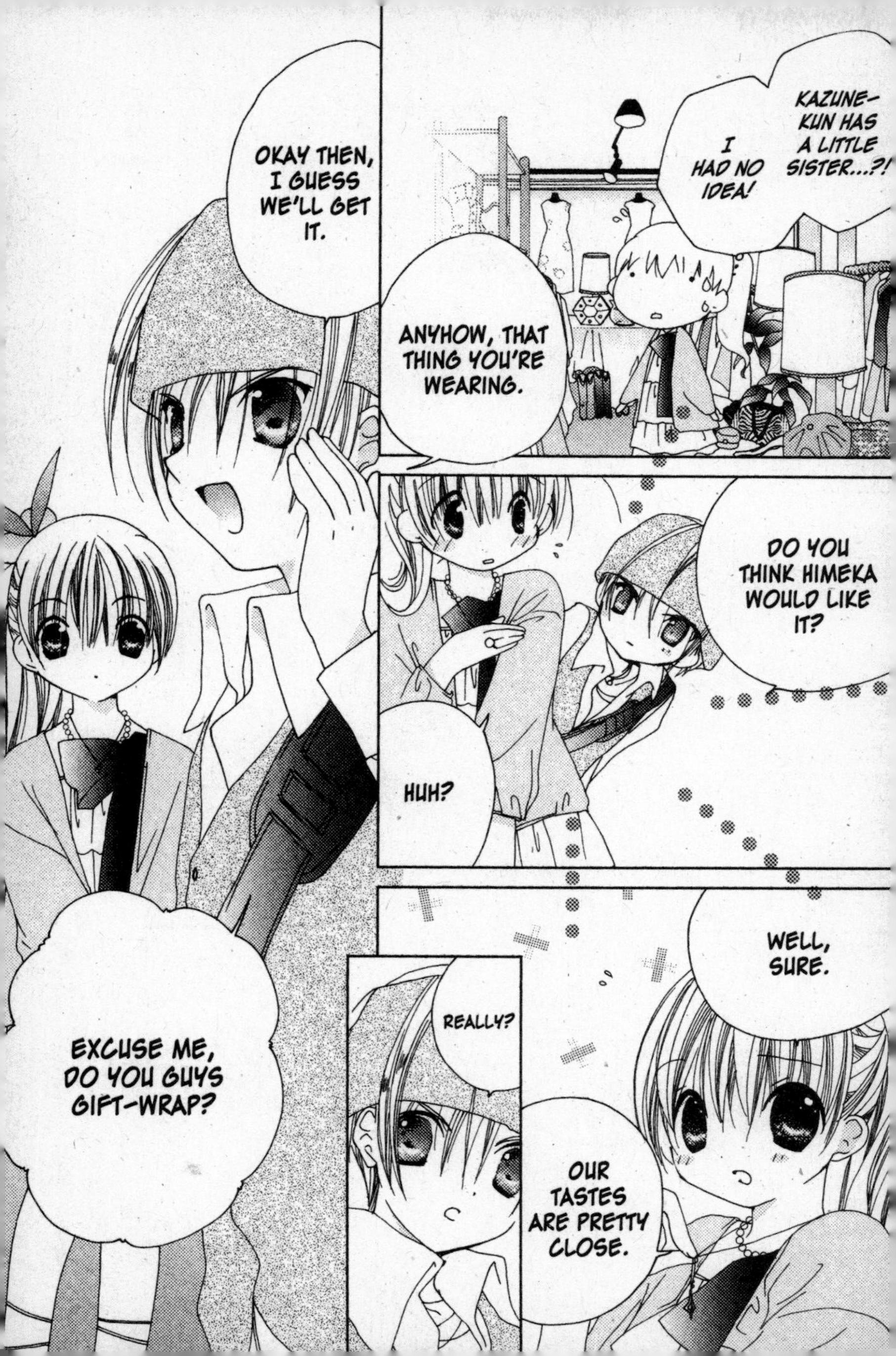
KAZUNE-KUN HAS A LITTLE SISTER...?!
I HAD NO IDEA!
ANYHOW, THAT THING YOU'RE WEARING.
DO YOU THINK HIMEKA WOULD LIKE IT?
HUH?
WELL, SURE.
REALLY?
OUR TASTES ARE PRETTY CLOSE.
OKAY THEN, I GUESS WE'LL GET IT.
EXCUSE ME, DO YOU GUYS GIFT-WRAP?

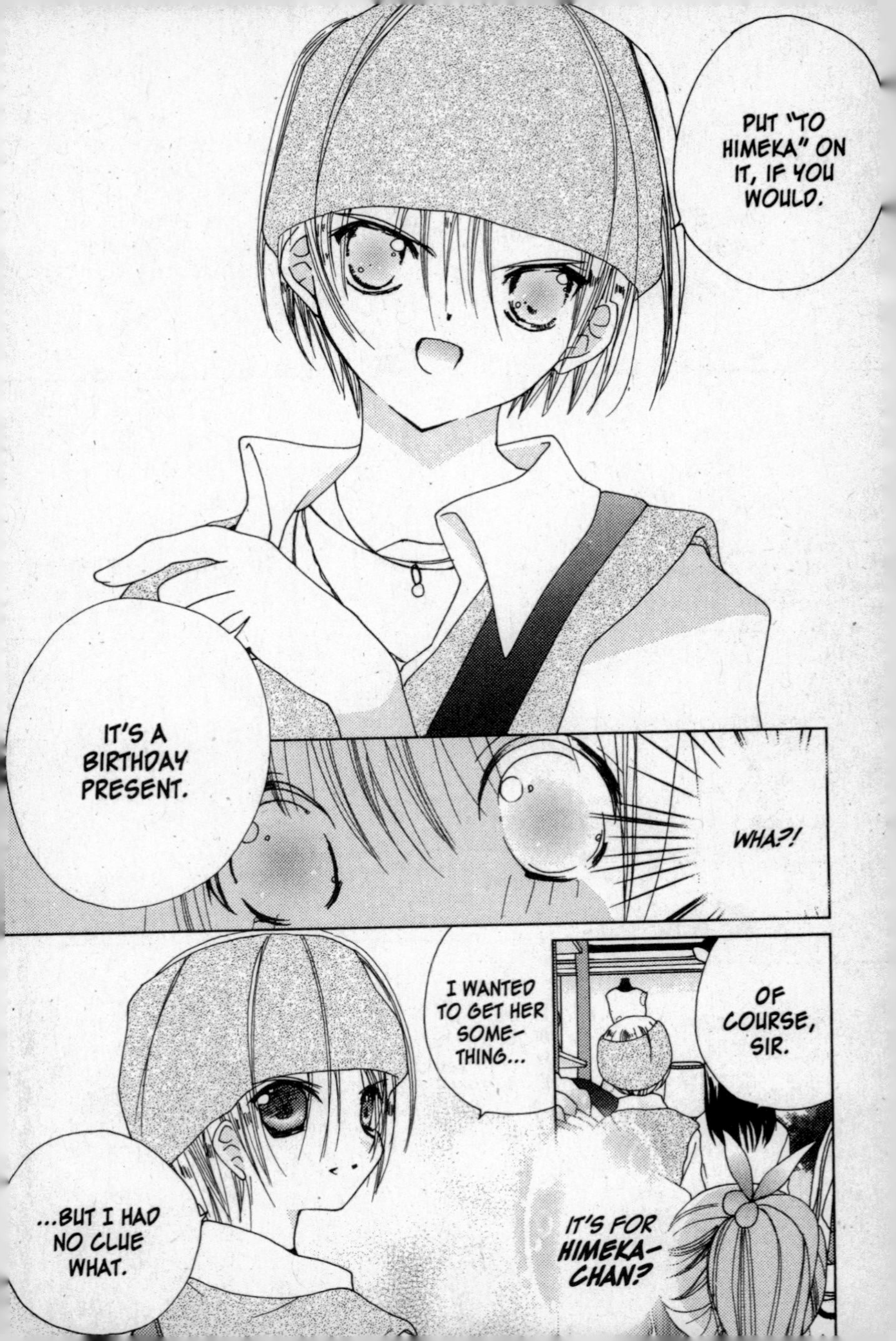
PUT "TO HIMEKA" ON IT, IF YOU WOULD.
IT'S A BIRTHDAY PRESENT.
WHA?!
OF COURSE, SIR.
IT'S FOR HIMEKA-CHAN?
I WANTED TO GET HER SOME-THING...
...BUT I HAD NO CLUE WHAT.

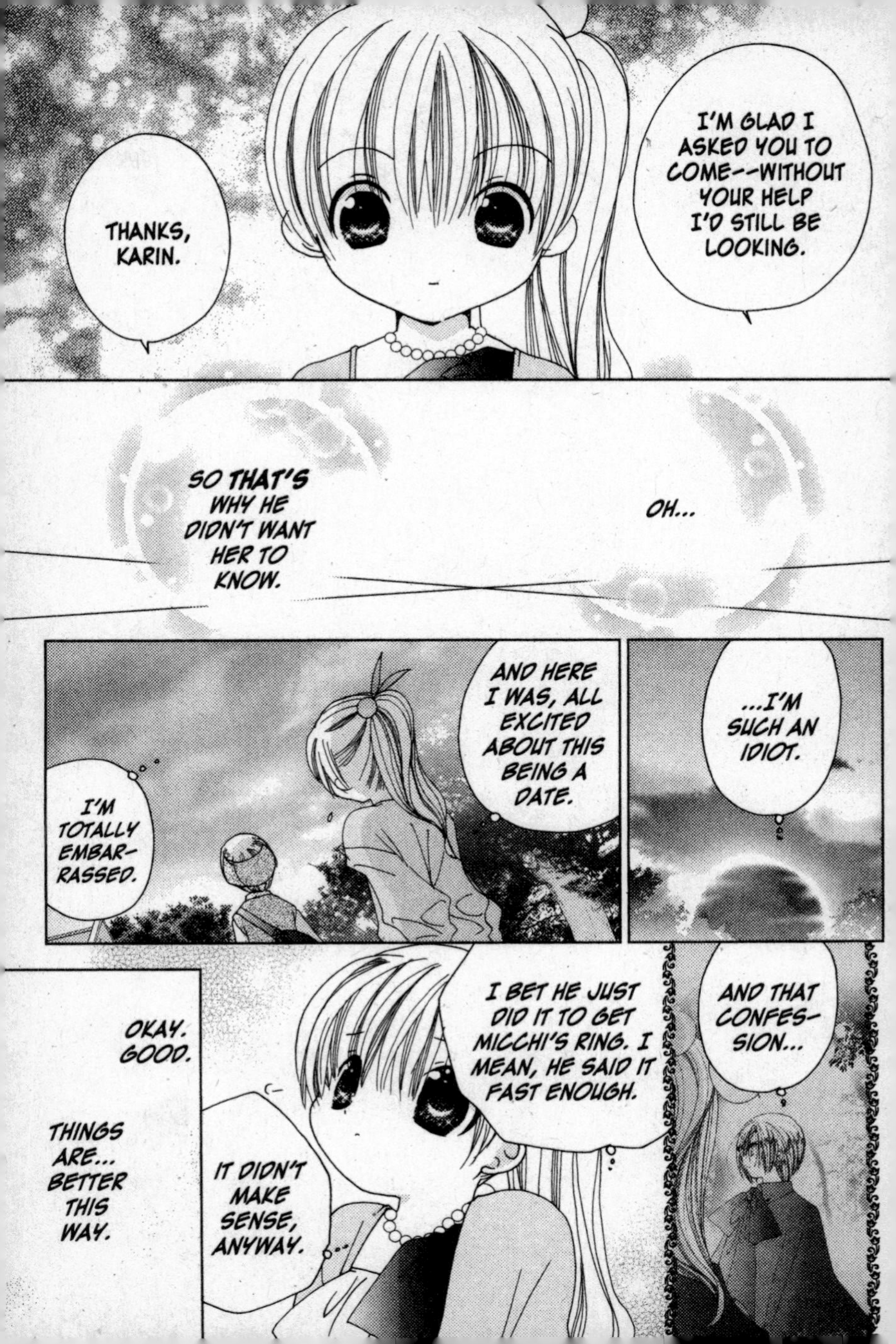
I'M GLAD I ASKED YOU TO COME--WITHOUT YOUR HELP I'D STILL BE LOOKING.
THANKS, KARIN.
OH...
SO THAT'S WHY HE DIDN'T WANT HER TO KNOW.
...I'M SUCH AN IDIOT.
AND HERE I WAS, ALL EXCITED ABOUT THIS BEING A DATE.
I'M TOTALLY EMBAR-RASSED.
AND THAT CONFES-SION...
I BET HE JUST DID IT TO GET MICCHI'S RING. I MEAN, HE SAID IT FAST ENOUGH.
IT DIDN'T MAKE SENSE, ANYWAY.
OKAY. GOOD.
THINGS ARE... BETTER THIS WAY.

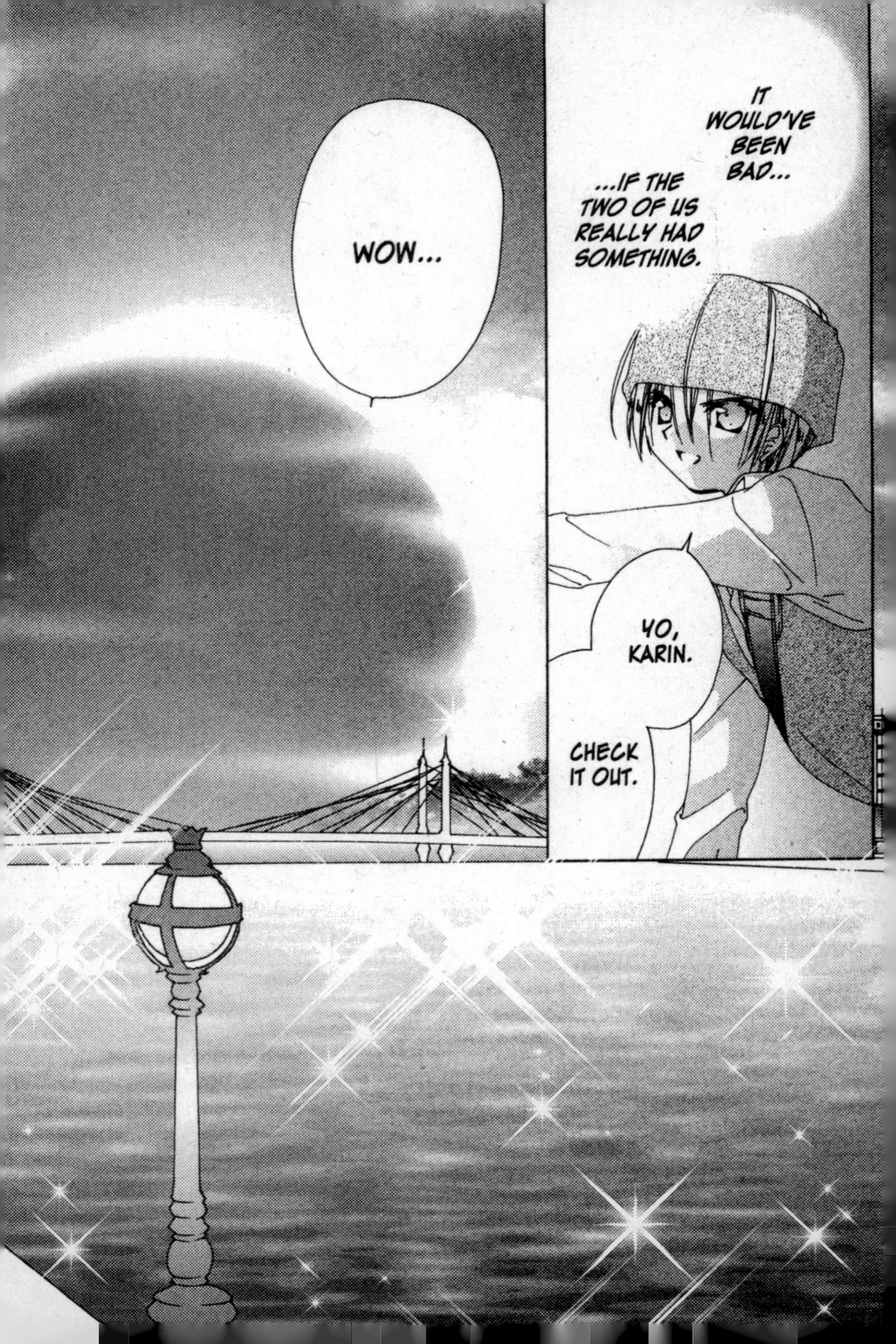
IT WOULD'VE BEEN BAD...
...IF THE TWO OF US REALLY HAD SOMETHING.
YO, KARIN.
CHECK IT OUT.
WOW...

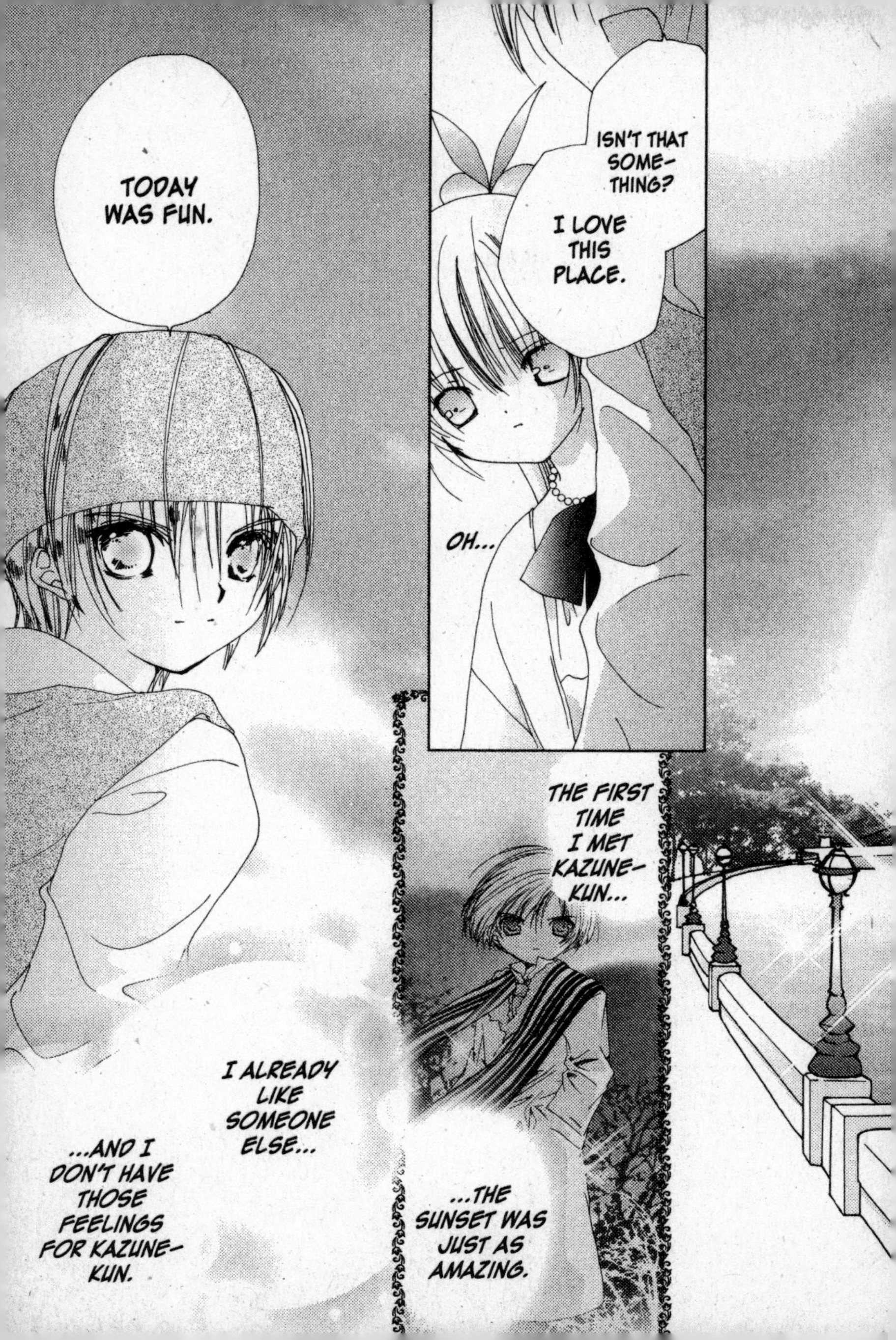
ISN'T THAT SOMETHING?
I LOVE THIS PLACE.
OH...
THE FIRST TIME I MET KAZUNE-KUN...
...THE SUNSET WAS JUST AS AMAZING.
TODAY WAS FUN.
I ALREADY LIKE SOMEONE ELSE...
...AND I DON'T HAVE THOSE FEELINGS FOR KAZUNE-KUN.

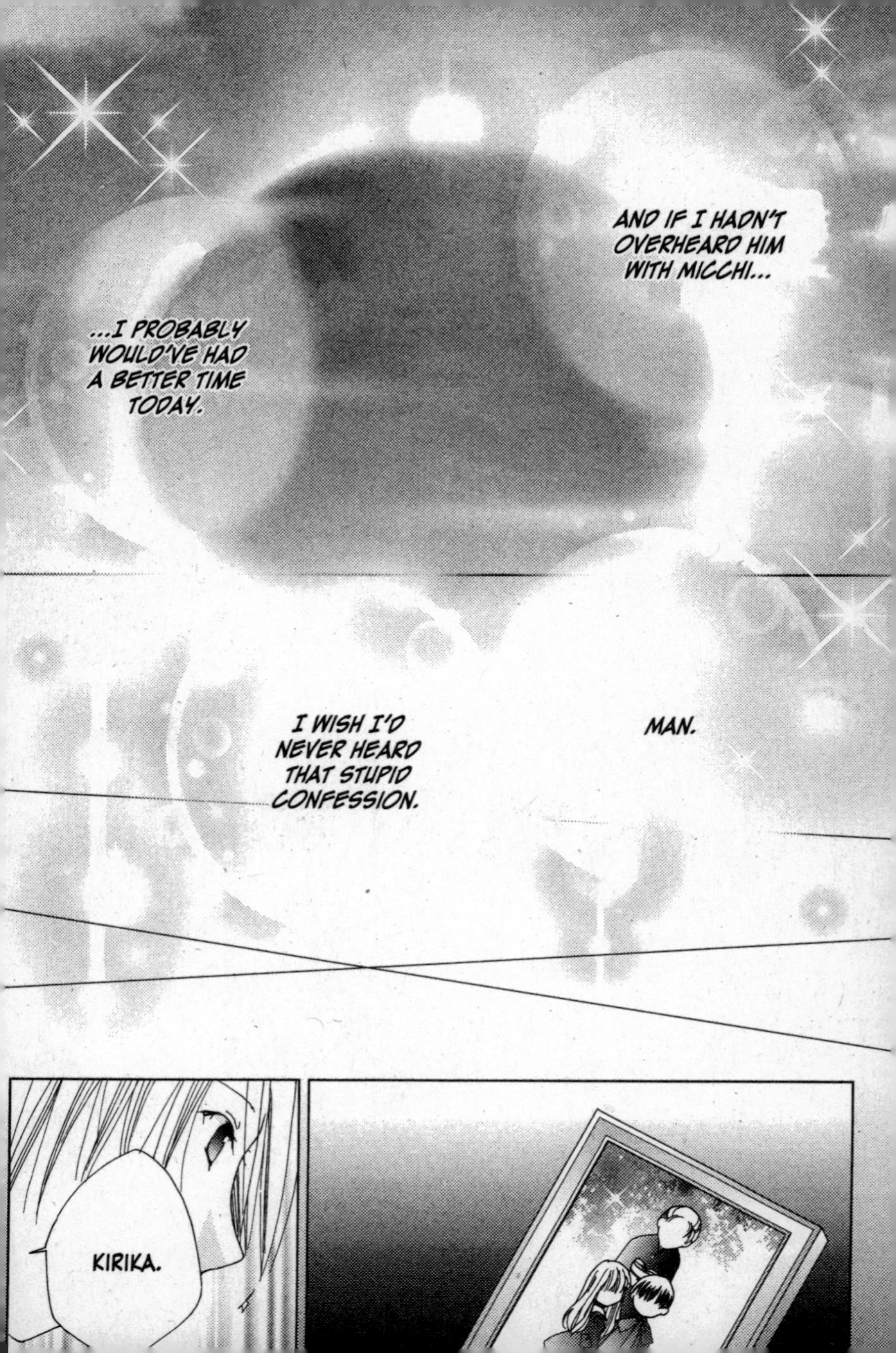
AND IF I HADN'T OVERHEARD HIM WITH MICCHI...
...I PROBABLY WOULD'VE HAD A BETTER TIME TODAY.
MAN.
I WISH I'D NEVER HEARD THAT STUPID CONFESSION.
KIRIKA.

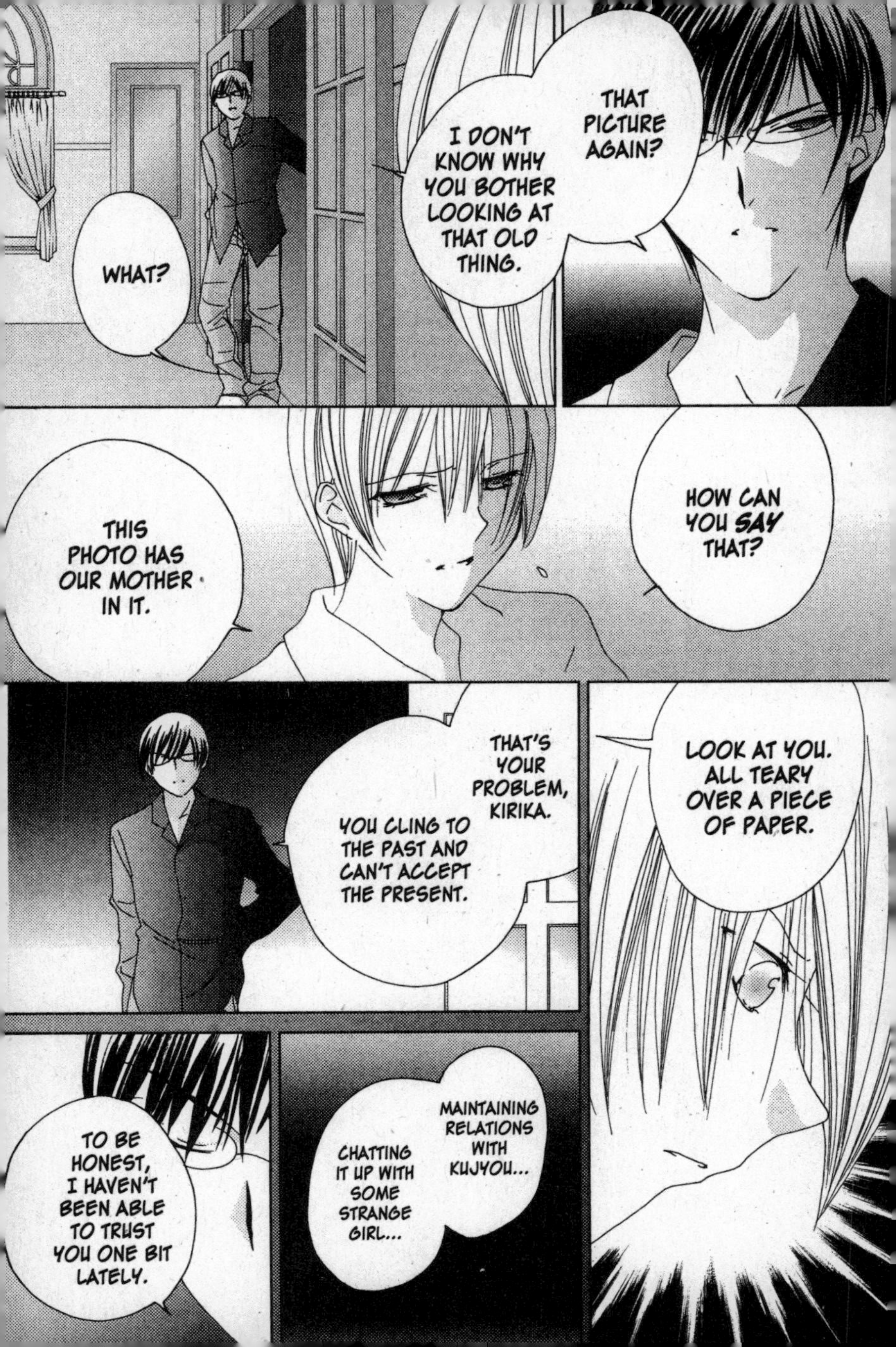
THAT PICTURE AGAIN?
I DON'T KNOW WHY YOU BOTHER LOOKING AT THAT OLD THING.
WHAT?
HOW CAN YOU *SAY* THAT?
THIS PHOTO HAS OUR MOTHER IN IT.
LOOK AT YOU. ALL TEARY OVER A PIECE OF PAPER.
THAT'S YOUR PROBLEM, KIRIKA.
YOU CLING TO THE PAST AND CAN'T ACCEPT THE PRESENT.
MAINTAINING RELATIONS WITH KUJYOU...
CHATTING IT UP WITH SOME STRANGE GIRL...
TO BE HONEST, I HAVEN'T BEEN ABLE TO TRUST YOU ONE BIT LATELY.

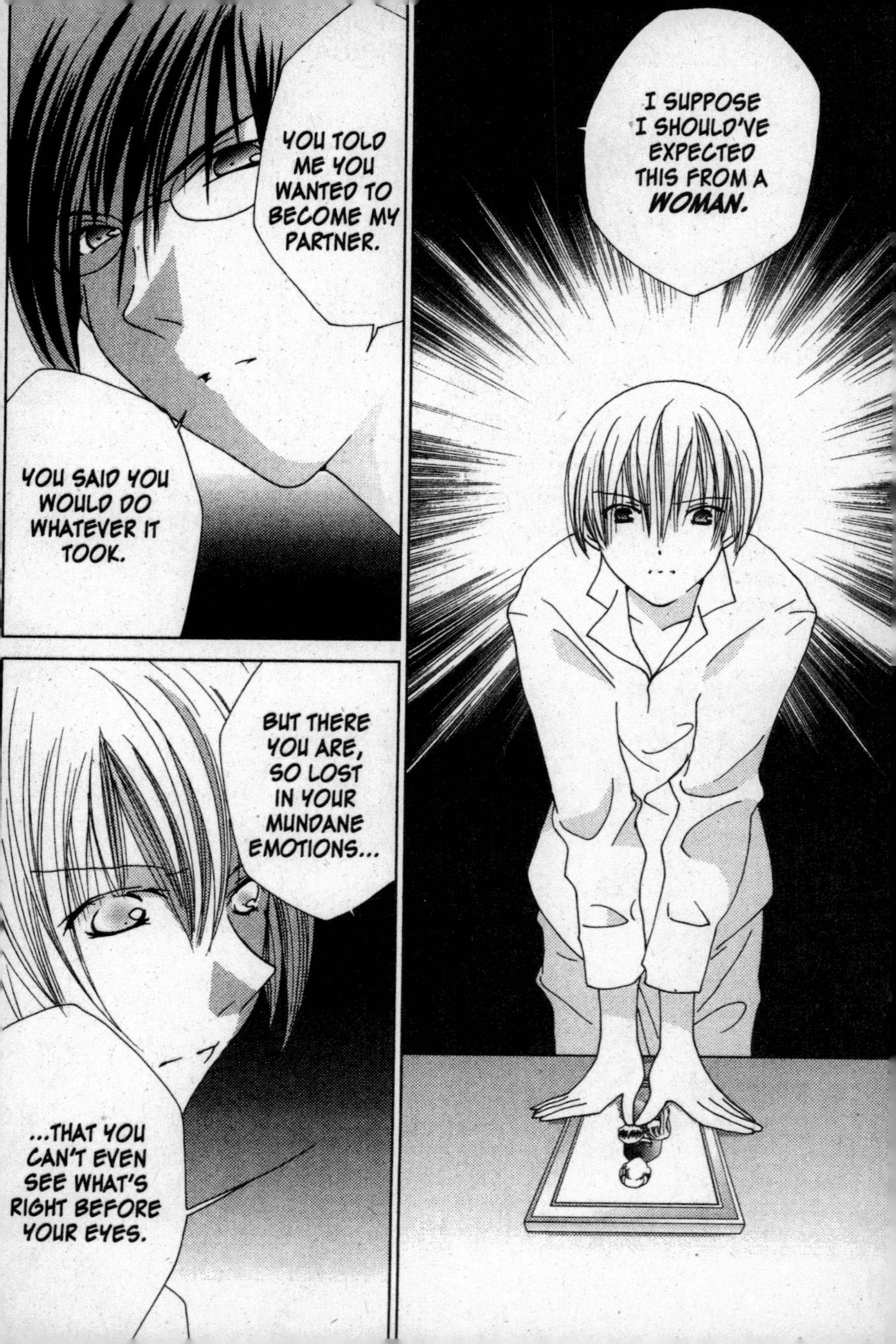
I SUPPOSE I SHOULD'VE EXPECTED THIS FROM A **WOMAN.**
YOU TOLD ME YOU WANTED TO BECOME MY PARTNER.
YOU SAID YOU WOULD DO WHATEVER IT TOOK.
BUT THERE YOU ARE, SO LOST IN YOUR MUNDANE EMOTIONS...
...THAT YOU CAN'T EVEN SEE WHAT'S RIGHT BEFORE YOUR EYES.

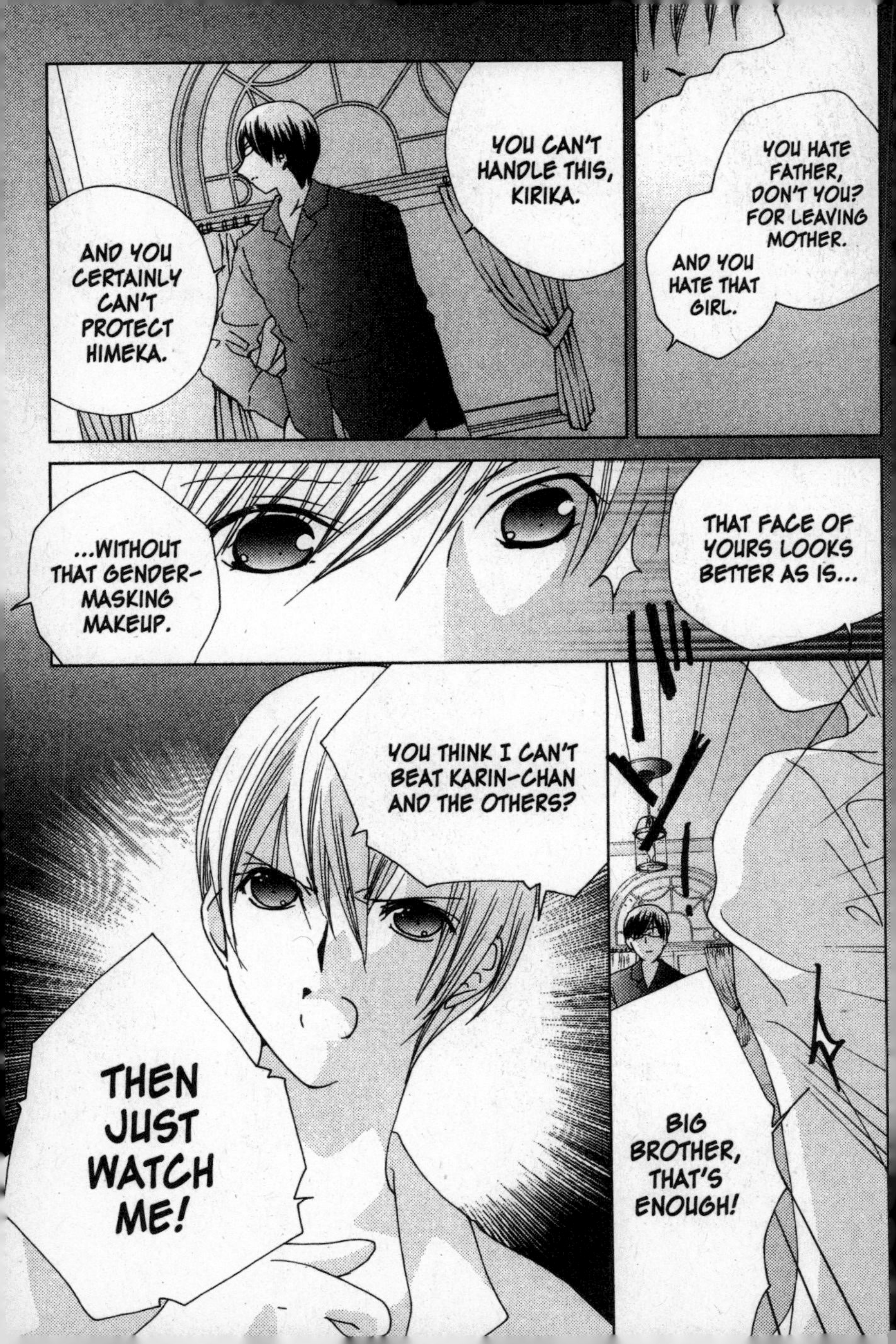
YOU HATE FATHER, DON'T YOU? FOR LEAVING MOTHER.
AND YOU HATE THAT GIRL.
YOU CAN'T HANDLE THIS, KIRIKA.
AND YOU CERTAINLY CAN'T PROTECT HIMEKA.
THAT FACE OF YOURS LOOKS BETTER AS IS...
...WITHOUT THAT GENDER-MASKING MAKEUP.
BIG BROTHER, THAT'S ENOUGH!
YOU THINK I CAN'T BEAT KARIN-CHAN AND THE OTHERS?
THEN JUST WATCH ME!

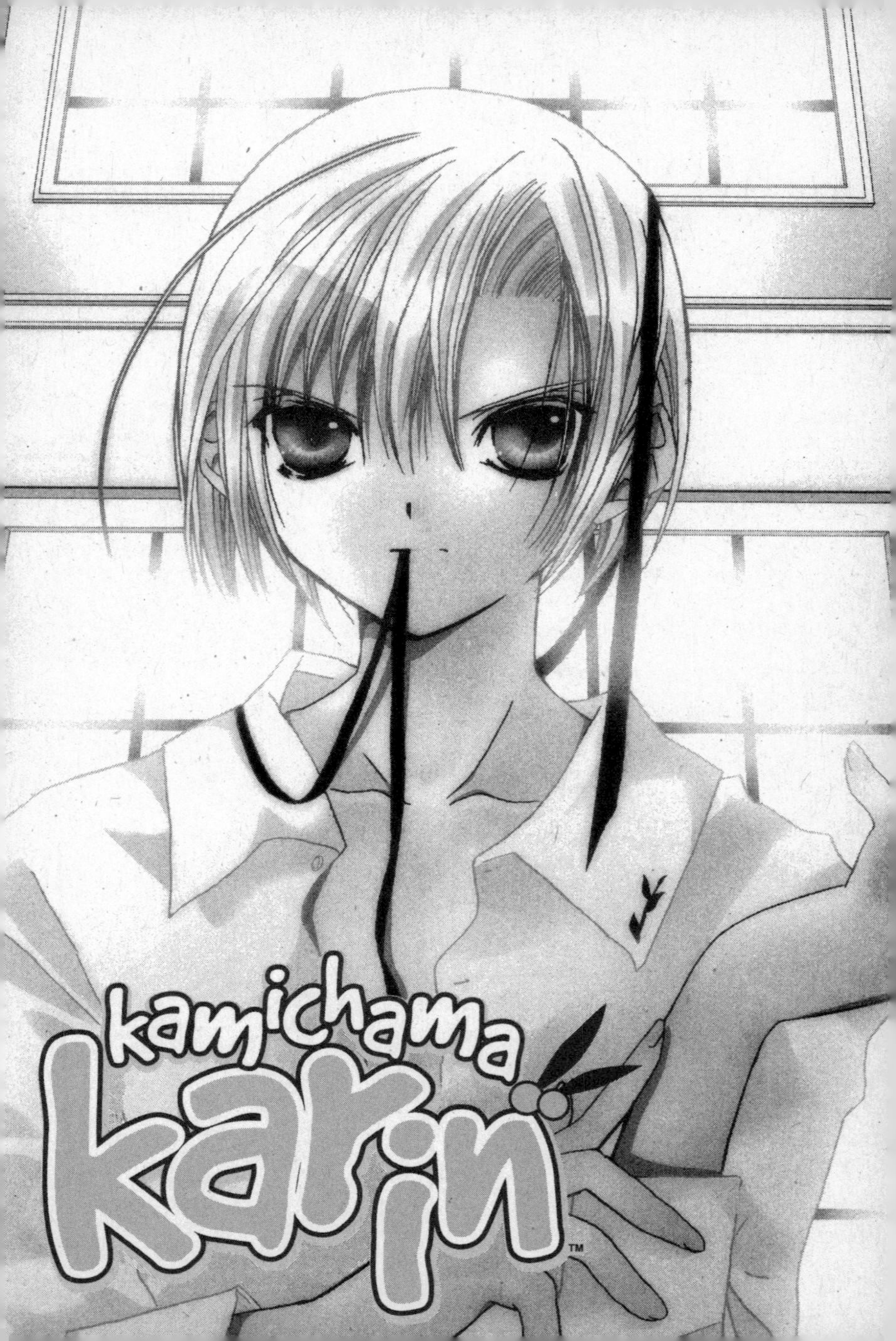
kamichama karin™

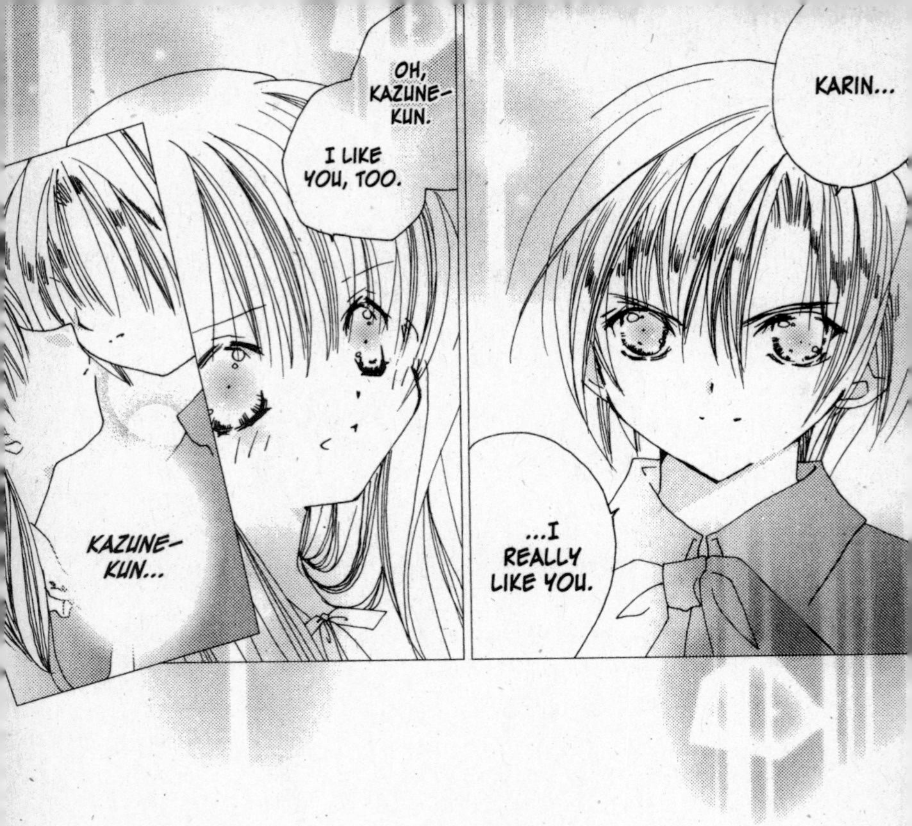
KARIN...
...I REALLY LIKE YOU.
OH, KAZUNE-KUN.
I LIKE YOU, TOO.
KAZUNE-KUN...

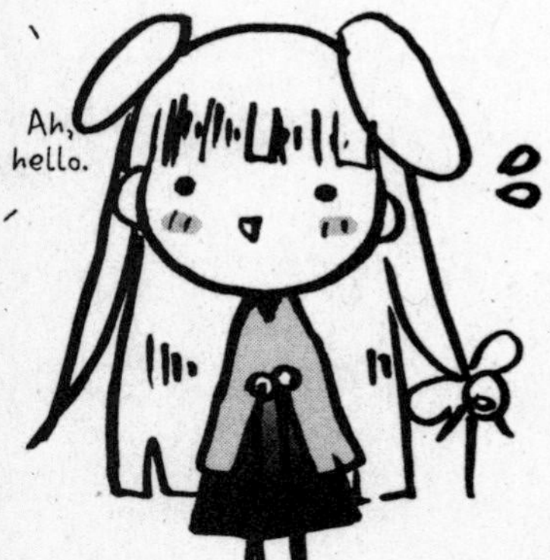
Ah, hello.

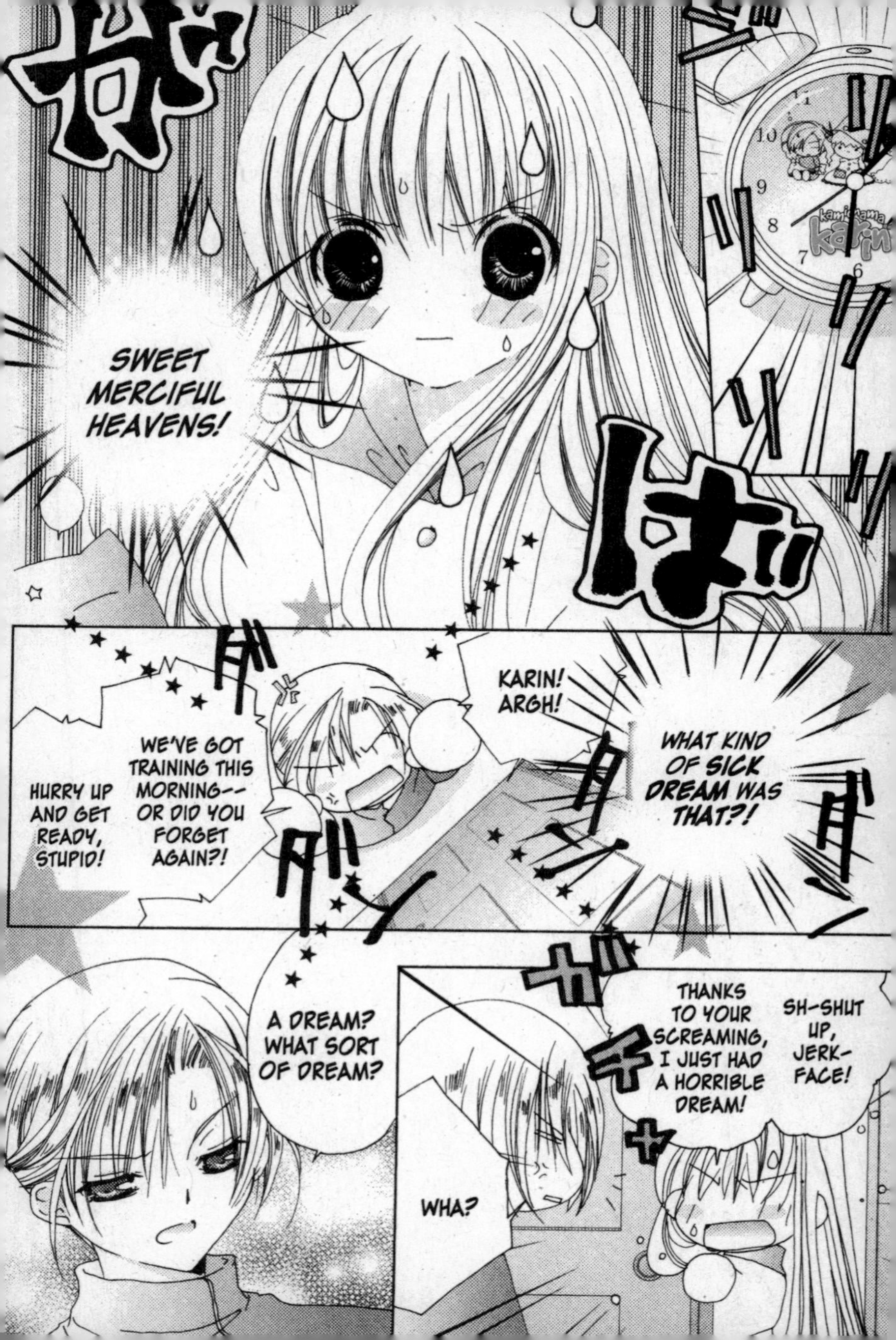
SWEET MERCIFUL HEAVENS!
WHAT KIND OF SICK DREAM WAS THAT?!
KARIN! ARGH!
WE'VE GOT TRAINING THIS MORNING-- OR DID YOU FORGET AGAIN?!
HURRY UP AND GET READY, STUPID!
SH-SHUT UP, JERK-FACE!
THANKS TO YOUR SCREAMING, I JUST HAD A HORRIBLE DREAM!
WHA?
A DREAM? WHAT SORT OF DREAM?

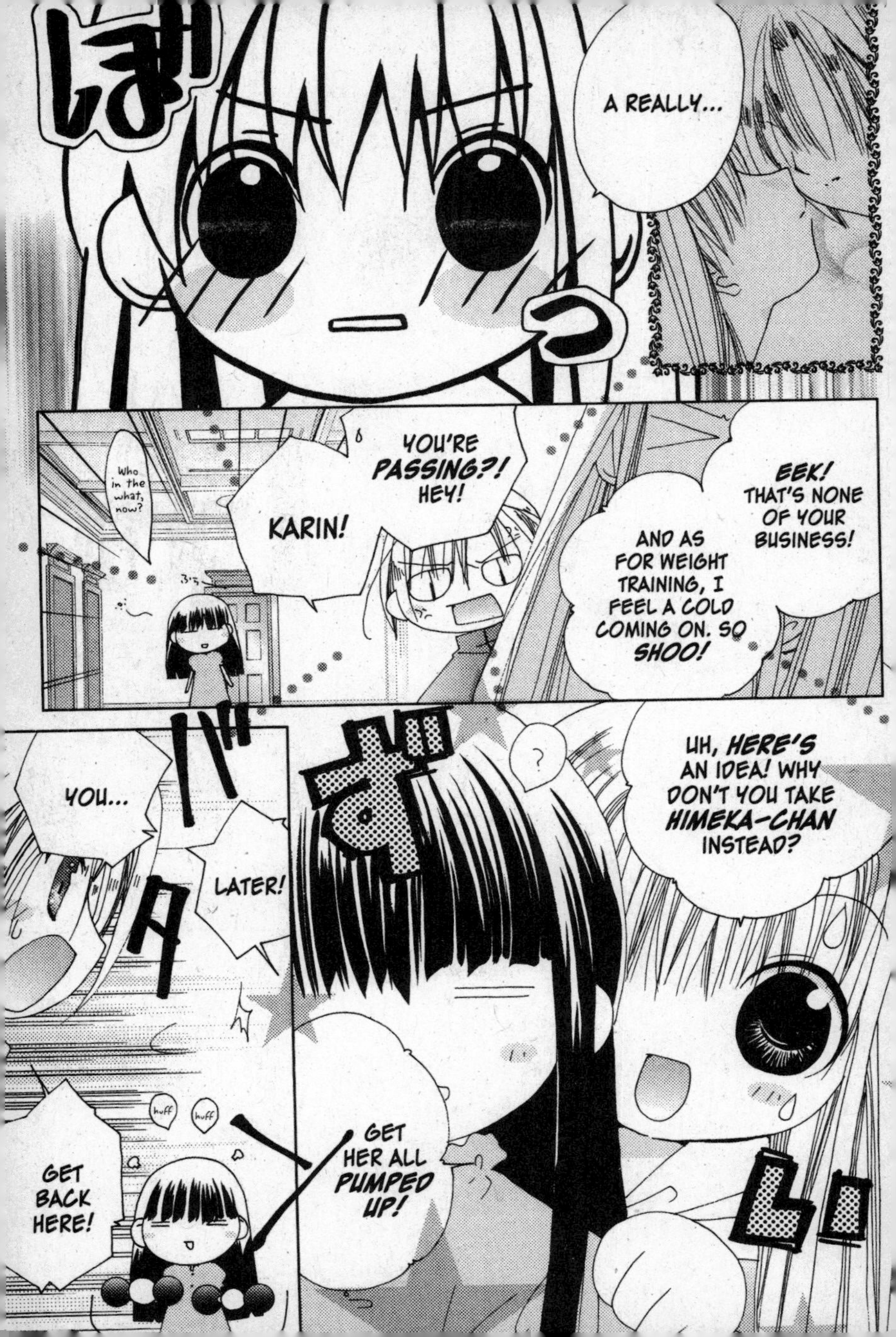

A REALLY...
EEK! THAT'S NONE OF YOUR BUSINESS!
AND AS FOR WEIGHT TRAINING, I FEEL A COLD COMING ON. SO SHOO!
YOU'RE PASSING?! HEY!
KARIN!
Who in the what, now?
UH, HERE'S AN IDEA! WHY DON'T YOU TAKE HIMEKA-CHAN INSTEAD?
?
GET HER ALL PUMPED UP!
YOU...
LATER!
huff
huff
GET BACK HERE!

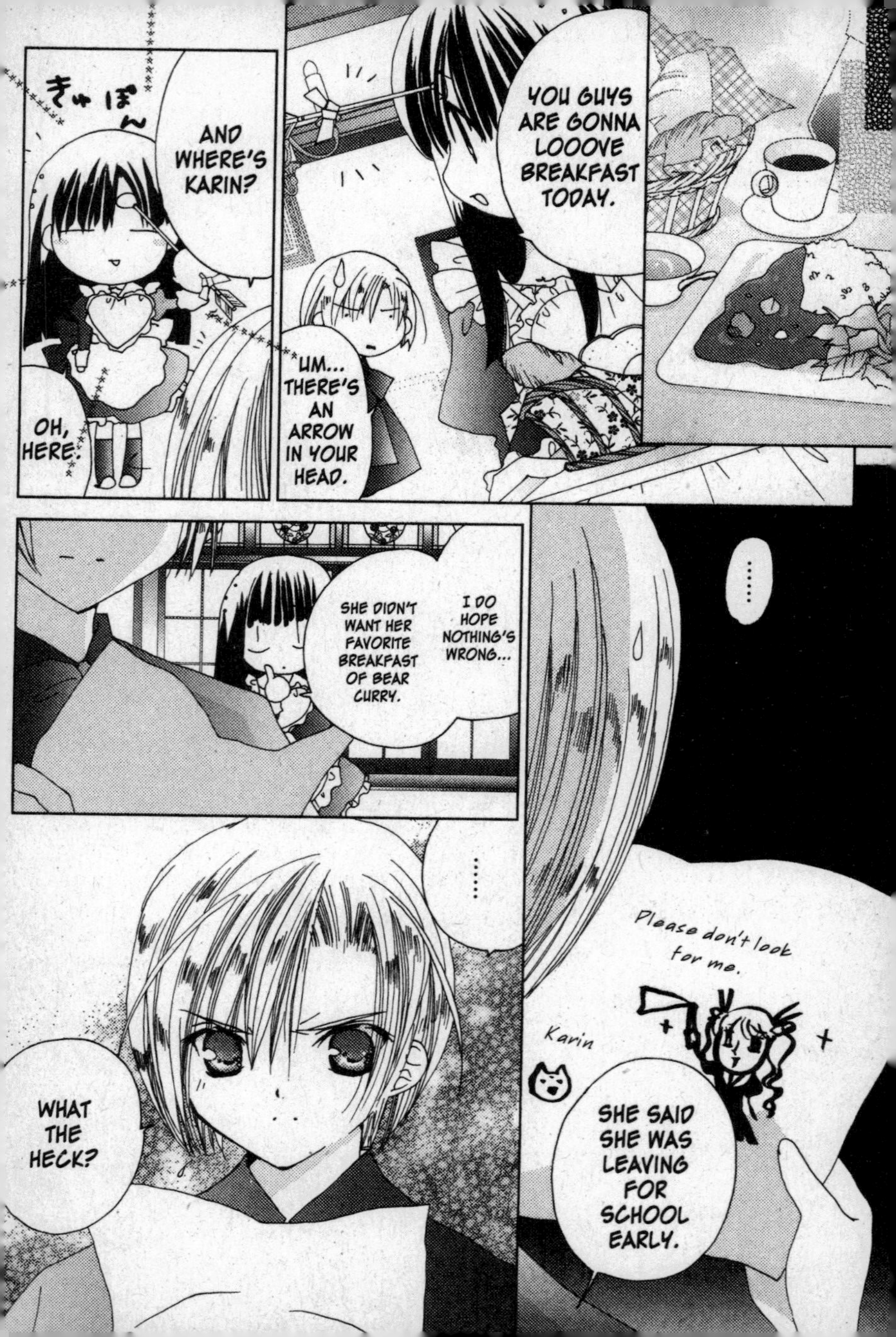

YOU GUYS ARE GONNA LOOOVE BREAKFAST TODAY.
UM... THERE'S AN ARROW IN YOUR HEAD.
きゅぽん
AND WHERE'S KARIN?
OH, HERE.
......
Please don't look for me.
Karin
SHE SAID SHE WAS LEAVING FOR SCHOOL EARLY.
I DO HOPE NOTHING'S WRONG...
SHE DIDN'T WANT HER FAVORITE BREAKFAST OF BEAR CURRY.
......
WHAT THE HECK?

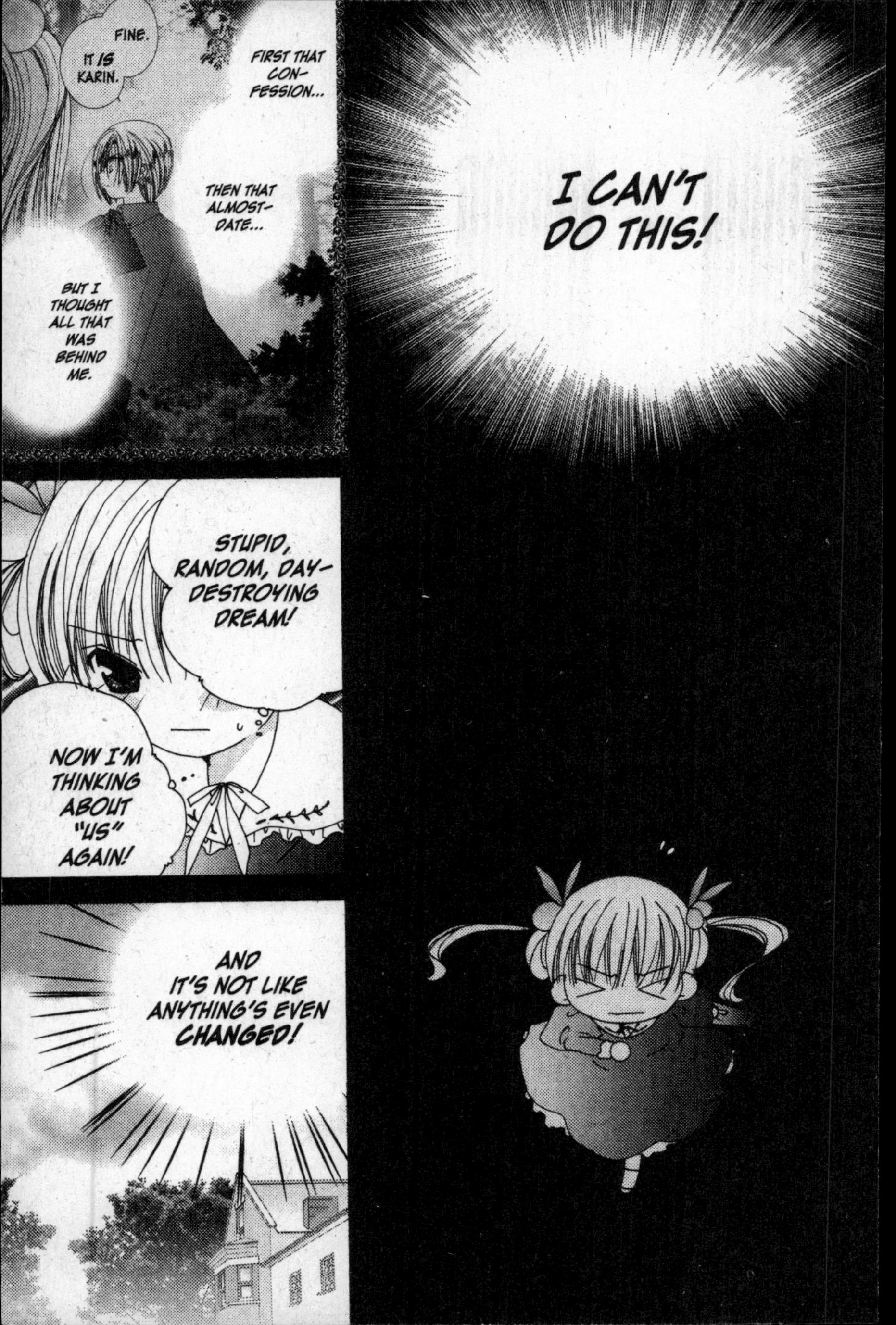
I CAN'T DO THIS!
FINE. IT IS KARIN.
FIRST THAT CON-FESSION...
THEN THAT ALMOST-DATE...
BUT I THOUGHT ALL THAT WAS BEHIND ME.
STUPID, RANDOM, DAY-DESTROYING DREAM!
NOW I'M THINKING ABOUT "US" AGAIN!
AND IT'S NOT LIKE ANYTHING'S EVEN CHANGED!

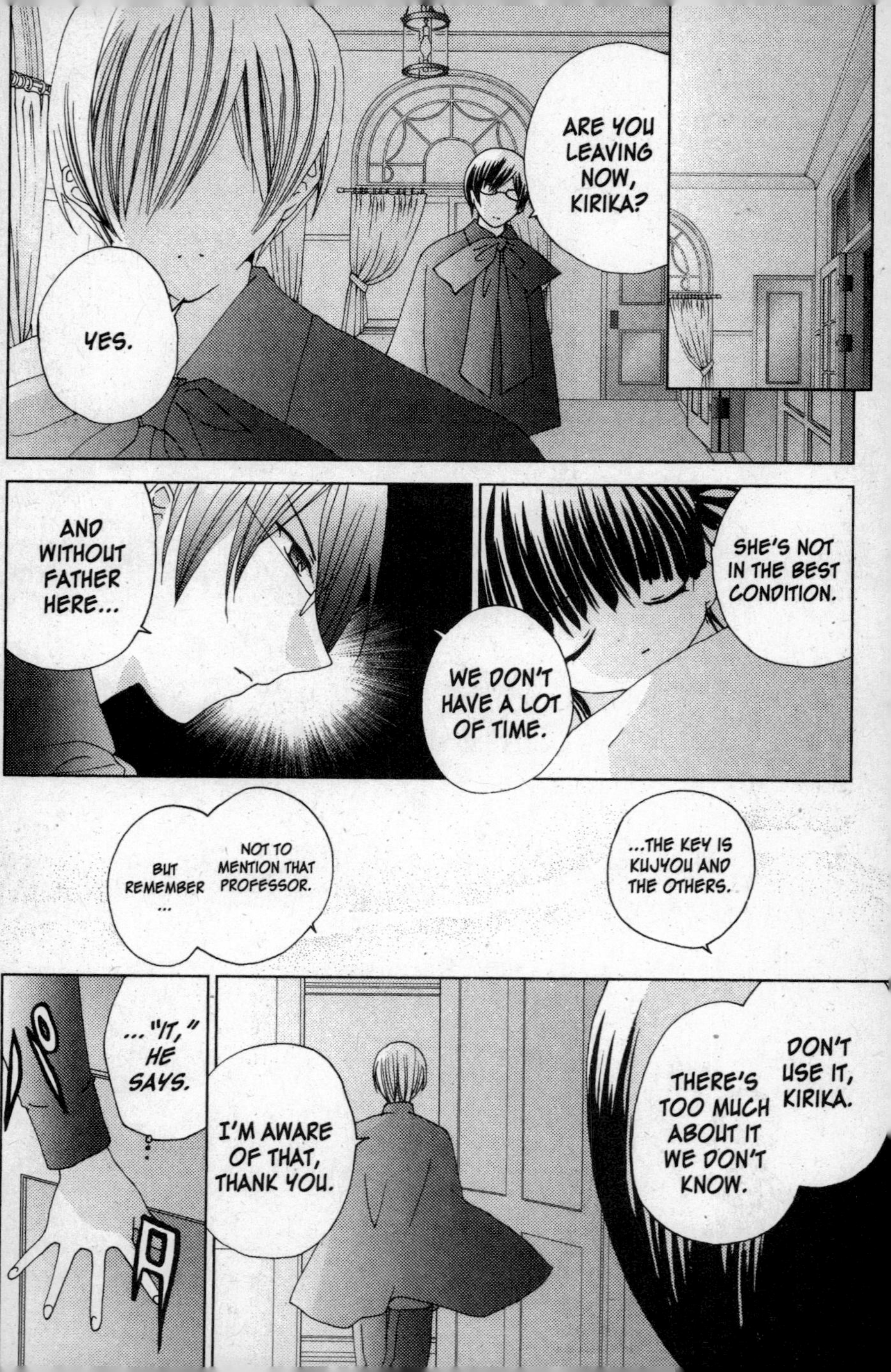
ARE YOU LEAVING NOW, KIRIKA?
YES.
SHE'S NOT IN THE BEST CONDITION.
WE DON'T HAVE A LOT OF TIME.
AND WITHOUT FATHER HERE...
NOT TO MENTION THAT PROFESSOR.
BUT REMEMBER ...
...THE KEY IS KUJYOU AND THE OTHERS.
DON'T USE IT, KIRIKA.
THERE'S TOO MUCH ABOUT IT WE DON'T KNOW.
I'M AWARE OF THAT, THANK YOU.
..."IT," HE SAYS.

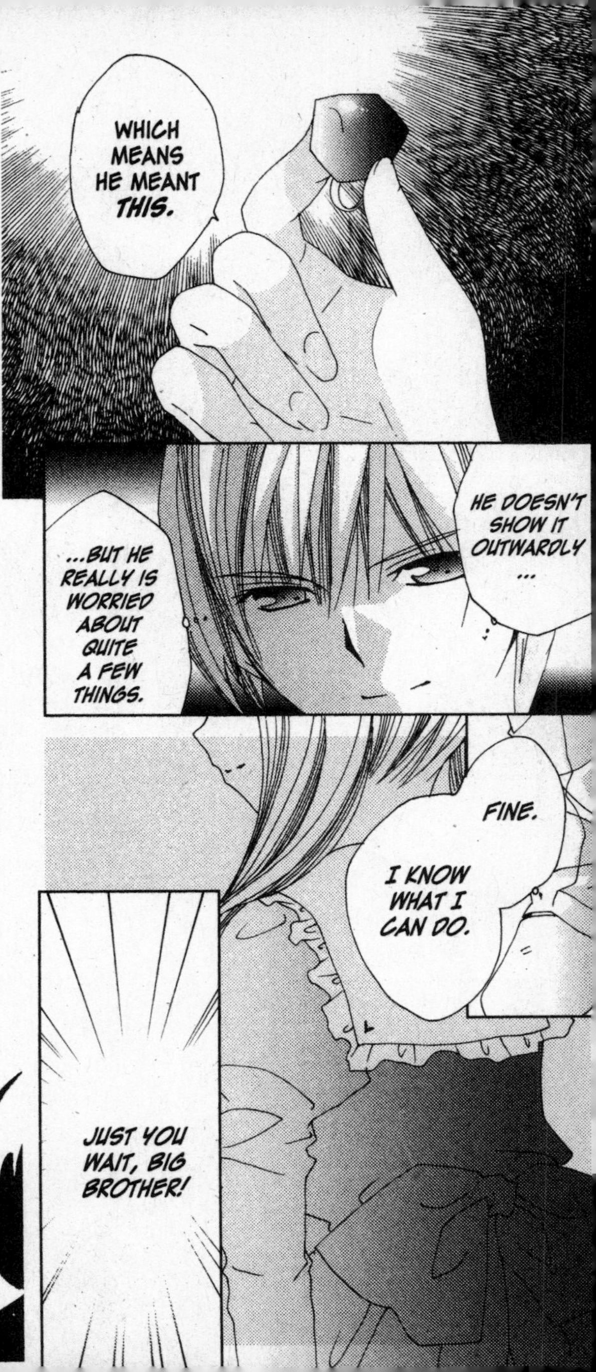
WHICH MEANS HE MEANT THIS.
HE DOESN'T SHOW IT OUTWARDLY ...
...BUT HE REALLY IS WORRIED ABOUT QUITE A FEW THINGS.
FINE.
I KNOW WHAT I CAN DO.
JUST YOU WAIT, BIG BROTHER!
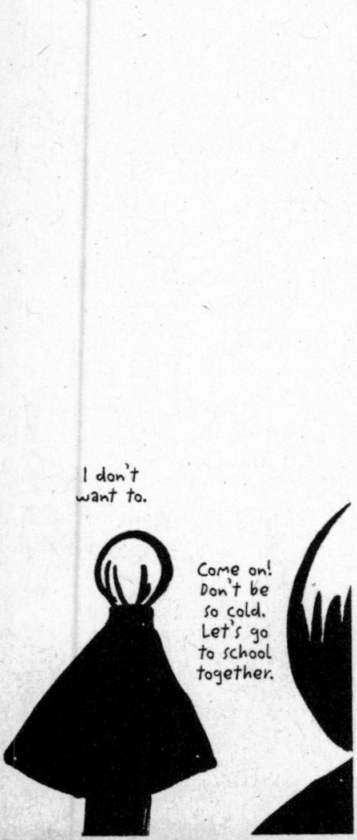
Come on! Don't be so cold. Let's go to school together.
I don't want to.

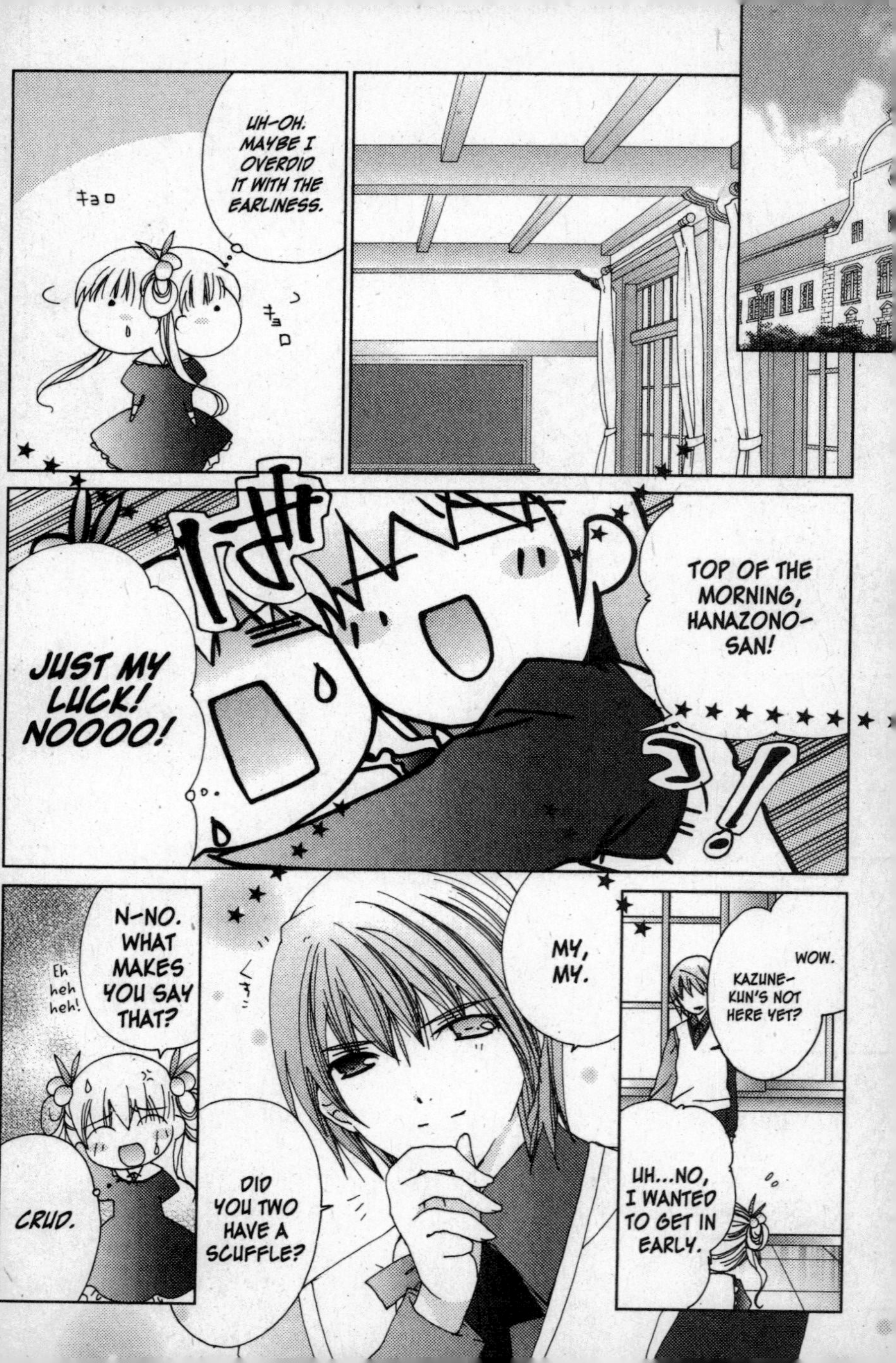

UH-OH. MAYBE I OVERDID IT WITH THE EARLINESS.
キョロ
キョロ
TOP OF THE MORNING, HANAZONO-SAN!
JUST MY LUCK! NOOOO!
WOW. KAZUNE-KUN'S NOT HERE YET?
UH...NO, I WANTED TO GET IN EARLY.
MY, MY.
くすっ
DID YOU TWO HAVE A SCUFFLE?
N-NO. WHAT MAKES YOU SAY THAT?
Eh heh heh!
CRUD.

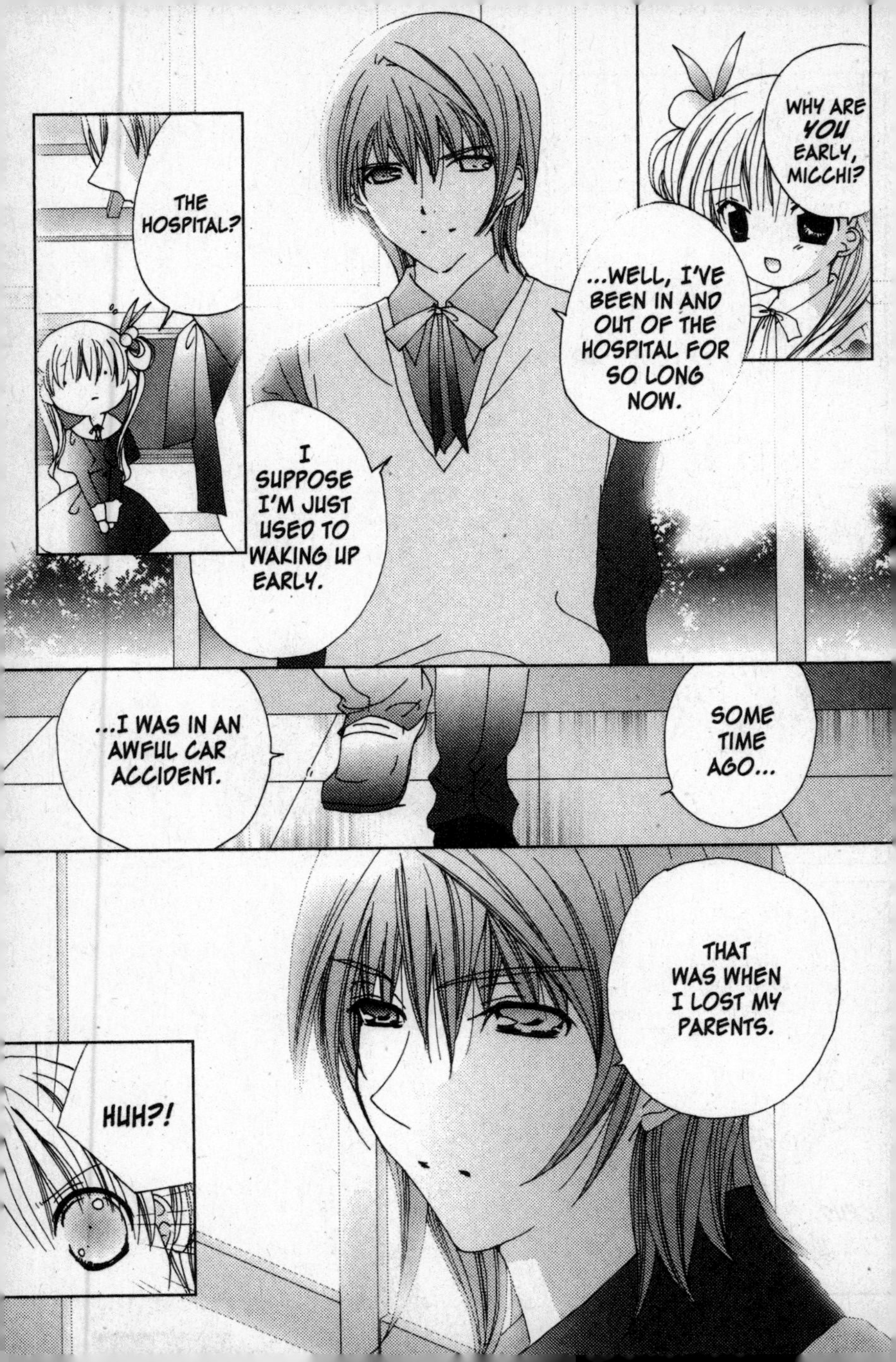
WHY ARE YOU EARLY, MICCHI?
...WELL, I'VE BEEN IN AND OUT OF THE HOSPITAL FOR SO LONG NOW.
I SUPPOSE I'M JUST USED TO WAKING UP EARLY.
THE HOSPITAL?
SOME TIME AGO...
...I WAS IN AN AWFUL CAR ACCIDENT.
THAT WAS WHEN I LOST MY PARENTS.
HUH?!

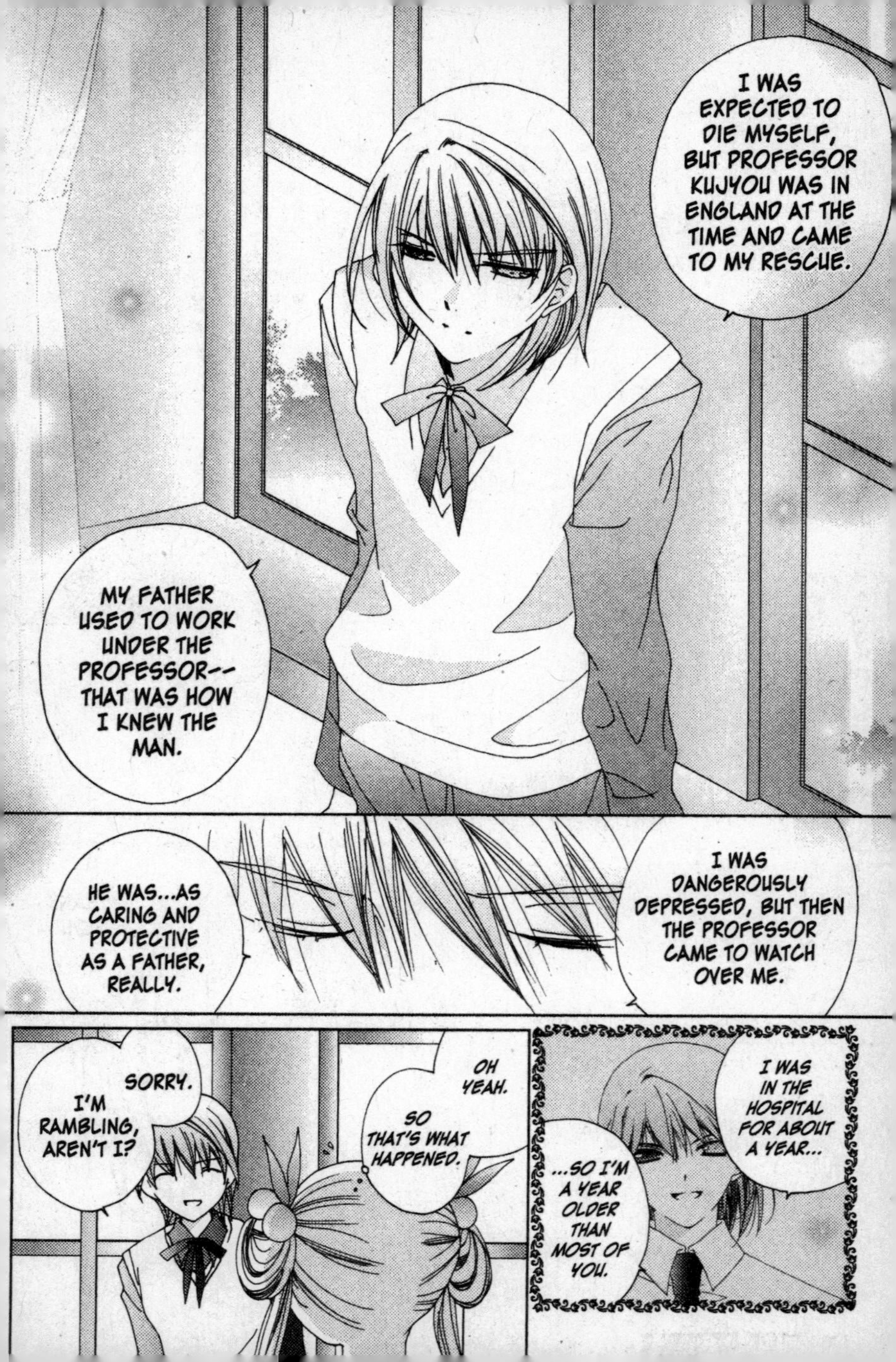
I WAS EXPECTED TO DIE MYSELF, BUT PROFESSOR KUJYOU WAS IN ENGLAND AT THE TIME AND CAME TO MY RESCUE.
MY FATHER USED TO WORK UNDER THE PROFESSOR--THAT WAS HOW I KNEW THE MAN.
I WAS DANGEROUSLY DEPRESSED, BUT THEN THE PROFESSOR CAME TO WATCH OVER ME.
HE WAS...AS CARING AND PROTECTIVE AS A FATHER, REALLY.
I WAS IN THE HOSPITAL FOR ABOUT A YEAR...
...SO I'M A YEAR OLDER THAN MOST OF YOU.
OH YEAH.
SO THAT'S WHAT HAPPENED.
SORRY.
I'M RAMBLING, AREN'T I?

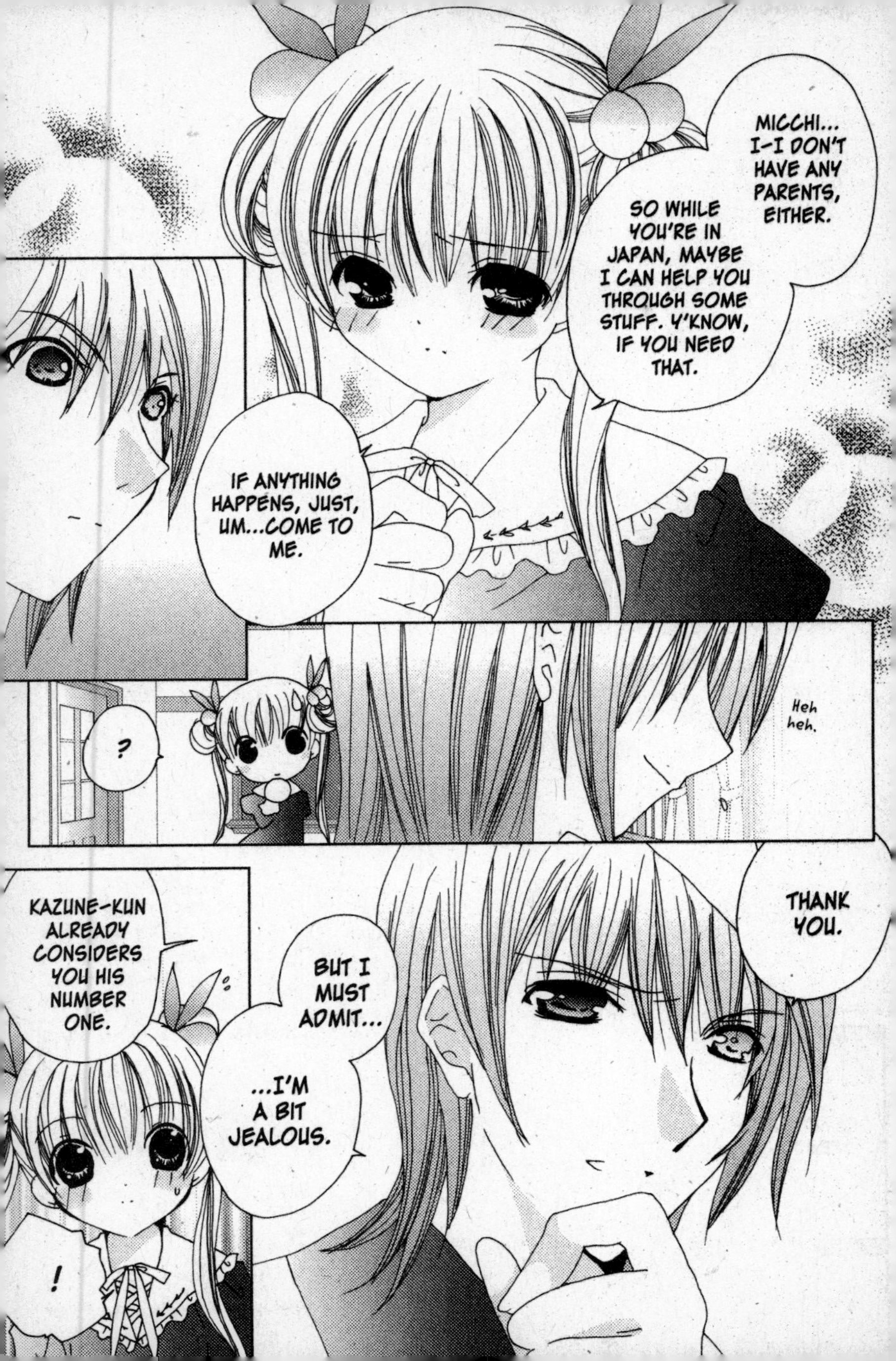
MICCHI... I-I DON'T HAVE ANY PARENTS, EITHER.
SO WHILE YOU'RE IN JAPAN, MAYBE I CAN HELP YOU THROUGH SOME STUFF. Y'KNOW, IF YOU NEED THAT.
IF ANYTHING HAPPENS, JUST, UM...COME TO ME.
Heh heh.
?
THANK YOU.
BUT I MUST ADMIT...
...I'M A BIT JEALOUS.
KAZUNE-KUN ALREADY CONSIDERS YOU HIS NUMBER ONE.
!

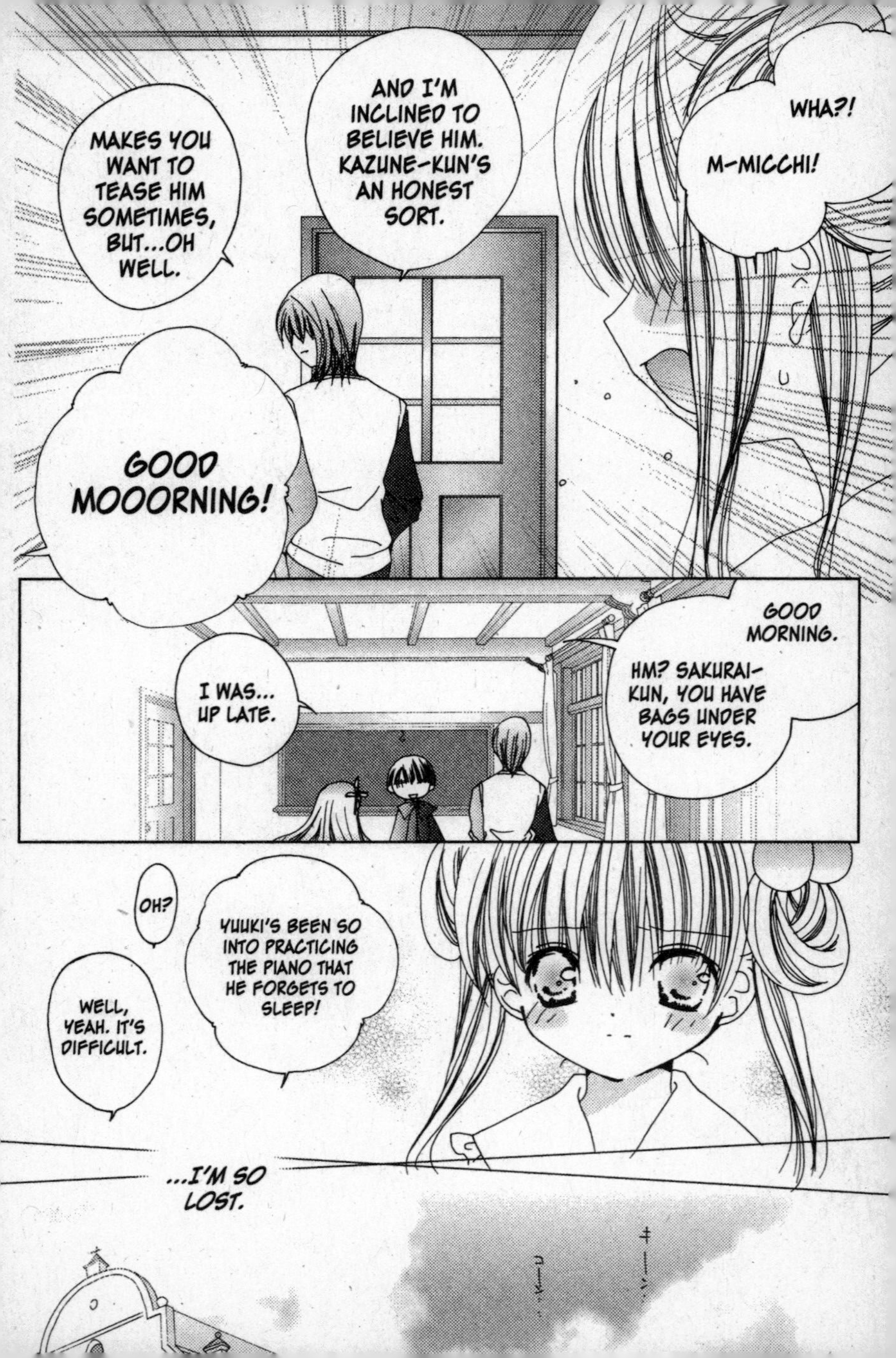
WHA?!
M-MICCHI!
AND I'M INCLINED TO BELIEVE HIM. KAZUNE-KUN'S AN HONEST SORT.
MAKES YOU WANT TO TEASE HIM SOMETIMES, BUT...OH WELL.
GOOD MOOORNING!
GOOD MORNING.
HM? SAKURAI-KUN, YOU HAVE BAGS UNDER YOUR EYES.
I WAS... UP LATE.
YUUKI'S BEEN SO INTO PRACTICING THE PIANO THAT HE FORGETS TO SLEEP!
OH?
WELL, YEAH. IT'S DIFFICULT.
...I'M SO LOST.

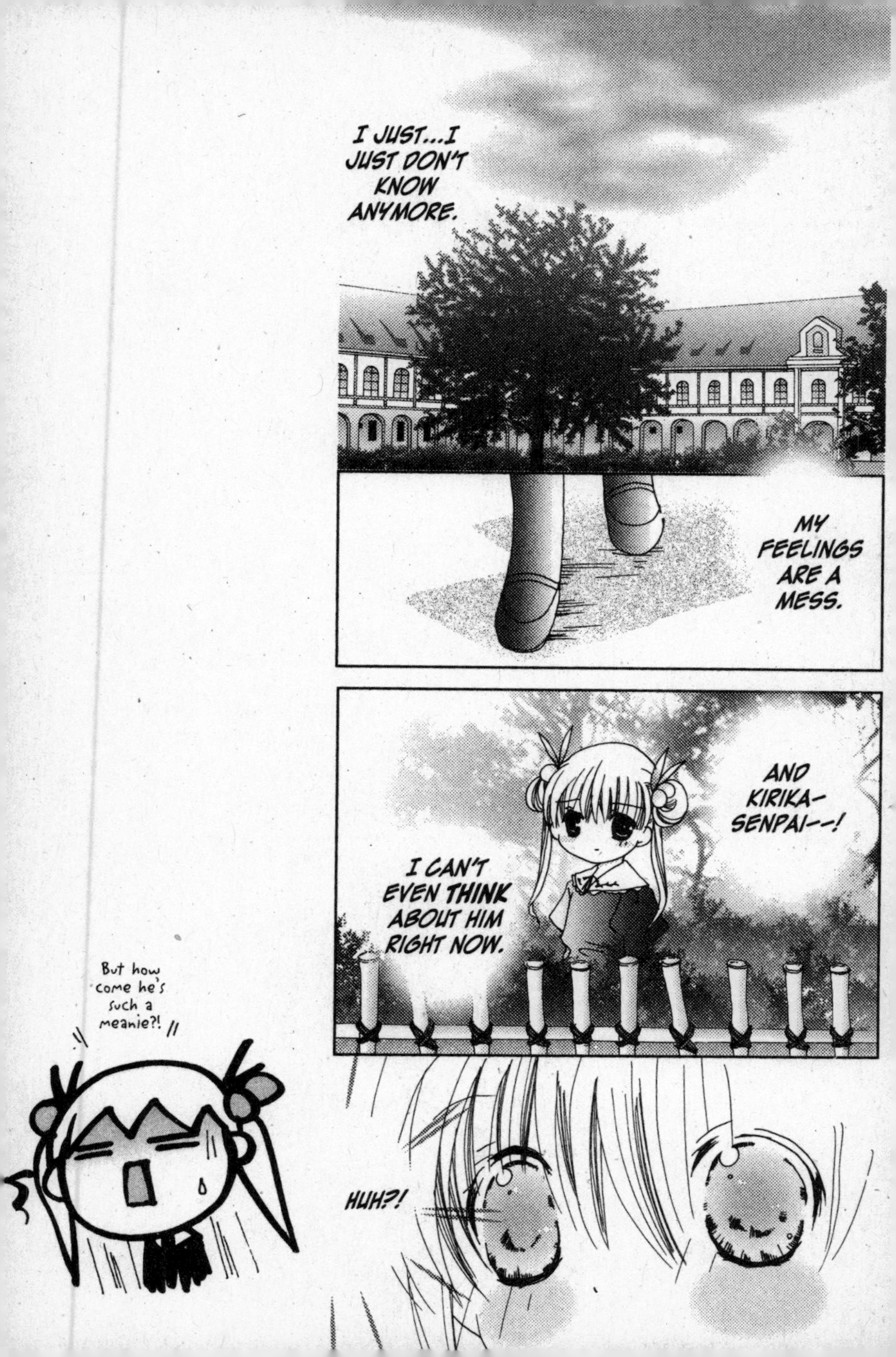
I JUST...I JUST DON'T KNOW ANYMORE.
MY FEELINGS ARE A MESS.
AND KIRIKA-SENPAI--!
I CAN'T EVEN THINK ABOUT HIM RIGHT NOW.
HUH?!
But how come he's such a meanie?!

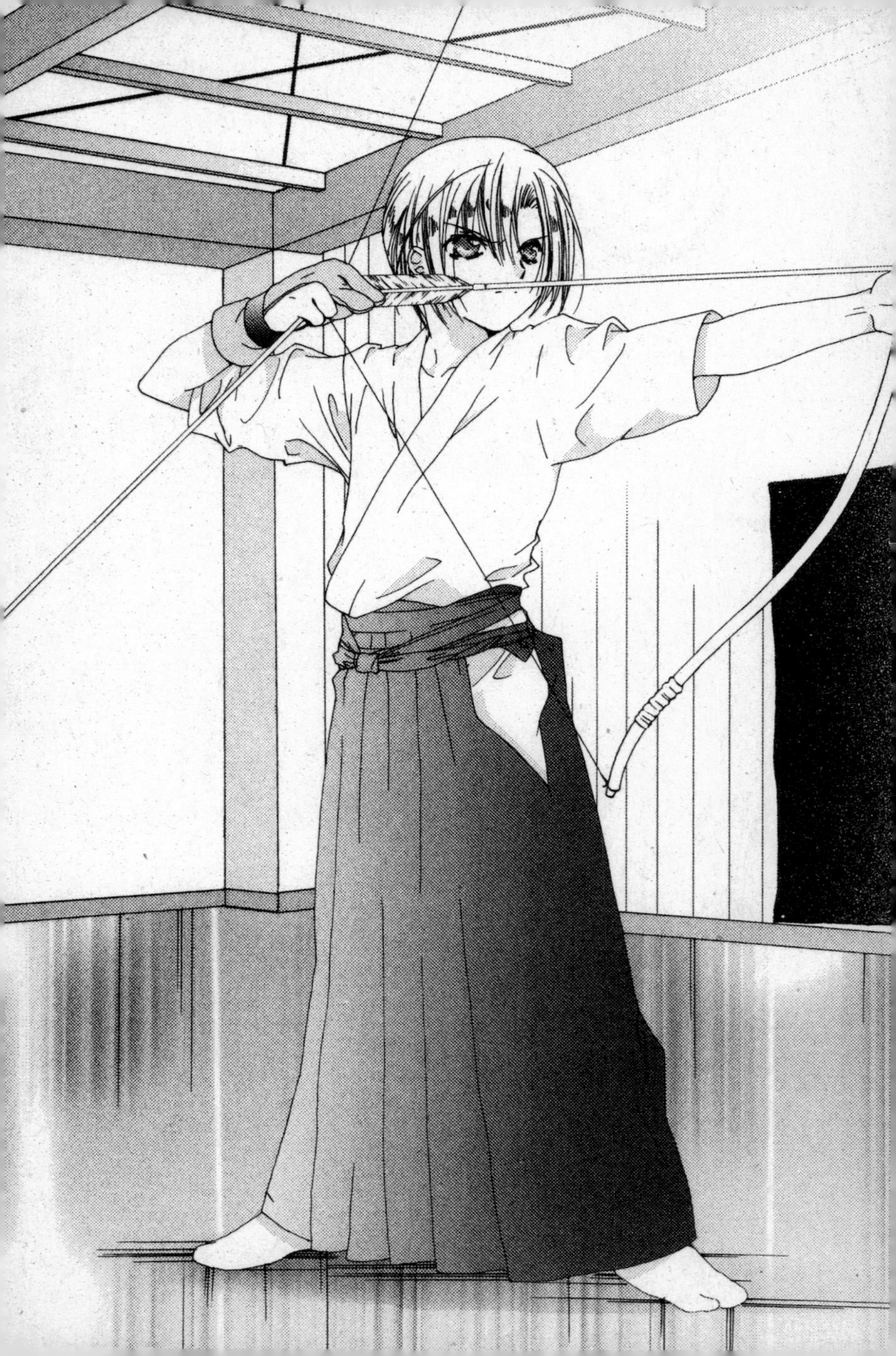

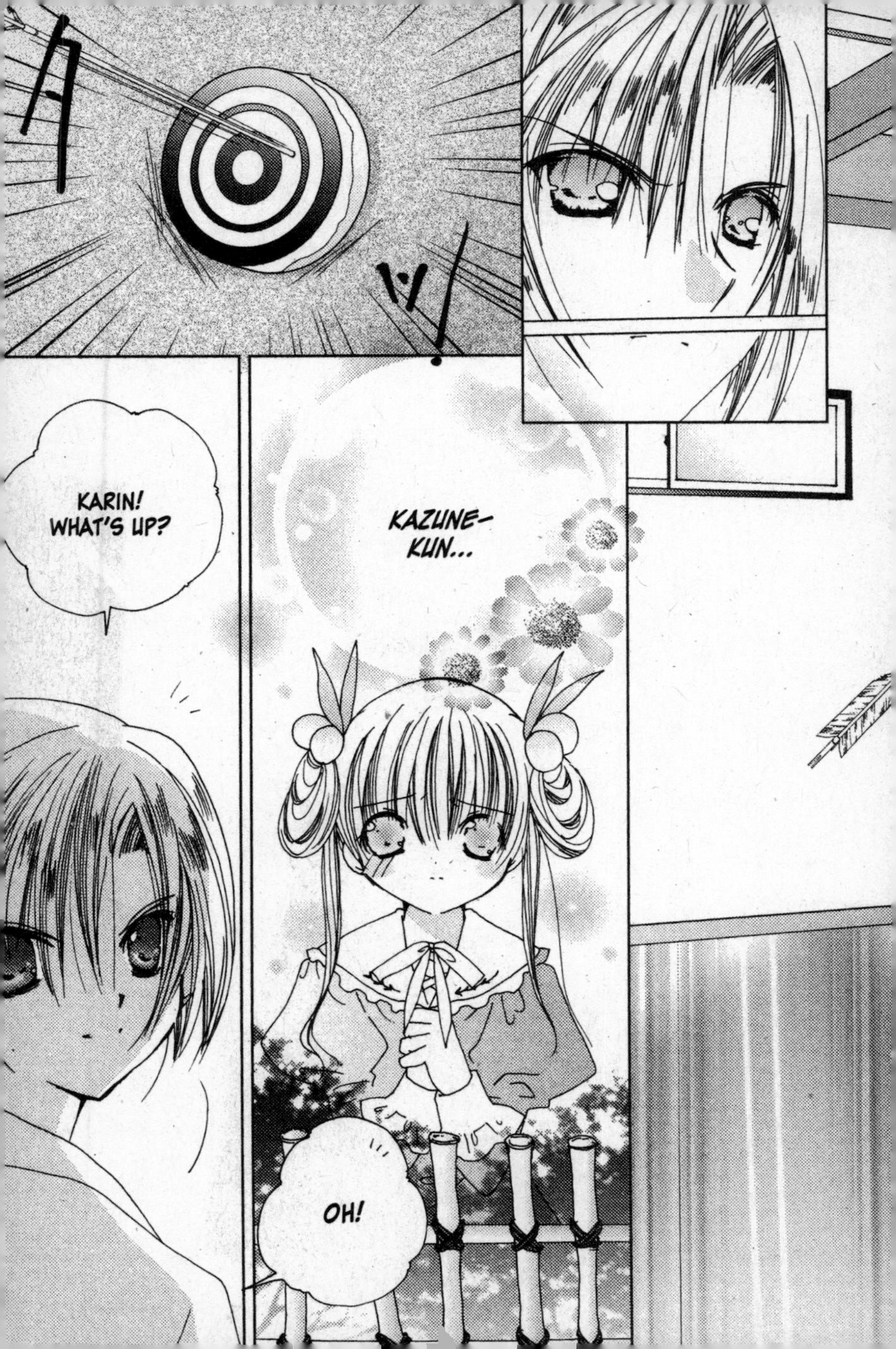
KAZUNE-KUN...
OH!
KARIN! WHAT'S UP?

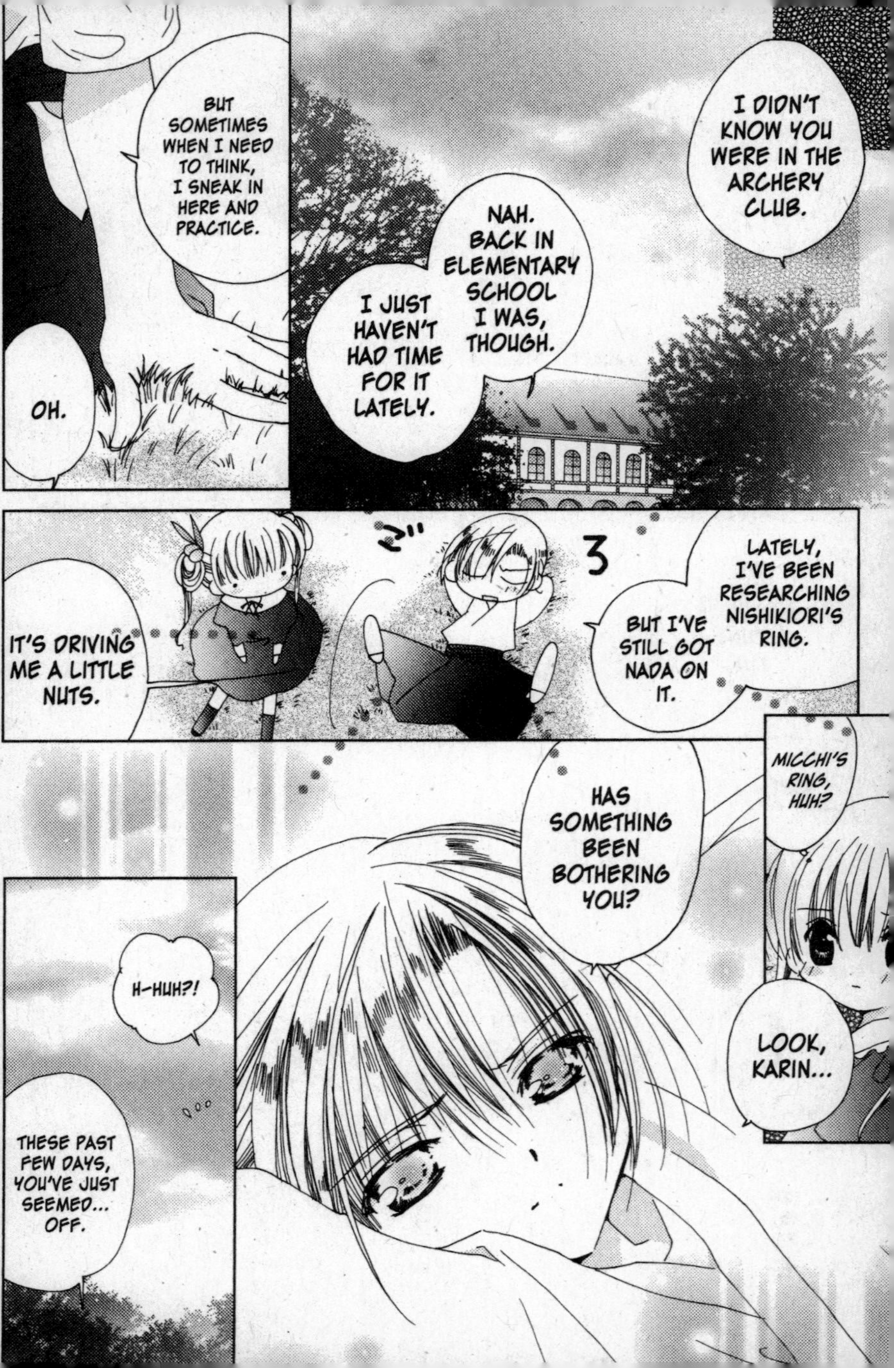
I DIDN'T KNOW YOU WERE IN THE ARCHERY CLUB.
NAH. BACK IN ELEMENTARY SCHOOL I WAS, THOUGH.
I JUST HAVEN'T HAD TIME FOR IT LATELY.
BUT SOMETIMES WHEN I NEED TO THINK, I SNEAK IN HERE AND PRACTICE.
OH.
LATELY, I'VE BEEN RESEARCHING NISHIKIORI'S RING.
BUT I'VE STILL GOT NADA ON IT.
IT'S DRIVING ME A LITTLE NUTS.
MICCHI'S RING, HUH?
LOOK, KARIN...
HAS SOMETHING BEEN BOTHERING YOU?
H-HUH?!
THESE PAST FEW DAYS, YOU'VE JUST SEEMED... OFF.

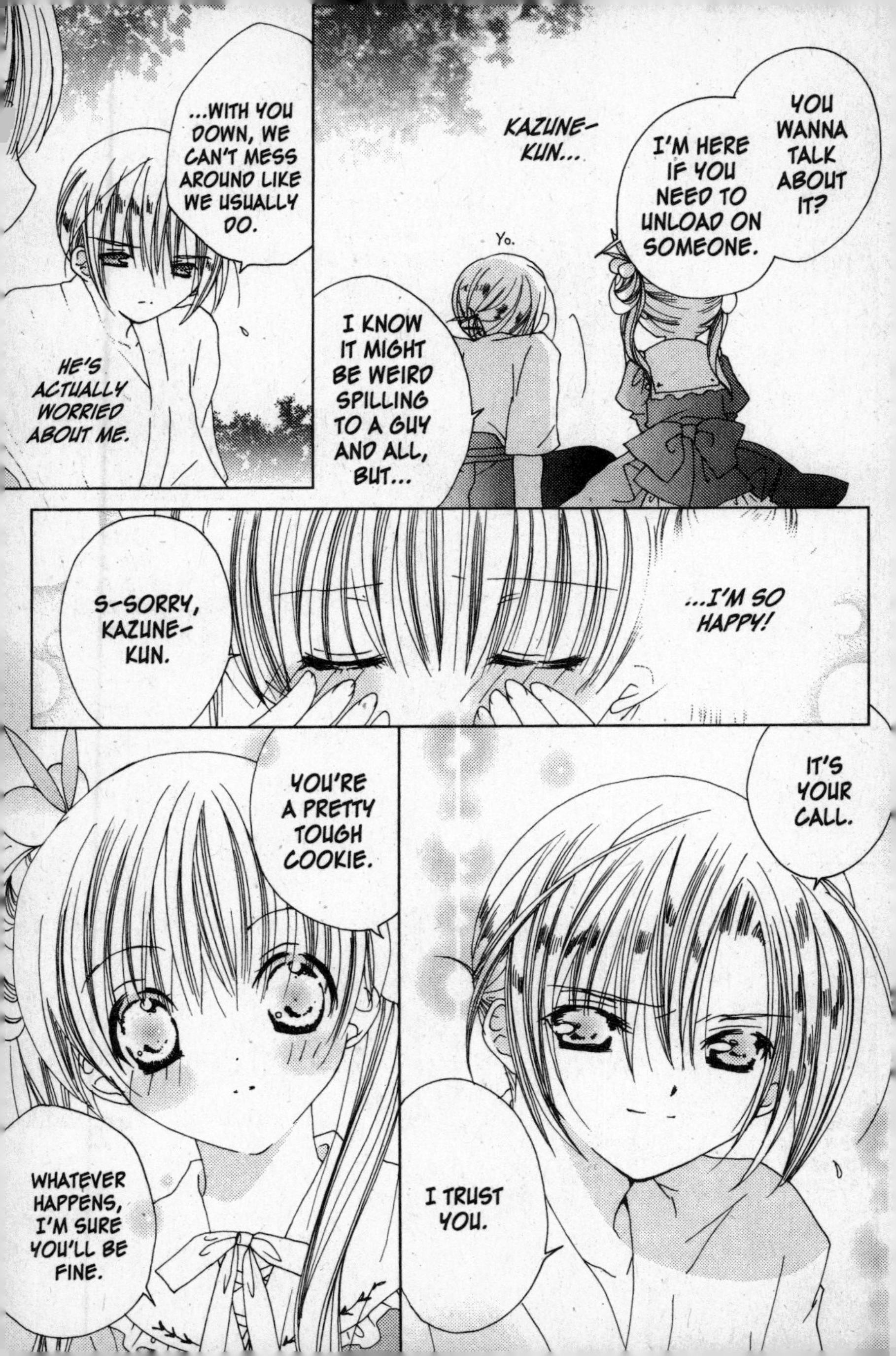
YOU WANNA TALK ABOUT IT?
I'M HERE IF YOU NEED TO UNLOAD ON SOMEONE.
KAZUNE-KUN...
Yo.
I KNOW IT MIGHT BE WEIRD SPILLING TO A GUY AND ALL, BUT...
...WITH YOU DOWN, WE CAN'T MESS AROUND LIKE WE USUALLY DO.
HE'S ACTUALLY WORRIED ABOUT ME.
...I'M SO HAPPY!
S-SORRY, KAZUNE-KUN.
IT'S YOUR CALL.
I TRUST YOU.
YOU'RE A PRETTY TOUGH COOKIE.
WHATEVER HAPPENS, I'M SURE YOU'LL BE FINE.

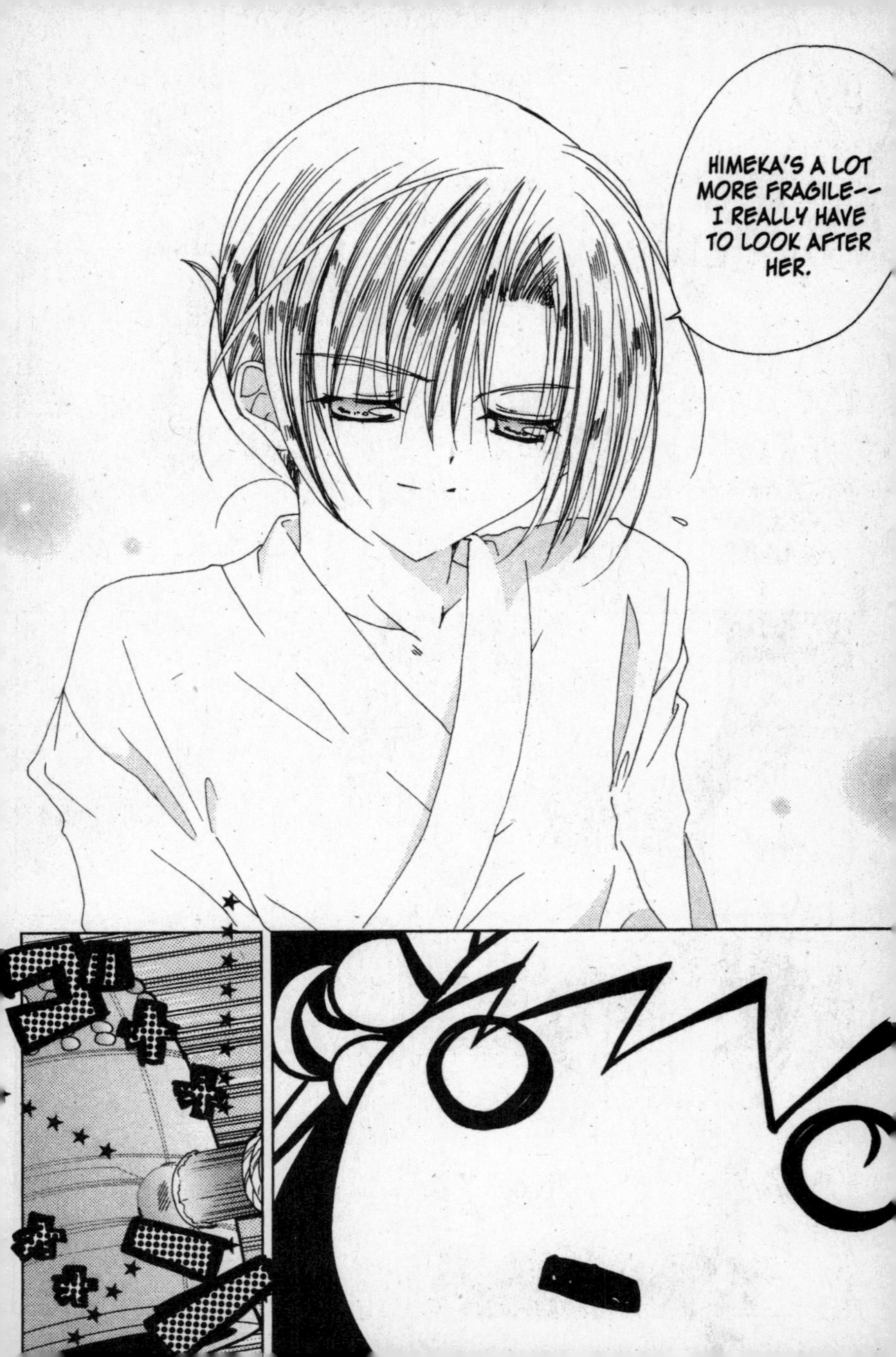
HIMEKA'S A LOT MORE FRAGILE-- I REALLY HAVE TO LOOK AFTER HER.

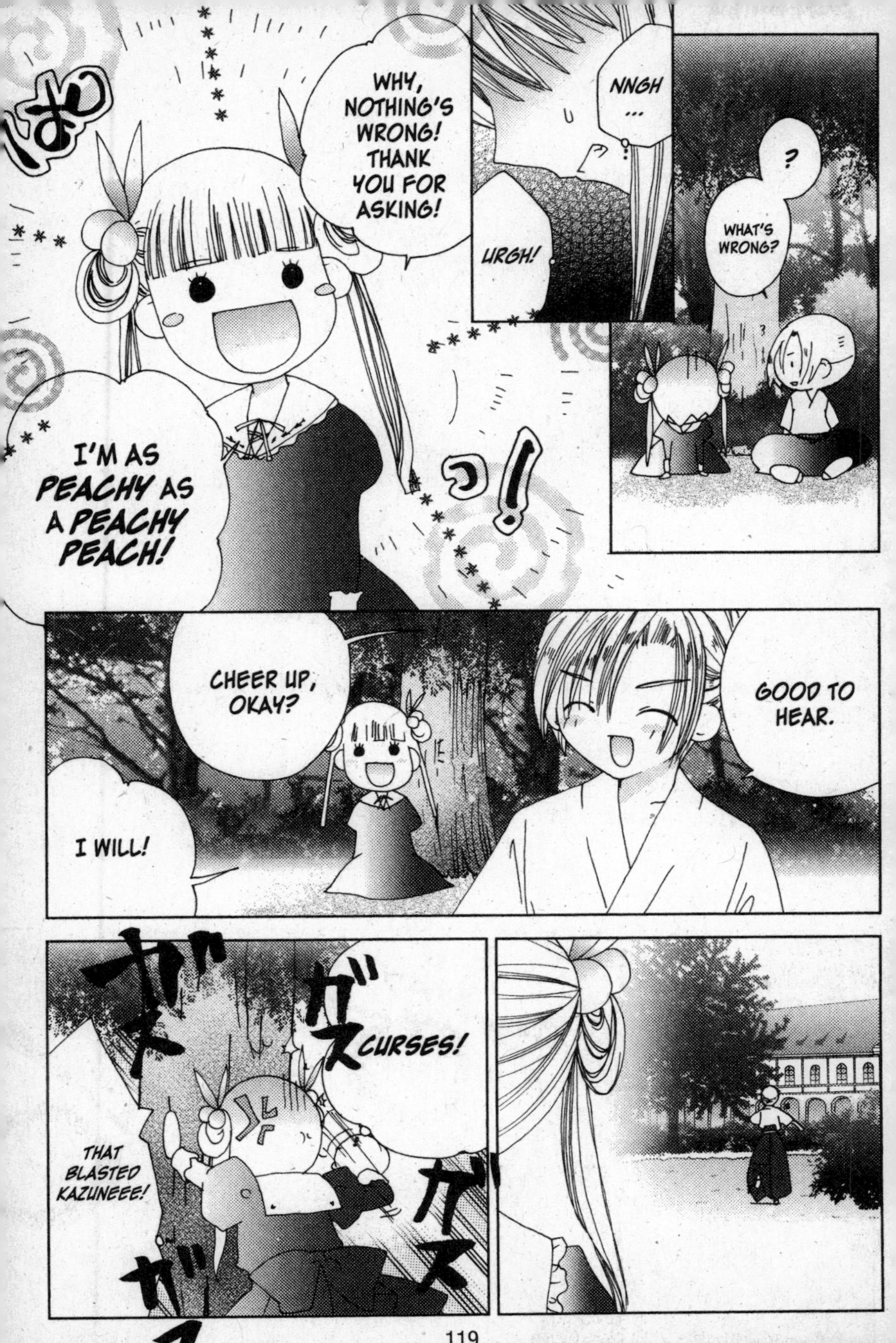
?
WHAT'S WRONG?
NNGH ...
URGH!
WHY, NOTHING'S WRONG! THANK YOU FOR ASKING!
I'M AS PEACHY AS A PEACHY PEACH!
GOOD TO HEAR.
CHEER UP, OKAY?
I WILL!
CURSES!
THAT BLASTED KAZUNEEE!

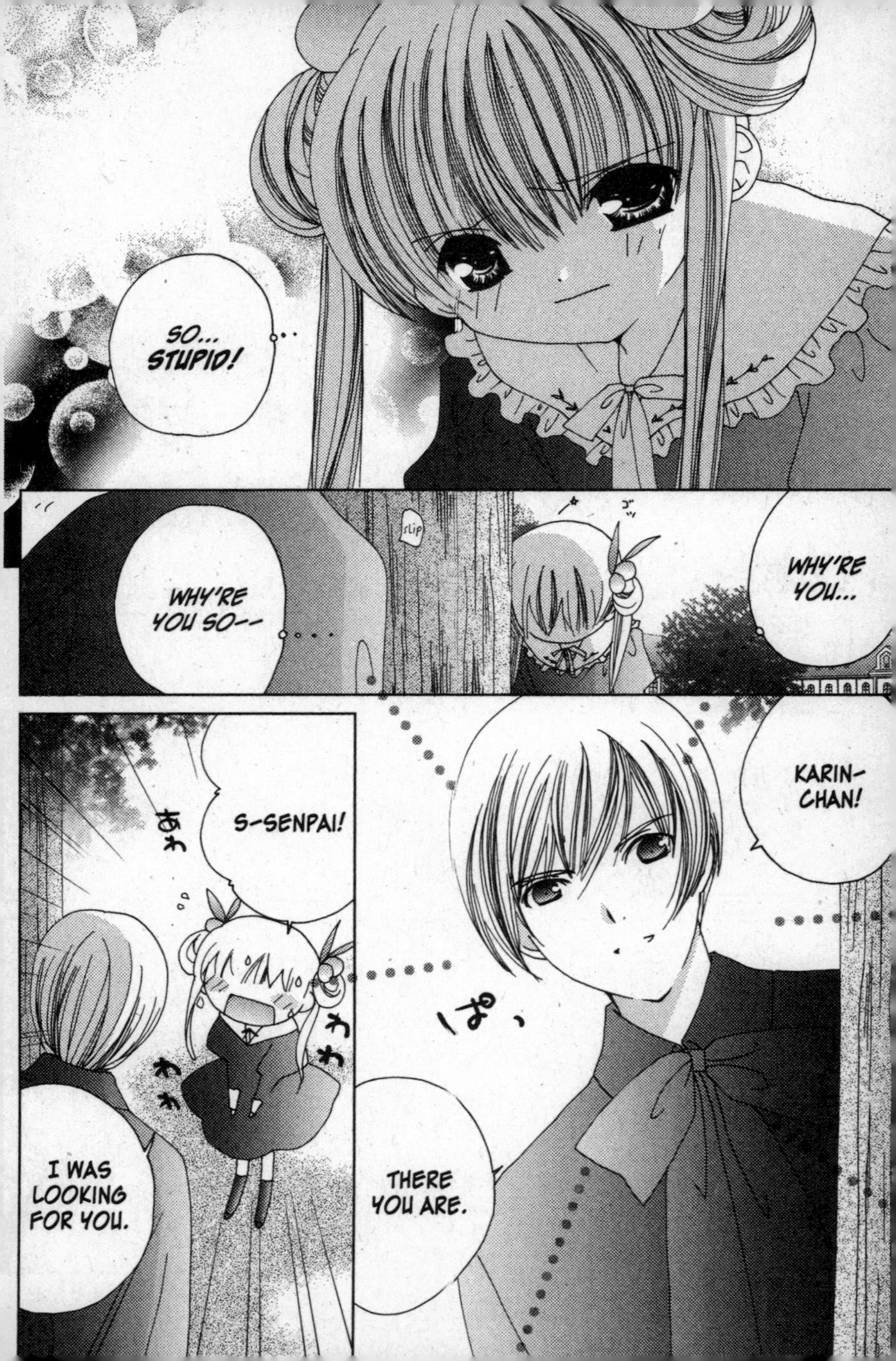
SO... STUPID!
WHY'RE YOU...
slip
WHY'RE YOU SO--
KARIN-CHAN!
ぱ、
THERE YOU ARE.
S-SENPAI!
あわ
わわ
わわ
I WAS LOOKING FOR YOU.

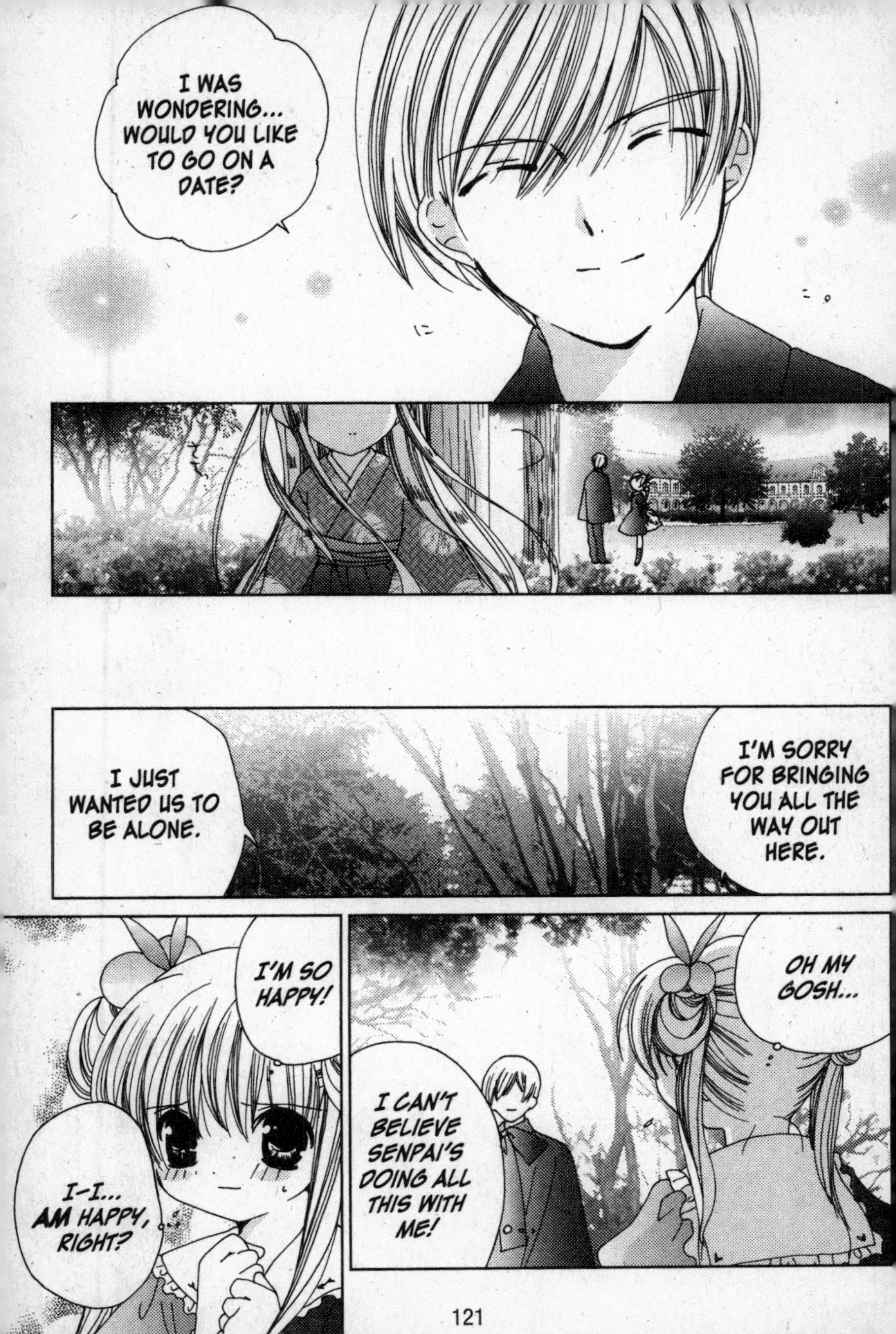
I WAS WONDERING... WOULD YOU LIKE TO GO ON A DATE?
I'M SORRY FOR BRINGING YOU ALL THE WAY OUT HERE.
I JUST WANTED US TO BE ALONE.
OH MY GOSH...
I CAN'T BELIEVE SENPAI'S DOING ALL THIS WITH ME!
I'M SO HAPPY!
I-I... AM HAPPY, RIGHT?

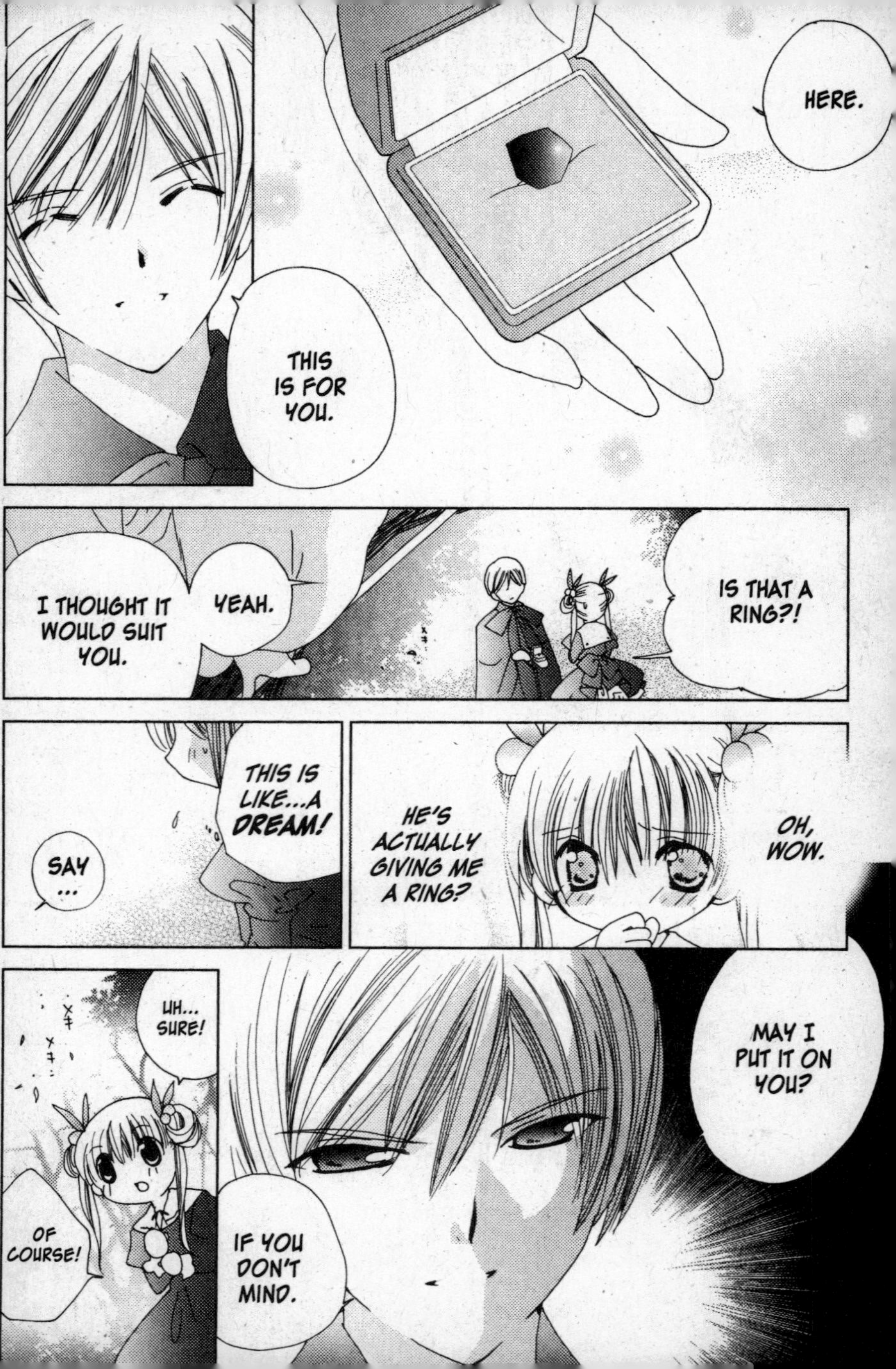
HERE.
THIS IS FOR YOU.
IS THAT A RING?!
YEAH.
I THOUGHT IT WOULD SUIT YOU.
OH, WOW.
HE'S ACTUALLY GIVING ME A RING?
THIS IS LIKE...A DREAM!
SAY ...
MAY I PUT IT ON YOU?
IF YOU DON'T MIND.
UH... SURE!
OF COURSE!

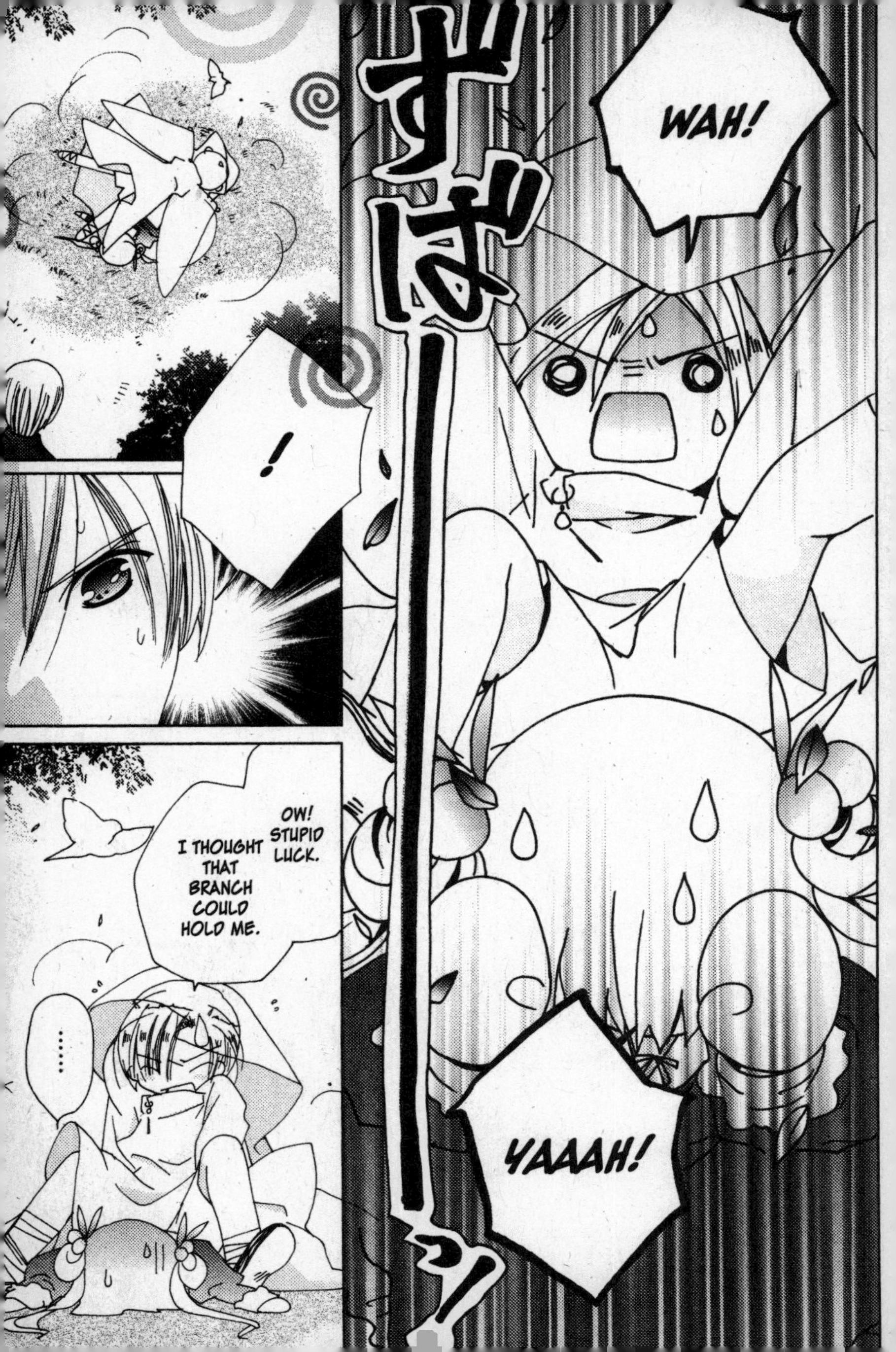
WAH!
ずばーっ!
YAAAH!
!
OW! STUPID LUCK.
I THOUGHT THAT BRANCH COULD HOLD ME.
......

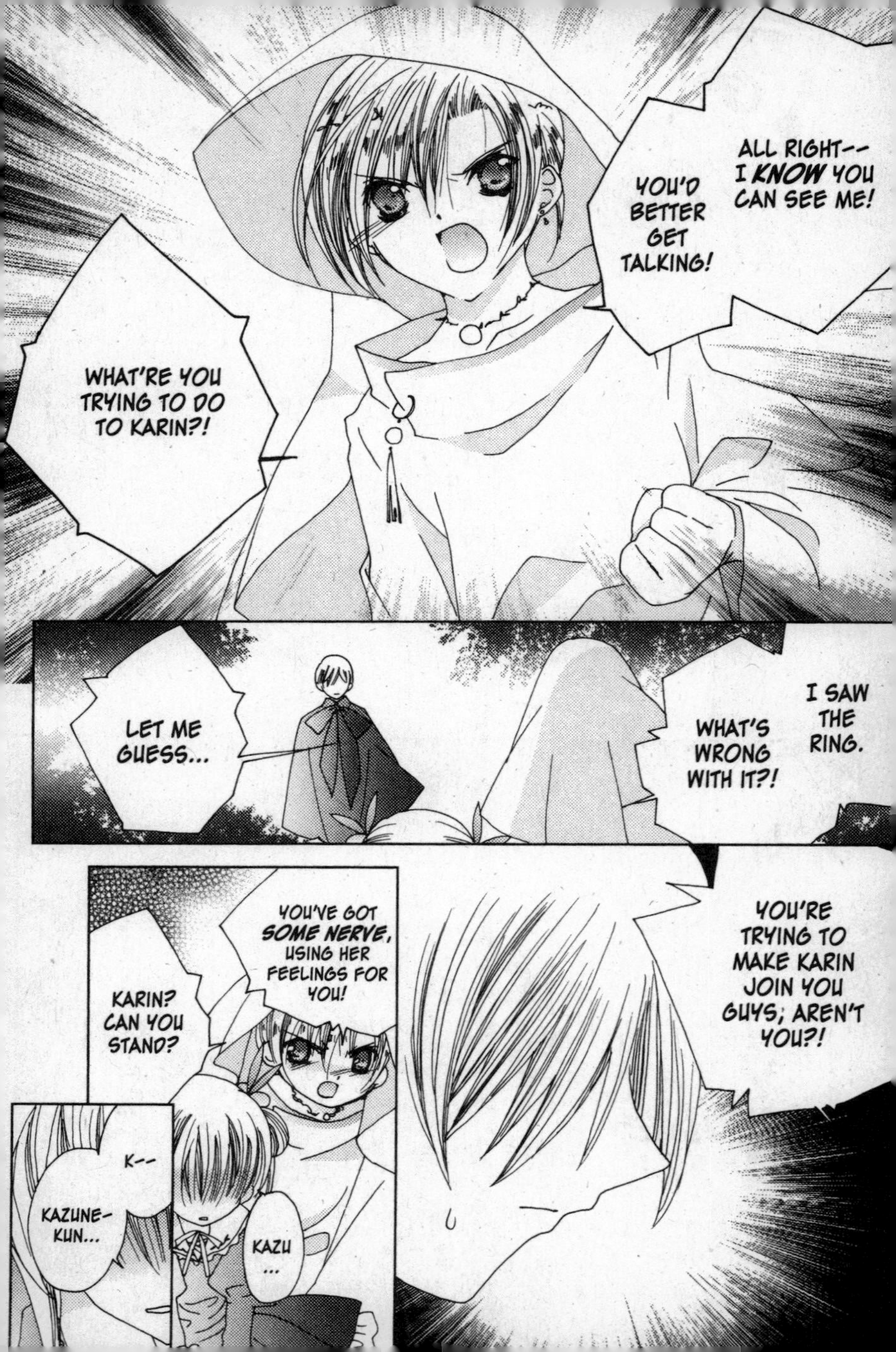
ALL RIGHT-- I KNOW YOU CAN SEE ME!
YOU'D BETTER GET TALKING!
WHAT'RE YOU TRYING TO DO TO KARIN?!
I SAW THE RING.
WHAT'S WRONG WITH IT?!
LET ME GUESS...
YOU'RE TRYING TO MAKE KARIN JOIN YOU GUYS; AREN'T YOU?!
YOU'VE GOT SOME NERVE, USING HER FEELINGS FOR YOU!
KARIN? CAN YOU STAND?
KAZU ...
K-- KAZUNE-KUN...

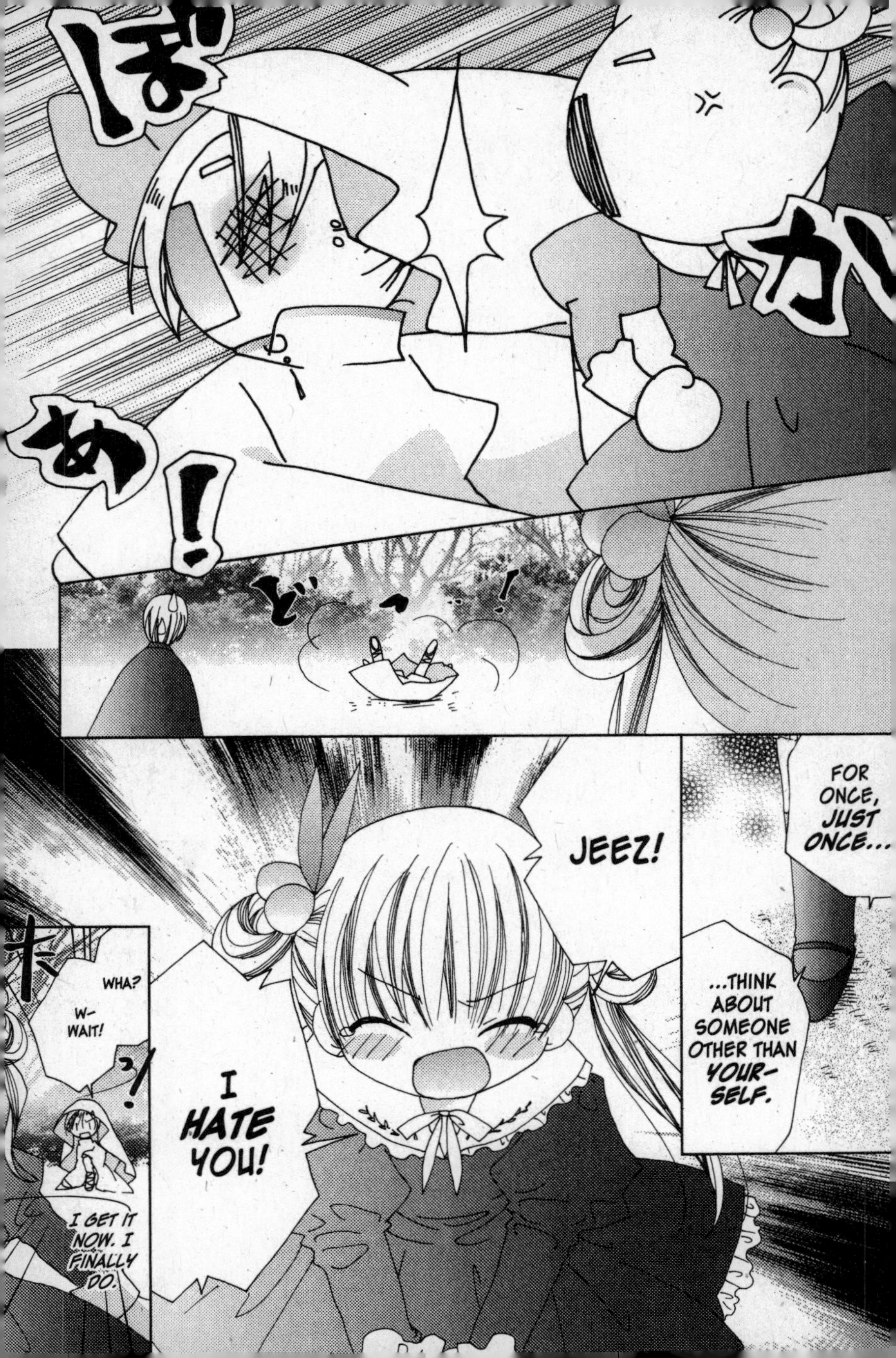
FOR ONCE, JUST ONCE...
...THINK ABOUT SOMEONE OTHER THAN YOURSELF.
JEEZ!
I HATE YOU!
WHA?
W-WAIT!
I GET IT NOW. I FINALLY DO.

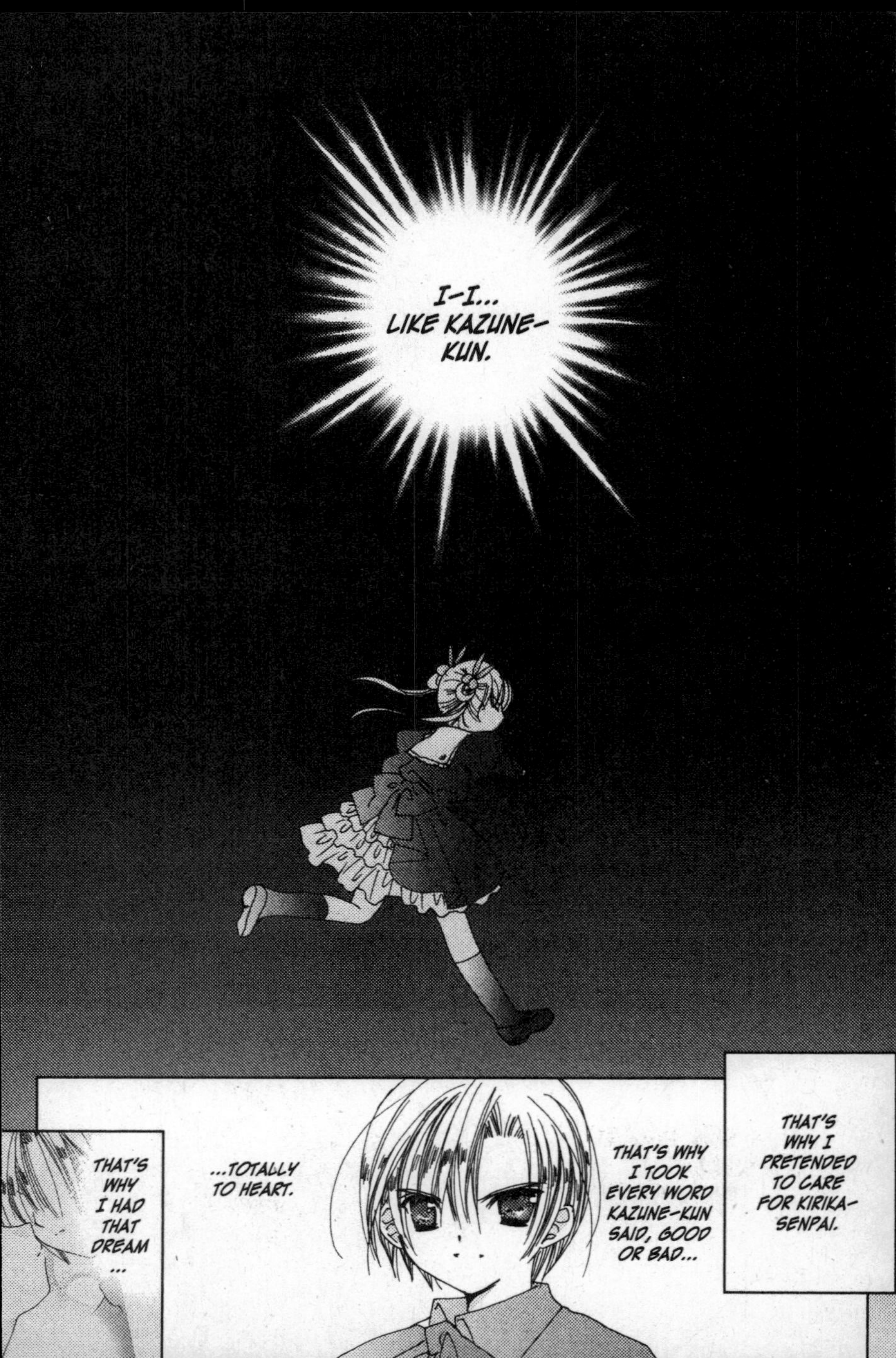
I-I... LIKE KAZUNE-KUN.
THAT'S WHY I PRETENDED TO CARE FOR KIRIKA-SENPAI.
THAT'S WHY I TOOK EVERY WORD KAZUNE-KUN SAID, GOOD OR BAD...
...TOTALLY TO HEART.
THAT'S WHY I HAD THAT DREAM ...

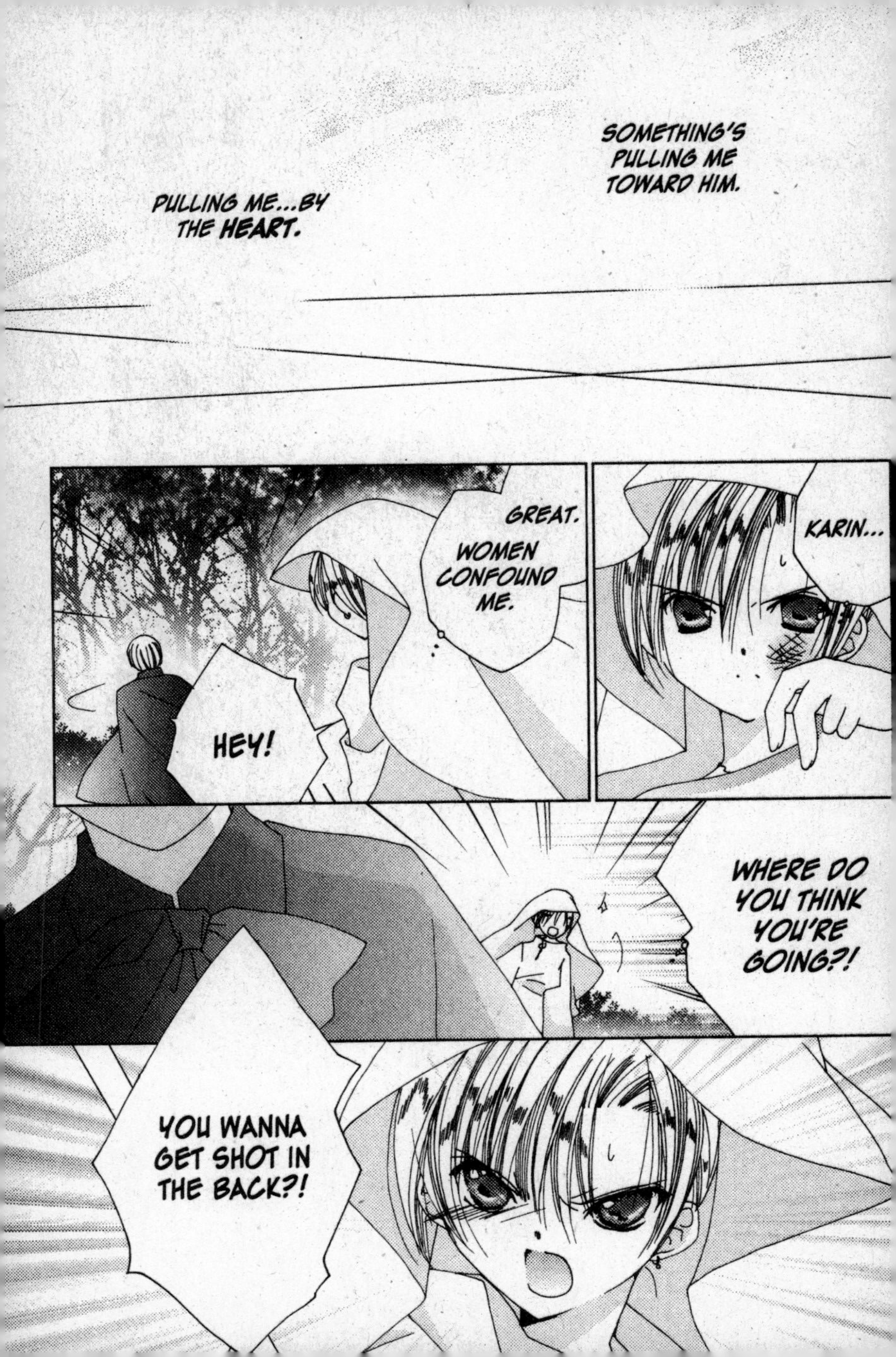
SOMETHING'S PULLING ME TOWARD HIM.
PULLING ME...BY THE HEART.
KARIN...
GREAT. WOMEN CONFOUND ME.
HEY!
WHERE DO YOU THINK YOU'RE GOING?!
YOU WANNA GET SHOT IN THE BACK?!

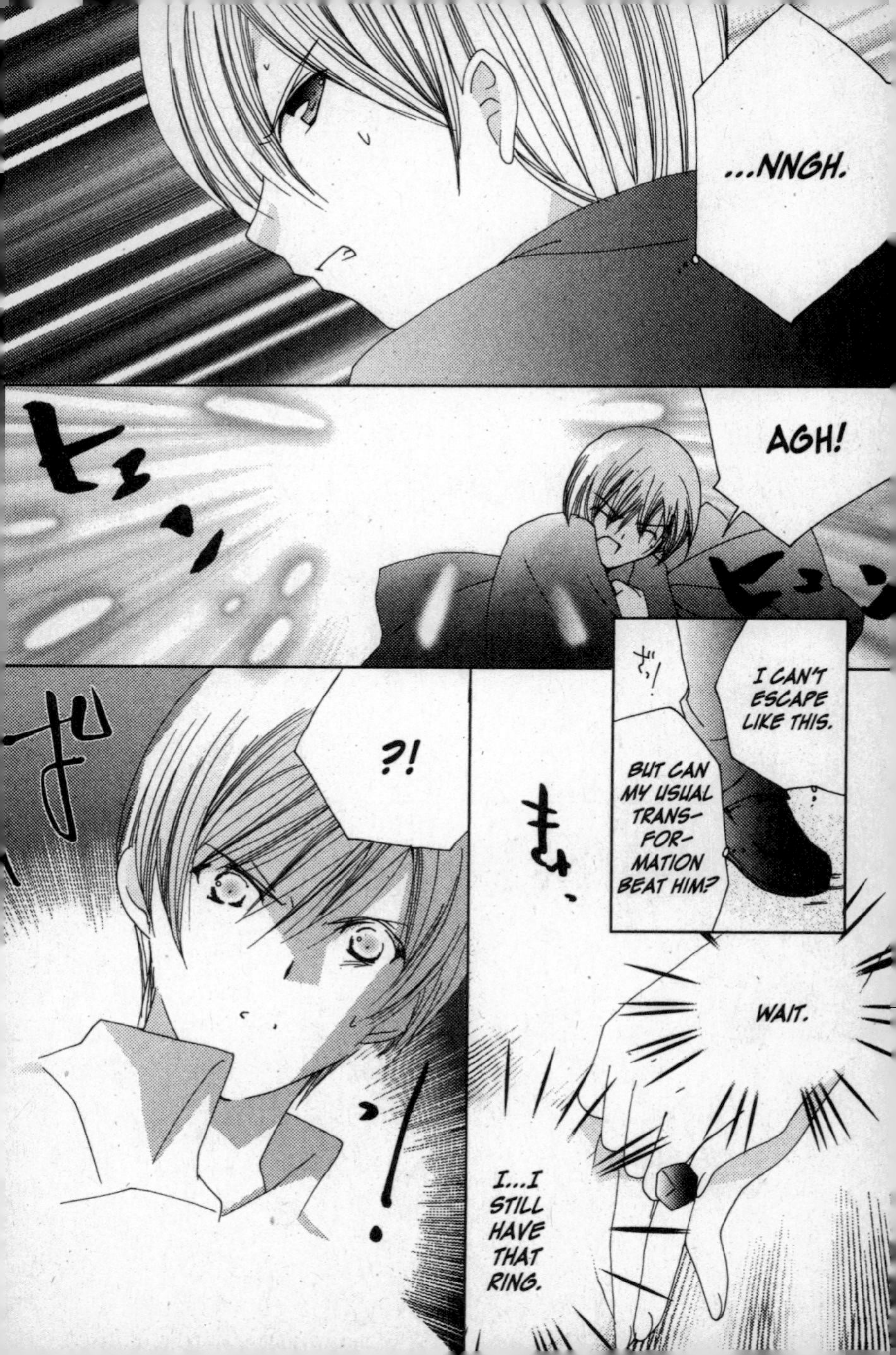
...NNGH.
AGH!
I CAN'T ESCAPE LIKE THIS.
BUT CAN MY USUAL TRANS-FOR-MATION BEAT HIM?
WAIT.
I...I STILL HAVE THAT RING.
?!

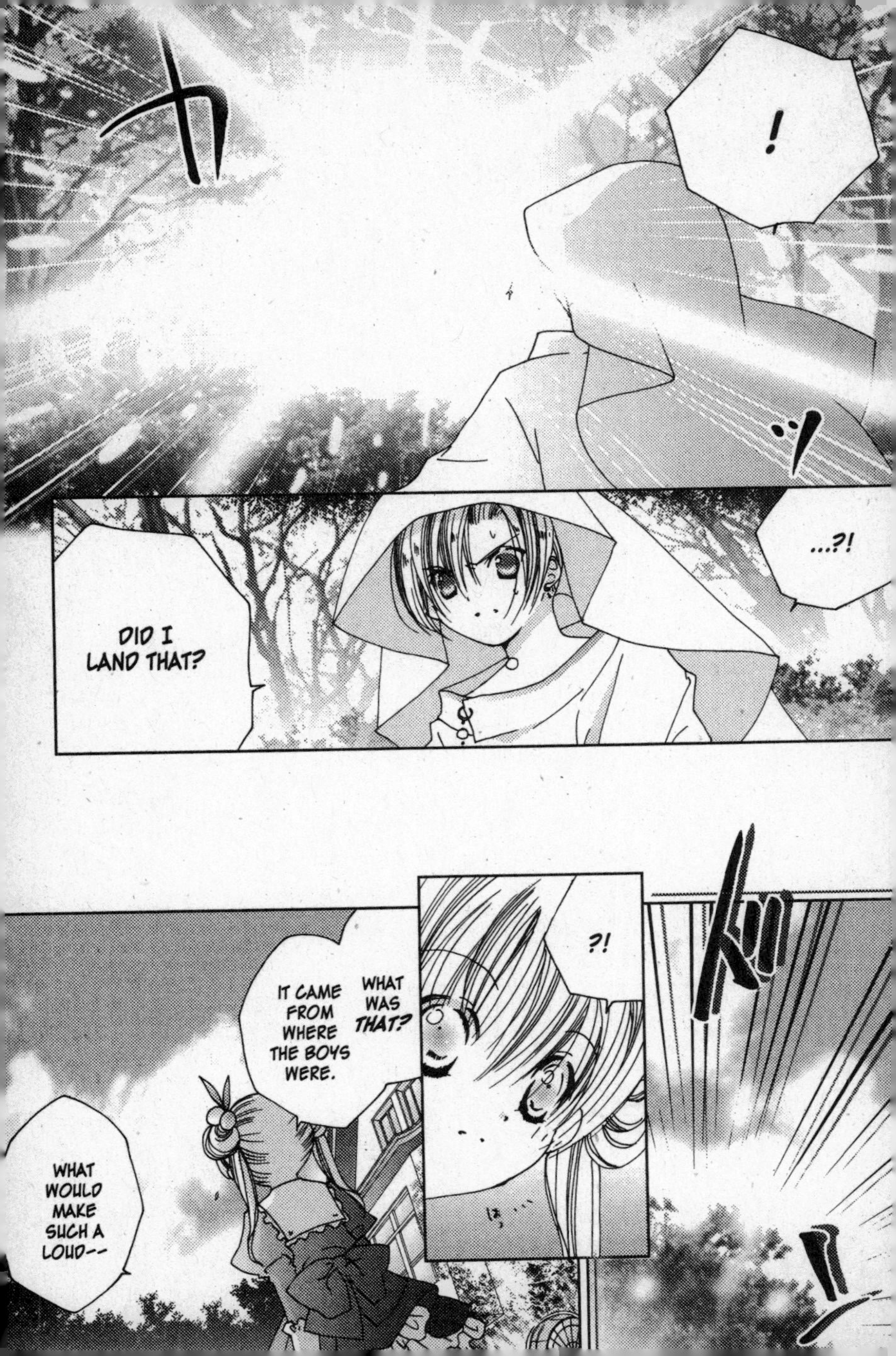
!
...?!
DID I LAND THAT?
?!
WHAT WAS *THAT?*
IT CAME FROM WHERE THE BOYS WERE.
WHAT WOULD MAKE SUCH A LOUD--

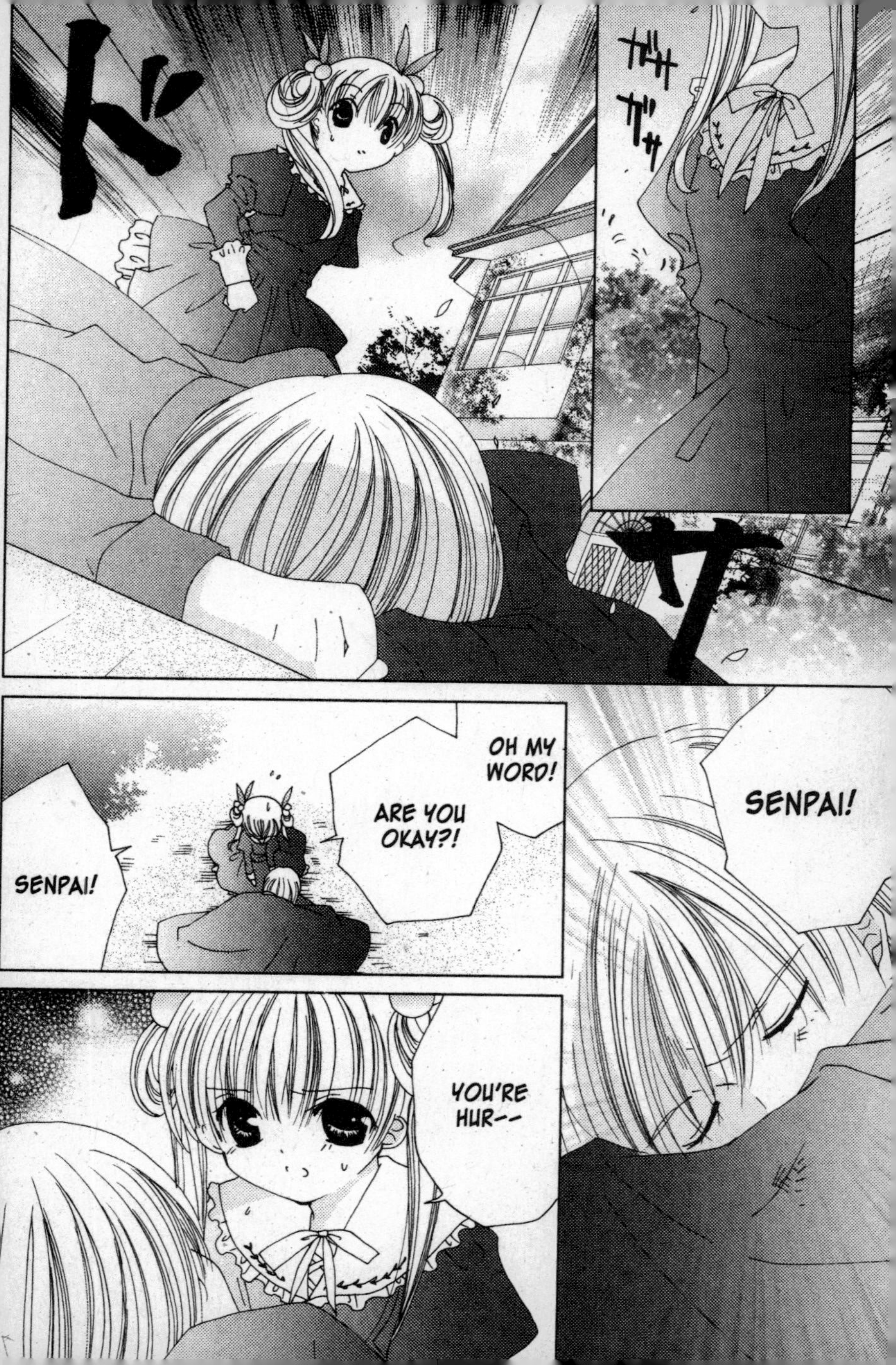
ガサ
ガサ
ド
ヤ
SENPAI!
OH MY WORD!
ARE YOU OKAY?!
SENPAI!
YOU'RE HUR--

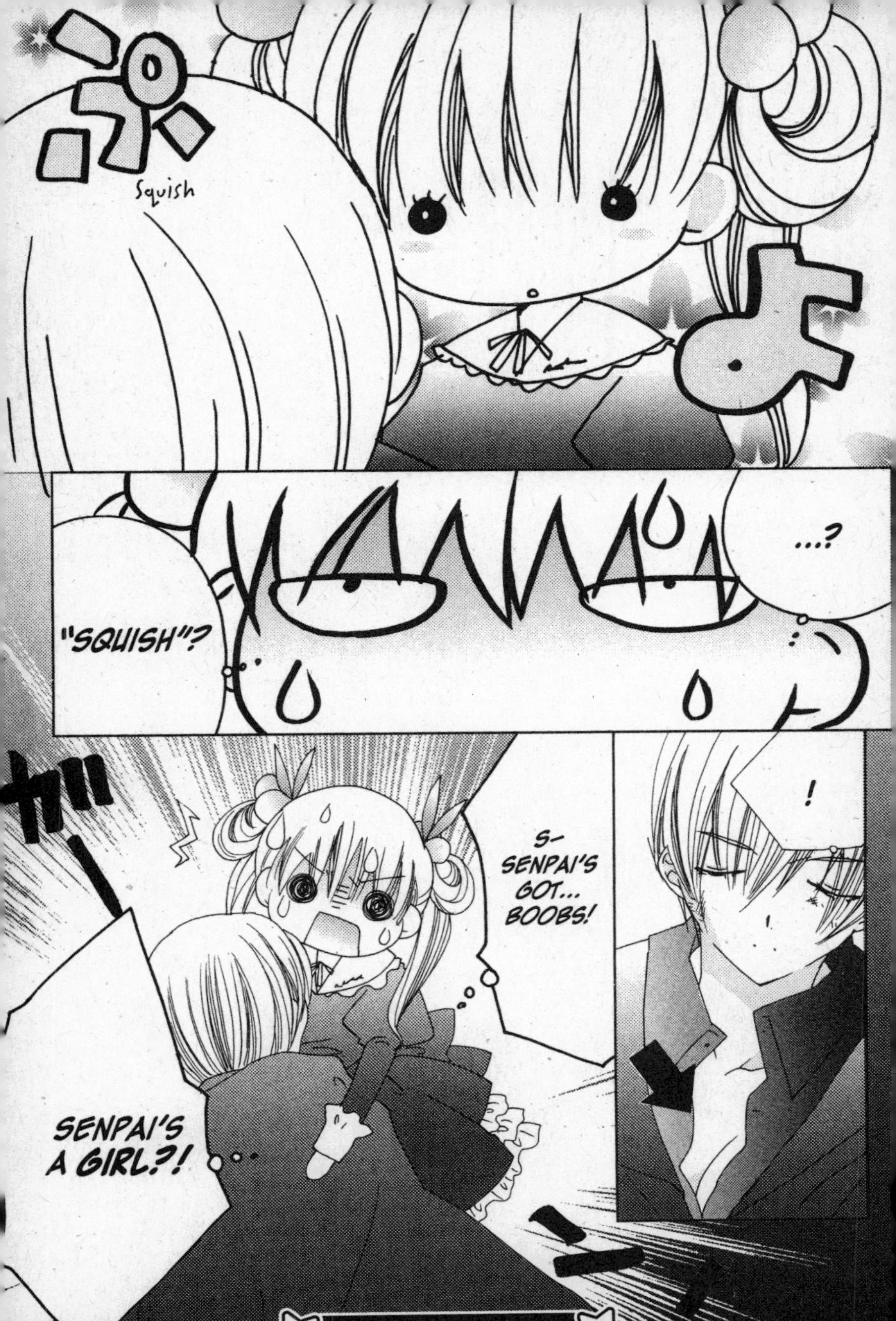
Squish
...?
"SQUISH"?
!
S-SENPAI'S GOT... BOOBS!
SENPAI'S A GIRL?!

Continued in Book 5!

Hey! Koge-Donbo here. Can you believe Kamichama Karin is on its 4th volume already? Thanks so much for picking it up and reading it! Although you're not really done, I guess--you still have a side story to read.

In Volume 4, there was all this talk about whether or not Kirika-san was a boy or a girl. Since I began the initial designs for this series, I really couldn't decide on what to make her, so there was always that tension there. Sometimes I drew her as a man, sometimes as a woman...it was really all over the place. Then again, maybe on her end she had lapses in her "disguise"--some days putting on too much boy make-up, some days too little...
Still, I had a lot of fun drawing her androgynously, like she both was and wasn't a boy or a girl. (Okay, honestly--that "disguise make-up" excuse is really because I couldn't make up my mind, and at times drew her too masculine or too feminine.)

But enough about that! Things are gonna go full speed ahead now! (In theory.) Keep an eye out for *Kamichama Karin* Volume 5! (Of course, if you're really curious, the continuation of this book will be in this month's *Nakayoshi*. Feel free to check it out.)
'Til next time.
6/16/2004
Koge-Donbo

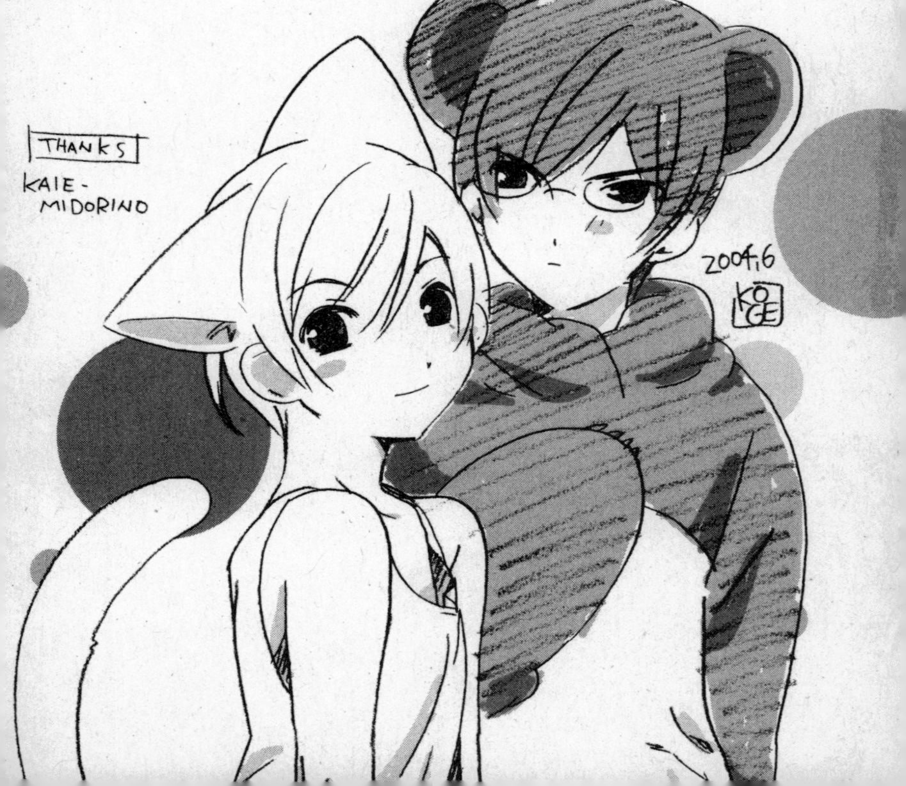
THANKS
KAIE-MIDORINO
2004.6
KOGE

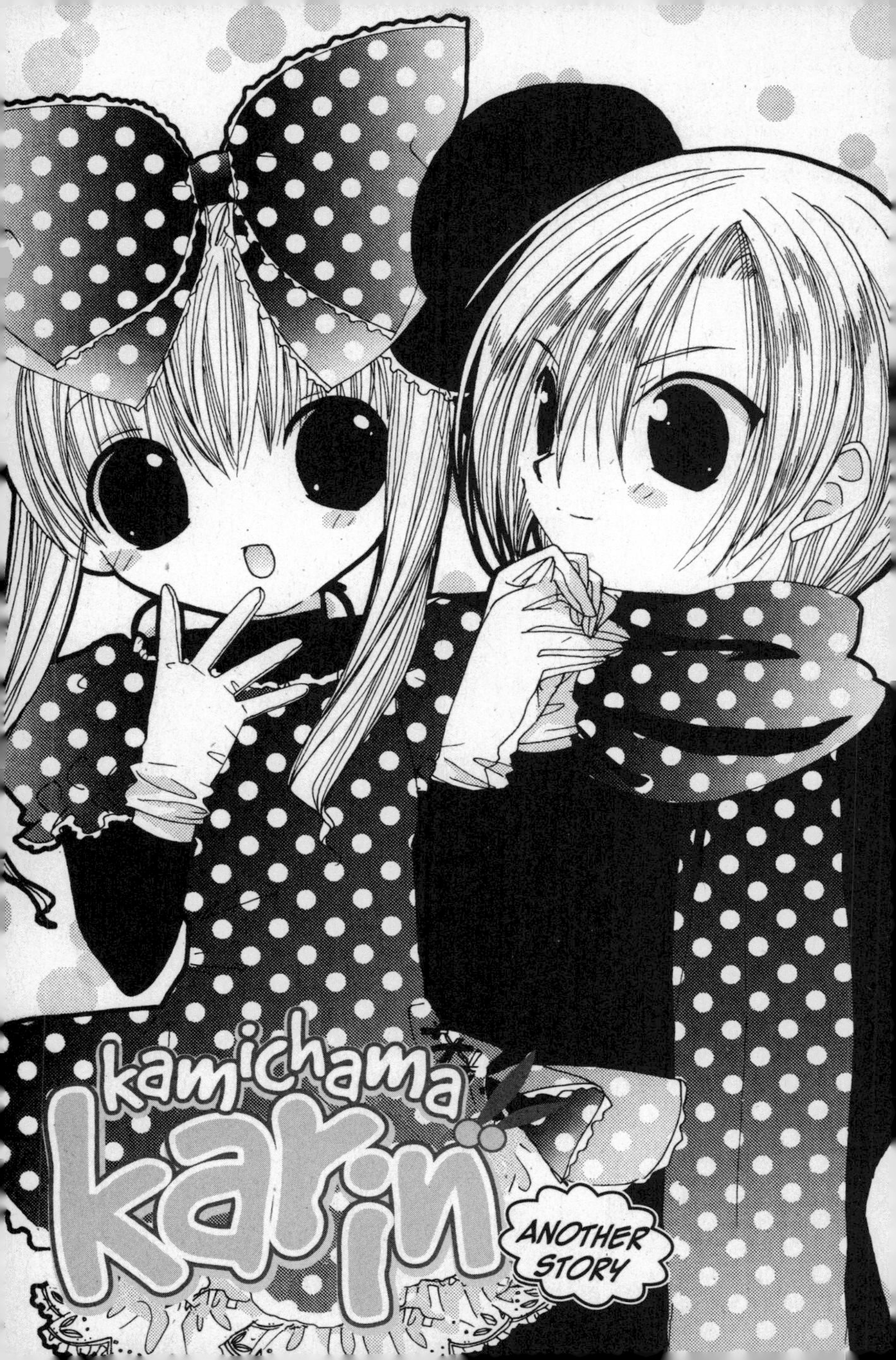
kamichama
karin
ANOTHER STORY

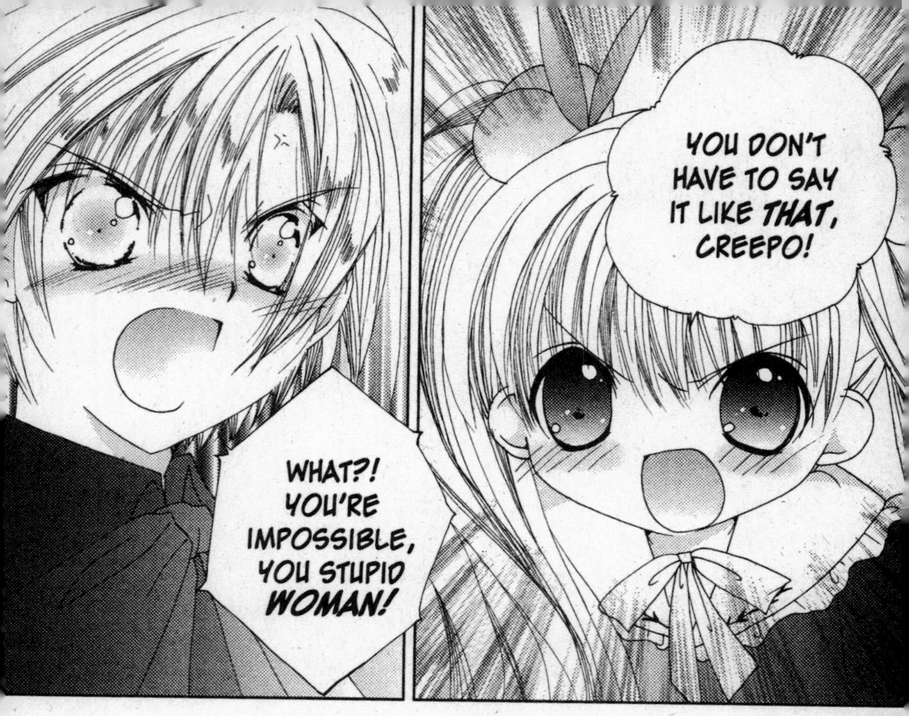
WHAT?! YOU'RE IMPOSSIBLE, YOU STUPID WOMAN!
YOU DON'T HAVE TO SAY IT LIKE THAT, CREEPO!

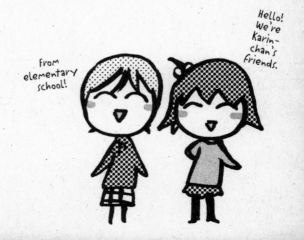

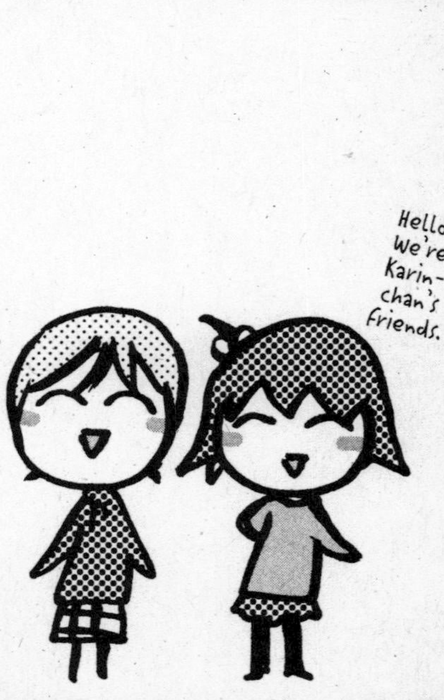
Hello! We're Karin-chan's friends.
From elementary school!

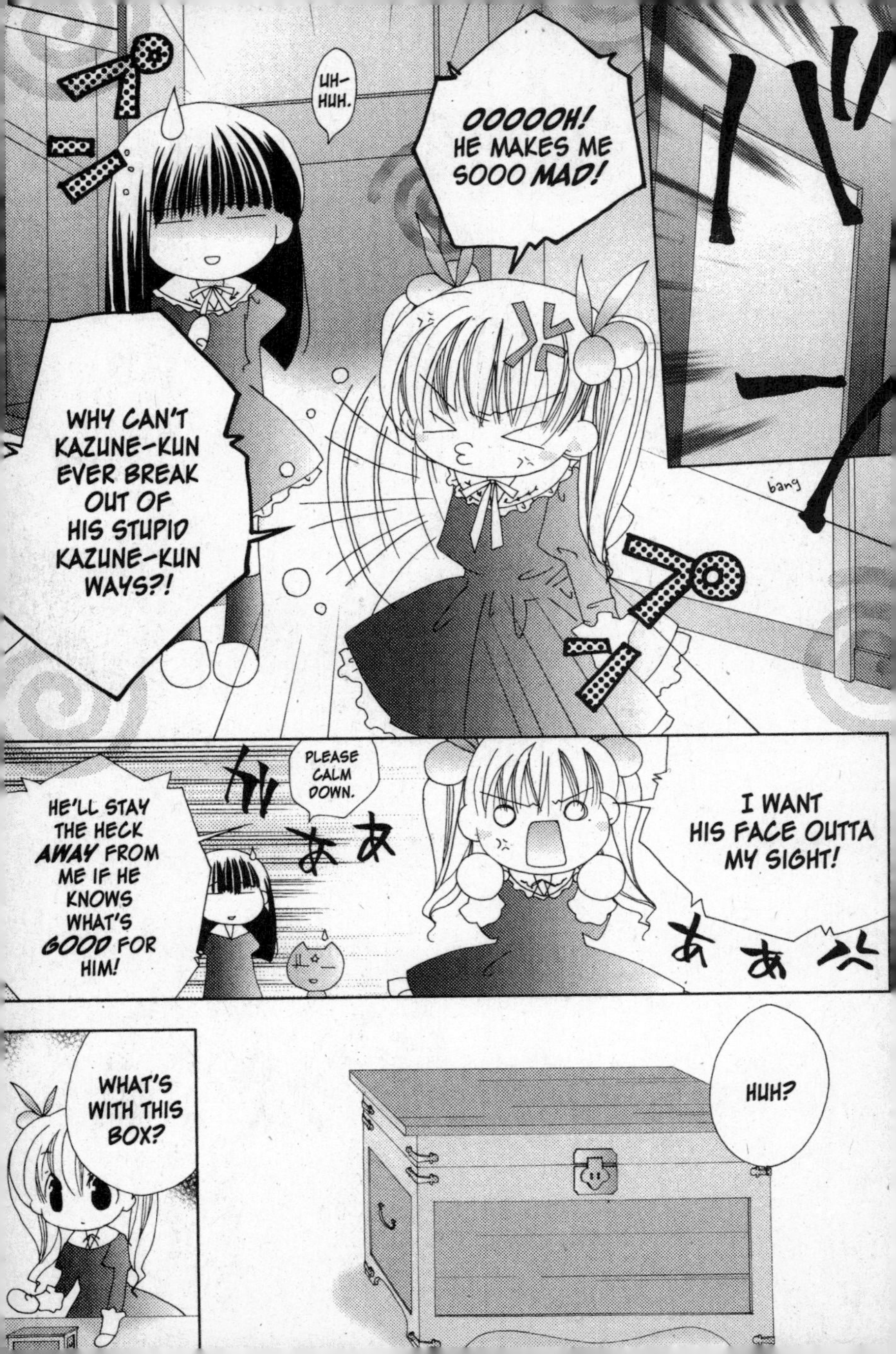

bang
OOOOOH! HE MAKES ME SOOO MAD!
UH-HUH.
WHY CAN'T KAZUNE-KUN EVER BREAK OUT OF HIS STUPID KAZUNE-KUN WAYS?!
I WANT HIS FACE OUTTA MY SIGHT!
PLEASE CALM DOWN.
HE'LL STAY THE HECK AWAY FROM ME IF HE KNOWS WHAT'S GOOD FOR HIM!
HUH?
WHAT'S WITH THIS BOX?

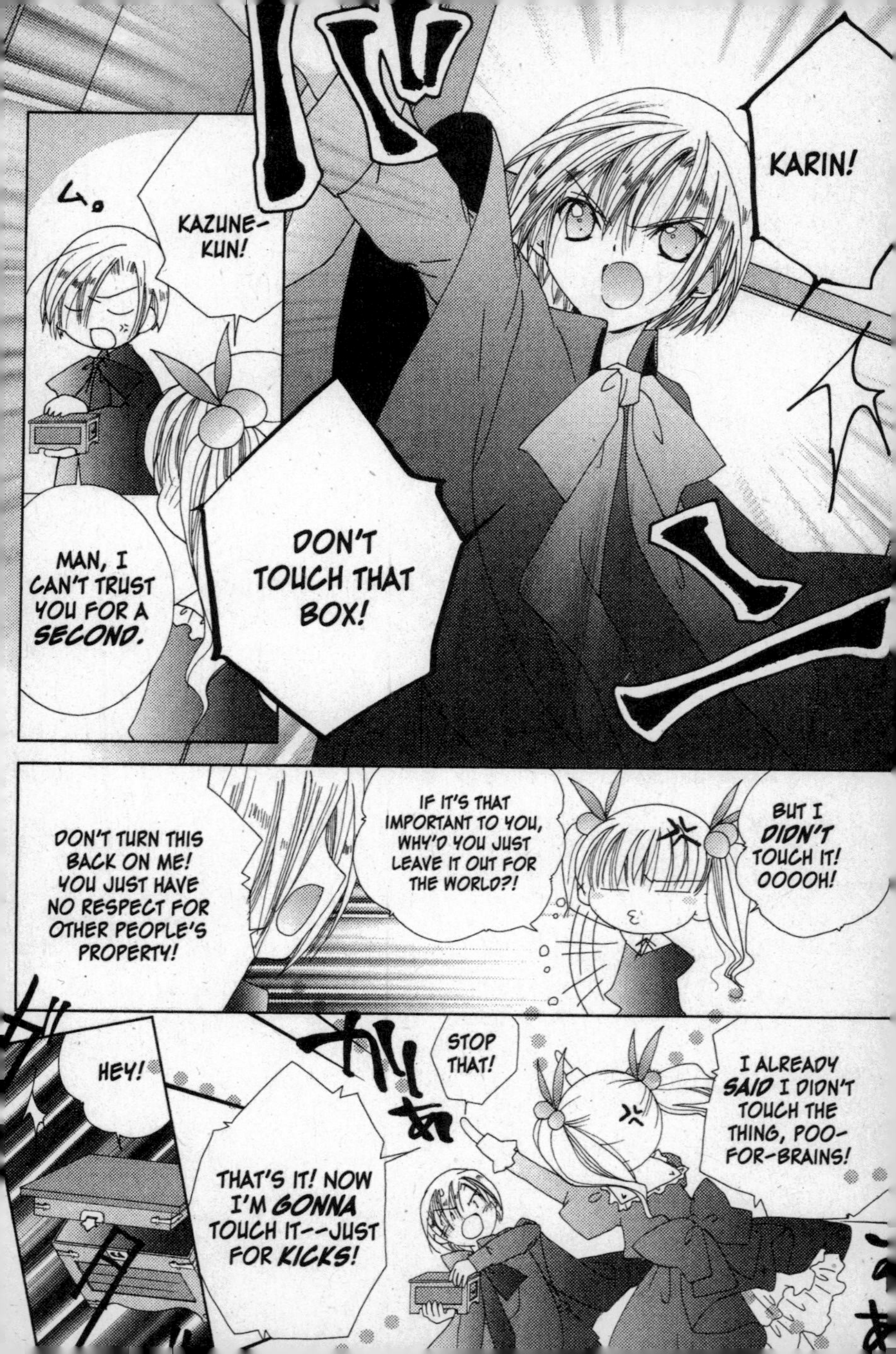
KARIN!
DON'T TOUCH THAT BOX!
む。
KAZUNE-KUN!
MAN, I CAN'T TRUST YOU FOR A SECOND.
BUT I DIDN'T TOUCH IT! OOOOH!
IF IT'S THAT IMPORTANT TO YOU, WHY'D YOU JUST LEAVE IT OUT FOR THE WORLD?!
DON'T TURN THIS BACK ON ME! YOU JUST HAVE NO RESPECT FOR OTHER PEOPLE'S PROPERTY!
I ALREADY SAID I DIDN'T TOUCH THE THING, POO-FOR-BRAINS!
STOP THAT!
THAT'S IT! NOW I'M GONNA TOUCH IT--JUST FOR KICKS!
HEY!

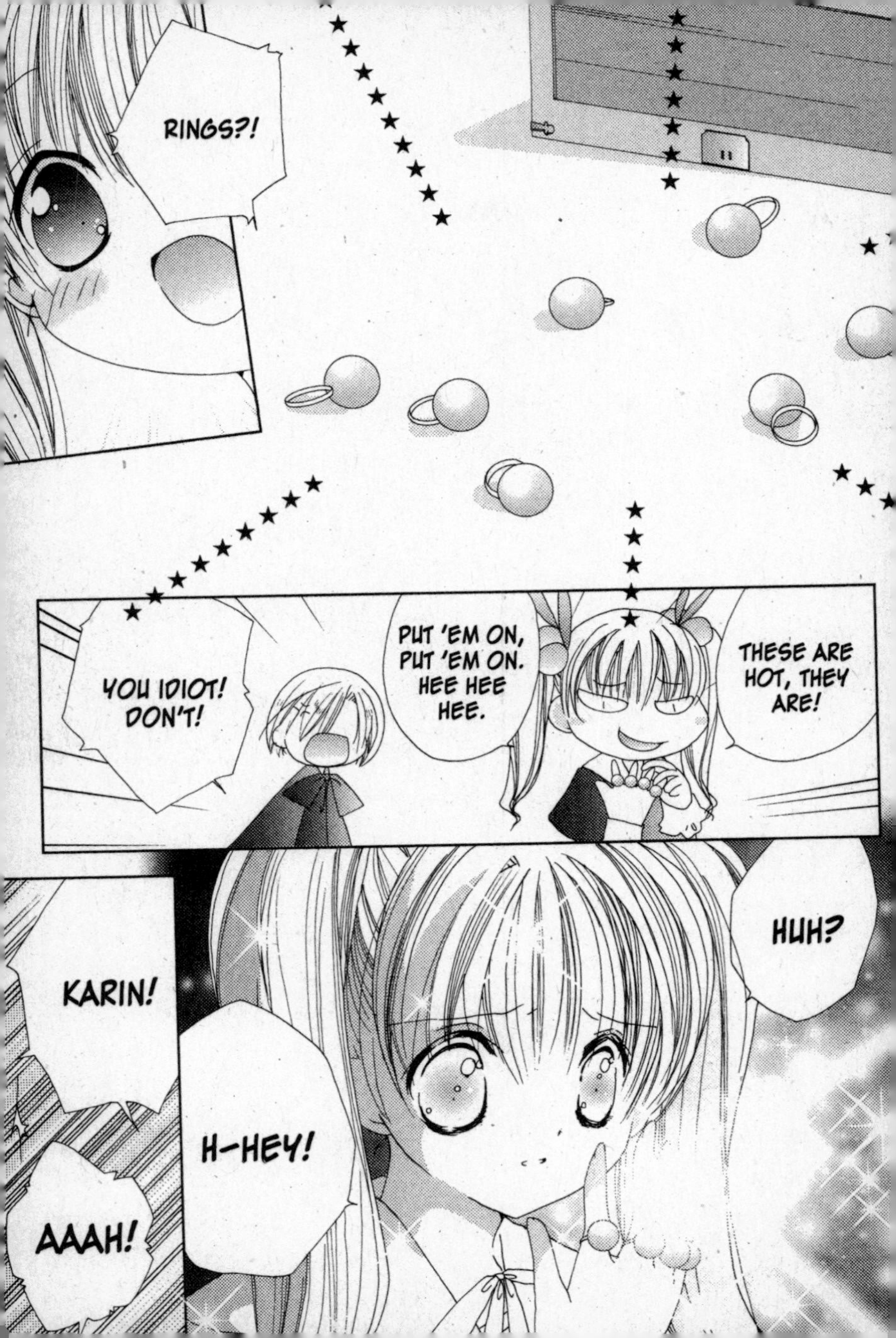
RINGS?!
THESE ARE HOT, THEY ARE!
PUT 'EM ON, PUT 'EM ON. HEE HEE HEE.
YOU IDIOT! DON'T!
HUH?
H-HEY!
KARIN!
AAAH!

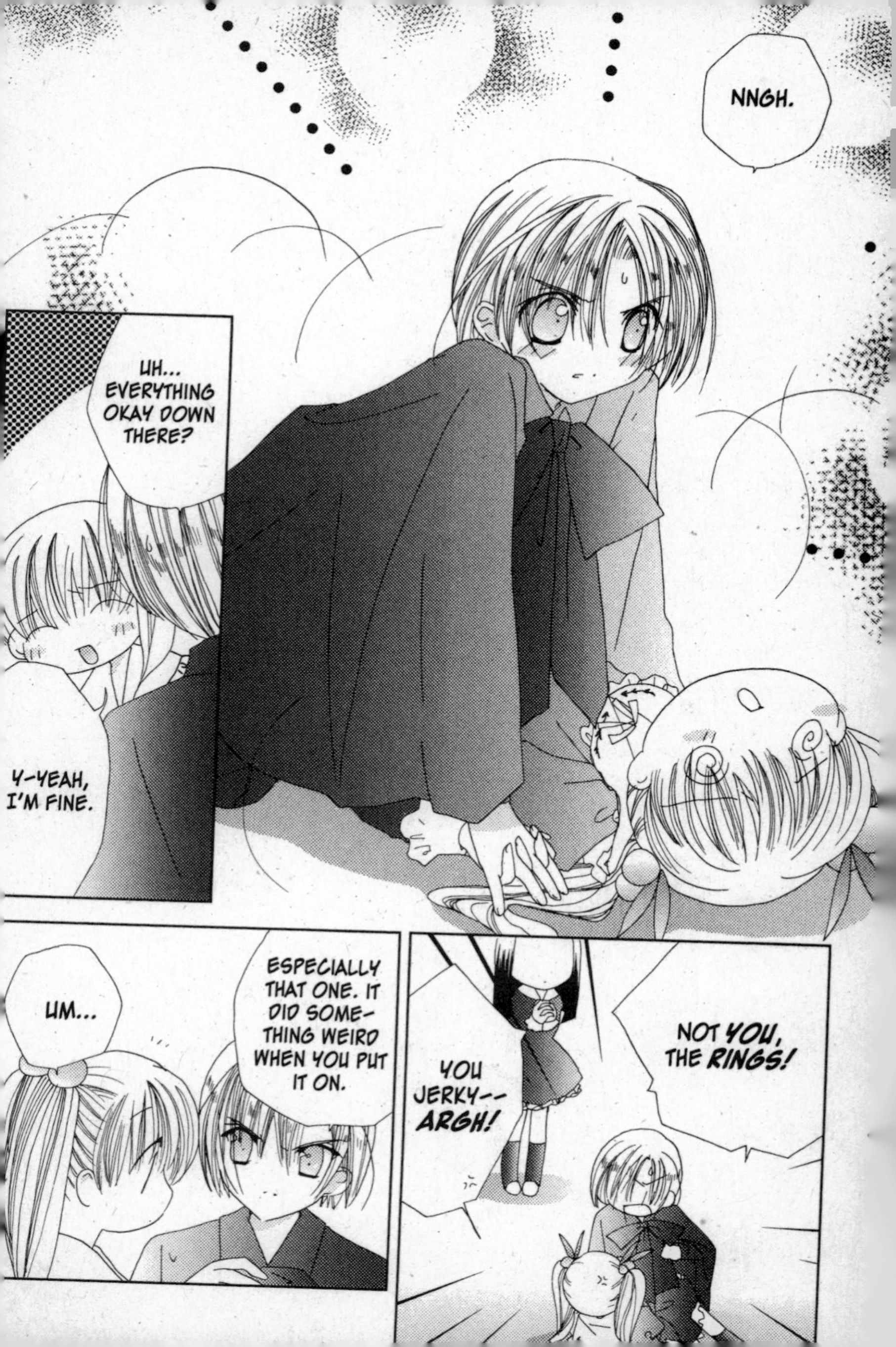
NNGH.
UH... EVERYTHING OKAY DOWN THERE?
Y-YEAH, I'M FINE.
UM...
ESPECIALLY THAT ONE. IT DID SOME-THING WEIRD WHEN YOU PUT IT ON.
YOU JERKY-- ARGH!
NOT YOU, THE RINGS!

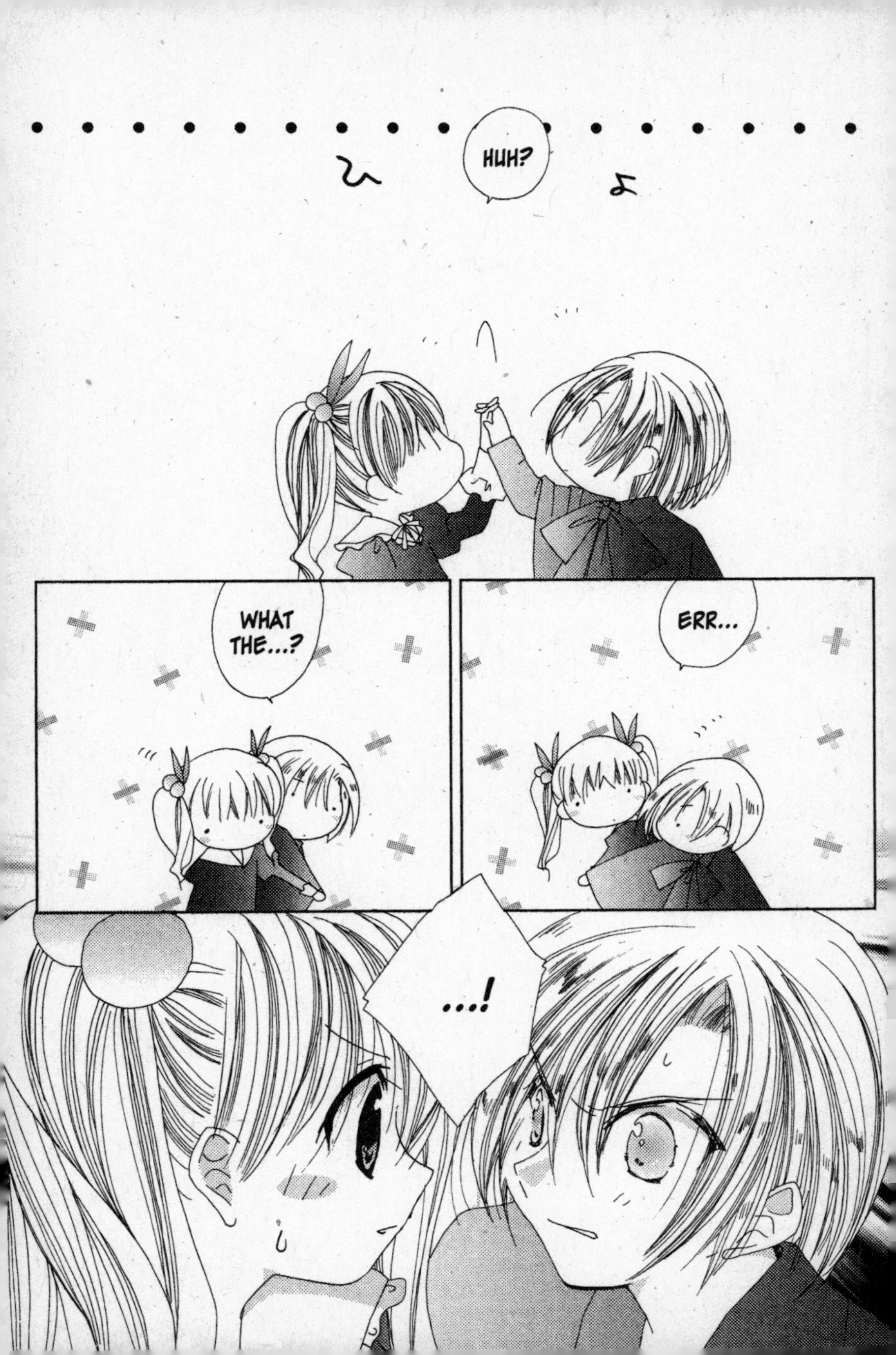
HUH?
ERR...
WHAT THE...?
...!

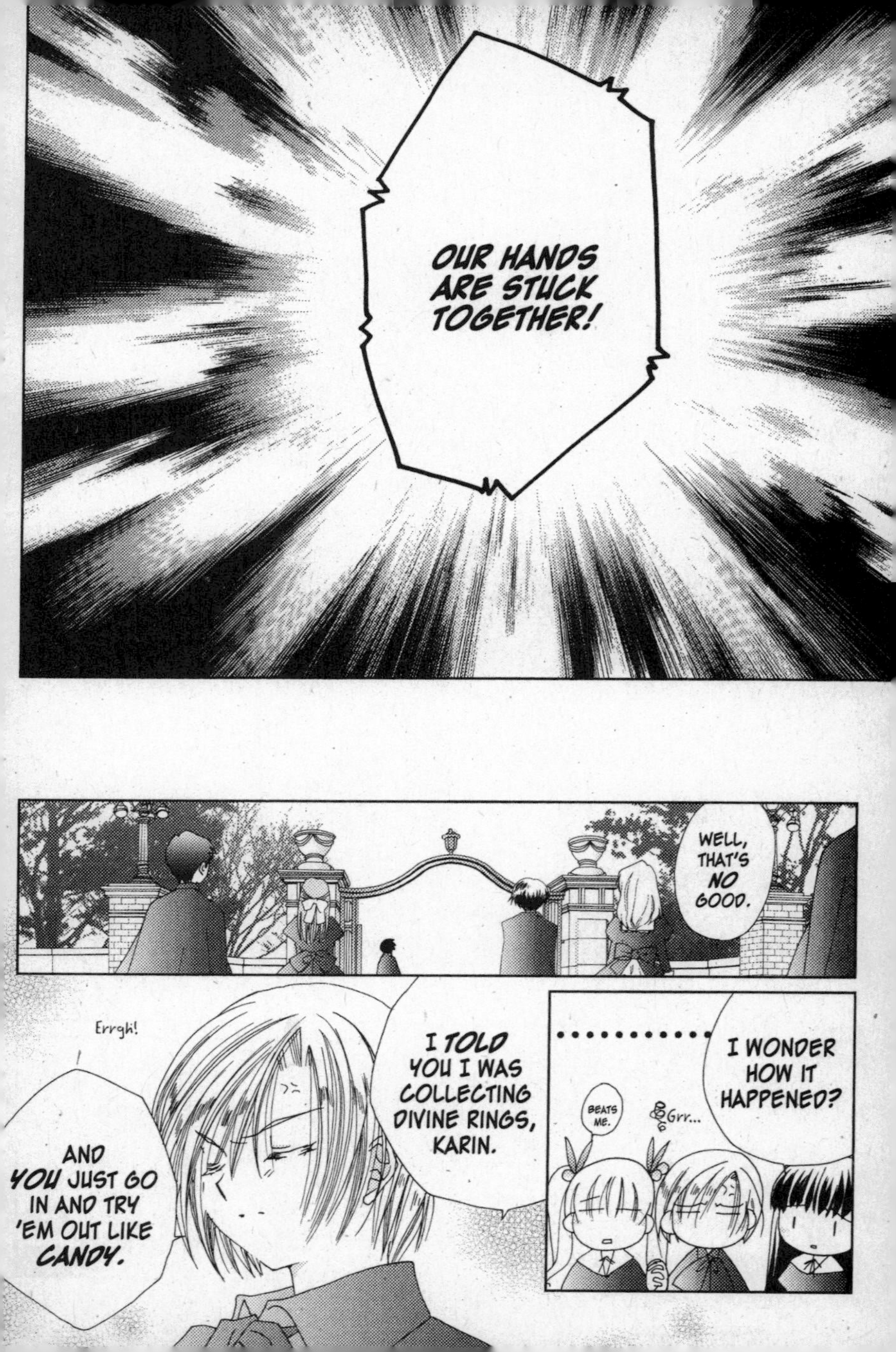
OUR HANDS ARE STUCK TOGETHER!
WELL, THAT'S NO GOOD.
....
I WONDER HOW IT HAPPENED?
Grr...
BEATS ME.
I TOLD YOU I WAS COLLECTING DIVINE RINGS, KARIN.
Errgh!
AND YOU JUST GO IN AND TRY 'EM OUT LIKE CANDY.

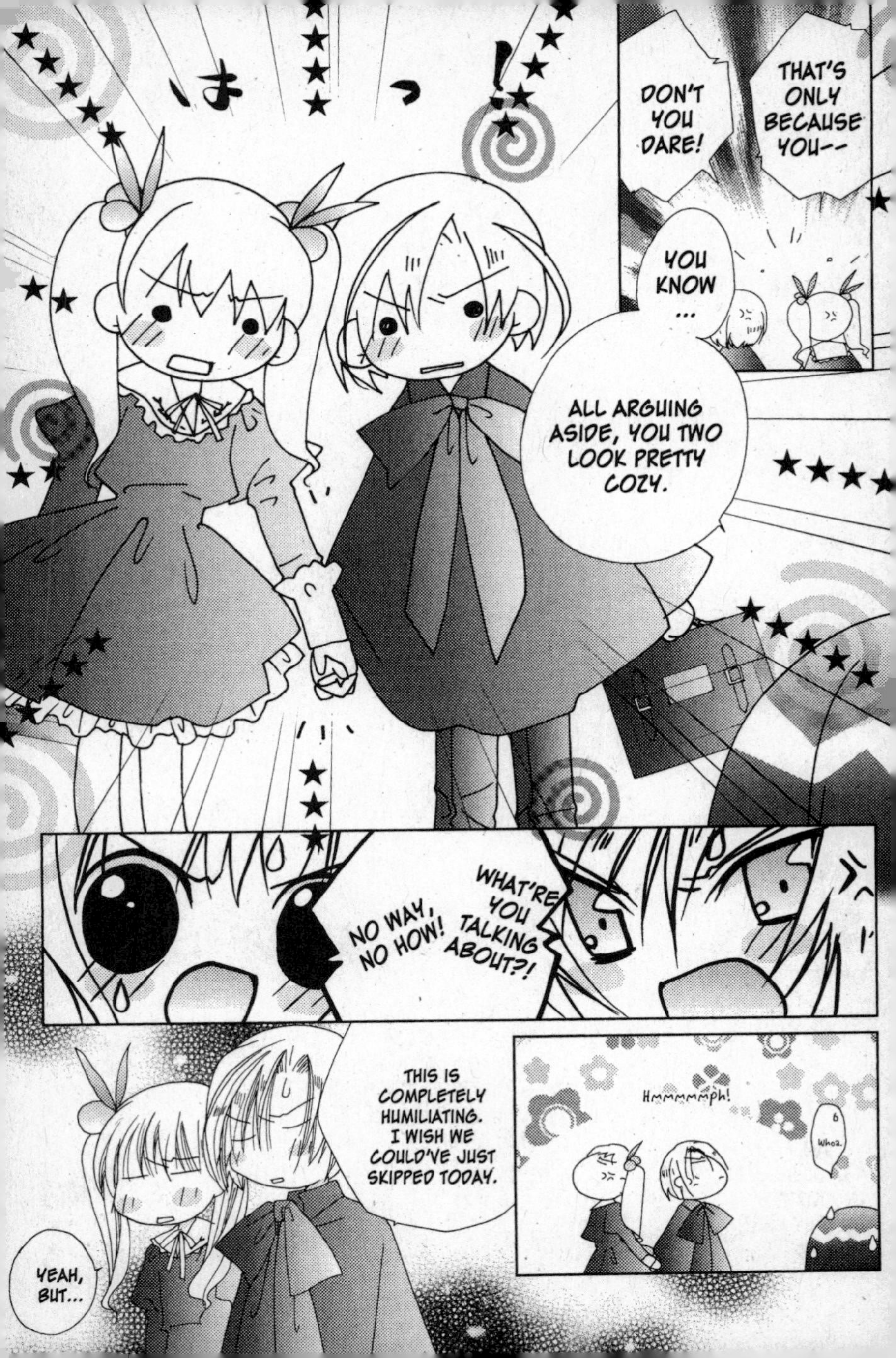
THAT'S ONLY BECAUSE YOU--
DON'T YOU DARE!
YOU KNOW...
ALL ARGUING ASIDE, YOU TWO LOOK PRETTY COZY.
はっ!
WHAT'RE YOU TALKING ABOUT?!
NO WAY, NO HOW!
Hmmmmmph!
Whoa.
THIS IS COMPLETELY HUMILIATING. I WISH WE COULD'VE JUST SKIPPED TODAY.
YEAH, BUT...

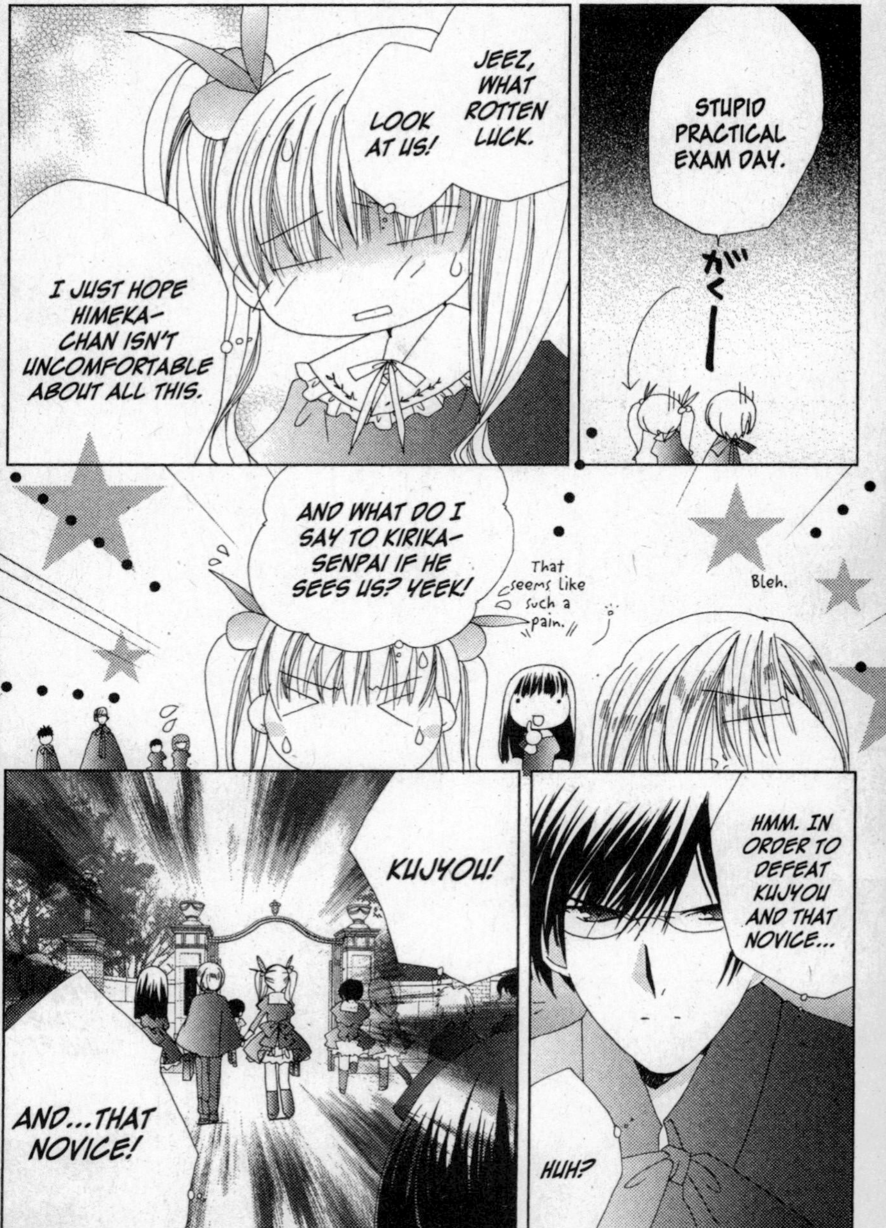
STUPID PRACTICAL EXAM DAY.
がくー
JEEZ, WHAT ROTTEN LUCK.
LOOK AT US!
I JUST HOPE HIMEKA-CHAN ISN'T UNCOMFORTABLE ABOUT ALL THIS.
Bleh.
That seems like such a pain.
AND WHAT DO I SAY TO KIRIKA-SENPAI IF HE SEES US? YEEK!
HMM. IN ORDER TO DEFEAT KUJYOU AND THAT NOVICE...
HUH?
KUJYOU!
AND...THAT NOVICE!

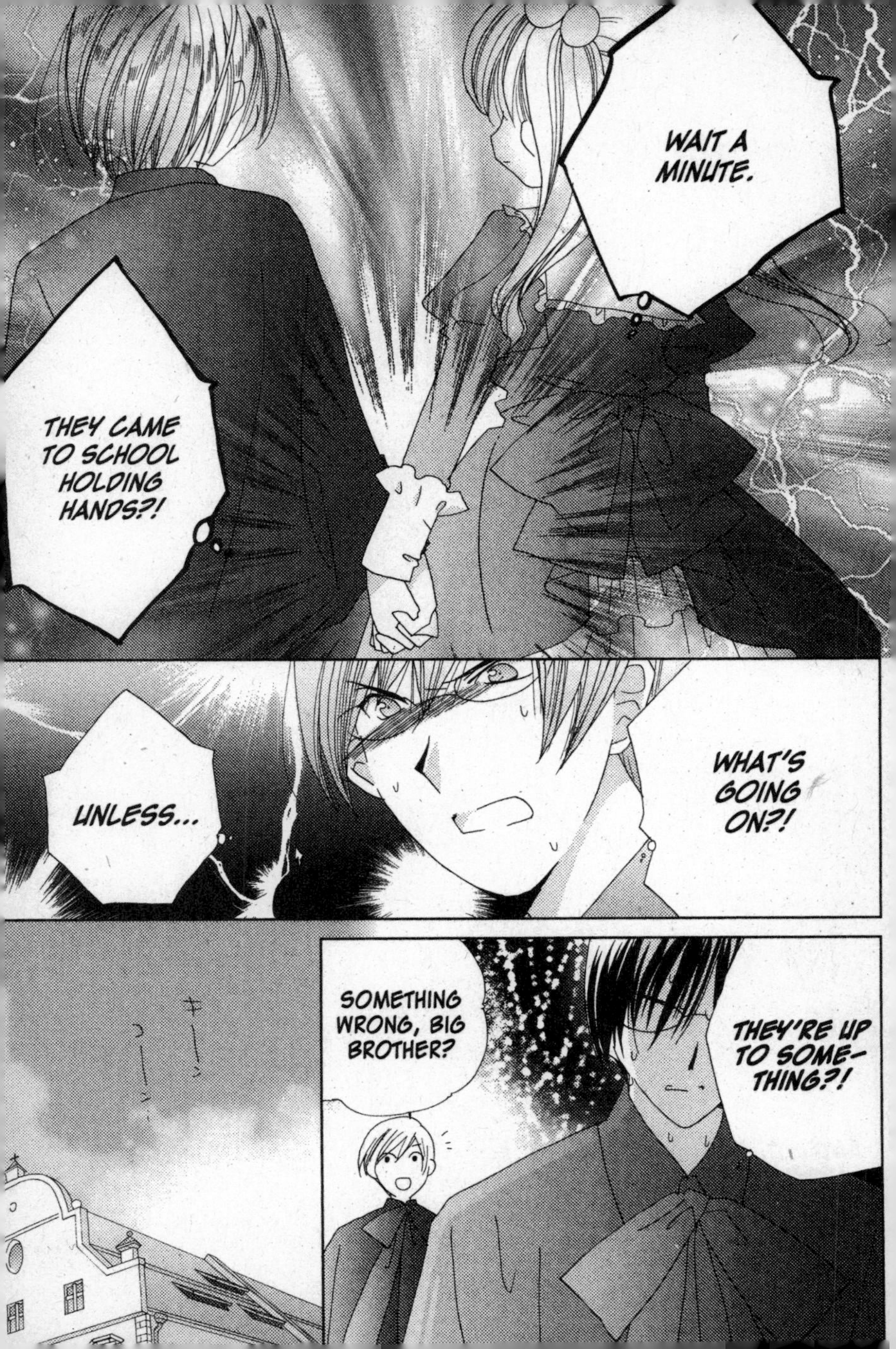
WAIT A MINUTE.
THEY CAME TO SCHOOL HOLDING HANDS?!
WHAT'S GOING ON?!
UNLESS...
THEY'RE UP TO SOME-THING?!
SOMETHING WRONG, BIG BROTHER?

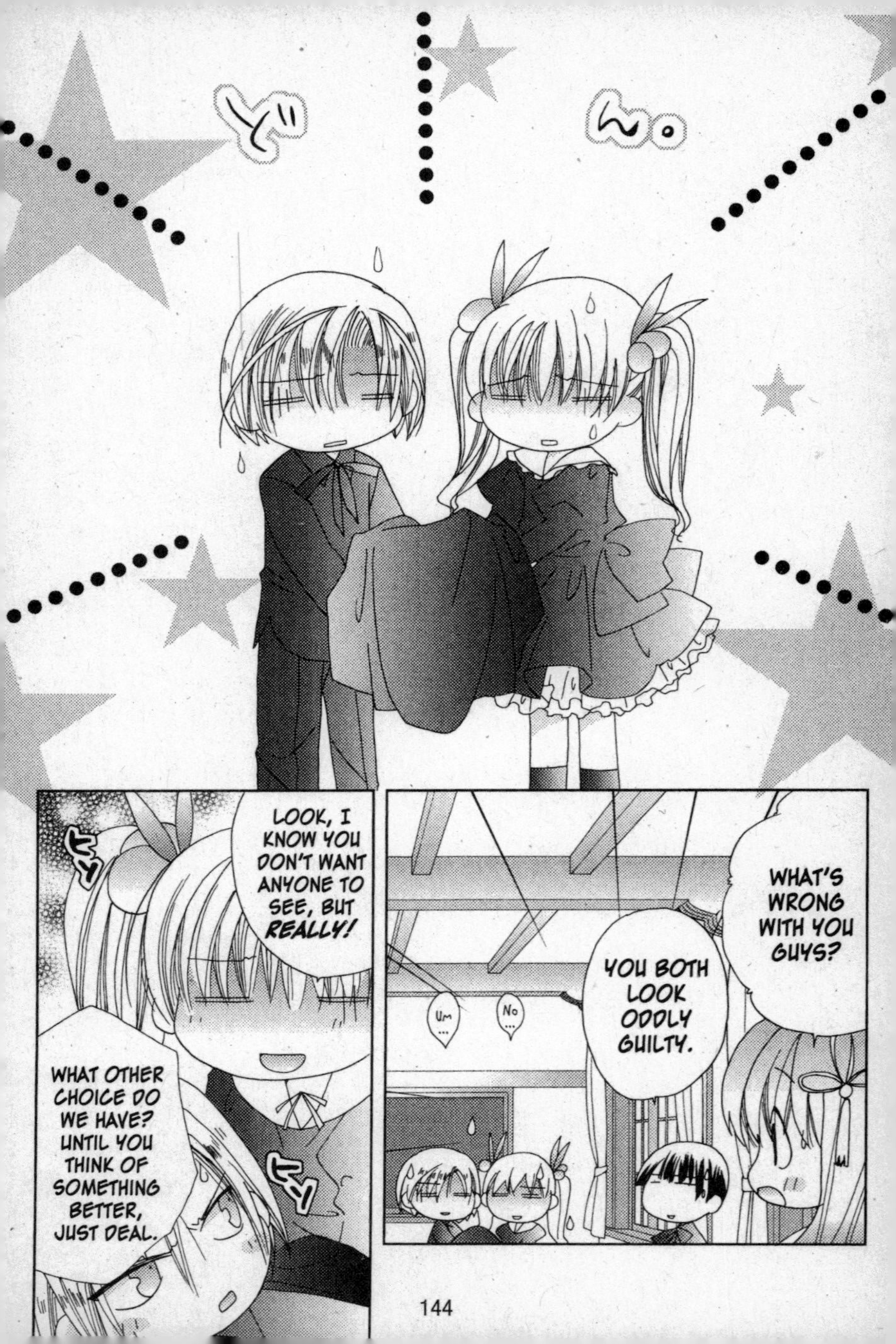

ど ん。
WHAT'S WRONG WITH YOU GUYS?
YOU BOTH LOOK ODDLY GUILTY.
No...
Um...
LOOK, I KNOW YOU DON'T WANT ANYONE TO SEE, BUT *REALLY!*
ヒソ
ヒソ
WHAT OTHER CHOICE DO WE HAVE? UNTIL YOU THINK OF SOMETHING BETTER, JUST DEAL.

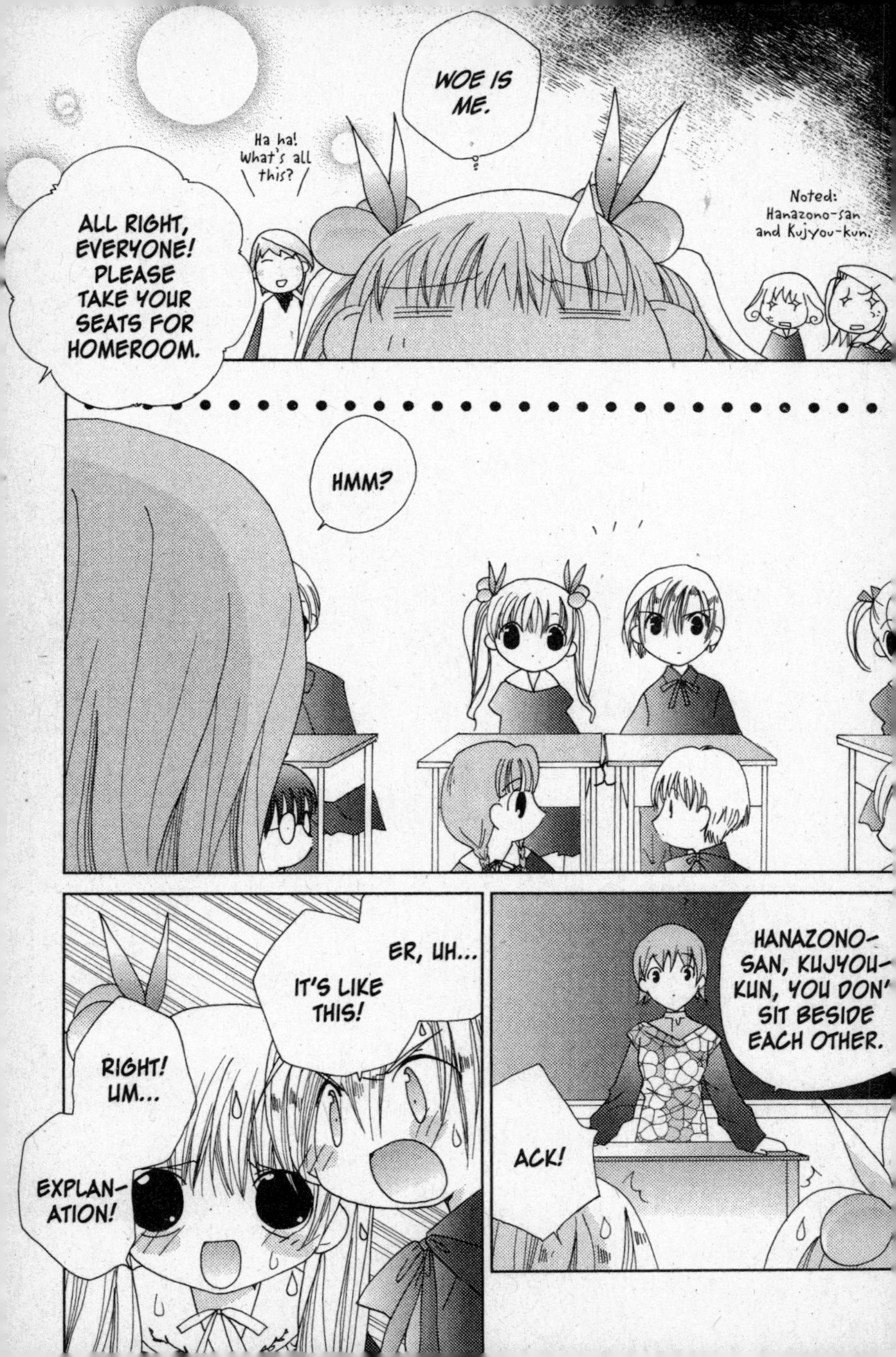
WOE IS ME.
Noted: Hanazono-san and Kujyou-kun.
Ha ha! What's all this?
ALL RIGHT, EVERYONE! PLEASE TAKE YOUR SEATS FOR HOMEROOM.
HMM?
HANAZONO-SAN, KUJYOU-KUN, YOU DON' SIT BESIDE EACH OTHER.
ACK!
ER, UH...
IT'S LIKE THIS!
RIGHT! UM...
EXPLANATION!

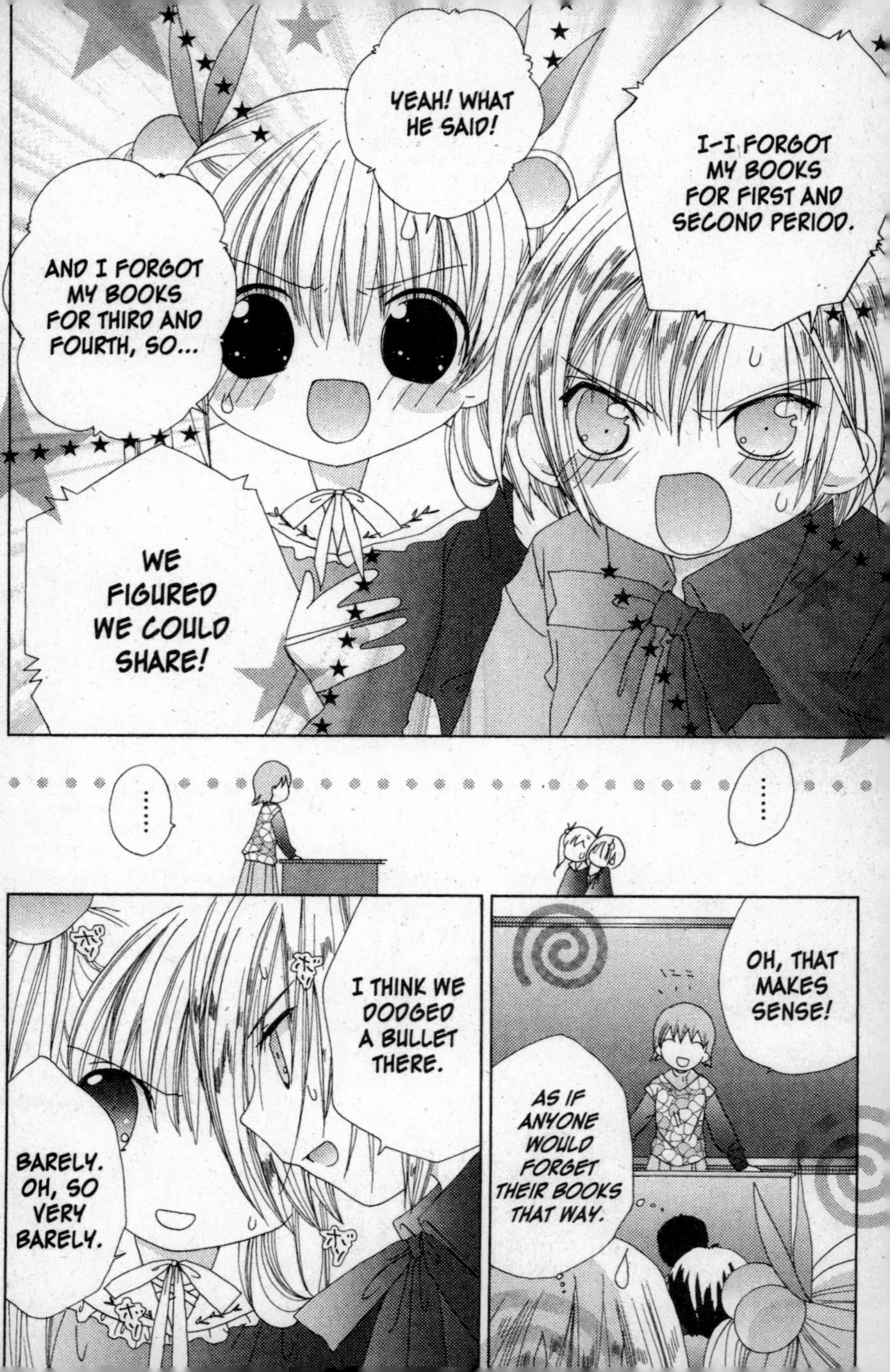
I-I FORGOT MY BOOKS FOR FIRST AND SECOND PERIOD.
YEAH! WHAT HE SAID!
AND I FORGOT MY BOOKS FOR THIRD AND FOURTH, SO...
WE FIGURED WE COULD SHARE!
......
......
OH, THAT MAKES SENSE!
AS IF ANYONE WOULD FORGET THEIR BOOKS THAT WAY.
I THINK WE DODGED A BULLET THERE.
BARELY. OH, SO VERY BARELY.

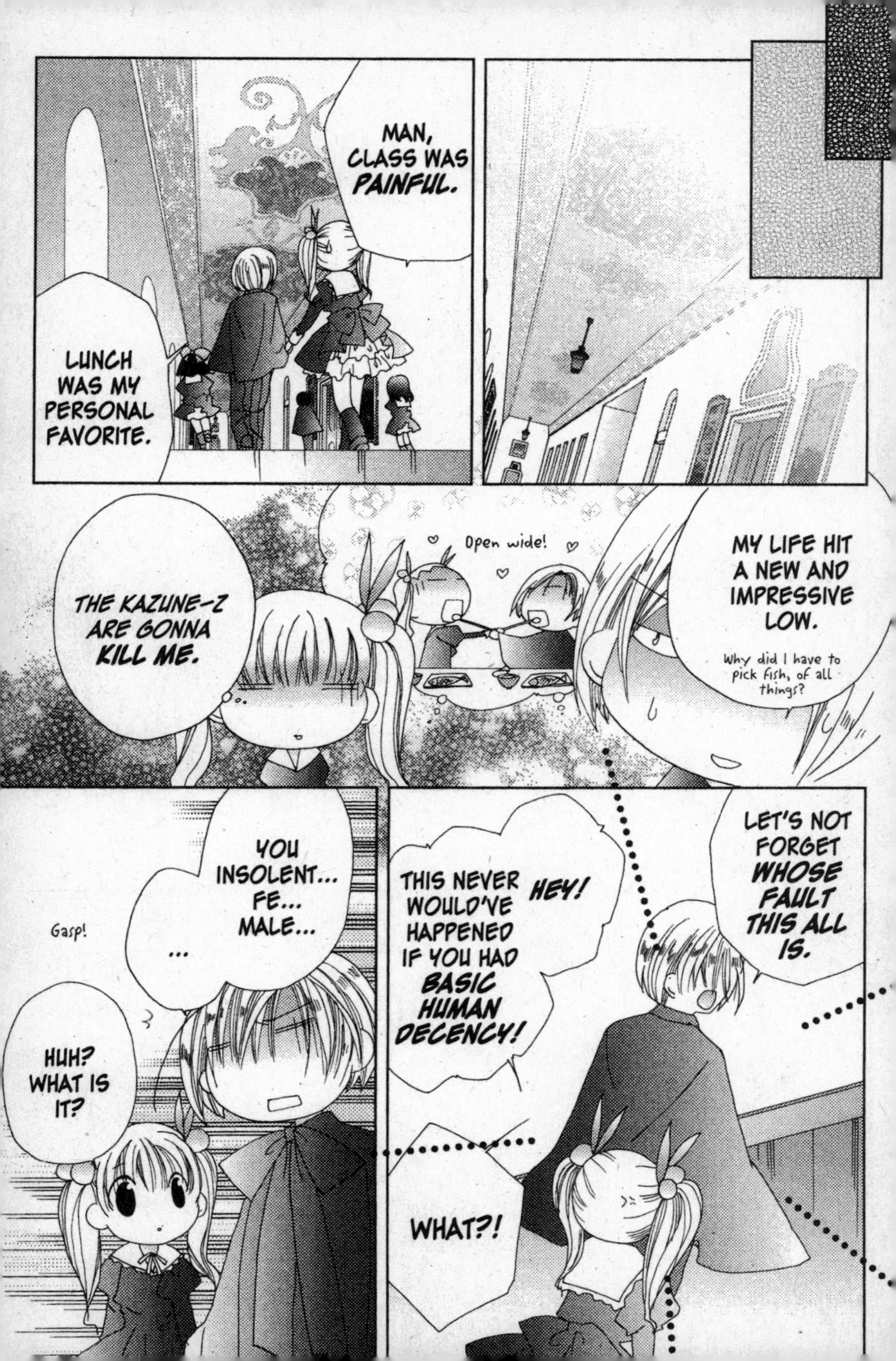
MAN, CLASS WAS PAINFUL.
LUNCH WAS MY PERSONAL FAVORITE.
MY LIFE HIT A NEW AND IMPRESSIVE LOW.
Why did I have to pick fish, of all things?
Open wide!
THE KAZUNE-Z ARE GONNA KILL ME.
LET'S NOT FORGET WHOSE FAULT THIS ALL IS.
HEY!
THIS NEVER WOULD'VE HAPPENED IF YOU HAD BASIC HUMAN DECENCY!
WHAT?!
YOU INSOLENT... FE... MALE...
...
Gasp!
HUH? WHAT IS IT?

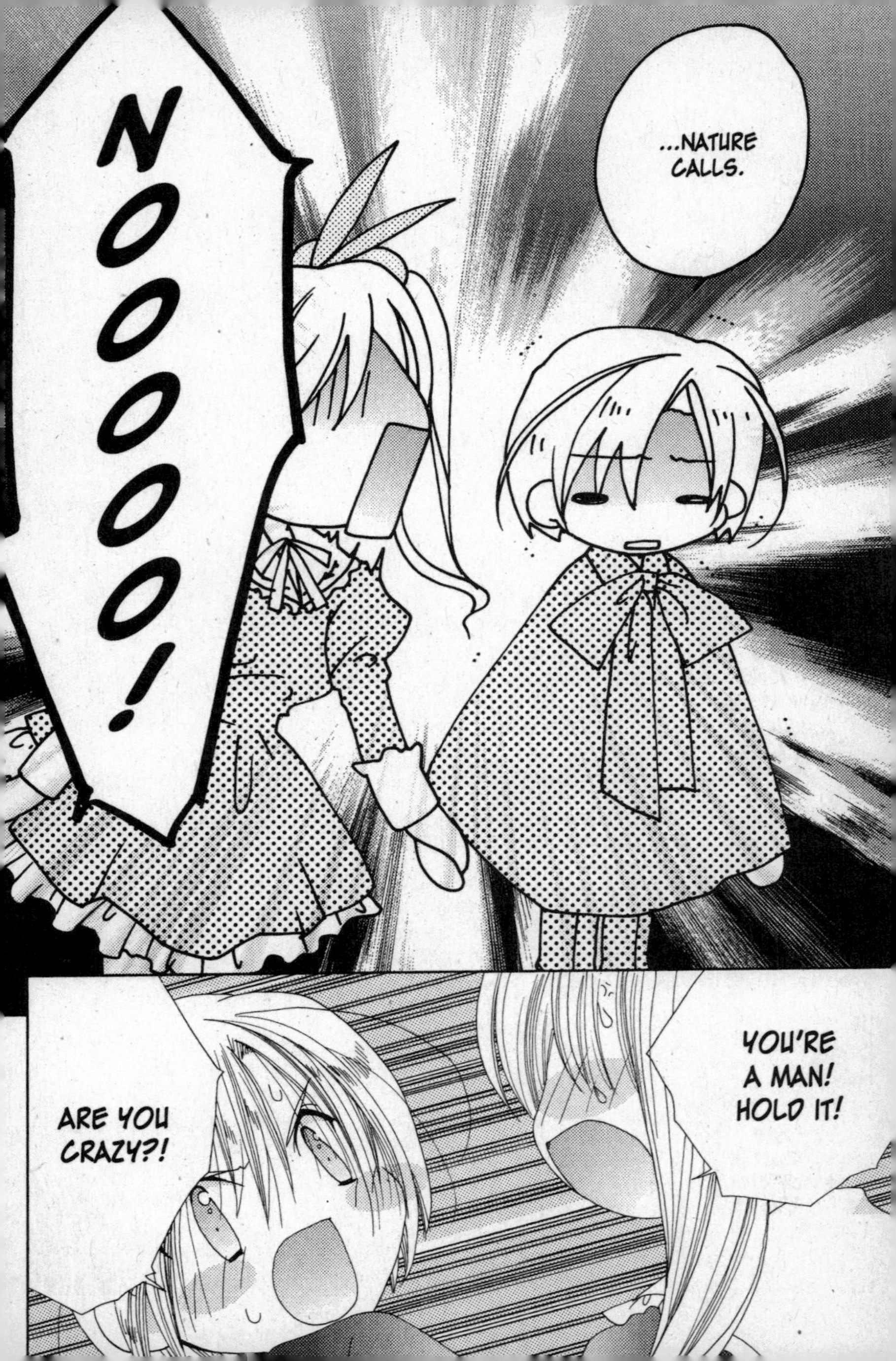
...NATURE CALLS.
NOOOOO!
YOU'RE A MAN! HOLD IT!
ARE YOU CRAZY?!

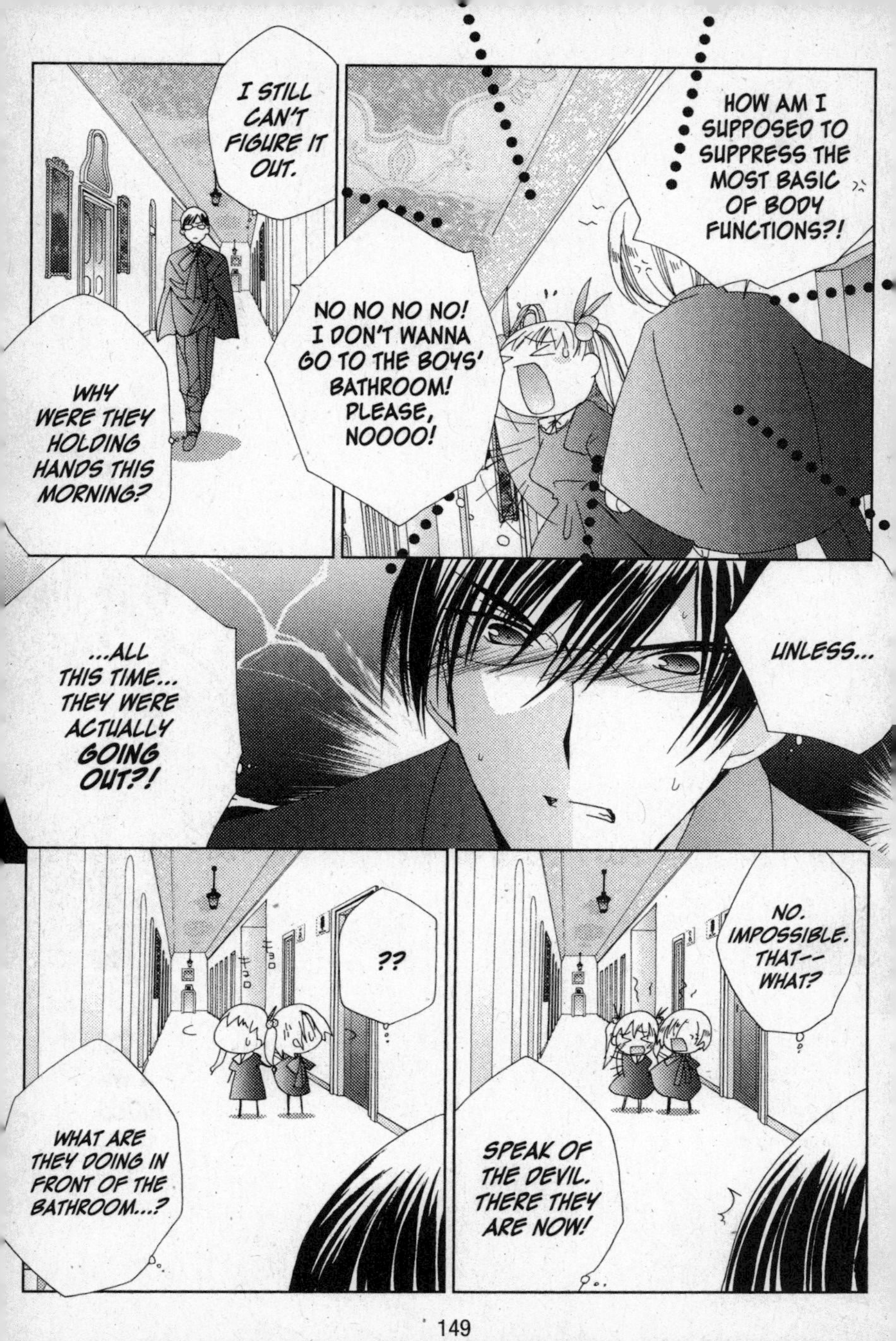
HOW AM I SUPPOSED TO SUPPRESS THE MOST BASIC OF BODY FUNCTIONS?!
NO NO NO NO! I DON'T WANNA GO TO THE BOYS' BATHROOM! PLEASE, NOOOO!
I STILL CAN'T FIGURE IT OUT.
WHY WERE THEY HOLDING HANDS THIS MORNING?
UNLESS...
...ALL THIS TIME... THEY WERE ACTUALLY GOING OUT?!
NO. IMPOSSIBLE. THAT-- WHAT?
SPEAK OF THE DEVIL. THERE THEY ARE NOW!
??
WHAT ARE THEY DOING IN FRONT OF THE BATHROOM...?

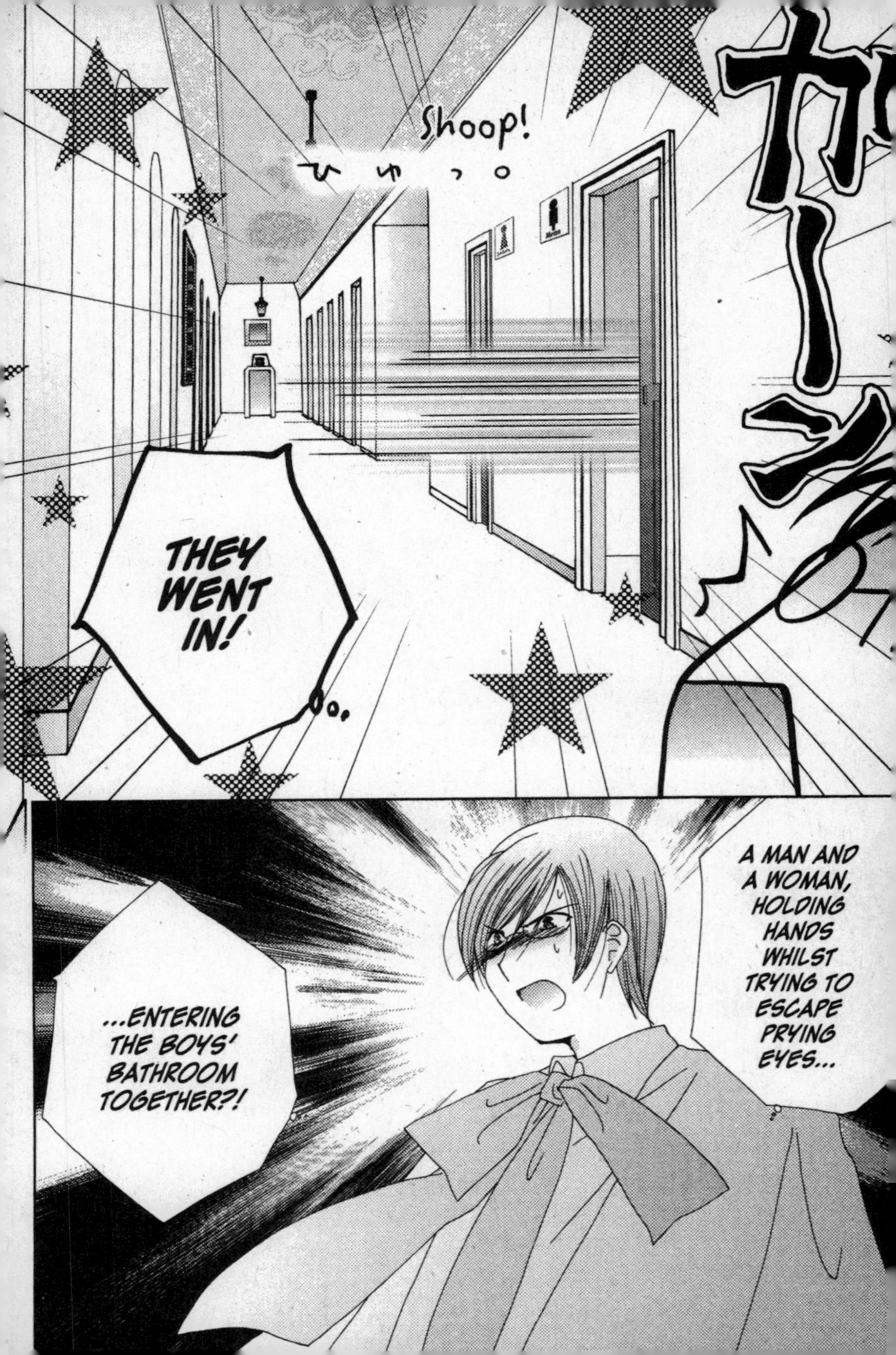
Shoop!
ひゅっ。
THEY WENT IN!
A MAN AND A WOMAN, HOLDING HANDS WHILST TRYING TO ESCAPE PRYING EYES...
...ENTERING THE BOYS' BATHROOM TOGETHER?!

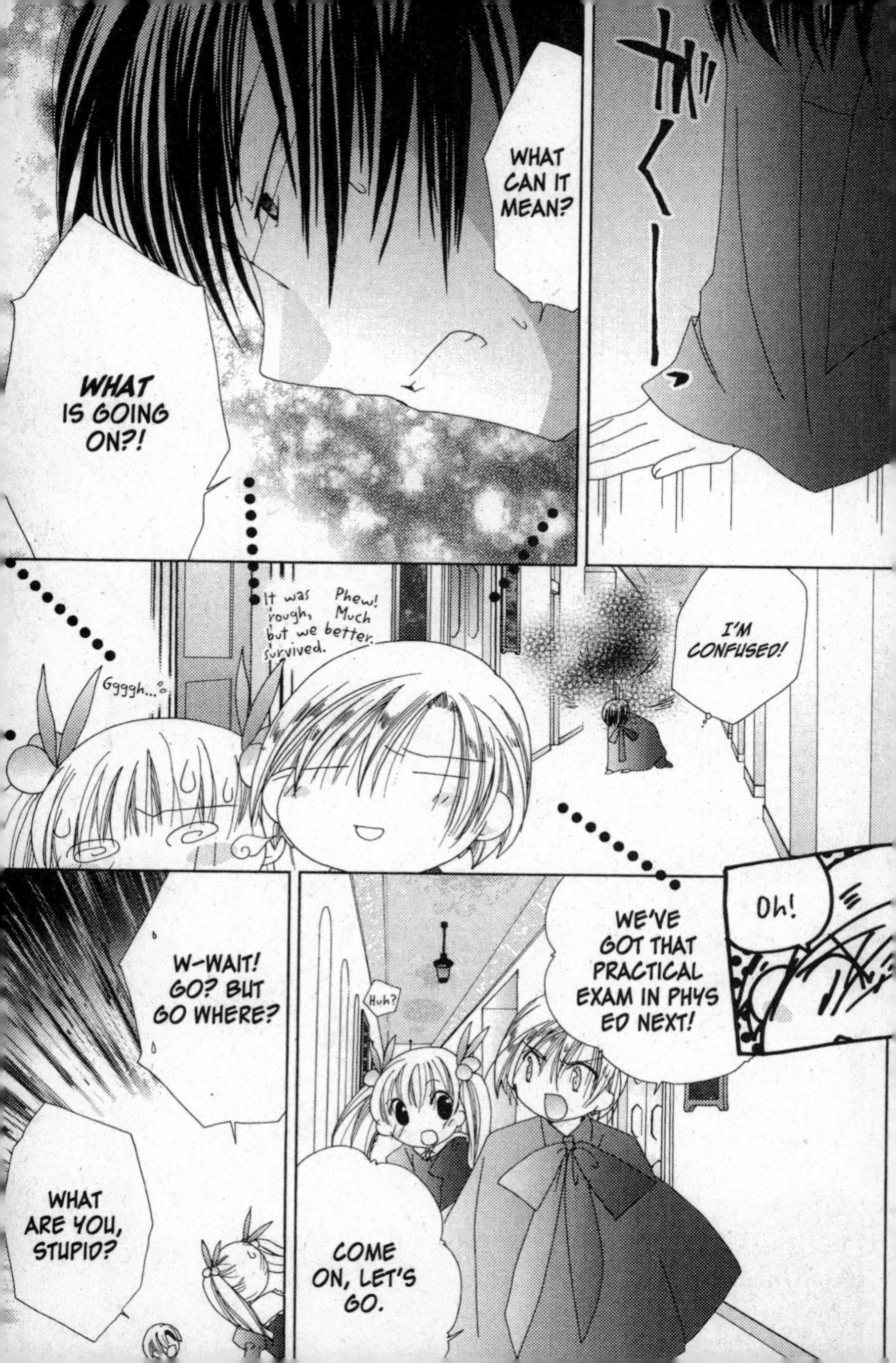
WHAT CAN IT MEAN?
WHAT IS GOING ON?!
I'M CONFUSED!
Phew! Much better.
It was rough, but we survived.
Ggggh...
Oh!
WE'VE GOT THAT PRACTICAL EXAM IN PHYS ED NEXT!
Huh?
COME ON, LET'S GO.
W-WAIT! GO? BUT GO WHERE?
WHAT ARE YOU, STUPID?

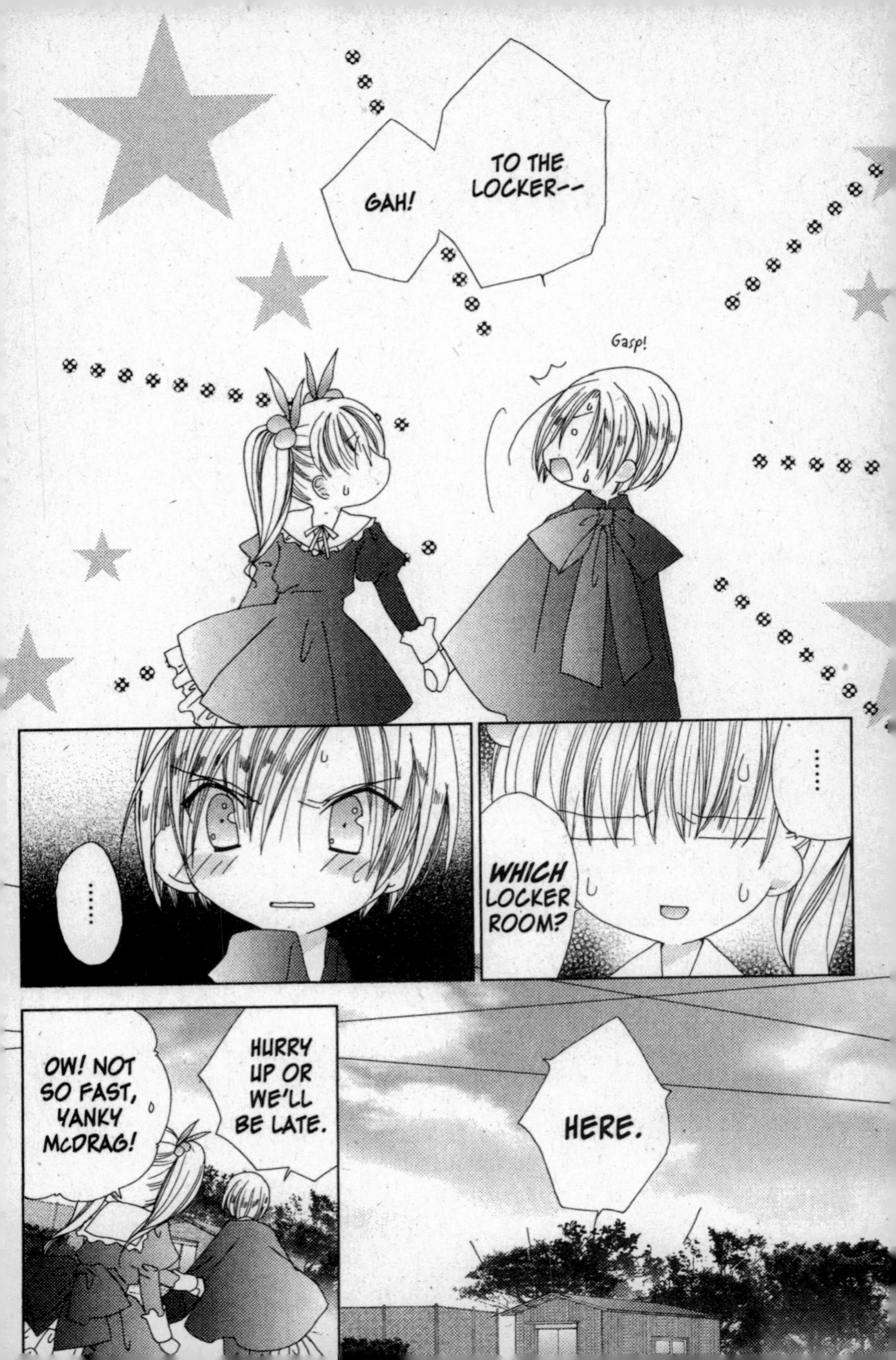
TO THE LOCKER--
GAH!
Gasp!
......
WHICH LOCKER ROOM?
......
HERE.
HURRY UP OR WE'LL BE LATE.
OW! NOT SO FAST, YANKY McDRAG!

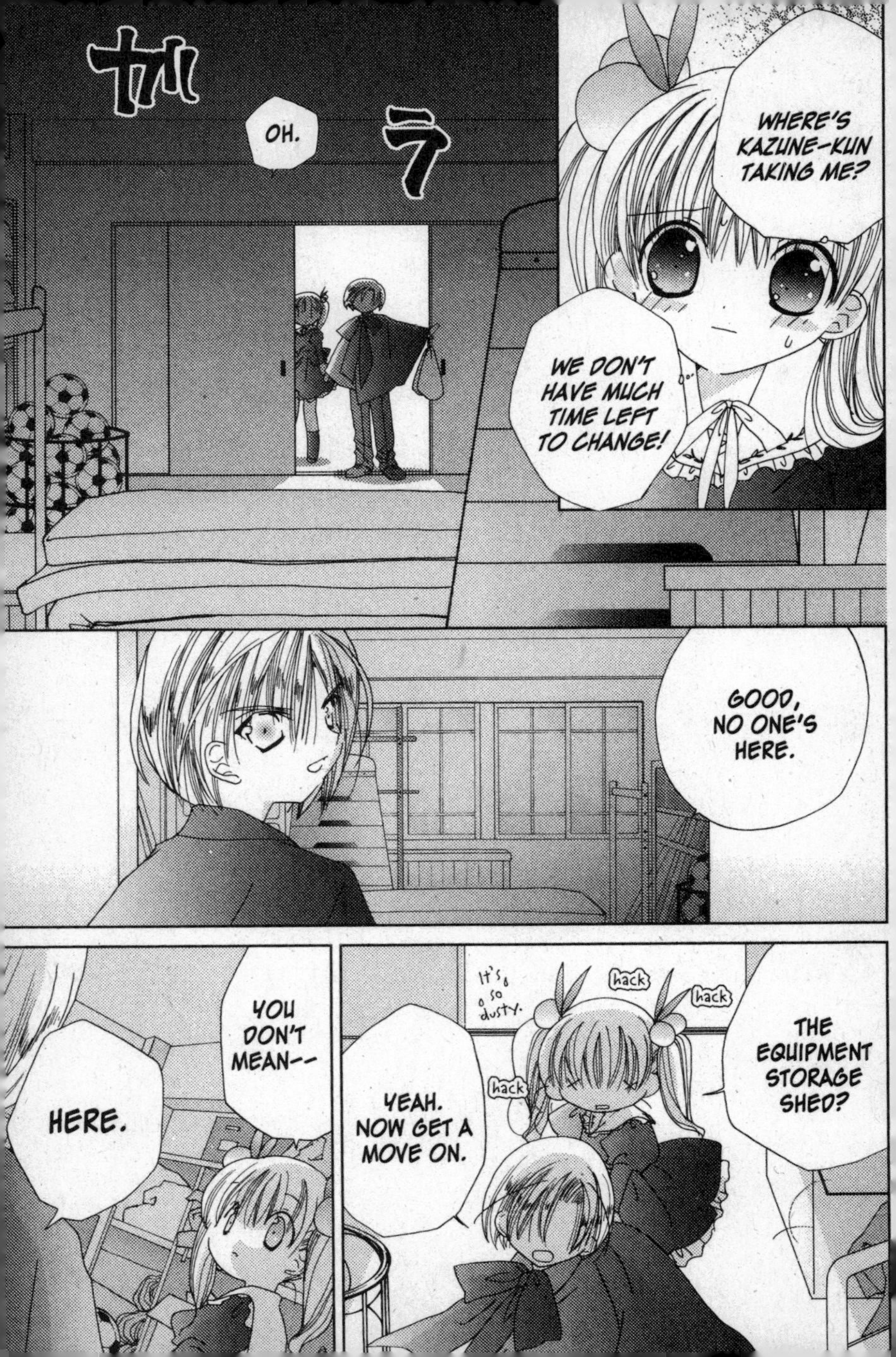
WHERE'S KAZUNE-KUN TAKING ME?
WE DON'T HAVE MUCH TIME LEFT TO CHANGE!
ガラ
OH.
GOOD, NO ONE'S HERE.
THE EQUIPMENT STORAGE SHED?
hack
hack
It's so dusty.
hack
YEAH. NOW GET A MOVE ON.
YOU DON'T MEAN--
HERE.

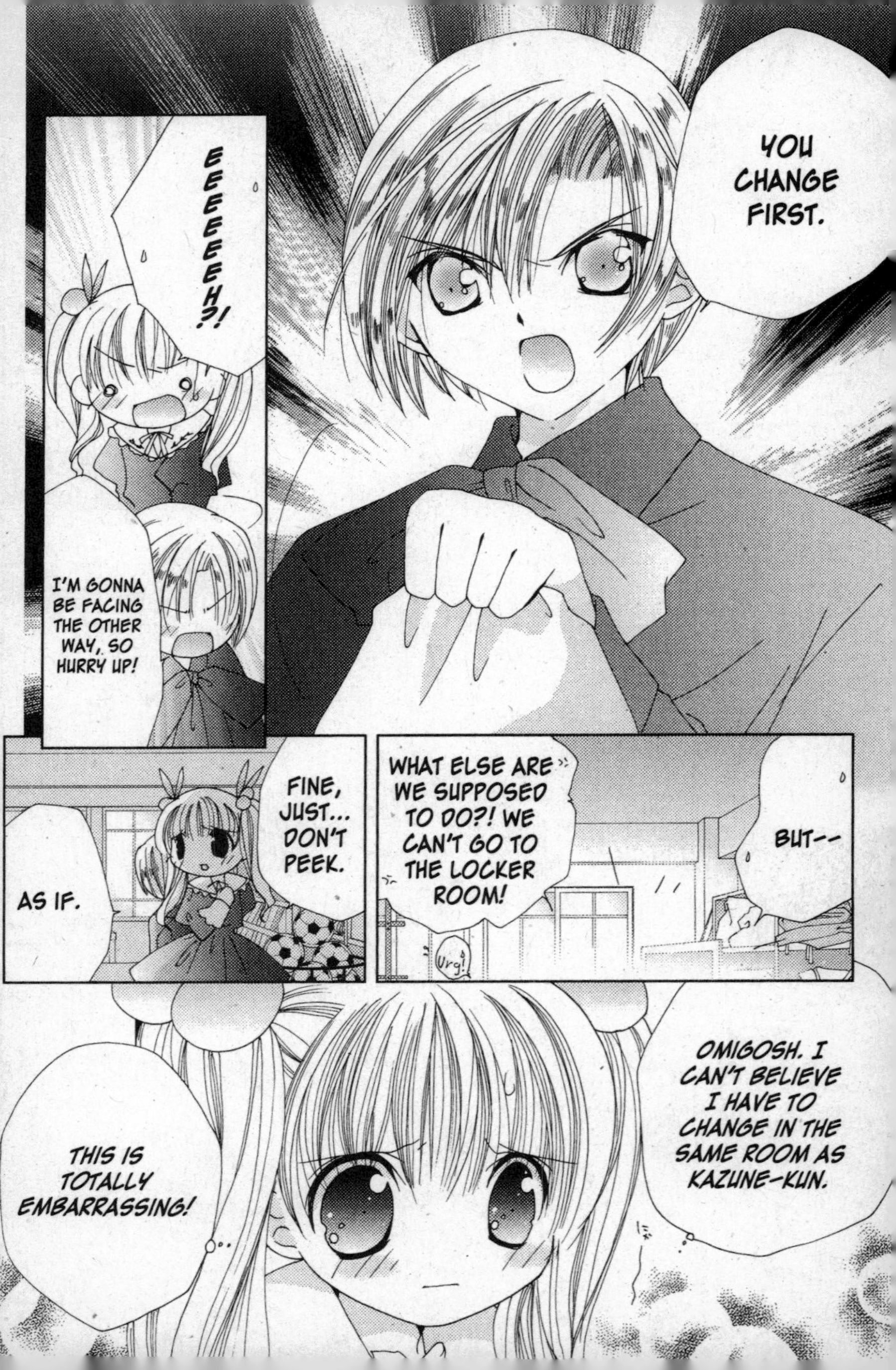
YOU CHANGE FIRST.
EEEEEEEH?!
I'M GONNA BE FACING THE OTHER WAY, SO HURRY UP!
BUT--
WHAT ELSE ARE WE SUPPOSED TO DO?! WE CAN'T GO TO THE LOCKER ROOM!
Urg!
FINE, JUST... DON'T PEEK.
AS IF.
OMIGOSH. I CAN'T BELIEVE I HAVE TO CHANGE IN THE SAME ROOM AS KAZUNE-KUN.
THIS IS TOTALLY EMBARRASSING!

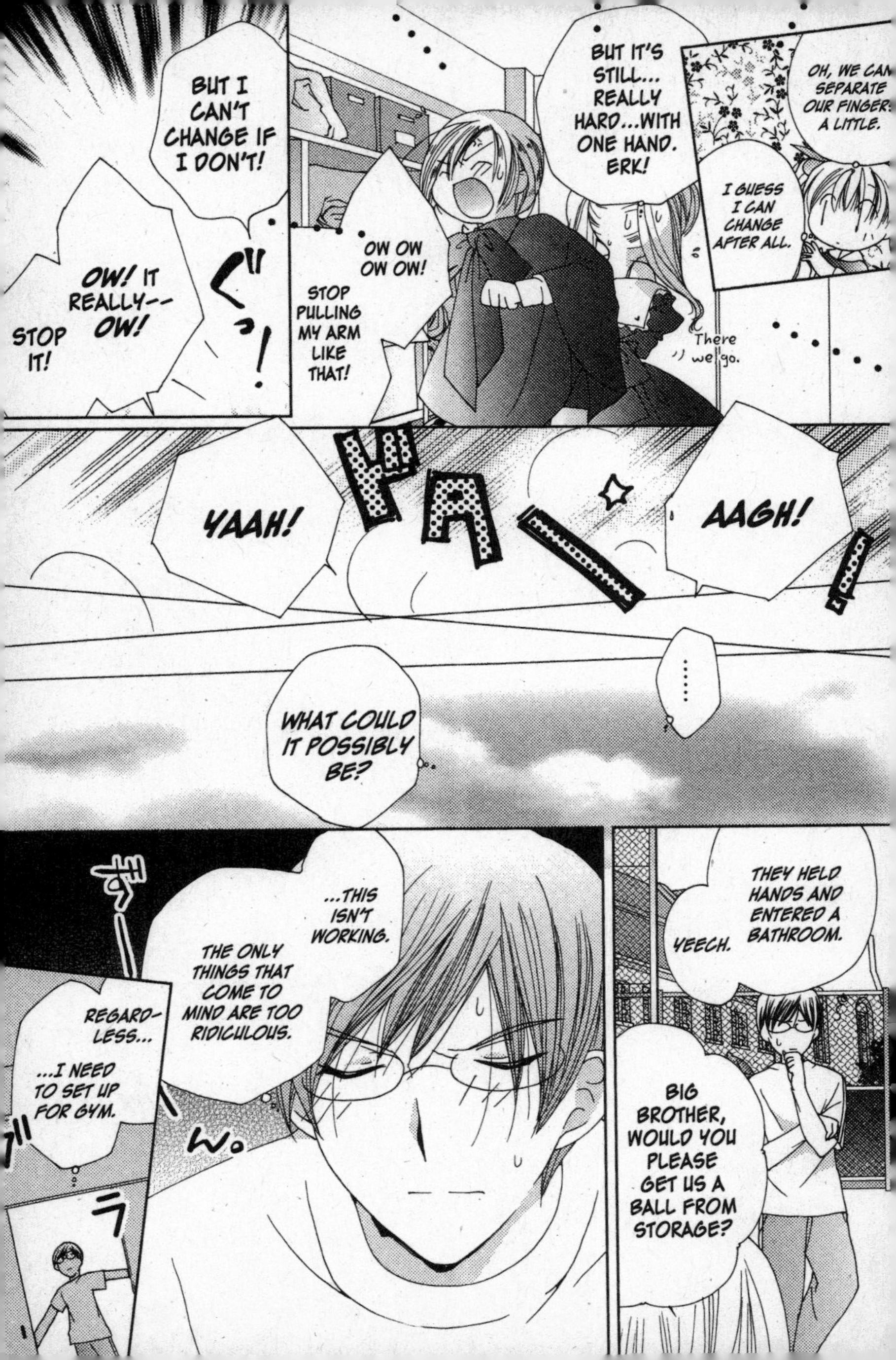
OH, WE CAN SEPARATE OUR FINGERS A LITTLE.
I GUESS I CAN CHANGE AFTER ALL.
BUT IT'S STILL... REALLY HARD...WITH ONE HAND. ERK!
There we go.
OW OW OW OW!
STOP PULLING MY ARM LIKE THAT!
BUT I CAN'T CHANGE IF I DON'T!
OW! IT REALLY--OW!
STOP IT!
AAGH!
YAAH!
......
WHAT COULD IT POSSIBLY BE?
THEY HELD HANDS AND ENTERED A BATHROOM.
YEECH.
BIG BROTHER, WOULD YOU PLEASE GET US A BALL FROM STORAGE?
...THIS ISN'T WORKING.
THE ONLY THINGS THAT COME TO MIND ARE TOO RIDICULOUS.
REGARDLESS...
...I NEED TO SET UP FOR GYM.

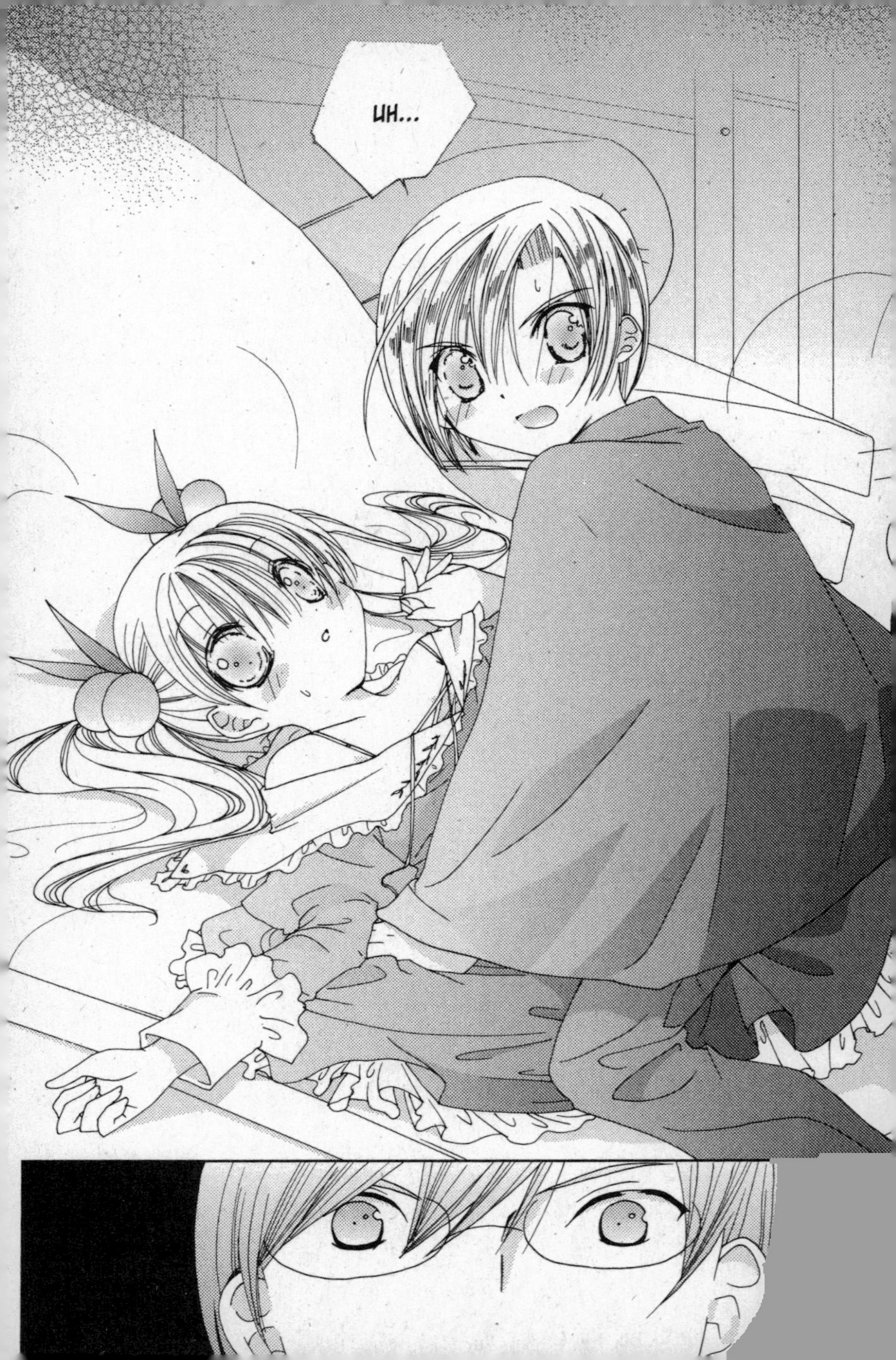
UH...

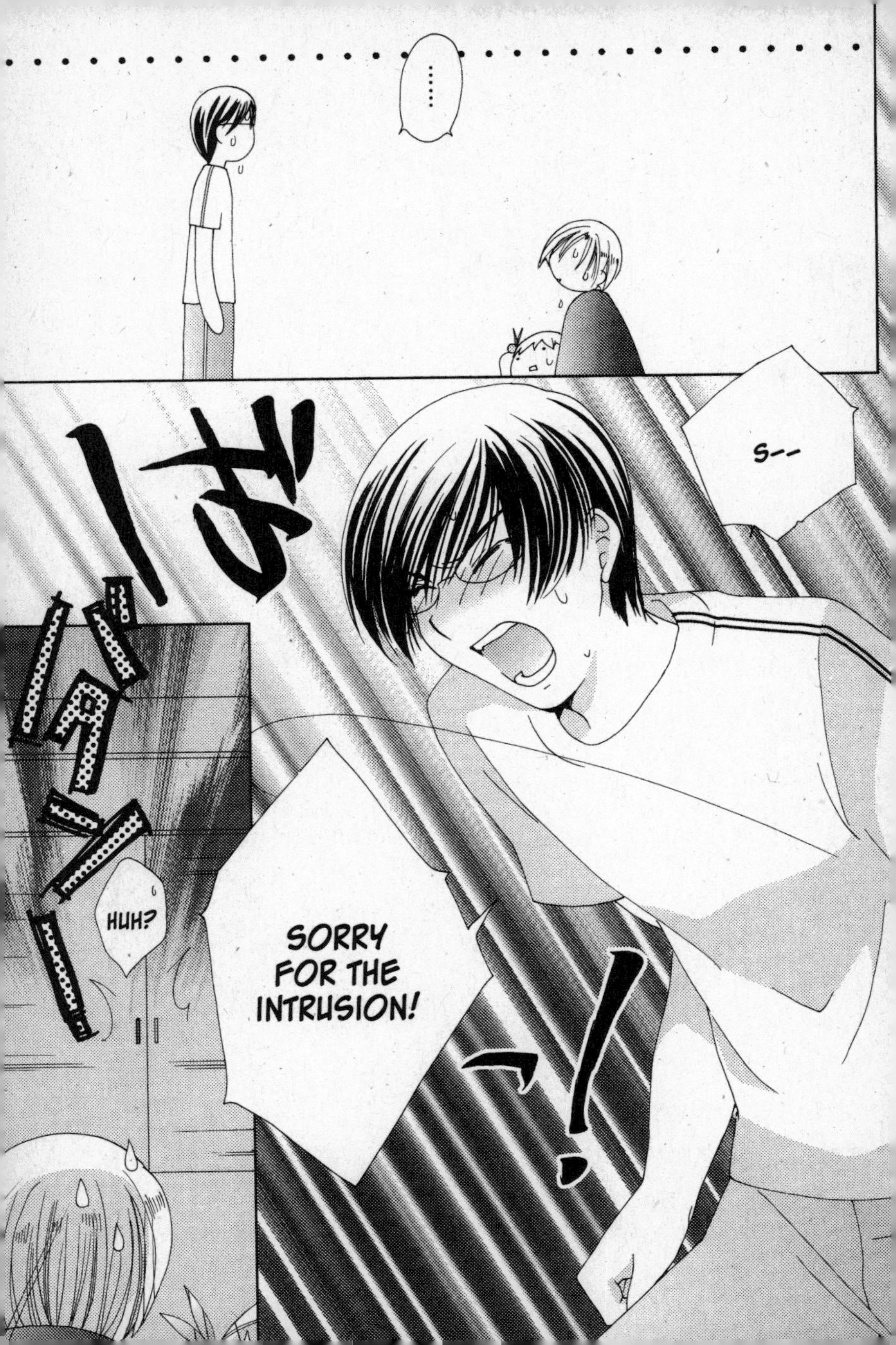
......
S--
SORRY FOR THE INTRUSION!
HUH?

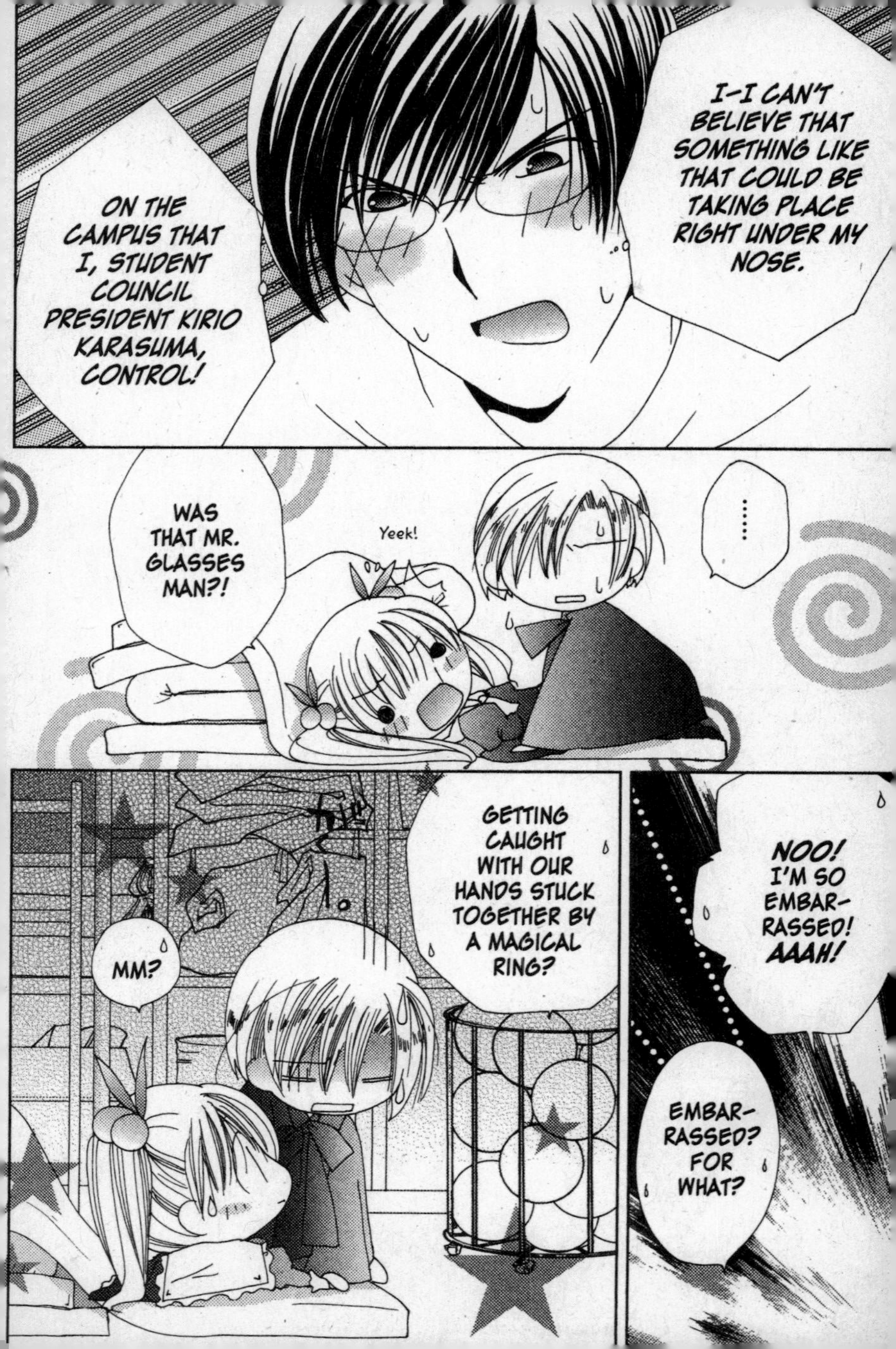
I-I CAN'T BELIEVE THAT SOMETHING LIKE THAT COULD BE TAKING PLACE RIGHT UNDER MY NOSE.
ON THE CAMPUS THAT I, STUDENT COUNCIL PRESIDENT KIRIO KARASUMA, CONTROL!
......
Yeek!
WAS THAT MR. GLASSES MAN?!
NOO! I'M SO EMBAR-RASSED! AAAH!
EMBAR-RASSED? FOR WHAT?
GETTING CAUGHT WITH OUR HANDS STUCK TOGETHER BY A MAGICAL RING?
MM?

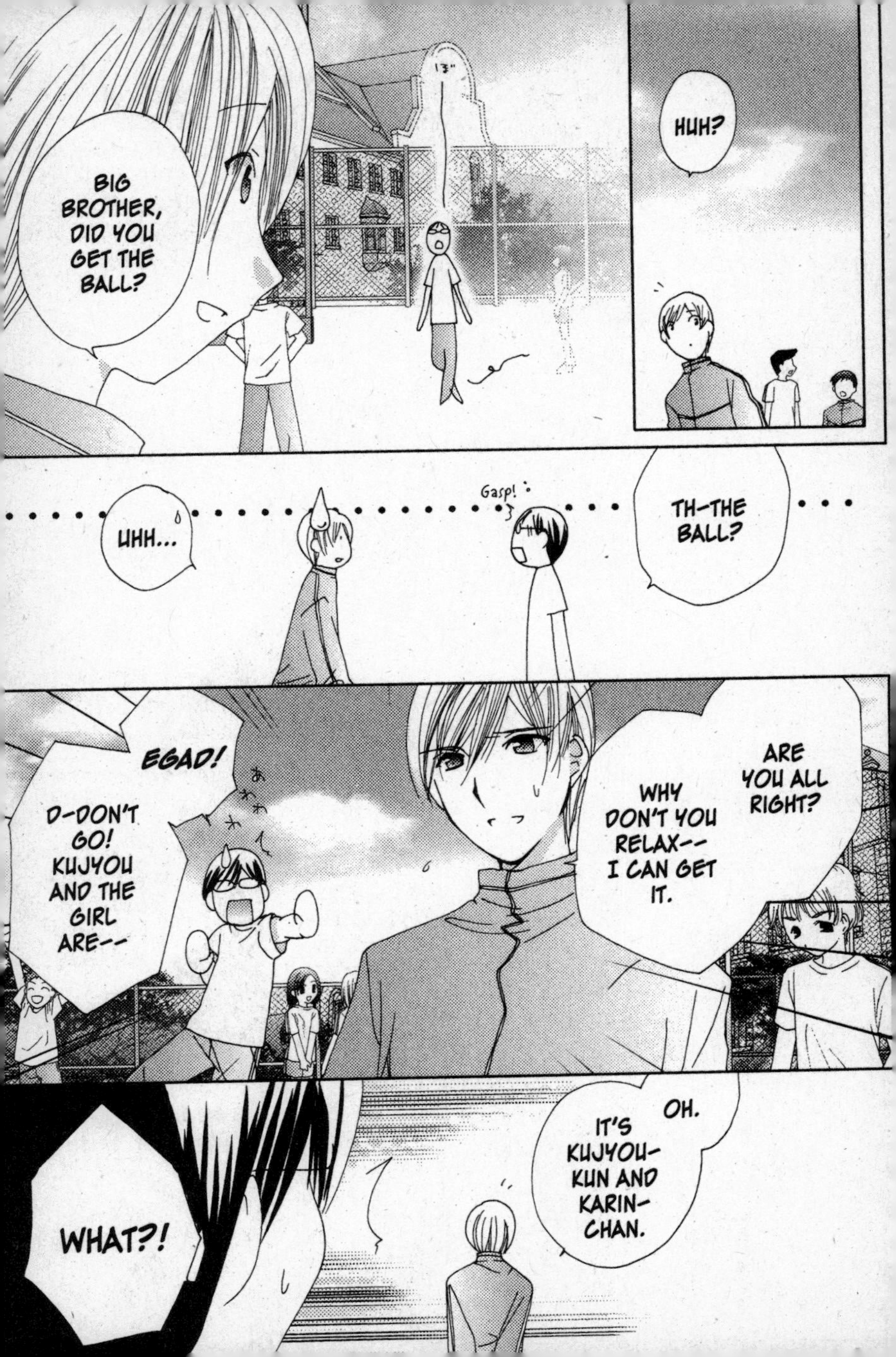
HUH?
BIG BROTHER, DID YOU GET THE BALL?
TH-THE BALL?
Gasp!
UHH...
ARE YOU ALL RIGHT?
WHY DON'T YOU RELAX-- I CAN GET IT.
EGAD!
D-DON'T GO! KUJYOU AND THE GIRL ARE--
OH. IT'S KUJYOU-KUN AND KARIN-CHAN.
WHAT?!

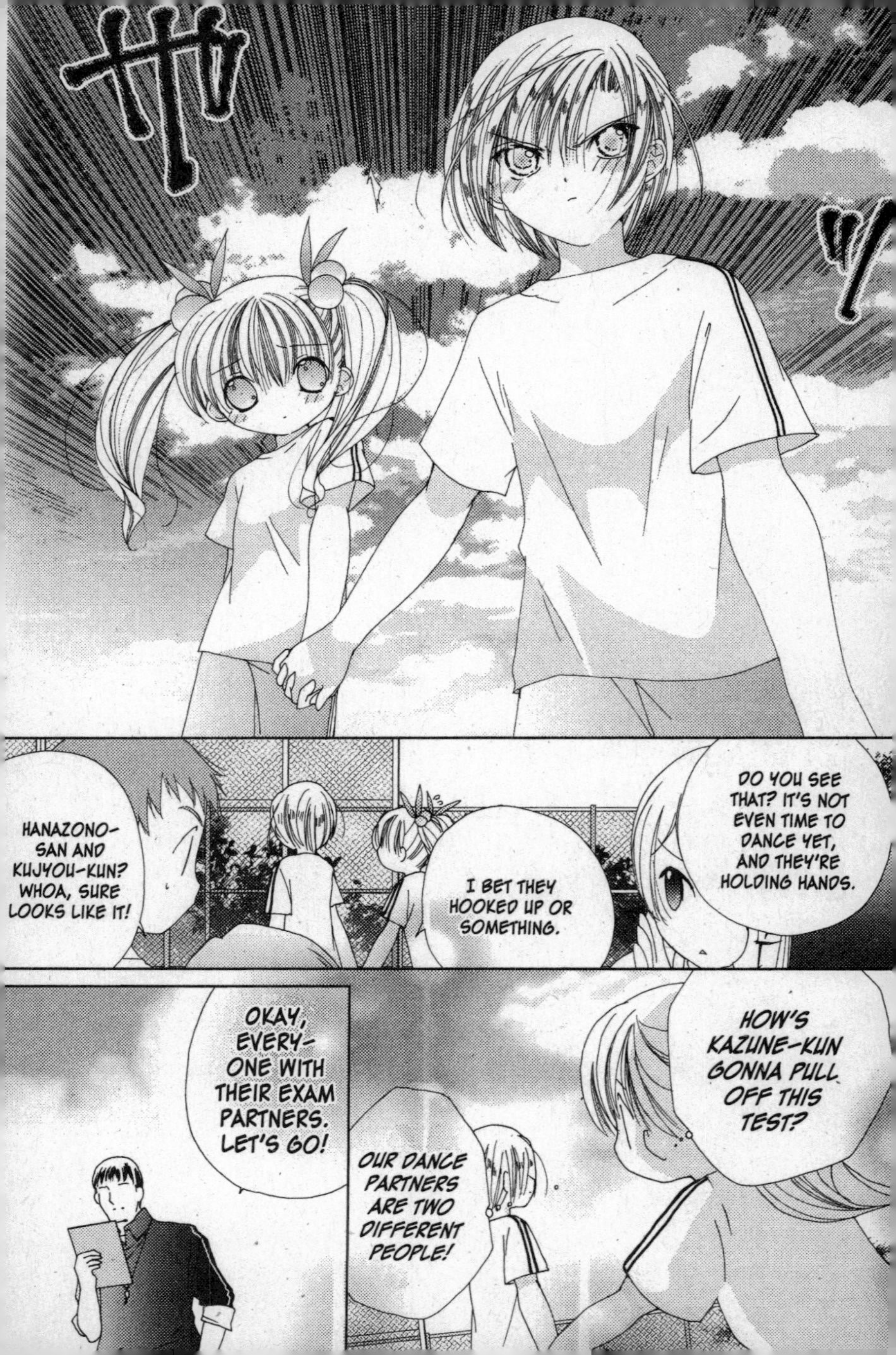
DO YOU SEE THAT? IT'S NOT EVEN TIME TO DANCE YET, AND THEY'RE HOLDING HANDS.
I BET THEY HOOKED UP OR SOMETHING.
HANAZONO-SAN AND KUJYOU-KUN? WHOA, SURE LOOKS LIKE IT!
HOW'S KAZUNE-KUN GONNA PULL OFF THIS TEST?
OUR DANCE PARTNERS ARE TWO DIFFERENT PEOPLE!
OKAY, EVERY-ONE WITH THEIR EXAM PARTNERS. LET'S GO!

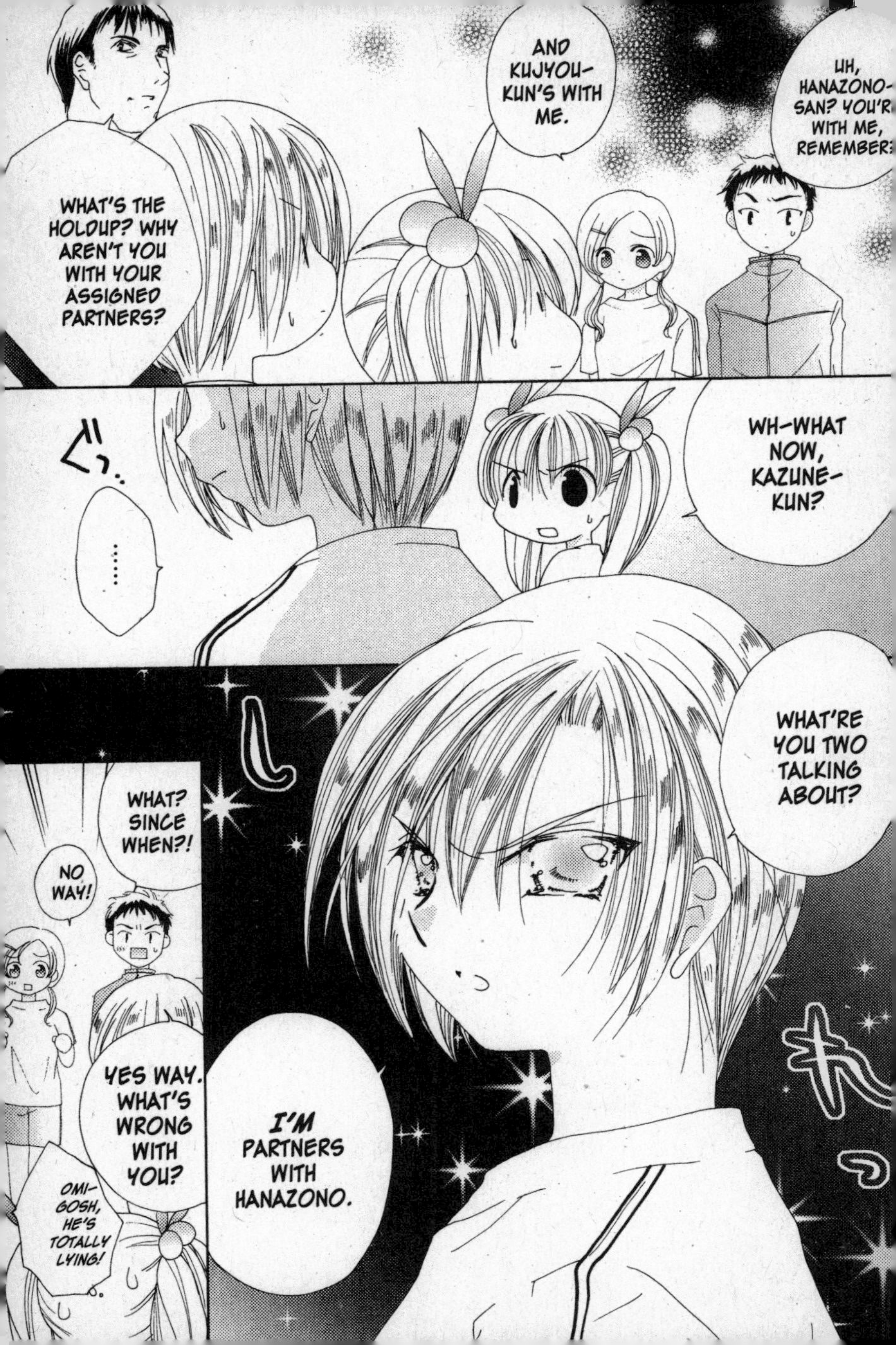
UH, HANAZONO-SAN? YOU'R WITH ME, REMEMBER
AND KUJYOU-KUN'S WITH ME.
WHAT'S THE HOLDUP? WHY AREN'T YOU WITH YOUR ASSIGNED PARTNERS?
WH-WHAT NOW, KAZUNE-KUN?
ぐ...
......
WHAT'RE YOU TWO TALKING ABOUT?
I'M PARTNERS WITH HANAZONO.
しれっ
WHAT? SINCE WHEN?!
NO WAY!
YES WAY. WHAT'S WRONG WITH YOU?
OMIGOSH, HE'S TOTALLY LYING!

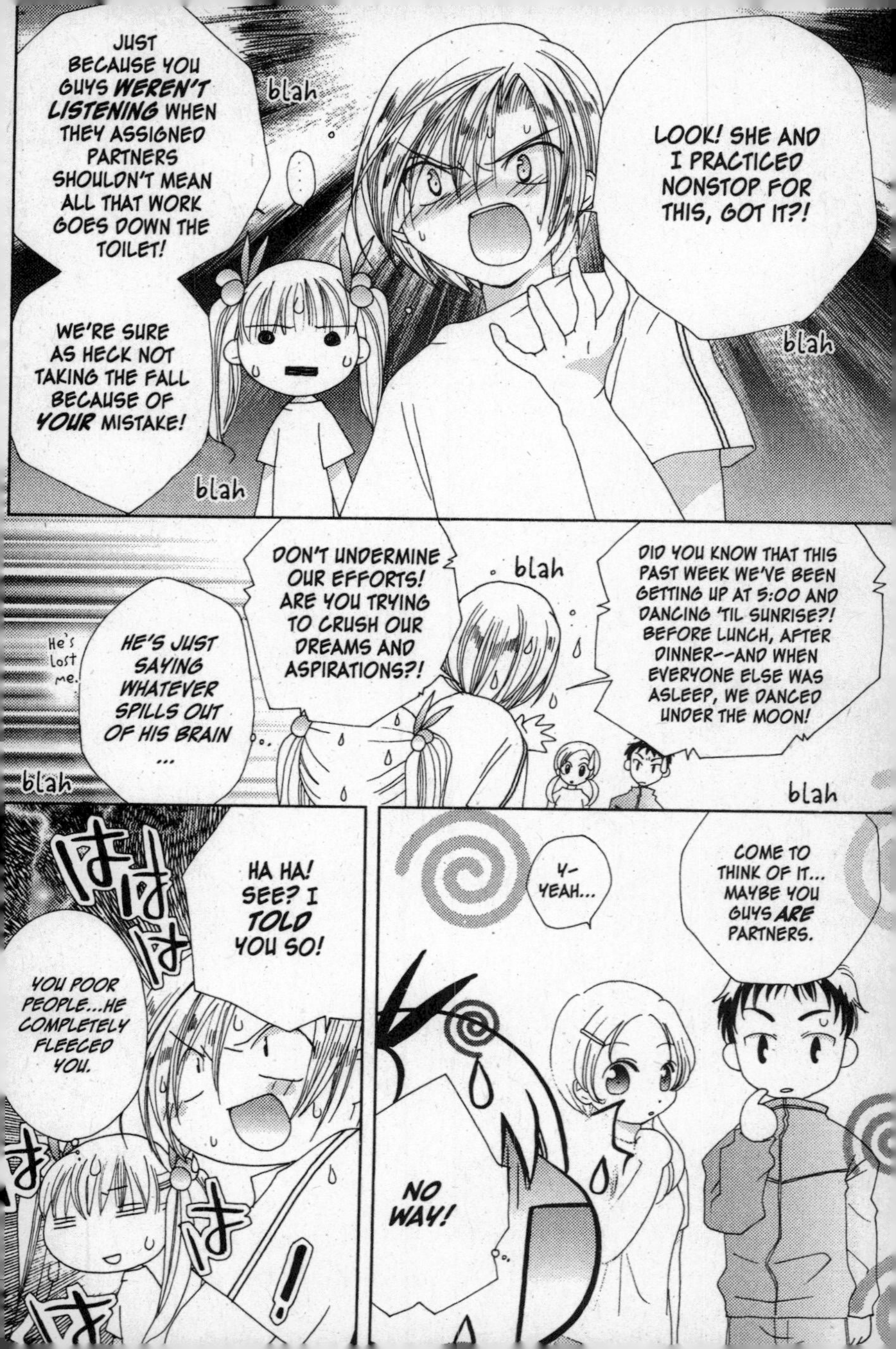

LOOK! SHE AND I PRACTICED NONSTOP FOR THIS, GOT IT?!
blah
JUST BECAUSE YOU GUYS **WEREN'T LISTENING** WHEN THEY ASSIGNED PARTNERS SHOULDN'T MEAN ALL THAT WORK GOES DOWN THE TOILET!
blah
...
WE'RE SURE AS HECK NOT TAKING THE FALL BECAUSE OF **YOUR** MISTAKE!
blah
DID YOU KNOW THAT THIS PAST WEEK WE'VE BEEN GETTING UP AT 5:00 AND DANCING 'TIL SUNRISE?! BEFORE LUNCH, AFTER DINNER--AND WHEN EVERYONE ELSE WAS ASLEEP, WE DANCED UNDER THE MOON!
blah
DON'T UNDERMINE OUR EFFORTS! ARE YOU TRYING TO CRUSH OUR DREAMS AND ASPIRATIONS?!
blah
HE'S JUST SAYING WHATEVER SPILLS OUT OF HIS BRAIN ...
He's lost me.
blah
COME TO THINK OF IT... MAYBE YOU GUYS **ARE** PARTNERS.
Y-YEAH...
NO WAY!
HA HA! SEE? I ***TOLD*** YOU SO!
ははは
YOU POOR PEOPLE...HE COMPLETELY FLEECED YOU.
は

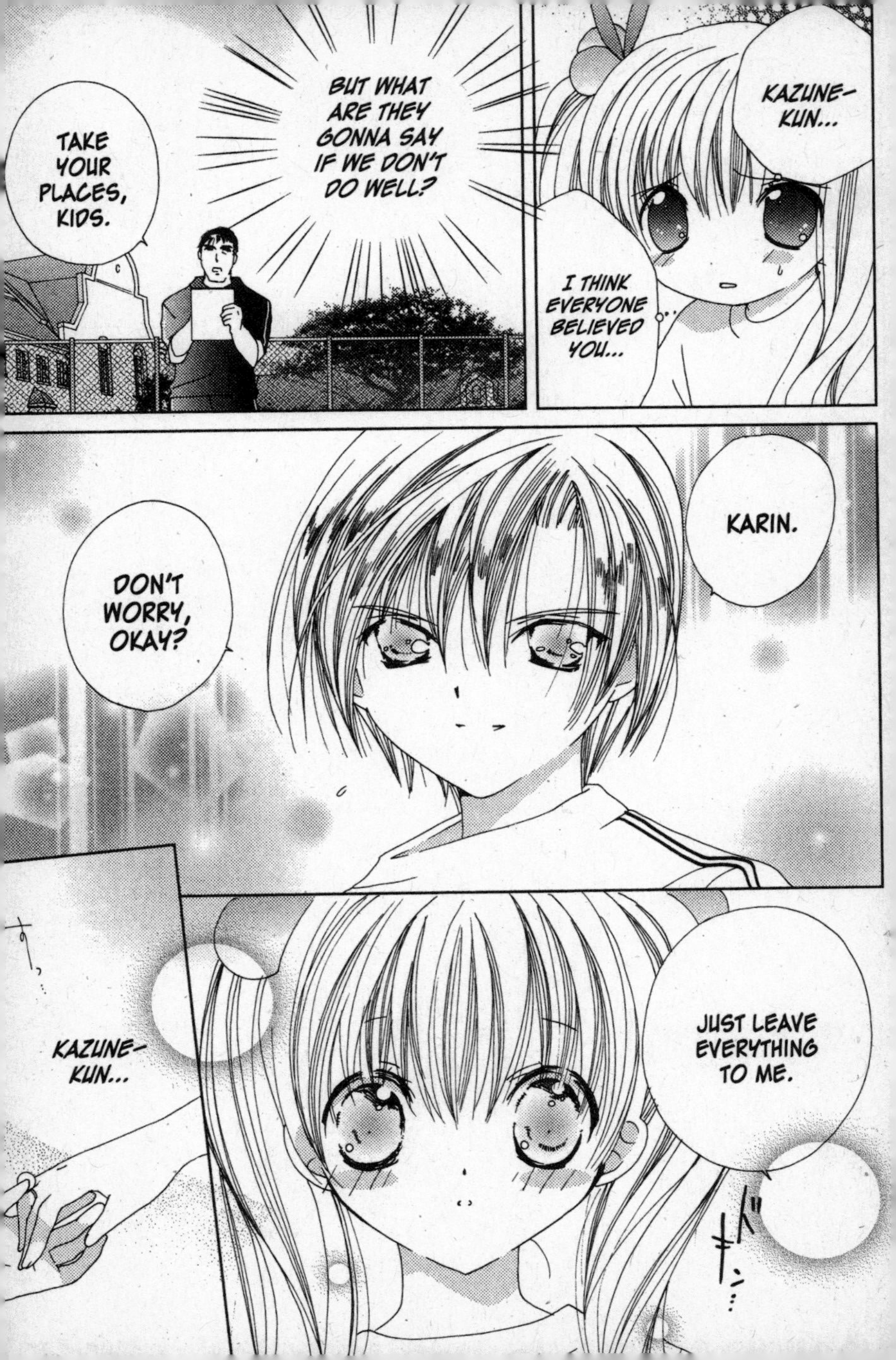
KAZUNE-KUN...
I THINK EVERYONE BELIEVED YOU...
BUT WHAT ARE THEY GONNA SAY IF WE DON'T DO WELL?
TAKE YOUR PLACES, KIDS.
KARIN.
DON'T WORRY, OKAY?
JUST LEAVE EVERYTHING TO ME.
KAZUNE-KUN...

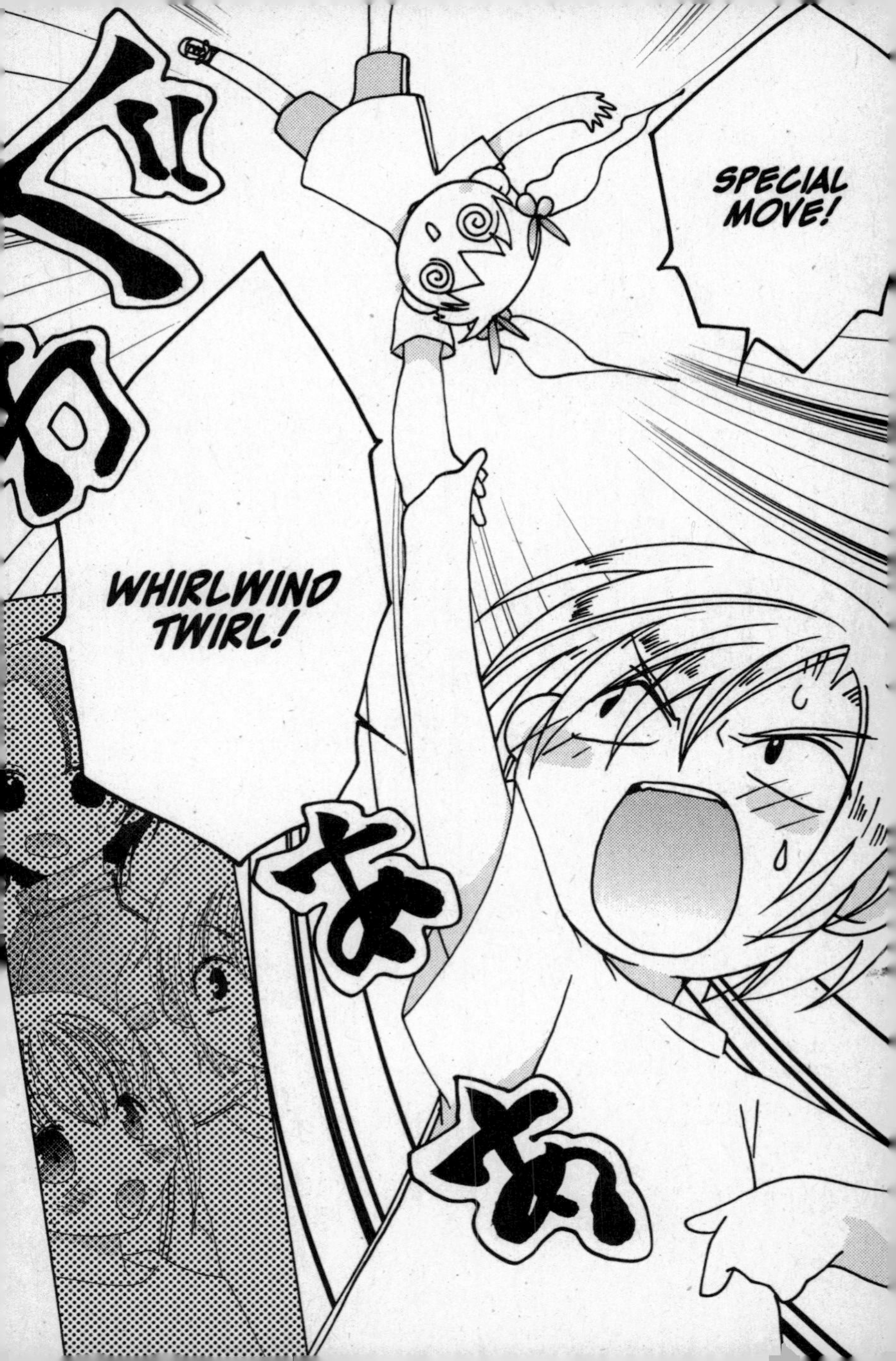
SPECIAL MOVE!
WHIRLWIND TWIRL!

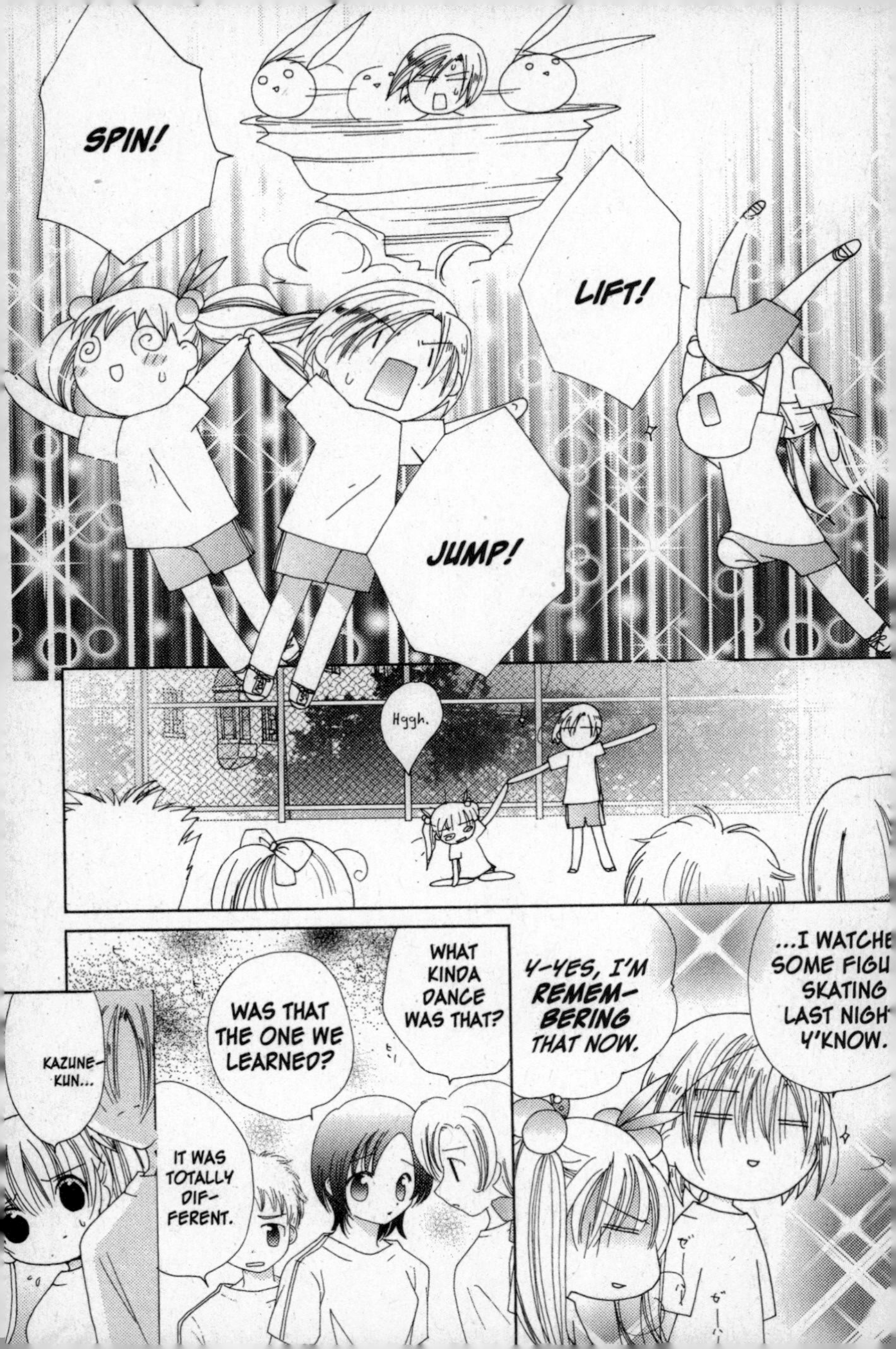
SPIN!
LIFT!
JUMP!
Hggh.
...I WATCHE SOME FIGU SKATING LAST NIGH Y'KNOW.
Y-YES, I'M REMEMBERING THAT NOW.
WHAT KINDA DANCE WAS THAT?
WAS THAT THE ONE WE LEARNED?
IT WAS TOTALLY DIFFERENT.
KAZUNE-KUN...

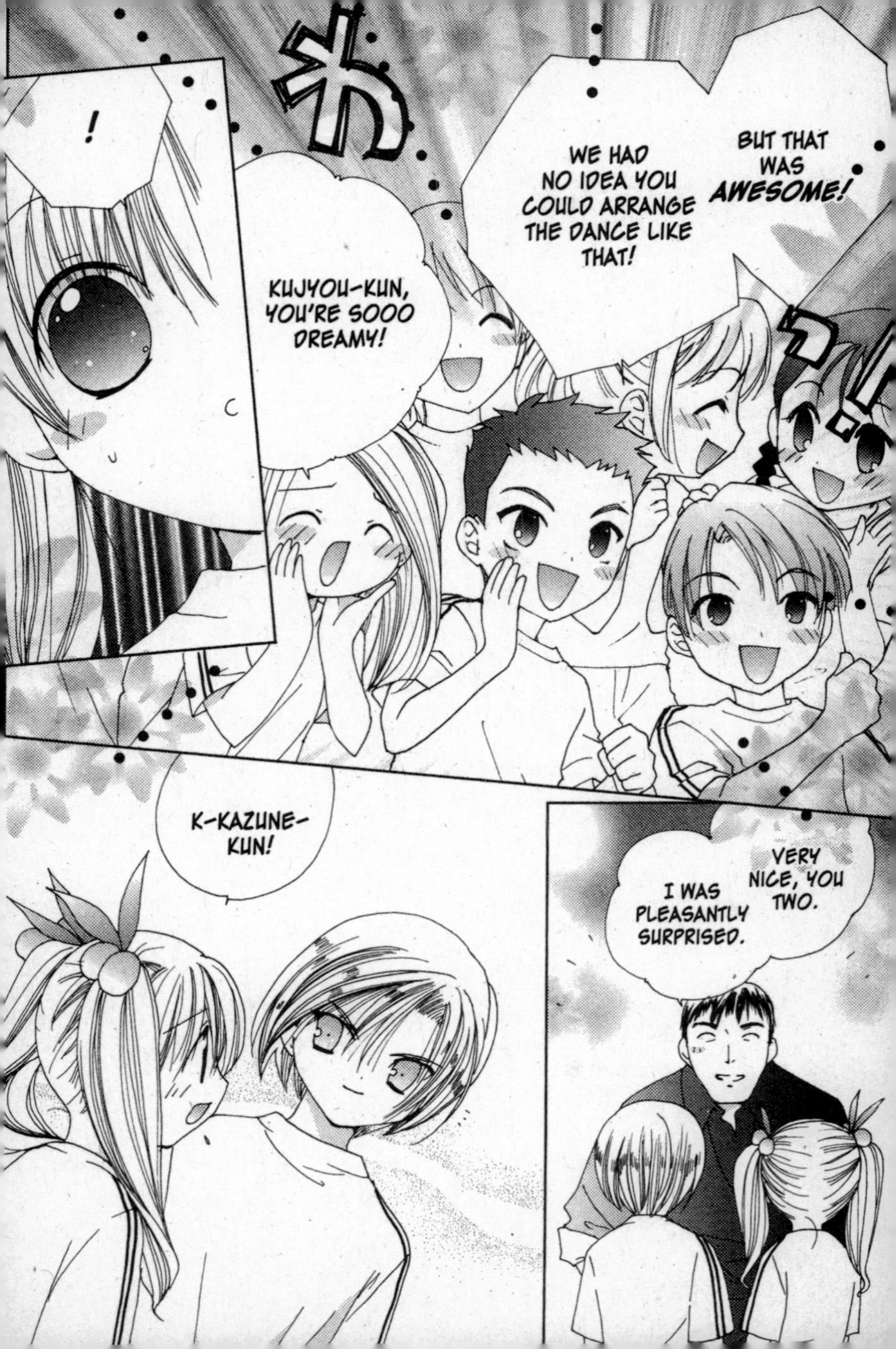
BUT THAT WAS AWESOME!
WE HAD NO IDEA YOU COULD ARRANGE THE DANCE LIKE THAT!
KUJYOU-KUN, YOU'RE SOOO DREAMY!
!
VERY NICE, YOU TWO.
I WAS PLEASANTLY SURPRISED.
K-KAZUNE-KUN!

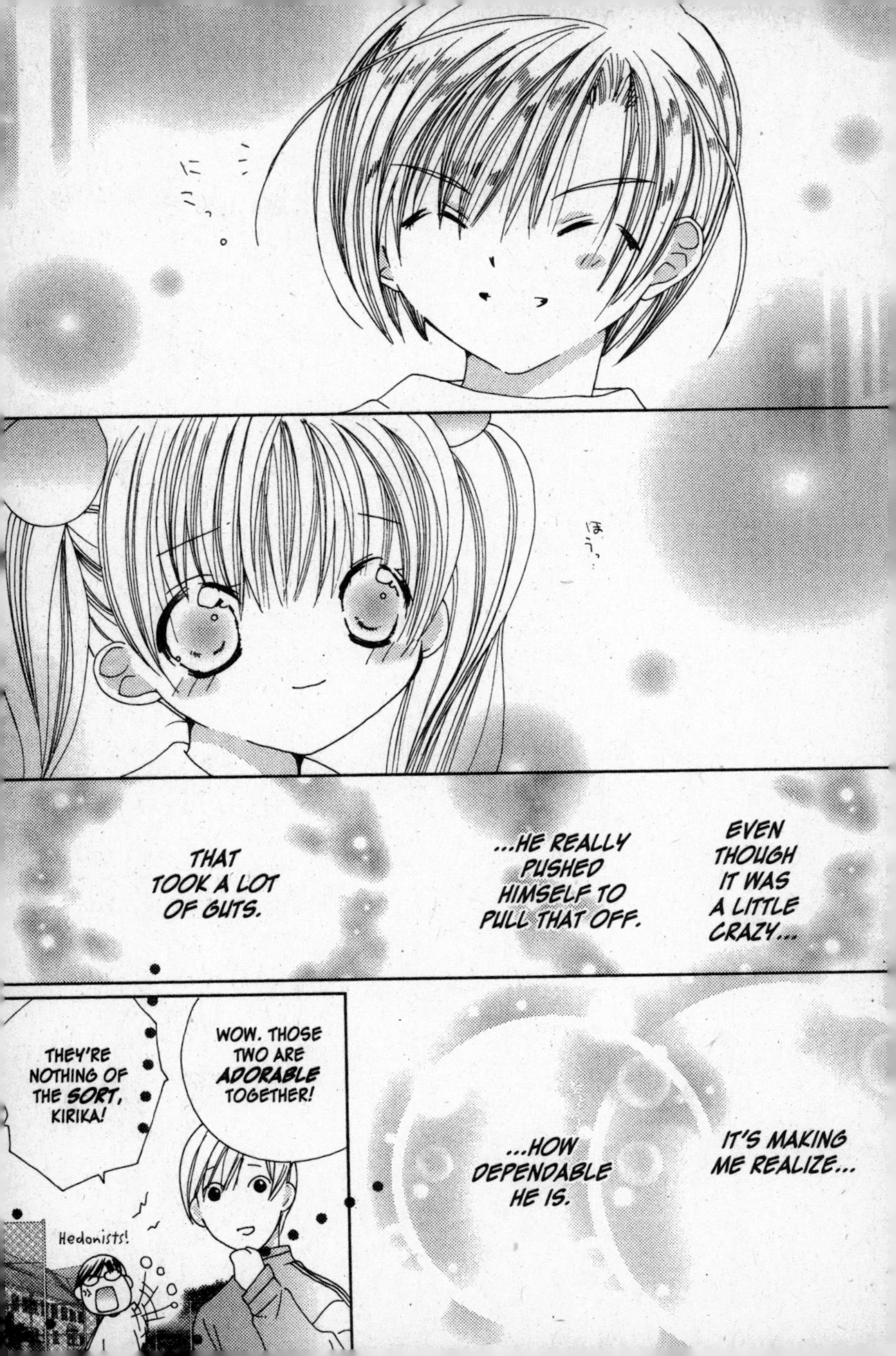
EVEN THOUGH IT WAS A LITTLE CRAZY...
...HE REALLY PUSHED HIMSELF TO PULL THAT OFF.
THAT TOOK A LOT OF GUTS.
IT'S MAKING ME REALIZE...
...HOW DEPENDABLE HE IS.
WOW. THOSE TWO ARE ADORABLE TOGETHER!
THEY'RE NOTHING OF THE SORT, KIRIKA!
Hedonists!

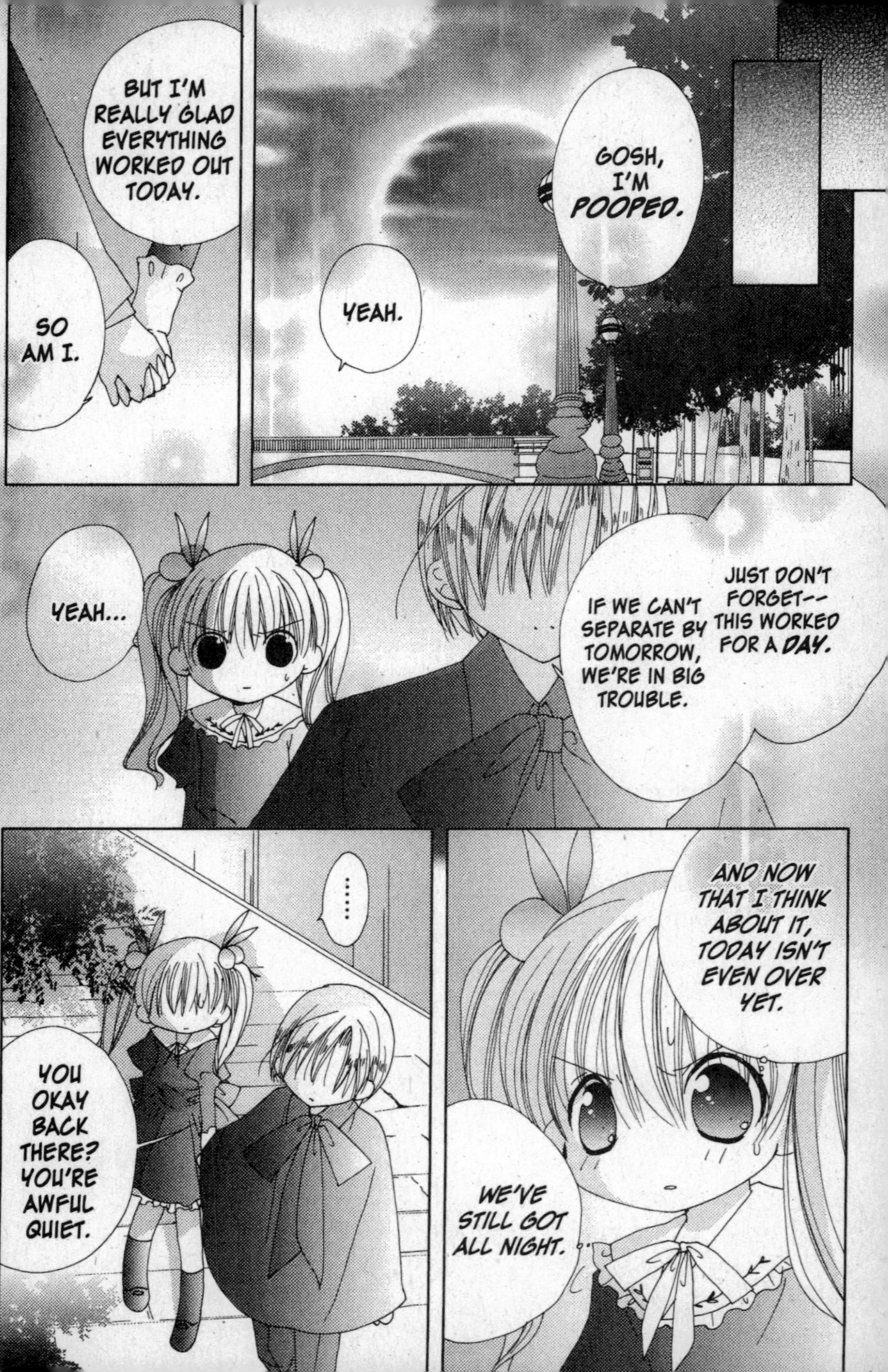
GOSH, I'M POOPED.
YEAH.
BUT I'M REALLY GLAD EVERYTHING WORKED OUT TODAY.
SO AM I.
JUST DON'T FORGET-- THIS WORKED FOR A DAY.
IF WE CAN'T SEPARATE BY TOMORROW, WE'RE IN BIG TROUBLE.
YEAH...
AND NOW THAT I THINK ABOUT IT, TODAY ISN'T EVEN OVER YET.
WE'VE STILL GOT ALL NIGHT.
......
YOU OKAY BACK THERE? YOU'RE AWFUL QUIET.

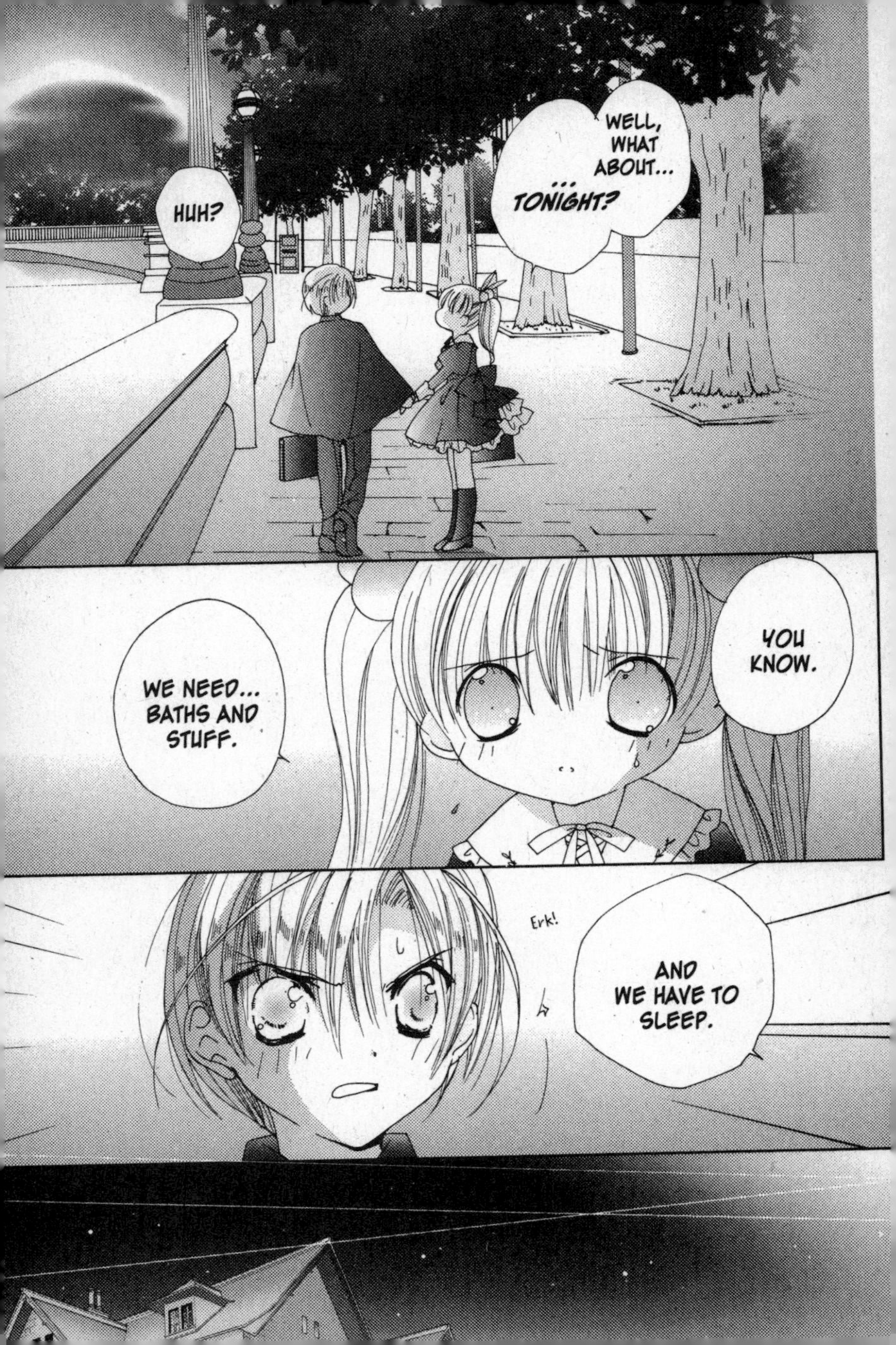
WELL, WHAT ABOUT... ...TONIGHT?
HUH?
YOU KNOW.
WE NEED... BATHS AND STUFF.
AND WE HAVE TO SLEEP.
Erk!

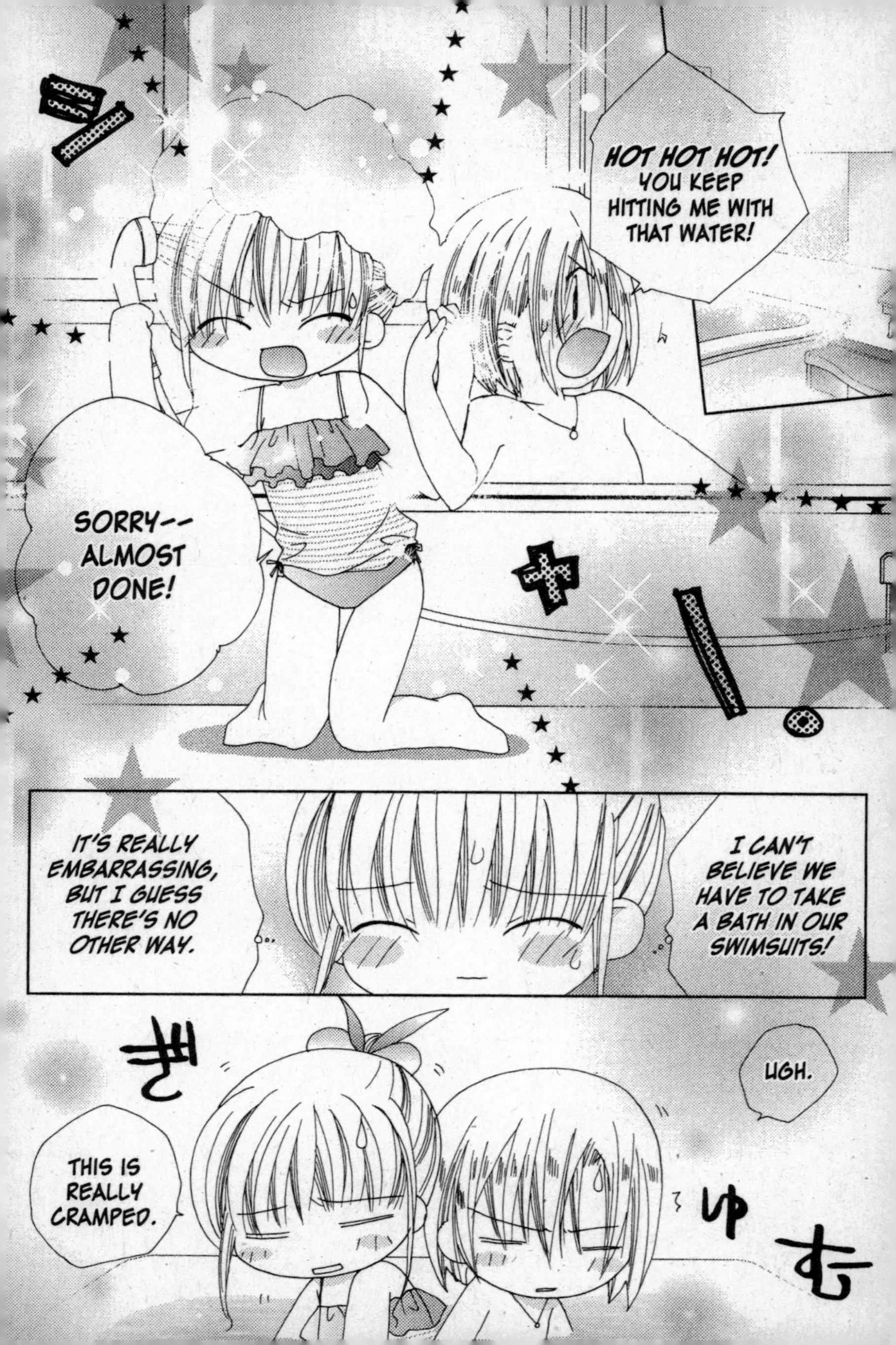
HOT HOT HOT! YOU KEEP HITTING ME WITH THAT WATER!
SORRY-- ALMOST DONE!
I CAN'T BELIEVE WE HAVE TO TAKE A BATH IN OUR SWIMSUITS!
IT'S REALLY EMBARRASSING, BUT I GUESS THERE'S NO OTHER WAY.
UGH.
THIS IS REALLY CRAMPED.

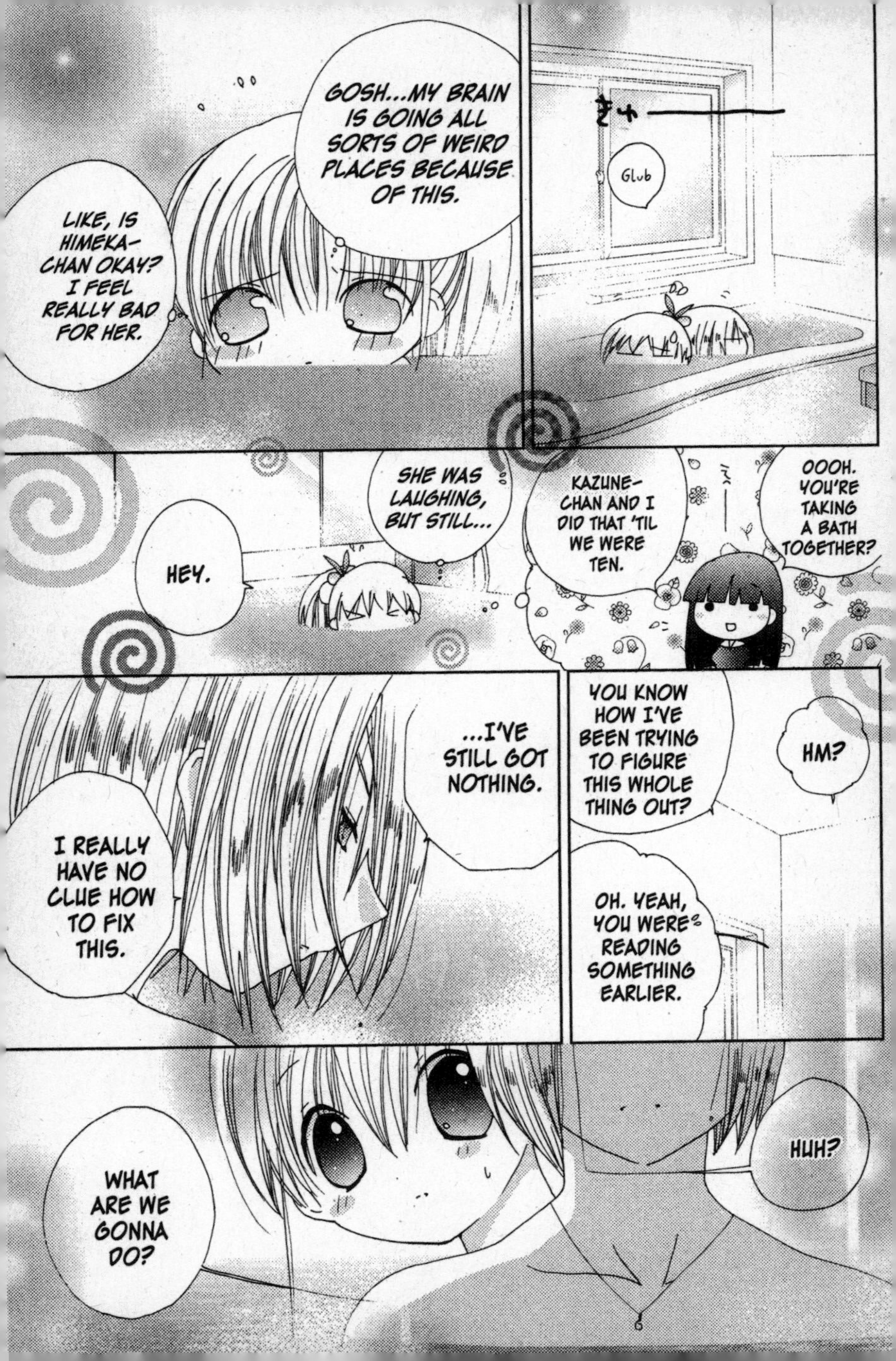
Glub
GOSH...MY BRAIN IS GOING ALL SORTS OF WEIRD PLACES BECAUSE OF THIS.
LIKE, IS HIMEKA-CHAN OKAY? I FEEL REALLY BAD FOR HER.
OOOH. YOU'RE TAKING A BATH TOGETHER?
KAZUNE-CHAN AND I DID THAT 'TIL WE WERE TEN.
SHE WAS LAUGHING, BUT STILL...
HEY.
HM?
YOU KNOW HOW I'VE BEEN TRYING TO FIGURE THIS WHOLE THING OUT?
OH. YEAH, YOU WERE READING SOMETHING EARLIER.
...I'VE STILL GOT NOTHING.
I REALLY HAVE NO CLUE HOW TO FIX THIS.
HUH?
WHAT ARE WE GONNA DO?

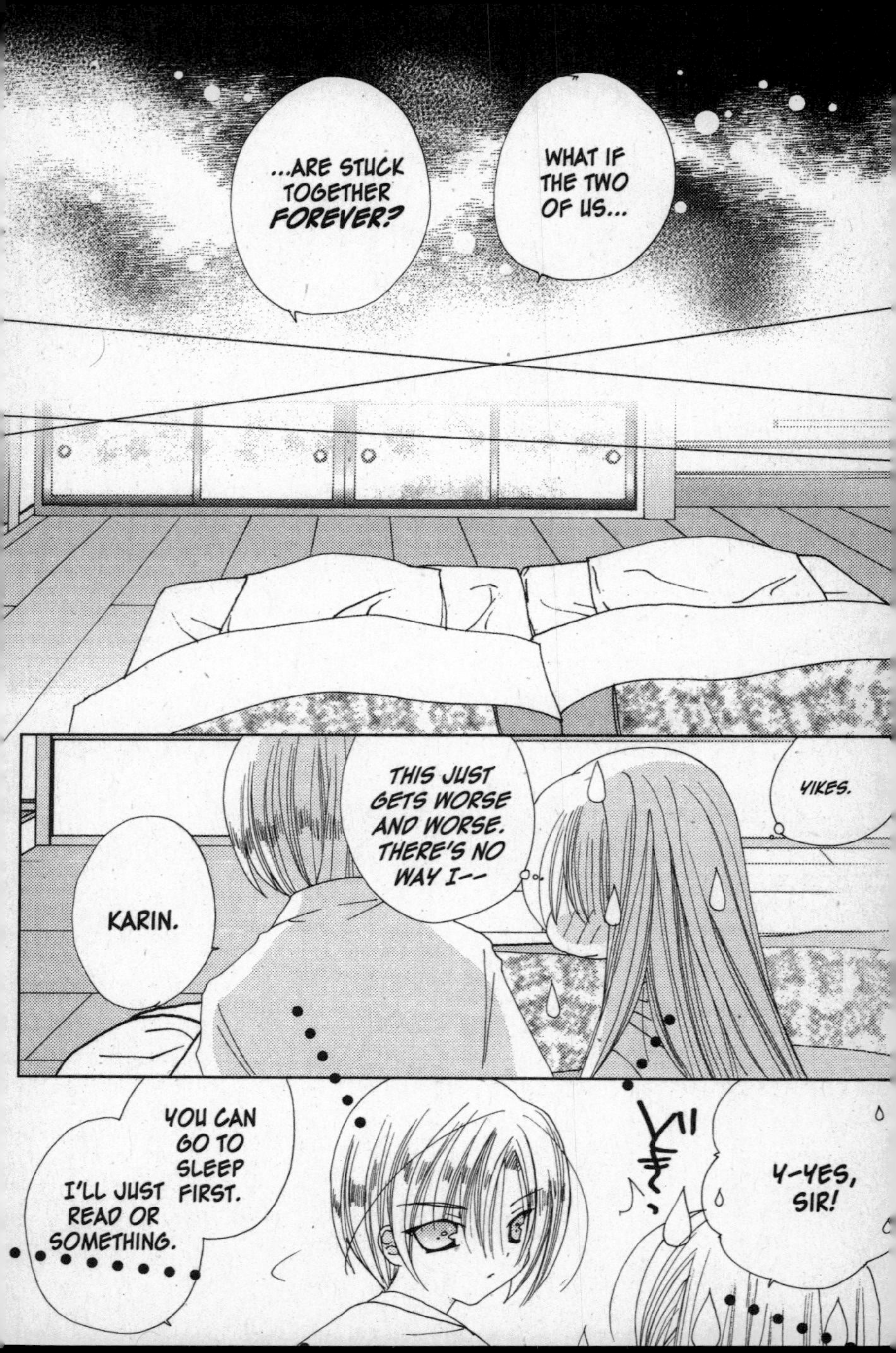
WHAT IF THE TWO OF US...
...ARE STUCK TOGETHER FOREVER?
YIKES.
THIS JUST GETS WORSE AND WORSE. THERE'S NO WAY I--
KARIN.
Y-YES, SIR!
YOU CAN GO TO SLEEP FIRST.
I'LL JUST READ OR SOMETHING.

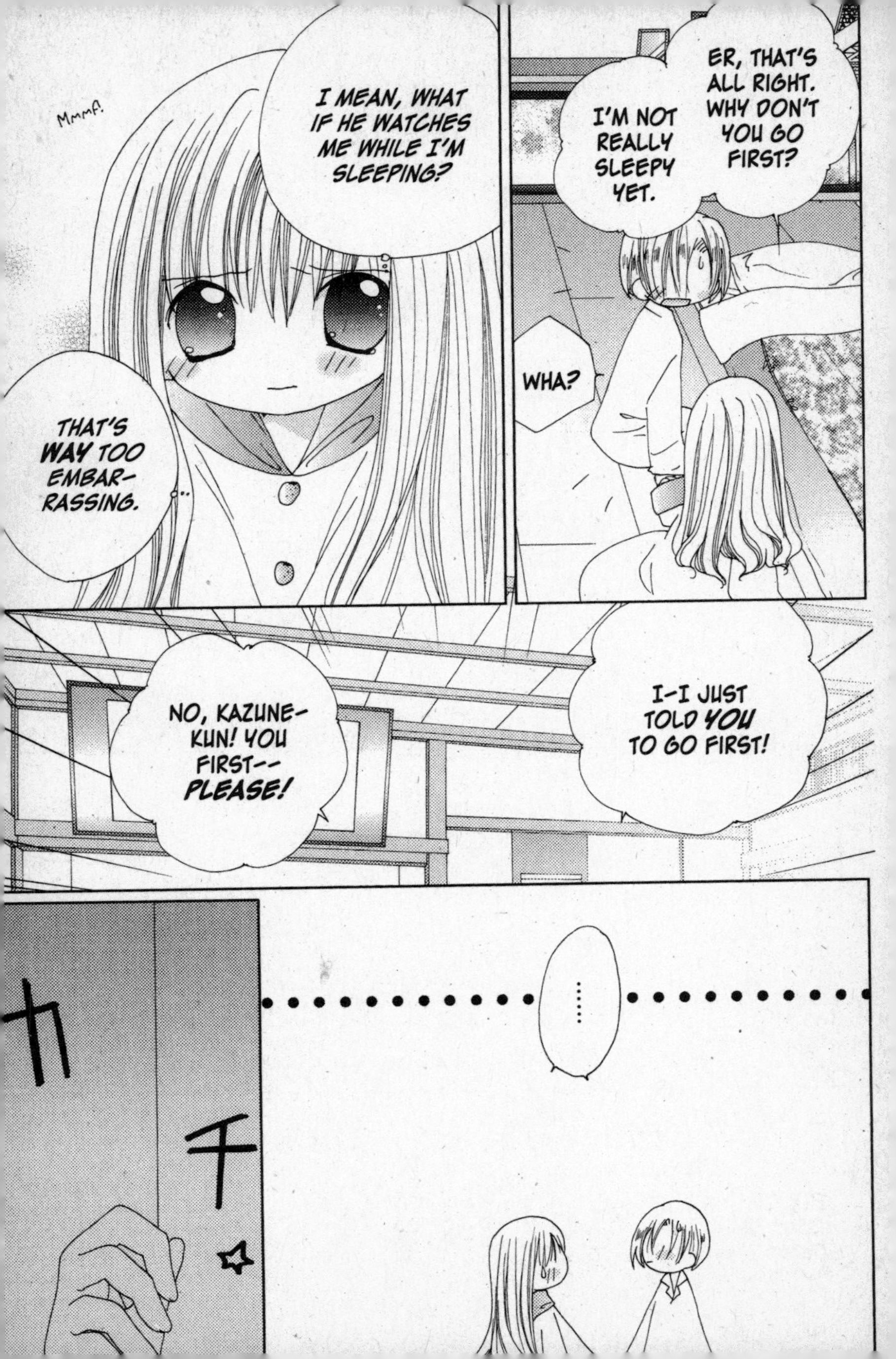
ER, THAT'S ALL RIGHT. WHY DON'T YOU GO FIRST?
I'M NOT REALLY SLEEPY YET.
WHA?
Mmmf.
I MEAN, WHAT IF HE WATCHES ME WHILE I'M SLEEPING?
THAT'S WAY TOO EMBARRASSING.
I-I JUST TOLD YOU TO GO FIRST!
NO, KAZUNE-KUN! YOU FIRST--PLEASE!
......
カチ

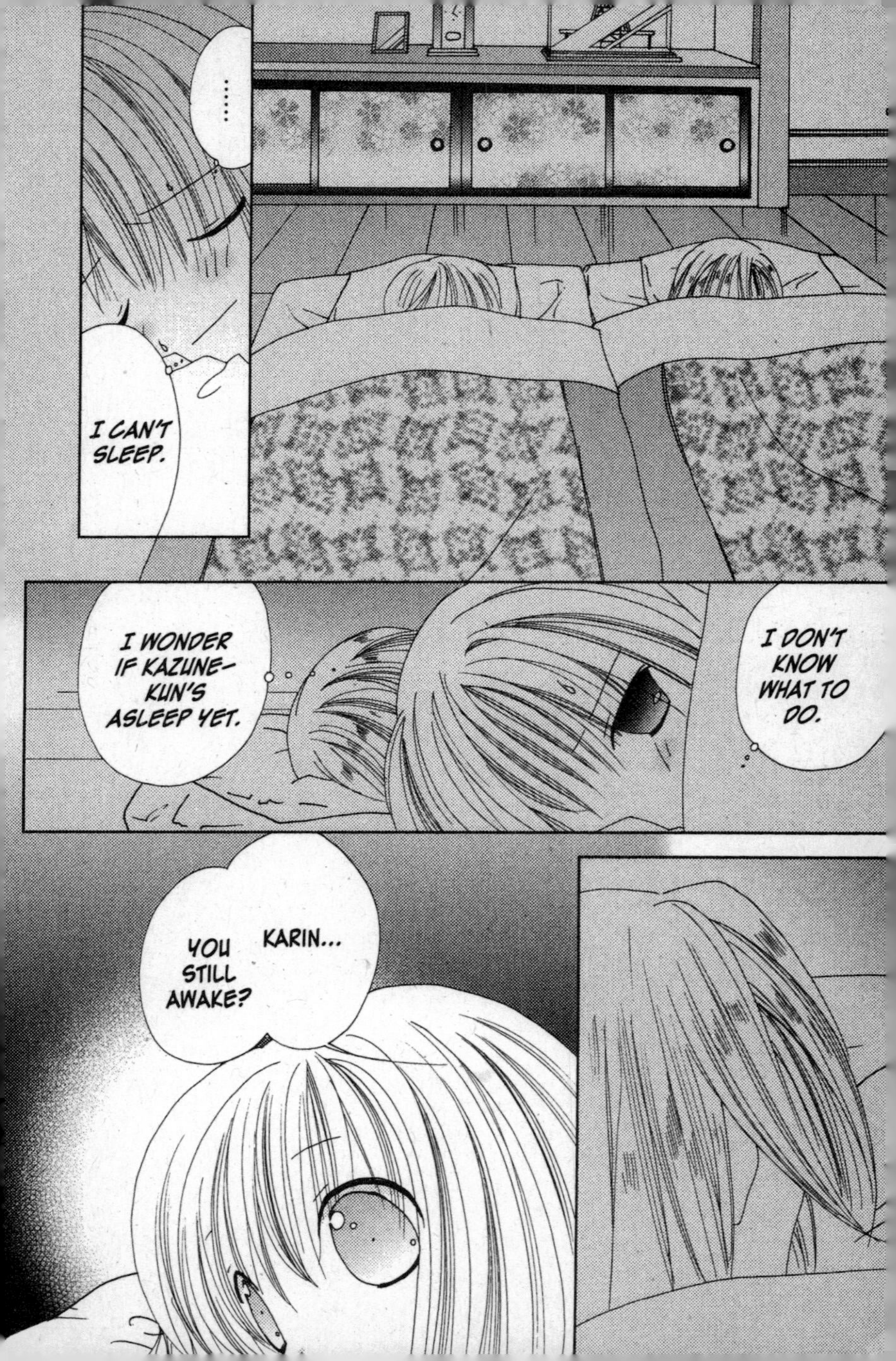
......
I CAN'T SLEEP.
I DON'T KNOW WHAT TO DO.
I WONDER IF KAZUNE-KUN'S ASLEEP YET.
KARIN...
YOU STILL AWAKE?

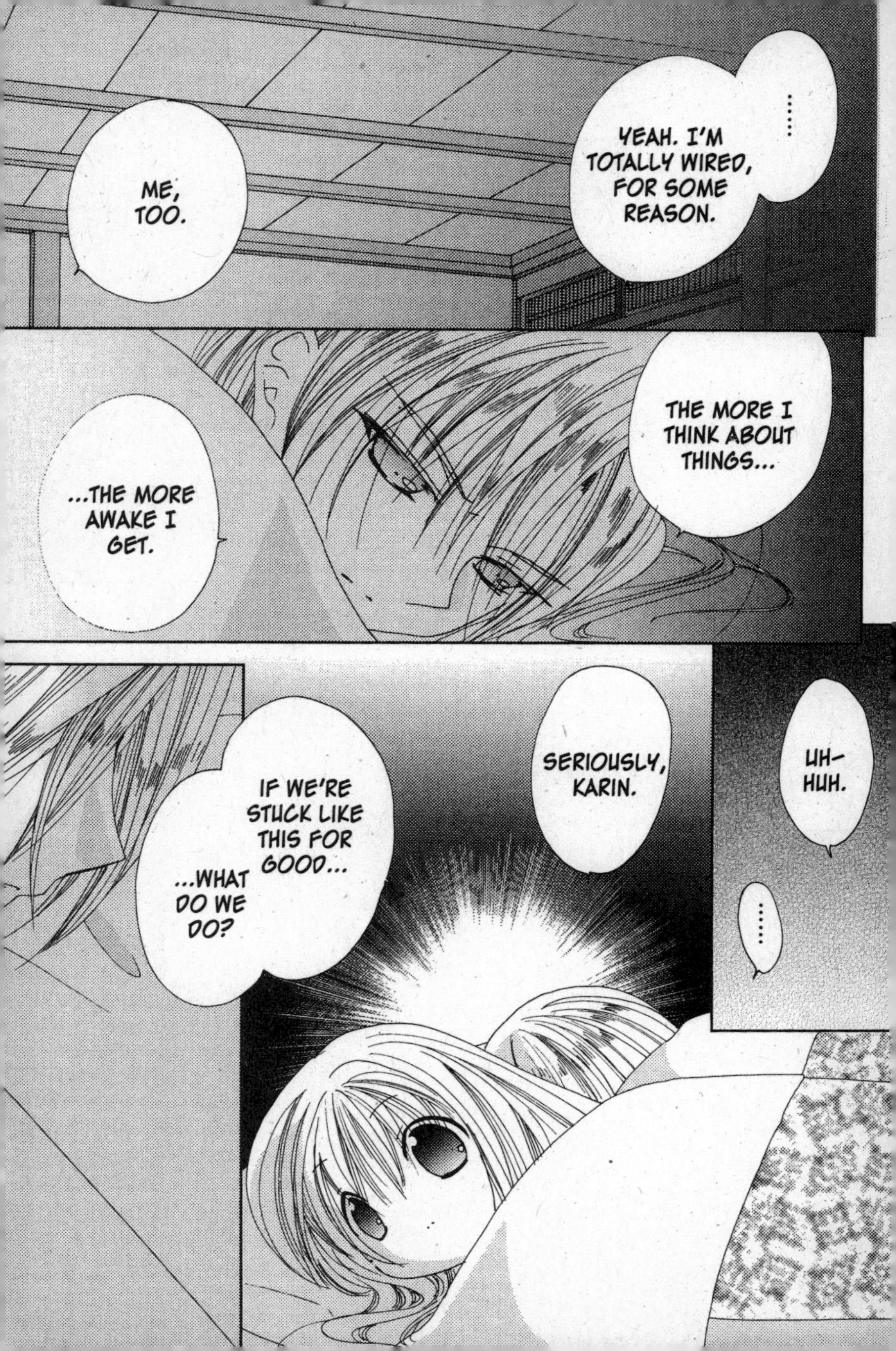
……
YEAH. I'M TOTALLY WIRED, FOR SOME REASON.
ME, TOO.
THE MORE I THINK ABOUT THINGS...
...THE MORE AWAKE I GET.
UH-HUH.
……
SERIOUSLY, KARIN.
IF WE'RE STUCK LIKE THIS FOR GOOD...
...WHAT DO WE DO?

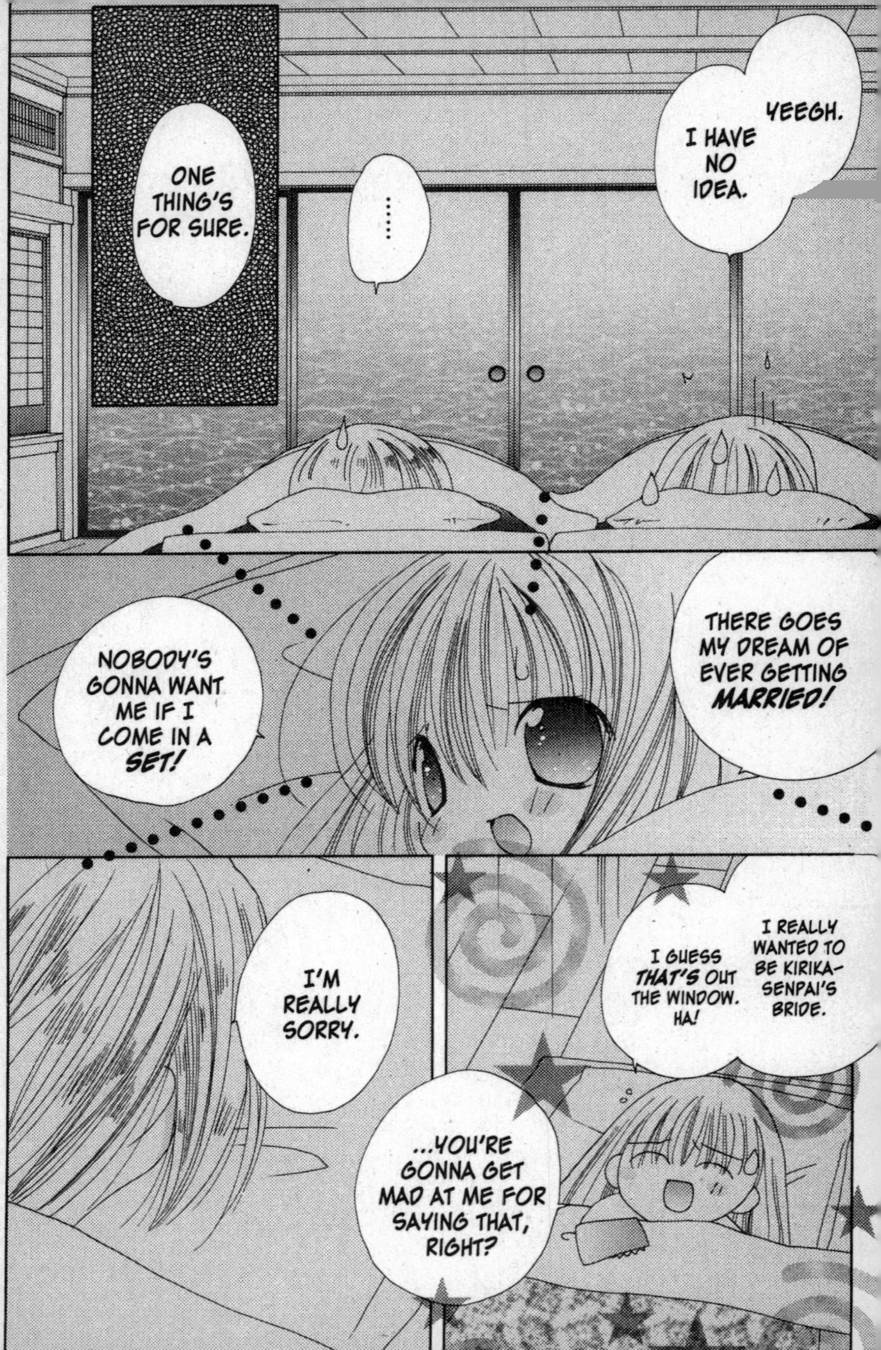
YEEGH. I HAVE NO IDEA.
......
ONE THING'S FOR SURE.
THERE GOES MY DREAM OF EVER GETTING *MARRIED!*
NOBODY'S GONNA WANT ME IF I COME IN A *SET!*
I REALLY WANTED TO BE KIRIKA-SENPAI'S BRIDE.
I GUESS *THAT'S* OUT THE WINDOW. HA!
...YOU'RE GONNA GET MAD AT ME FOR SAYING THAT, RIGHT?
I'M REALLY SORRY.

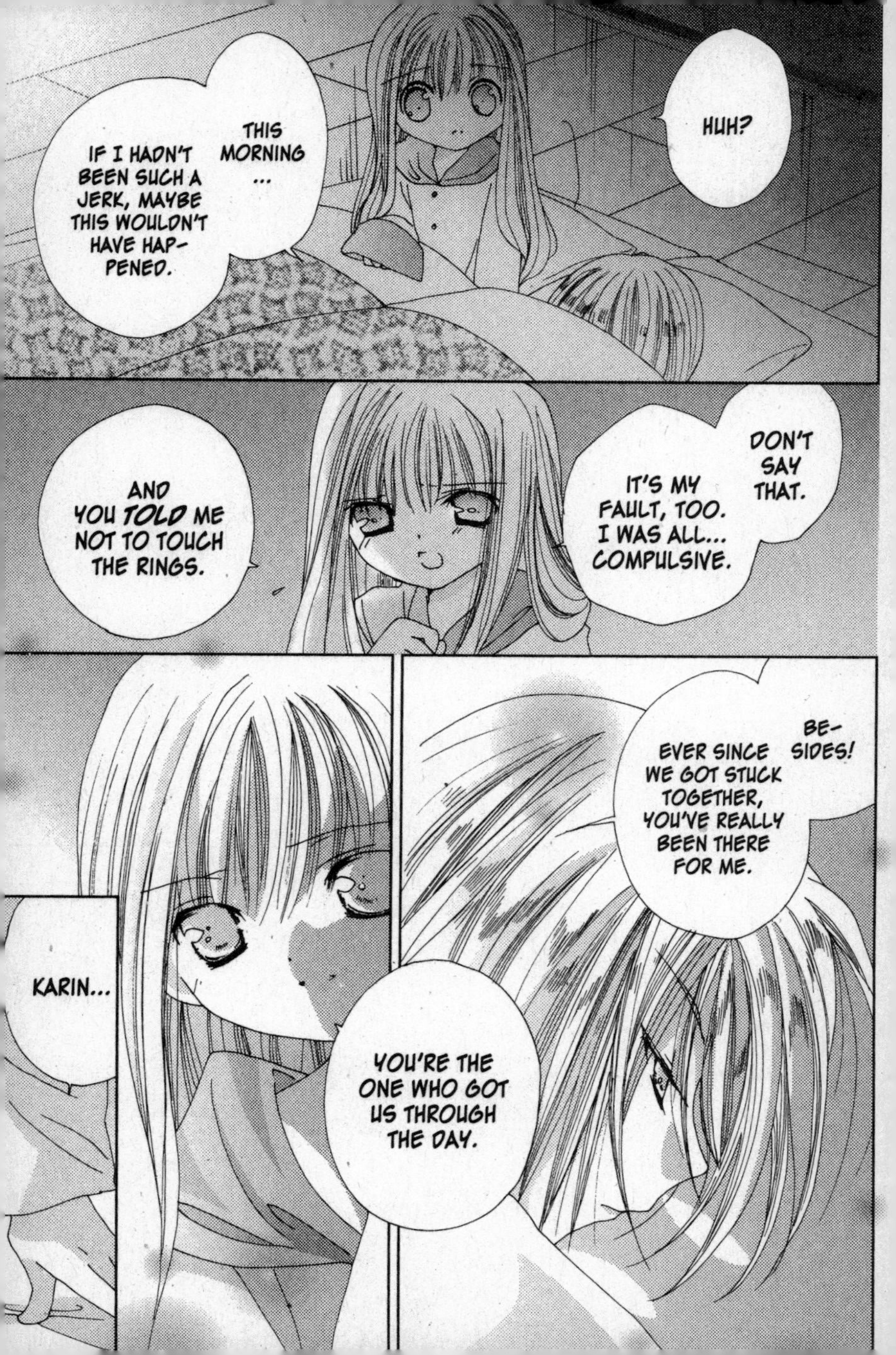
HUH?
THIS MORNING ... IF I HADN'T BEEN SUCH A JERK, MAYBE THIS WOULDN'T HAVE HAP-PENED.
DON'T SAY THAT. IT'S MY FAULT, TOO. I WAS ALL... COMPULSIVE.
AND YOU *TOLD* ME NOT TO TOUCH THE RINGS.
BE-SIDES! EVER SINCE WE GOT STUCK TOGETHER, YOU'VE REALLY BEEN THERE FOR ME.
YOU'RE THE ONE WHO GOT US THROUGH THE DAY.
KARIN...

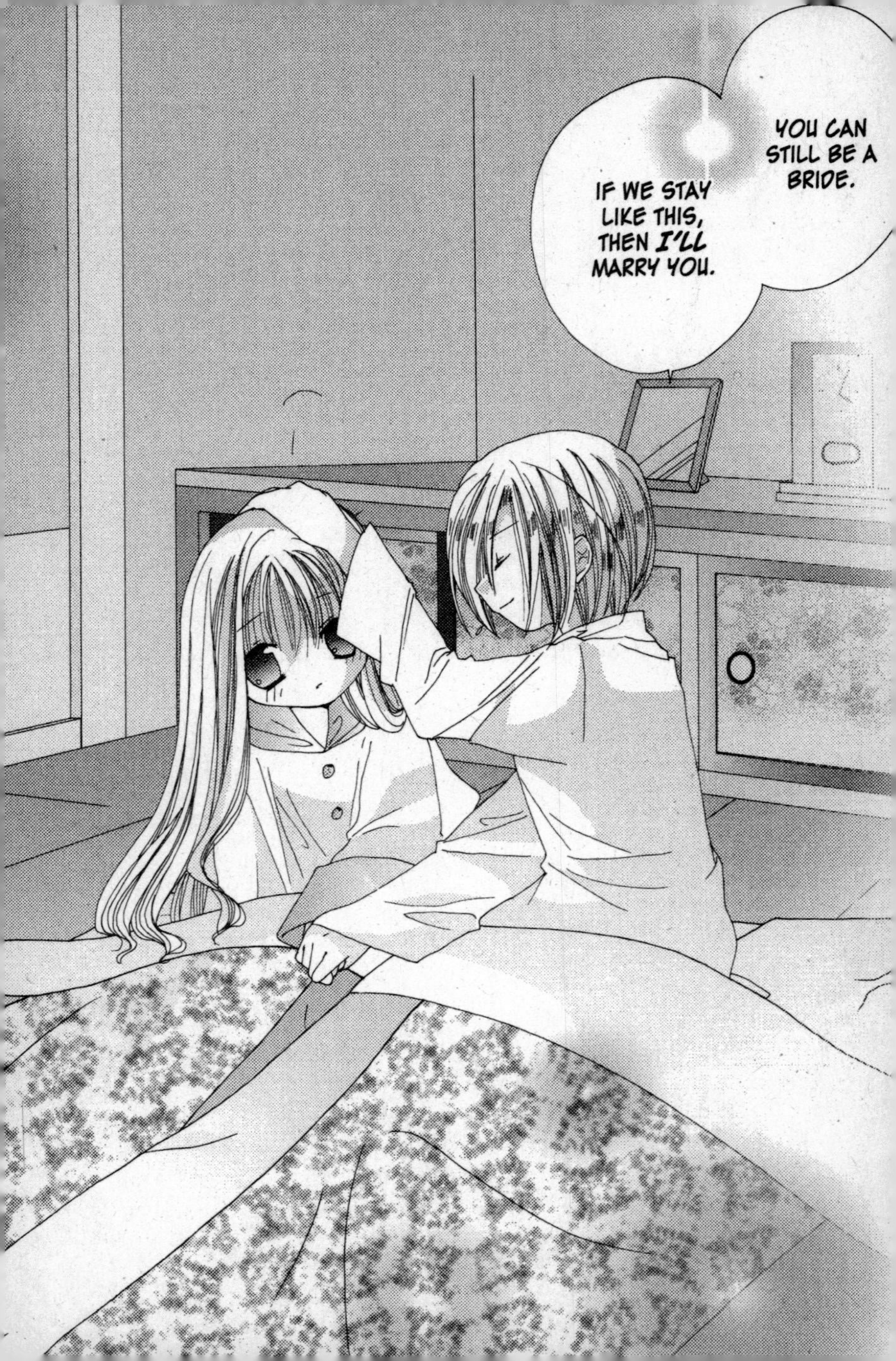
YOU CAN STILL BE A BRIDE.
IF WE STAY LIKE THIS, THEN *I'LL* MARRY YOU.

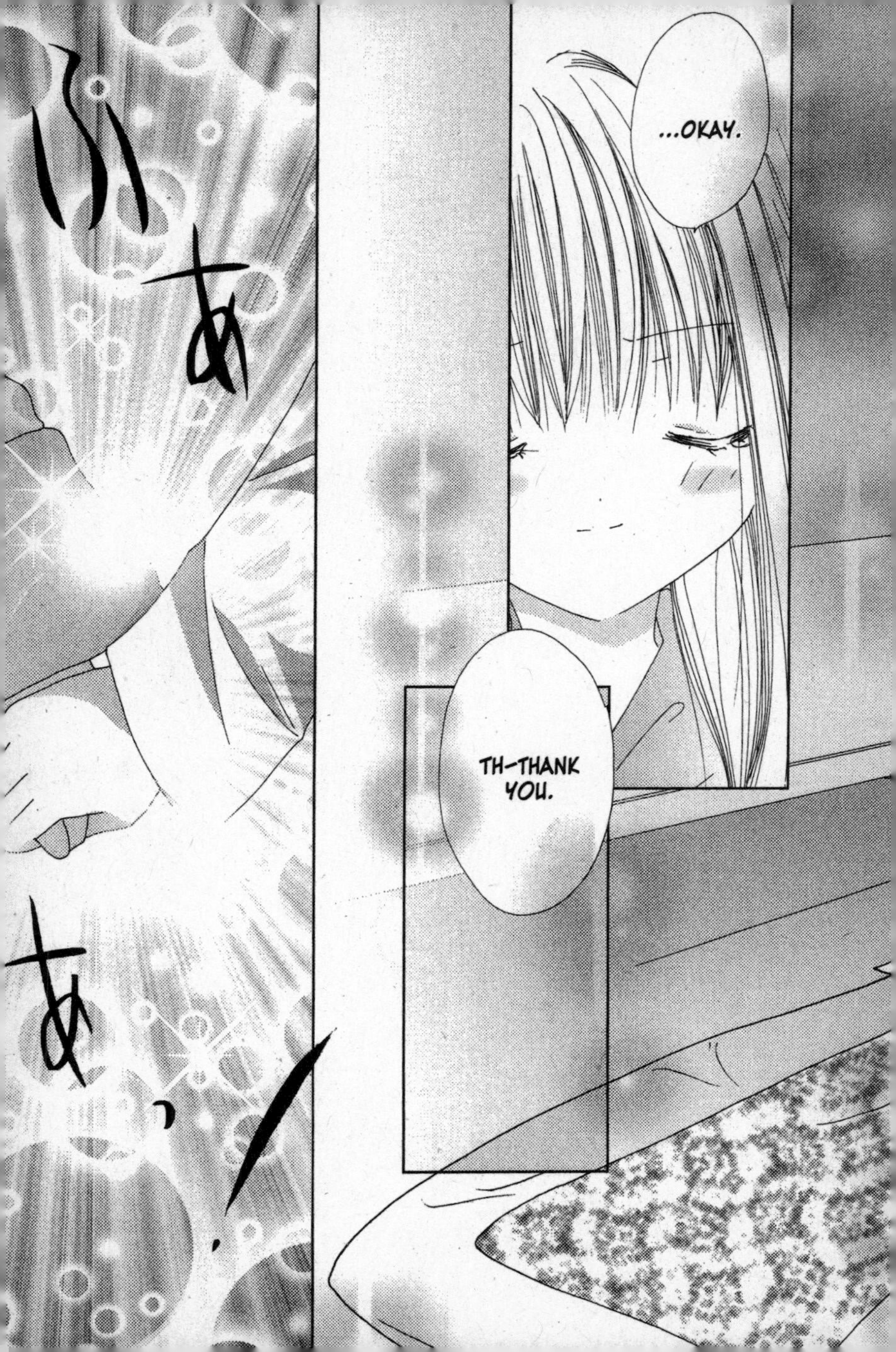
...OKAY.
TH-THANK YOU.
ふぁあっ!

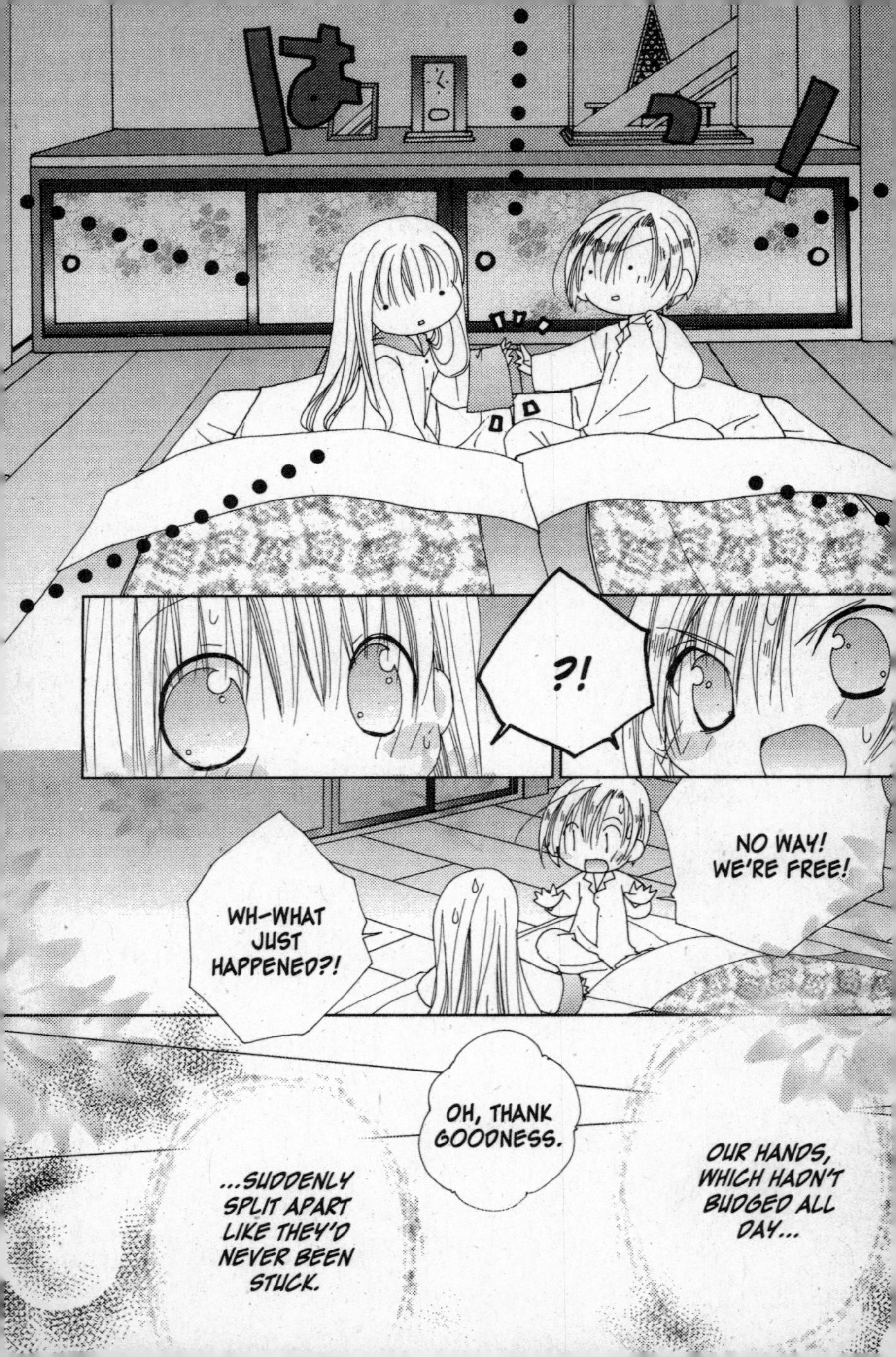
はっ!
?!
NO WAY! WE'RE FREE!
WH-WHAT JUST HAPPENED?!
OH, THANK GOODNESS.
OUR HANDS, WHICH HADN'T BUDGED ALL DAY...
...SUDDENLY SPLIT APART LIKE THEY'D NEVER BEEN STUCK.

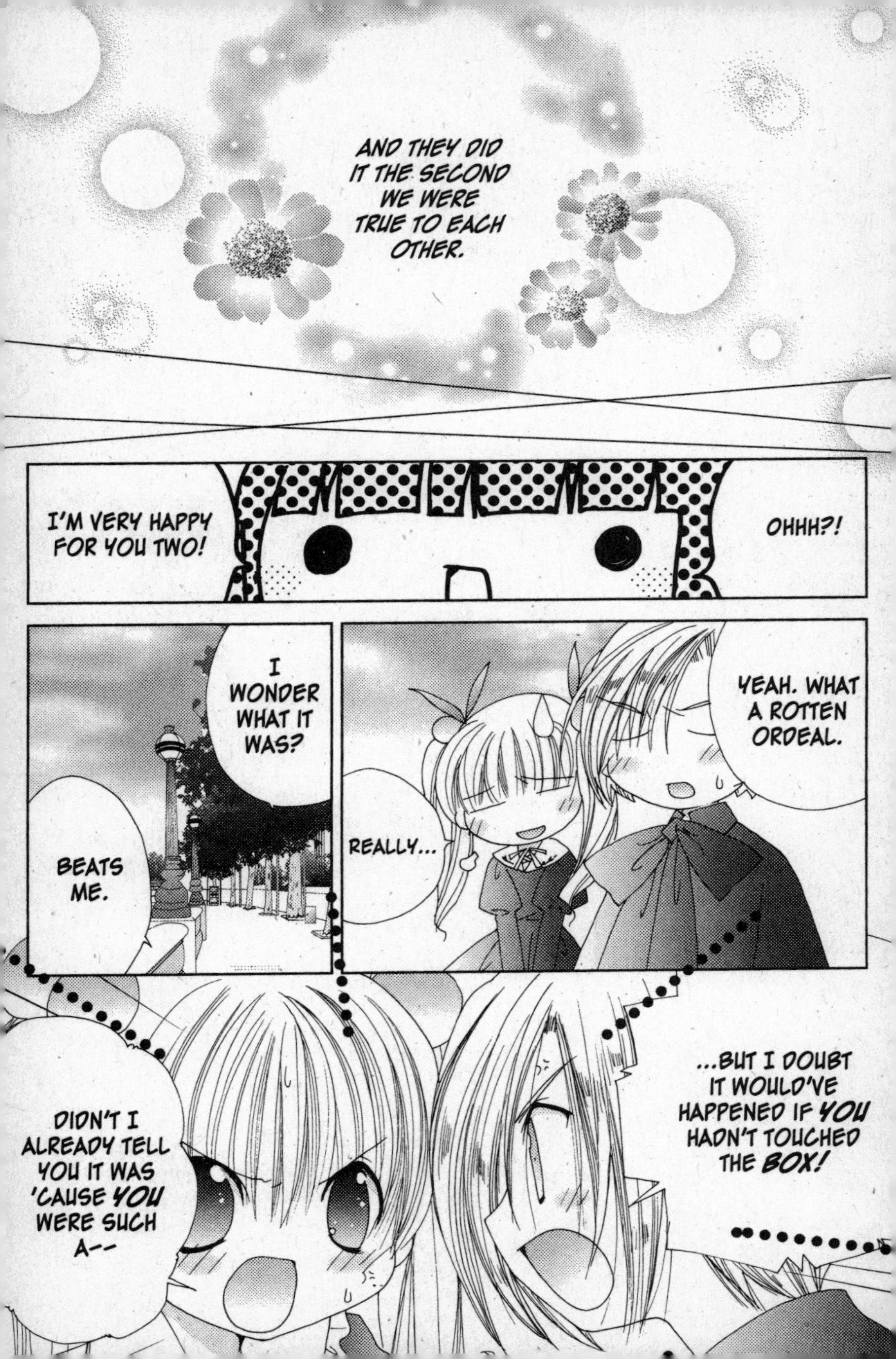
AND THEY DID IT THE SECOND WE WERE TRUE TO EACH OTHER.
OHHH?!
I'M VERY HAPPY FOR YOU TWO!
YEAH. WHAT A ROTTEN ORDEAL.
REALLY...
I WONDER WHAT IT WAS?
BEATS ME.
...BUT I DOUBT IT WOULD'VE HAPPENED IF *YOU* HADN'T TOUCHED THE *BOX*!
DIDN'T I ALREADY TELL YOU IT WAS 'CAUSE *YOU* WERE SUCH A--

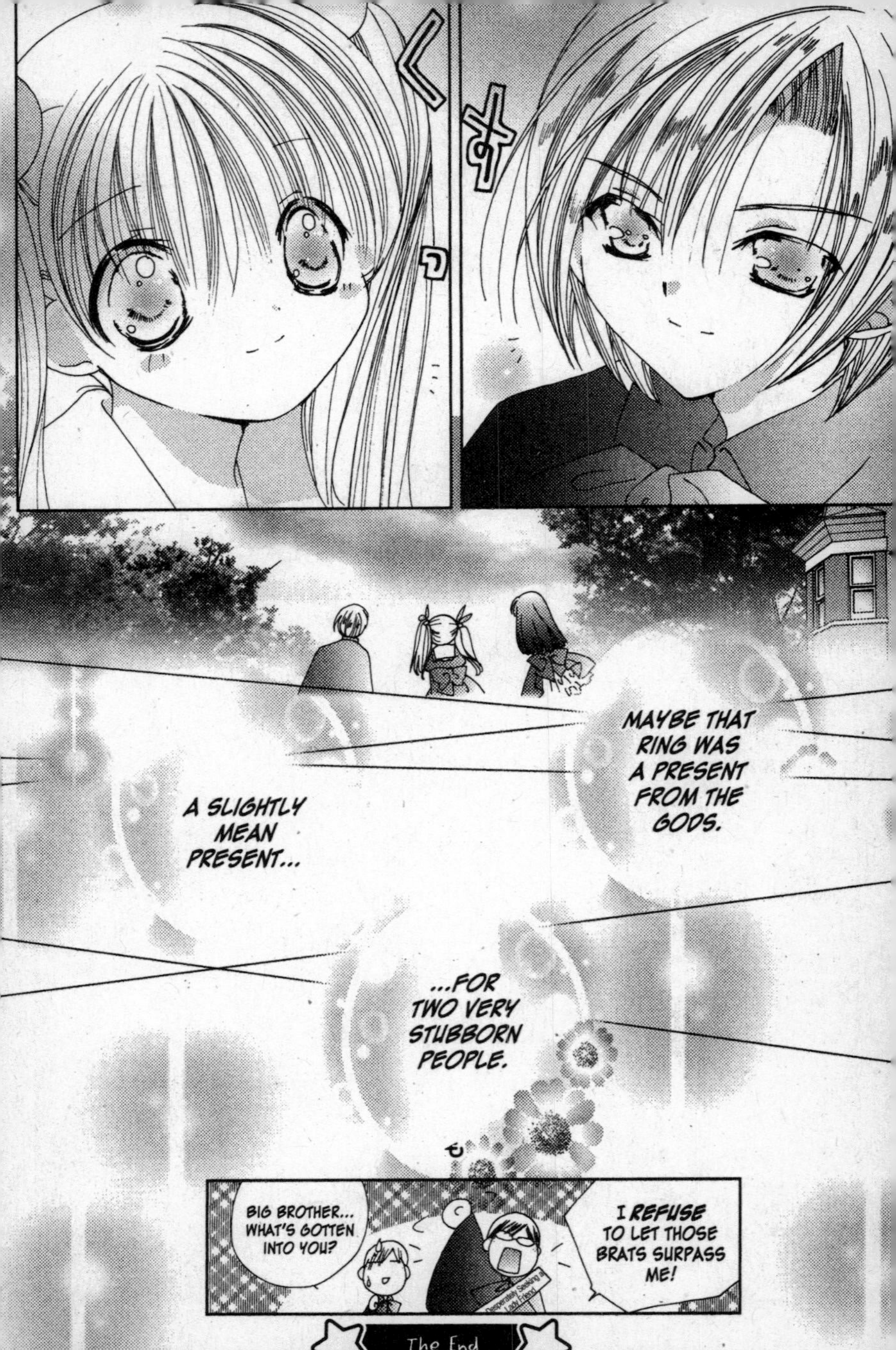
くすっ
MAYBE THAT RING WAS A PRESENT FROM THE GODS.
A SLIGHTLY MEAN PRESENT...
...FOR TWO VERY STUBBORN PEOPLE.
I *REFUSE* TO LET THOSE BRATS SURPASS ME!
BIG BROTHER... WHAT'S GOTTEN INTO YOU?
Desperately Seeking a Lady Friend!

The End

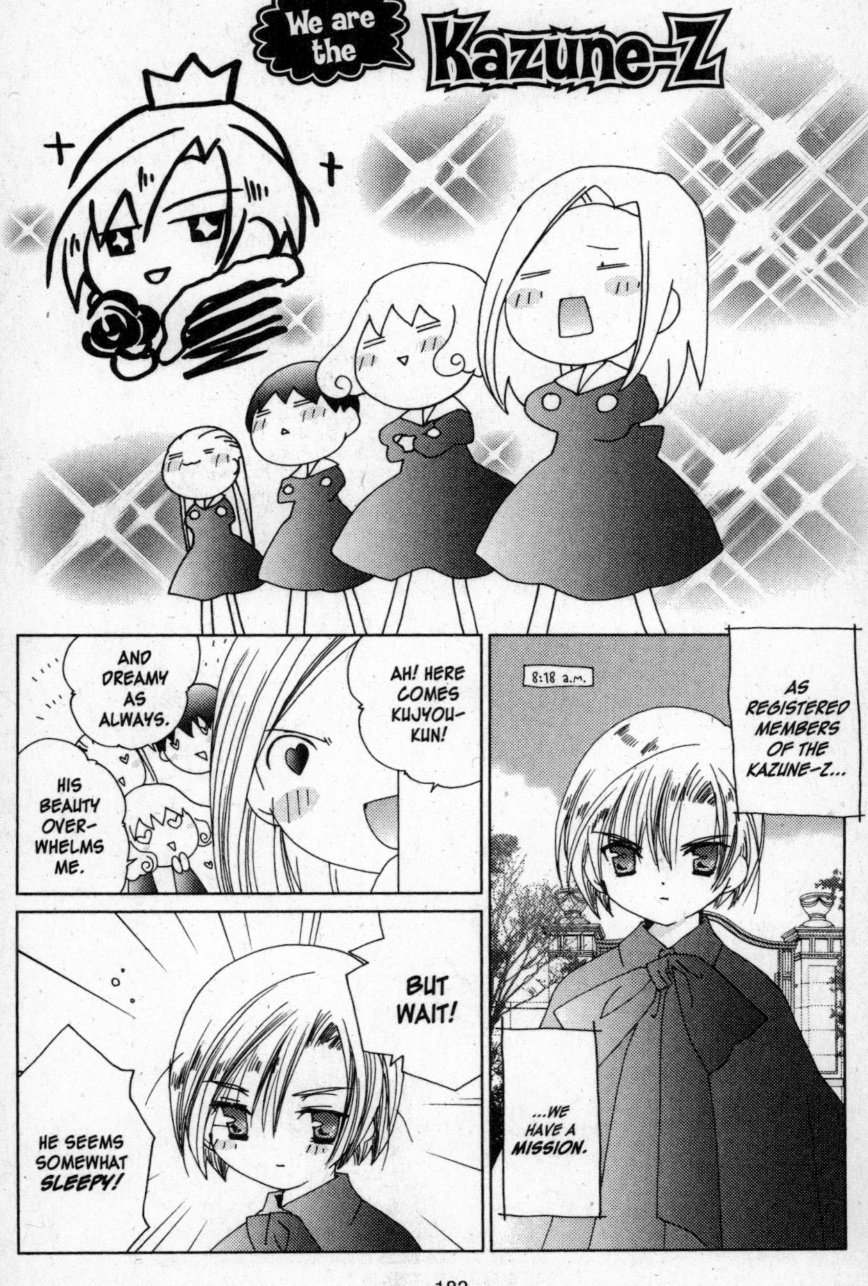
We are the
Kazune-Z
8:18 a.m.
AS REGISTERED MEMBERS OF THE KAZUNE-Z...
...WE HAVE A MISSION.
AH! HERE COMES KUJYOU-KUN!
AND DREAMY AS ALWAYS.
HIS BEAUTY OVERWHELMS ME.
BUT WAIT!
HE SEEMS SOMEWHAT SLEEPY!

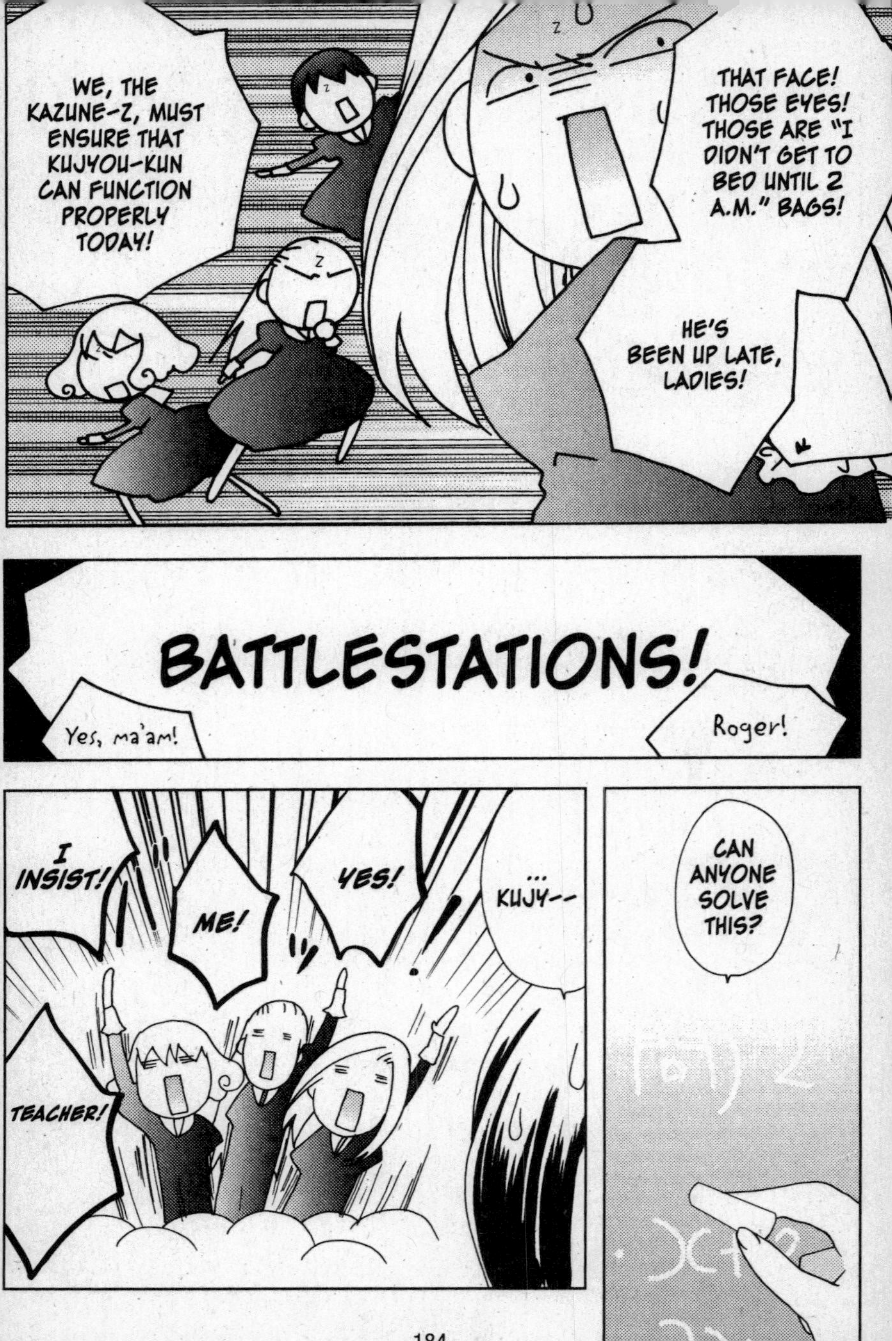
THAT FACE! THOSE EYES! THOSE ARE "I DIDN'T GET TO BED UNTIL 2 A.M." BAGS!
HE'S BEEN UP LATE, LADIES!
WE, THE KAZUNE-Z, MUST ENSURE THAT KUJYOU-KUN CAN FUNCTION PROPERLY TODAY!
BATTLESTATIONS!
Roger!
Yes, ma'am!
CAN ANYONE SOLVE THIS?
... KUJY--
YES!
ME!
I INSIST!
TEACHER!

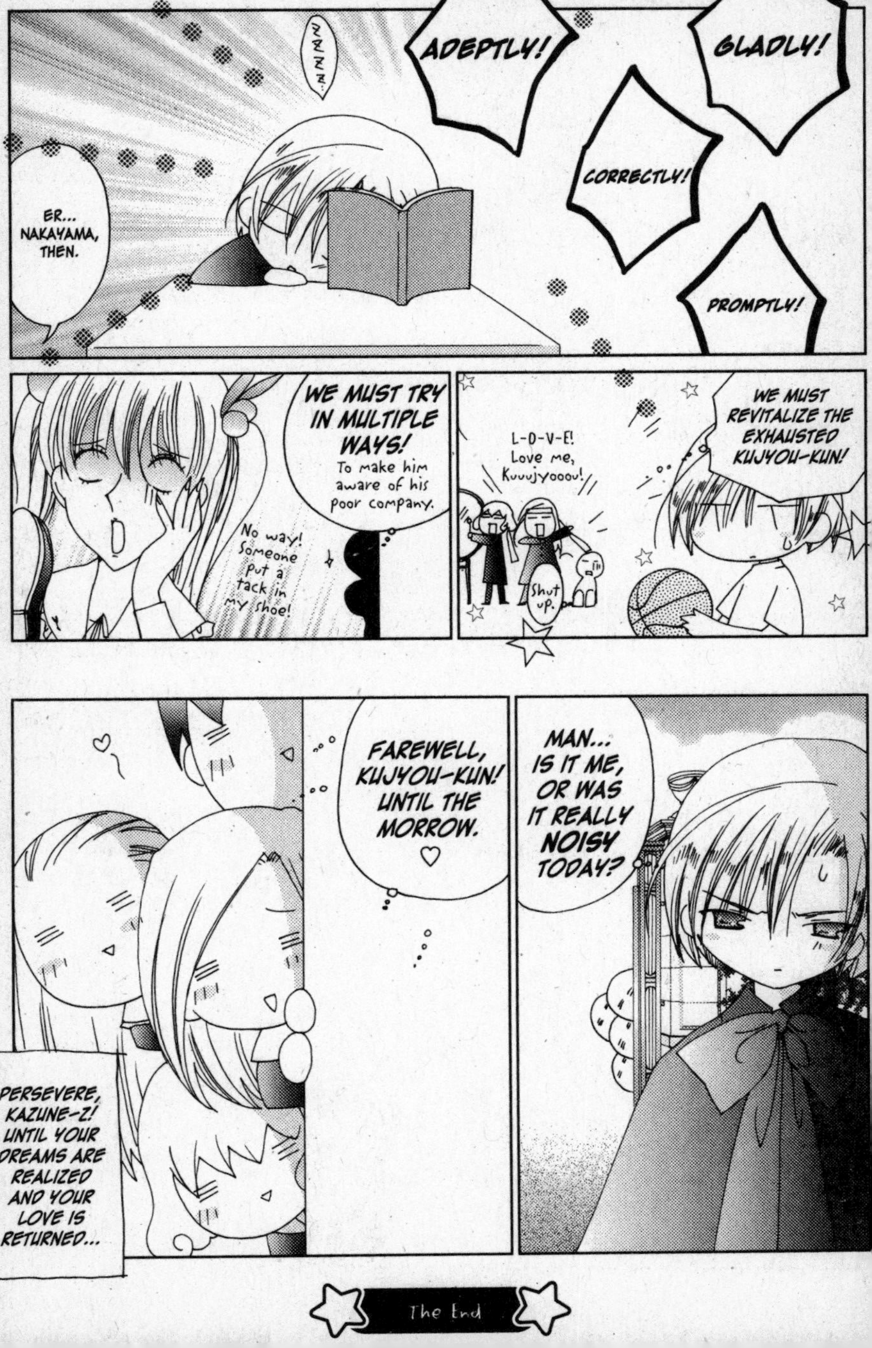
GLADLY!
ADEPTLY!
...ZZZ
CORRECTLY!
PROMPTLY!
ER... NAKAYAMA, THEN.
WE MUST REVITALIZE THE EXHAUSTED KUJYOU-KUN!
L-O-V-E! Love me, Kuuujyooou!
Shut up.
WE MUST TRY IN MULTIPLE WAYS! To make him aware of his poor company.
No way! Someone put a tack in my shoe!
MAN... IS IT ME, OR WAS IT REALLY NOISY TODAY?
FAREWELL, KUJYOU-KUN! UNTIL THE MORROW. ♡
PERSEVERE, KAZUNE-Z! UNTIL YOUR DREAMS ARE REALIZED AND YOUR LOVE IS RETURNED...
The End

And now, without further ado...

Kamichama Karin Fan Art!

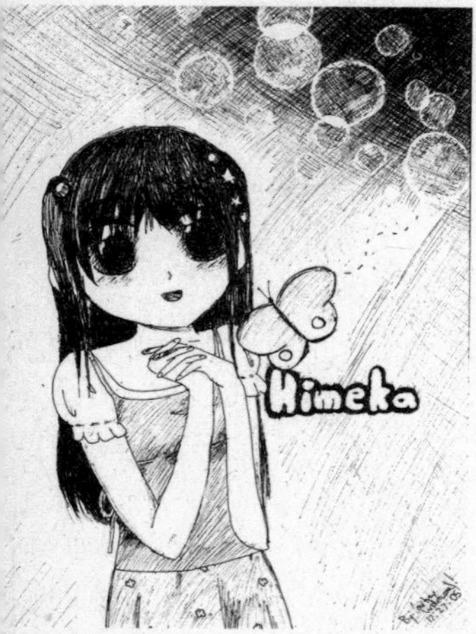
Himeka

Ah, that Himeka-chan.
Head in the clouds, stars in her eyes.

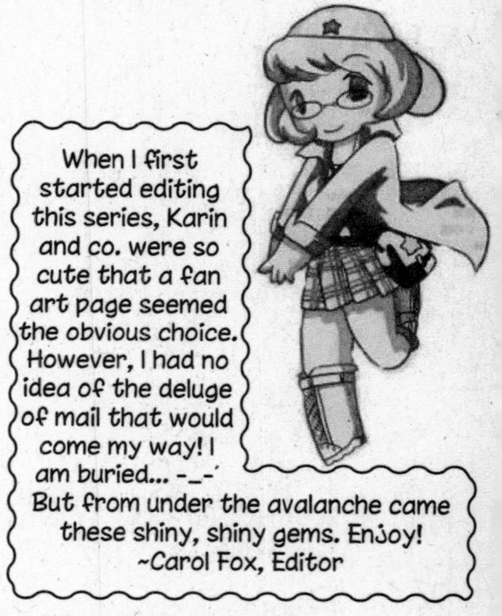

When I first started editing this series, Karin and co. were so cute that a fan art page seemed the obvious choice. However, I had no idea of the deluge of mail that would come my way! I am buried... -_-´
But from under the avalanche came these shiny, shiny gems. Enjoy!
~Carol Fox, Editor

It's a funky new take on Karin's signature style!

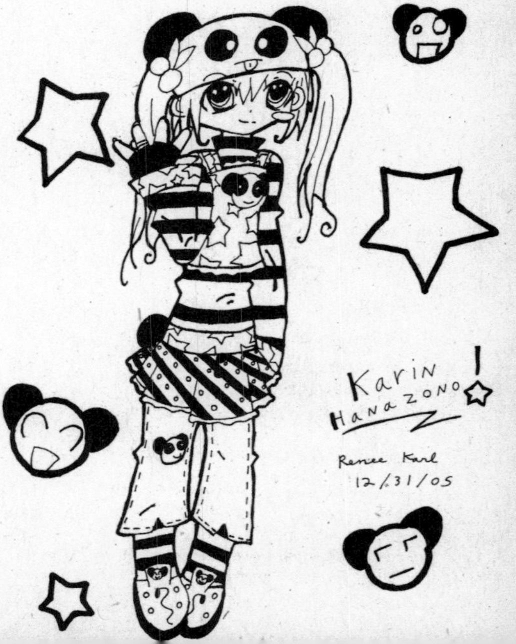
Karin HANAZONO!
Renee Karl
12/31/05

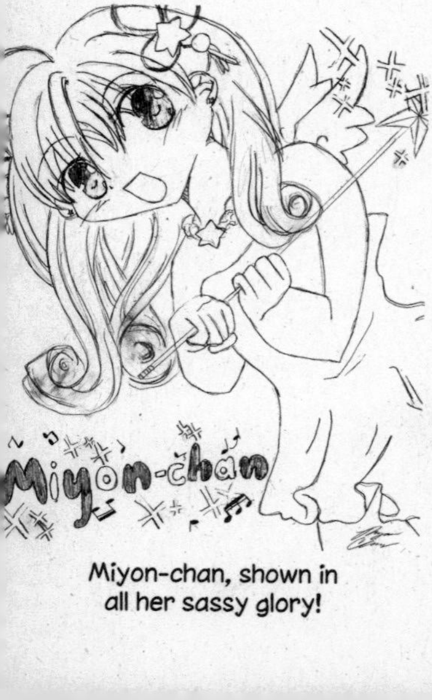
Miyon-chan

Miyon-chan, shown in all her sassy glory!

Don't you dare call it a dress, or he'll whack ya!

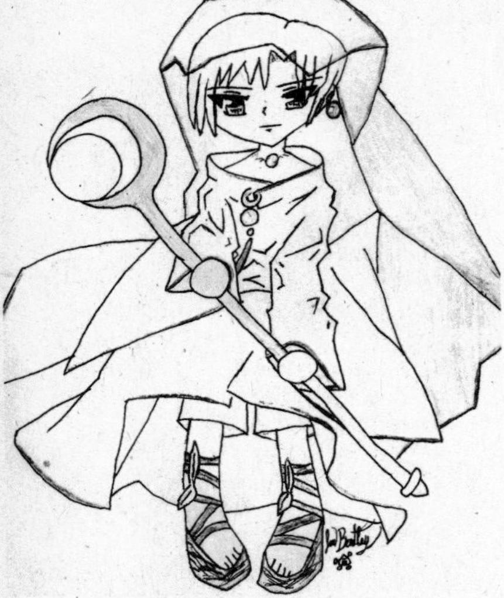

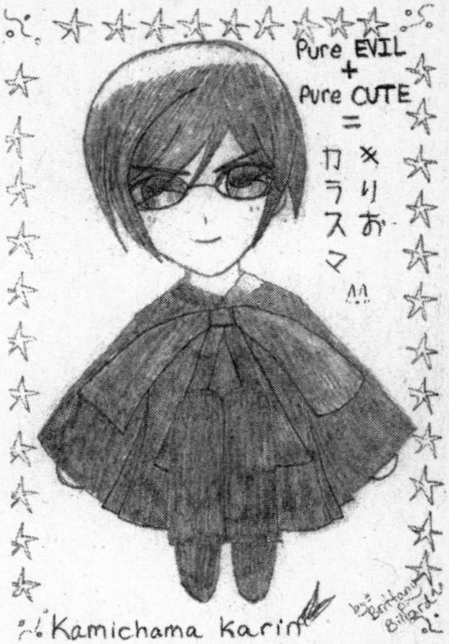

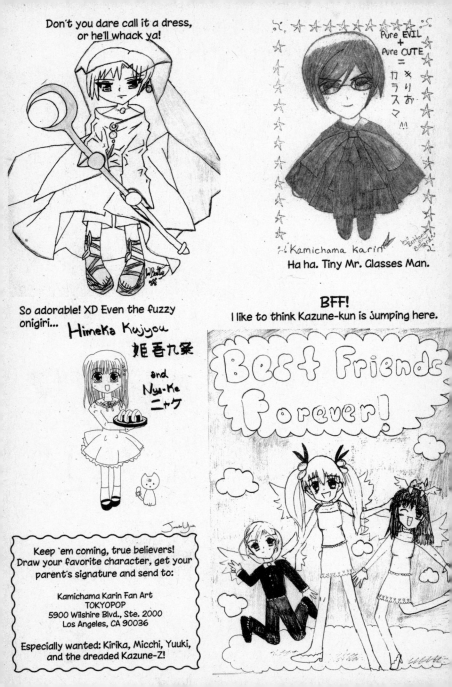

Pure EVIL
+
Pure CUTE
=
キりお
カラスマ
!!
Kamichama karin

Ha ha. Tiny Mr. Glasses Man.

So adorable! XD Even the fuzzy onigiri...

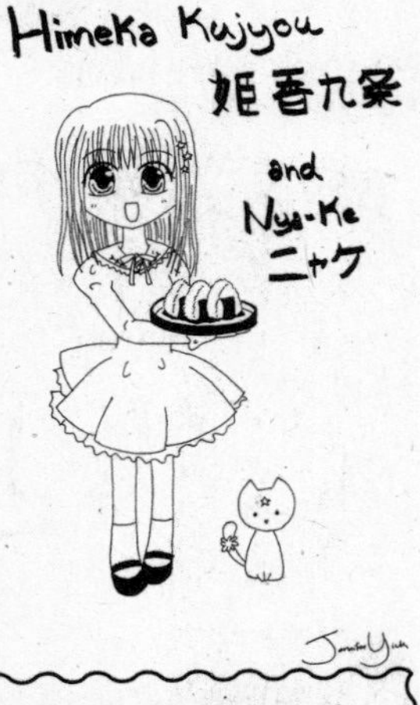

Himeka Kujyou
姫香九条
and
Nya-Ke
ニャケ

BFF!

I like to think Kazune-kun is jumping here.

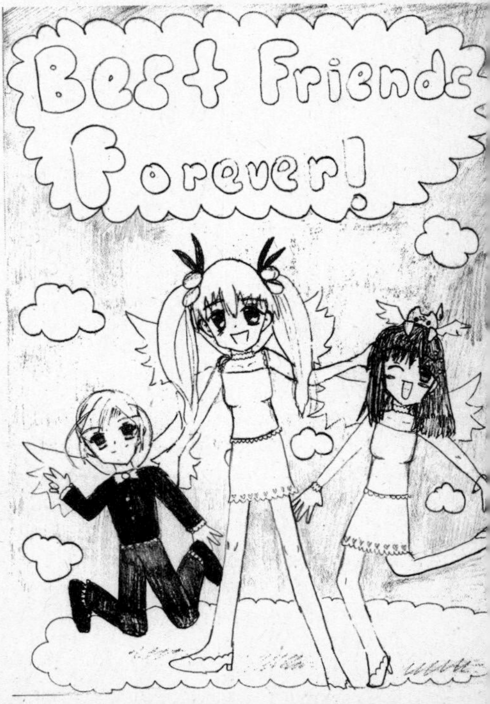

Best Friends Forever!

Keep 'em coming, true believers! Draw your favorite character, get your parent's signature and send to:

Kamichama Karin Fan Art
TOKYOPOP
5900 Wilshire Blvd., Ste. 2000
Los Angeles, CA 90036

Especially wanted: Kirika, Micchi, Yuuki, and the dreaded Kazune-Z!

Next time in...

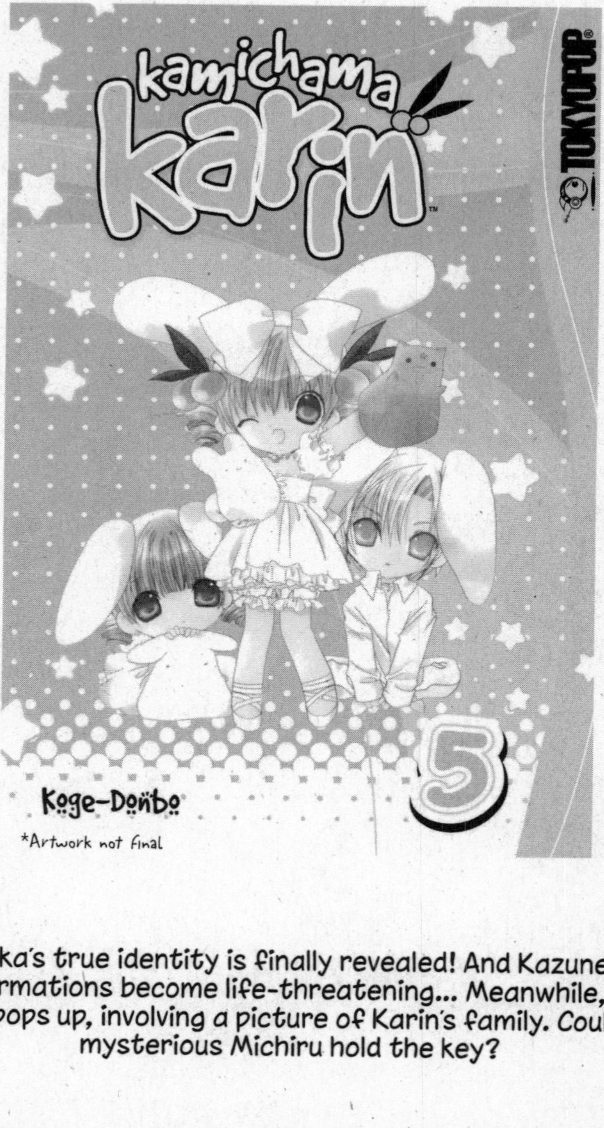
kamichama karin
TOKYOPOP
5
Koge-Donbo

*Artwork not final

Kirika's true identity is finally revealed! And Kazune's transformations become life-threatening... Meanwhile, a new puzzle pops up, involving a picture of Karin's family. Could the mysterious Michiru hold the key?

TOKYOPOP MANGA SUPPLEMENT

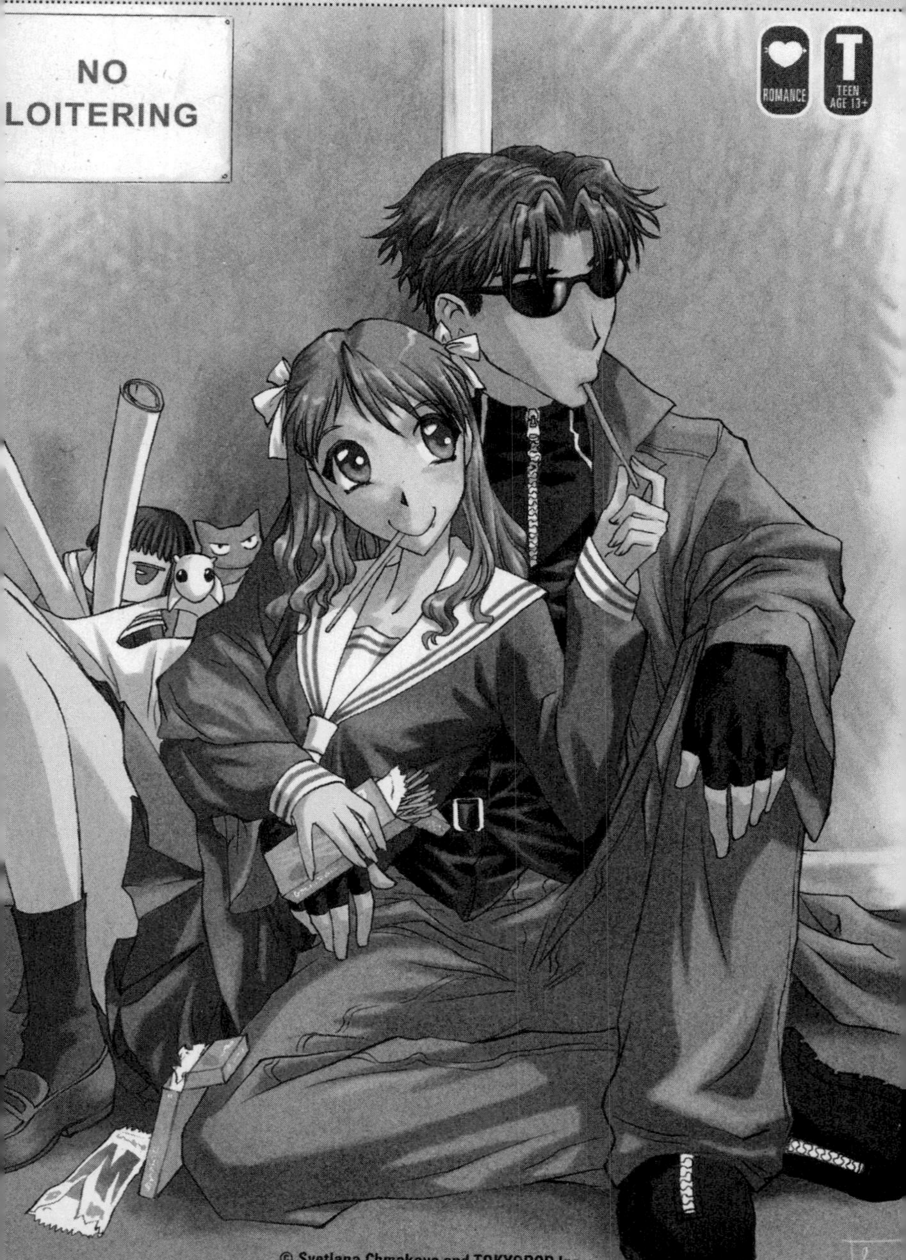
NO
LOITERING
ROMANCE
T
TEEN
AGE 13+

Sometimes even two's a crowd.

When Christie settles in the Artist Alley of her first-ever anime convention, she only sees it as an opportunity to promote the comic she has started with her boyfriend. But conventions are never what you expect, and soon a whirlwind of events sweeps Christie off her feet and changes her life. Who is the mysterious cosplayer who won't even take off his sunglasses indoors? What do you do when you fall in love with a guy who is going to be miles away from you in just a couple of days?

CREATED BY SVETLANA CHMAKOVA!

"YOU CAN'T AVOID FALLING UNDER ITS CHARM." -IGN.COM

READ AN ENTIRE CHAPTER ONLINE FOR FREE:
WWW.TOKYOPOP.COM/MANGAONLINE

STOP!

This is the back of the book.
You wouldn't want to spoil a great ending

This book is printed "manga-style," in the authentic Japanese right-to-le
format. Since none of the artwork has been flipped or altered, readers
get to experience the story just as the creator intended. You've been
asking for it, so TOKYOPOP® delivered: authentic, hot-off-the-press,
and far more fun!

DIRECTIONS

If this is your first time
reading manga-style, here's a
quick guide to help you
understand how it works.

It's easy... just start in the top
right panel and follow the
numbers. Have fun, and look for
more 100% authentic manga
from TOKYOPOP®!